Against All Odds

COINCIDENCE OR GOD'S PROVIDENCE?

Johnny Vaughan

Against All Odds

Published by
21st Century Press
Springfield, MO 65807

21st Century Press is a Christian publisher dedicated to publishing books that have a high standard of family values. We believe the vision for our companies is to provide families and individuals with user-friendly materials that will help them in their daily lives and experiences. It is our prayer that this book will help you discover biblical truth for your own life and help you meet the needs of others. May God richly bless you.

21st Century Press
2131 W. Republic Rd.
PMB 211
Springfield, MO 65807

Cover Design: Lee Fredrickson
Book Design: Lee Fredrickson
ISBN: Paperback: 978-1-951774-26-4
          Hardback: 978-1-951774-25-7
          Ebook: 978-1-951774-24-0

Visit our website at: www.21stcenturypress.com
Printed in the United States of America

CONTENTS

PREFACE

In a commentary by John W. Smith, a long–time evangelist and Christian author, he states, "One of those consequences (of faith) is that we believe that there is no such thing as luck, chance, happenstance, or fate. Accepting God, as He has revealed Himself in the Bible, means that when something "mysterious" happens – something for which we can't find a logical, rational explanation – we look to God." This implies that everything that happens is providential of God – either He causes it or He allows it. True believers really have no alternative other than to accept this. Either God is or He isn't. Either He created the universe or He didn't. And if He did then He is aware of everything that happens and has the power to cause or allow anything to happen. If God were indifferent to His creation it would devalue the concept of His being God.

This doesn't mean that God causes or allows only "happy" things to occur. Sometimes he causes or allows devastation in order to punish or to teach or to strengthen one's faith or to prepare the way for future blessings. Joseph was not taken into captivity as punishment but rather as a means of allowing the seed of Abraham to survive a famine. It was not an accident or "happenstance" that Moses was saved from the death edict for all male Jewish babies. Rather, it placed him in a position to ultimately lead the Israelites out of Egypt into the Promised Land. King David experienced both extremes of God's providence when he was first punished for his sins involving Bathsheba and Uriah and then blessed not only as becoming a critical link in the lineage of Jesus but then being referred to as "a man after God's own heart." Jesus' mistreatment and cruel death were necessary elements in the eternal salvation of mankind. God is providentially involved in every element of every person's life. If not, then what is the point of it all?

While this book is an autobiography it is not intended to inform the reader of any great or extraordinary accomplishments I may have achieved in my lifetime. In the first place, I highly doubt that anything I have accomplished on my own during my life would warrant such attention. Rather, this book is intended to serve as a witness to what I call the Providence of God – a recounting of numerous times I believe God has intervened in my life to my ultimate benefit. I call such interventions miracles, because I have no other explanation for them. No, I don't believe God any longer deals in "spectacular" miracles such as raising the dead or making the sun stand still. However, I believe He still intervenes, usually subtly but sometimes almost blatantly, in the lives of those who love Him. After all, Romans 8:28 unambiguously states, "And we know that in all things God works for the good of those who love him, who have been called according to his purpose." If we don't believe the literal meaning of this verse – "God works" – then how can we say we believe in anything the Bible says? It all comes down to faith. Do we have faith in God and scripture?

While my life would likely be considered mundane – even dull – in the view of many, it has nevertheless been filled with a myriad of unexplained events. The events which will be described are eerily timely, seemingly closely choreographed, and irrefutably related, and they inevitably benefitted me in some way, in one instance actually sparing my life. In addition I have experienced numerous "small world" events which have greatly enriched my life. I have encountered friends, friends of friends and celebrities – once and future presidents, governors, actors and athletes – in unusual places and circumstances so frequently that I cannot attribute it to chance or luck.

In this book I will reveal many narratives and anecdotes which, on the whole, defy any explanation other than being God's Providence and intervention in my life. As the book will note, the nature of the events and their very specific sequence and timing lend compelling support to this thesis. This is not an action–packed novel, so I encourage you to read the book slowly and savor the events and unusual circumstances.

I hope you will find the read interesting and thought–provoking and that it will strengthen your faith in God and His word.

FOREWORD

Perhaps a more meaningful title for this book would be "Hither by Thy Help I've Come." These words found in the fourth stanza of the old Christian hymn "O Thou Found of Every Blessing", written by Robert Robinson in the year 1758. The words reference an incident found in the Bible, in 1 Samuel, where is recorded an attempt by the Philistines to attack and destroy the Israelites. In response to the threat the prophet Samuel sacrificed a lamb and cried out to the Lord on Israel's behalf, and the Lord answered him.

1 Samuel 7:10–13

[10] *While Samuel was sacrificing the burnt offering, the Philistines drew near to engage Israel in battle. But that day the Lord thundered with loud thunder against the Philistines and threw them into such a panic that they were routed before the Israelites.* [11] *The men of Israel rushed out of Mizpah and pursued the Philistines, slaughtering them along the way to a point below Betha Kar.* [12] *Then Samuel took a stone and set it up between Mizpah and Shen. He named it Ebenezer, saying, "Thus far the Lord has helped us."* [13] *So the Philistines were subdued and they stopped invading Israel's territory.*

Samuel rightfully attributed the Israelites' victory over the Philistines to the intervention of God, and in response he built a stone memorial in recognition of the fact that it was only by God's help that it had come to pass. He named the stone memorial "Ebenezer," which in Hebrew means "stone of help," which is a very appropriate name for the memorial. This, then, within the context of this book, is the provenance – origin – of the name "Ebenezer" as it refers to a memorial stone raised in praise of and thanks to God.

In addition, Ebenezer just happened to be the name of the site where the Israelites defeated the Philistines in the battle described in the scripture above. Samuel likely drew his inspiration for the name of his memorial from the name of the site where the battle occurred. Was it just happenstance that the name of the site of the Israelite victory was translated "stone of help?" I think not. I believe it was another opportunity for God to demonstrate his Providence.

When I was younger we sang this hymn frequently in our worship services, and I always wondered who Ebenezer was. Was it Scrooge from Dickens' novel "A Christmas Carol", or was it some other historical person? Eventually I read the scripture and learned the back story of the writing of the hymn.

Over the years I have come to believe that the scripture, particularly as paraphrased by Mr. Robinson, has applied to every victory I have enjoyed in this life. I have come to believe that God has been with me every step of the way and that I could have achieved nothing without His help. At this late stage of my life I reverently and respectfully raise my own personal Ebenezer, for truly, hither (old English meaning "to this point") by God's help I have come.

Consequently, I write this book not out of some grandiose belief that my life is of any interest to anyone, except perhaps to a few family members and close friends. Rather, I write it to tell of scores of significant events in my life that I cannot believe were just some sort of random cosmic accidents. The events of which I write were very personal and frequently irrefutably connected together, as if some greater power had a hand in their orchestration. Every such event ultimately and unbelievably contributed to my wellbeing, even though some of them were uncomfortable and unappreciated at the time. When the uncomfortable events occurred I reminded myself that sometimes discipline is more effective than reward. And later on, when the ultimate value of those events was revealed, I came to treasure them as necessary steps in my Christian walk. On those occasions I would remember 1 Thessalonians 5:16–18, where it says, "Rejoice always, pray continually, give thanks in all circumstances; for this is God's will for you in Christ Jesus." Should I give thanks when I am being beaten down in, it seems, every possible way? Give me a break! However, those circumstances alluded to in 1 Thessalonians segue nicely into Romans 8:28, where it says, "And we know that in all things God works for the good of those who love him, who have been called according to his purpose."

From this scripture I gathered that, although sometimes we face misfortunes in life, God works in those misfortunes for the good of those who love Him. Sometimes a carrot, sometimes a stick, whichever is most effective at the time and under the circumstances. We cannot avoid trials and tribulations of this world, but when they occur God does not abandon us but rather is still with us and working for our good. In my personal case, those trials and tribulations turned out to be both educational and faith–strengthening, because, ultimately, I was able to gain a better understanding and appreciation of what God has done for me, and I was able to use those adversities to grow in every way – spiritually, socially and even financially.

I also fully believe Hebrews 13:2, where it says, "Do not forget to show hospitality to strangers, for by so doing some people have shown hospitality to angels without knowing it." Sometimes in our life we may encounter "angels unaware" (KJV). From this I can only believe that at critical times in our lives we may be visited by actual angels sent by God to help us through a trying situation. Such visits occurred in Biblical times, and scripture does not suggest that they were limited to the times of the Patriarchs, Judges, Prophets and Apostles. I don't know how else to interpret that verse in Hebrews except to concede that God has the power and wisdom to allow such things to happen even today. I have experienced such phenomena in my life which are otherwise inexplicable. In each case the "visitors', whether supernatural or impossibly coincidental, helped me through a very difficult situation.

I have also experienced an extraordinary number of "small world" events in my life which are seemingly statistically impossible and that I can only attribute to the grace and good will of God as He makes my life more interesting.

As to the major theme of this book . . . while I have enjoyed "small world" events and possibly entertained "angels unaware", those events pale in comparison to the number and significance of the times that Romans 8:28 has apparently manifested itself in my life, and in each such case, although sometimes belatedly, I raised my Ebenezer, recognizing from whence the help came. It is my hope that this book will strengthen the reader's faith in that scripture.

I became a Christian at the age of 15, but even prior to that, through the efforts of my parents and our church affiliations, I came to believe in God and, to some youthful extent, in the power of prayer. However, I was also taught that although prayer is powerful we sometimes don't get exactly what we pray for, a lesson I was to learn powerfully and repeatedly over the next several decades. Over the years, even during my pre–teen years, I challenged God regarding situations and events in my life which I felt were to my disadvantage and in which I sought different outcomes. At those times I held many one–sided conversations (prayers) with God and asked a lot of "Why?" questions, particularly asking why things had happened as they did.

In every "conversation" I pleaded with God to favorably resolve the dilemma which I was facing at the time, and of course in most of the pleas I was very short sighted and selfish. Since I am not Abraham, Moses or the Apostle Peter, I never received any direct spoken responses from God nor did

I receive any miraculous revelations through dreams over the years. However, I do firmly believe He responded to my pleas – just in a different way and in his own time.

Blessed with the benefit of hindsight, it has become very clear to me that in every one of those situations God providentially responded to my benefit, providing much more dynamic and wonderful outcomes than I could have ever imagined. Sometimes the interim between my petition and the eventual outcome was years in the making. Frequently the steps taken by God to deliver those blessings to me made me uncomfortable, sometimes angry, and sometimes they appeared to be diametrically opposed to what I was seeking. However, in every case they resulted in blessings for me. When I later reflected on things that have happened in my life it chills me to the bone to realize what I might have missed had those things had turned out differently.

I believe the way He responded to me was by allowing me, perhaps actually inspiring me, to experience "Aha" moments later in life. For instance, one day many years after the fact, I suddenly realized the positive personal impact of my dad's taking a new job, which at the time required our moving from my birthplace of Seminole, Oklahoma, to Ada, Oklahoma. At another time I realized how my dad's job transfer from Ada to Bartlesville, Oklahoma, had resulted in additional positive, life–changing influences on my future. Still later the significance of my dad's job transfer from Bartlesville to Okemah, Oklahoma – after I was already in college – became crystal clear. In each case, my dad's move permitted me to meet people who heavily and positively influenced my life. These were people whom I would not otherwise have met, and my life most certainly would have turned out radically different had the job transfers not occurred. All of these examples, and others, are described in this book. I have to believe that my actions, my attitudes and my prayers influenced God to place me, frequently against my will, in situations that would ultimately accrue to great benefit in my life. I believe He answered my pleas and complaints by "working for the good of one who loves Him."

There are so many of these unexplainable beneficial events that have occurred in my life, at specific times and in specific sequences, that it is not reasonable to believe they happened by accident. I don't believe in coincidences, and I am enough of a mathematician to understand the very long odds of such interconnected events actually occurring randomly. I have to believe that the only explanation is the intervention of God, frequently and ultimately beneficially, in my life – as I believe He does daily in the lives of innumerable believers. In this book I will attempt to highlight many of those events – both the beneficial and the "instructive" (translation: painful at the time but ultimately beneficial) events.

In addition to describing some of these unexplainable events that have occurred in my life I will also mention an encounter with what I call angels unaware, and I will also relate many of the small world events I have enjoyed.

I can only attribute these events to the Providence of God. In each instance, as mentioned in the hymn, I ultimately – sometimes years later – raised my Ebenezer, realizing that hither by His help, by the Providence of God, I had come.

My journey has covered more than seven decades thus far, and to enable the reader to keep track of the what, when and where of the events I have displayed the year or years in many of the chapter titles. That the Providence of God did not occur overnight but rather required many years to fully manifest itself convinces me that God never ceases working in our lives. It is my hope you will be inspired likewise.

One

EBENEZER

For years I have enjoyed a weekly early morning coffee with some close friends at Jude's Coffee House in Bartlesville, Oklahoma, my frequent and long–time home town. Our coffees are politically incorrect as we unabashedly discuss religion, politics, and economics in depth. Opinions are offered without apology, and good-natured trash talk abounds. Someone with thin skin need not show up.

At coffee one morning, one of my friends asked me, "How did you wind up in Bartlesville?" He was aware that I had lived in Bartlesville on several occasions and lived in several different cities in several other states – stories to be revealed later in this book. "With all the experiences you have had with living in so many different places, how did you end up here?"

"Which time?" I replied. "I have lived in Bartlesville six times in five different houses."

He said, "I guess I am curious as to how you arrived in Bartlesville at this point in your life. How did you and your wife meet? What about your career?"

These were fascinating questions, ones that I had never pondered deeply. It begged some other questions: How did a boy born into semi–poverty during World War II while his dad was in the South Pacific dodging bombs and bullets, a boy whose entire youth was lived in lower middle class financially, a boy who married a girl raised in poverty and whose house didn't even have running water, a boy who often didn't know the difference between "come here and sic 'em" – how did this boy wind up in a coffee shop in Bartlesville, Oklahoma, on this day?

These were not simple questions to answer. Before I could answer, I felt the need to also reflect on those things I had experienced that don't usually evolve from such unpretentious beginnings.

To begin with, for my entire life from puberty until now, I have been focused on several significant objectives in life:

• A happy marriage to a wonderful woman and, later, children

• A college education – a first for my immediate family

• A good job which would support my family

• An opportunity serve my country honorably

• A life situation which would enhance my walk with God

I believe these objectives were born of my early family life. I was an only child until I was 12 years old. Somewhere around the time my sister, Drew, was born, I began to notice my home life. My parents' marriage was probably typical of the time – the husband worked and put food on the table and a roof over the family's head, and the wife cooked and cleaned and bore children – and was probably devoid of true love. That's just how things were in the 1950s.

Consequently, my home life was not like that of Ozzie and Harriett. My parents were stubborn and occasionally a touch vindictive, and around my age 10 or 12, I took notice of the verbal fights they frequently engaged in. There was no philandering on either parent's part, no physical abuse, just disagreements from time to time that wound up in an almost violent argument. My sister told me that years later, after I had gone off to college, the arguments would often culminate in one or the other of my parents leaving home for a few days.

It is ironic that my parents celebrated their golden wedding anniversary in 1992 and were divorced five years later. My mom initiated the divorce, and it was likely precipitated by dementia brought on by a stroke she suffered in 1996.

I hated those arguments, and as a child I always feared the worst – that one or the other would leave or that someone would get physically hurt. It was as a result of those events I focused on my life objectives. Everything I would do in the future, every step I would take, and essentially every decision I would make were influenced by my attempted adherence to those objectives. The last thing I wanted in life was to have a marriage and subsequent family life remotely resembling that of my parents.

Having been raised in this family environment, in very modest financial and social circumstances, and with my attitudes tempered by church attendance and Bible stories, I had no interest in the three popular goals in life – Fame, Fortune, and Power. I would have had no clue how to handle any of them. Instead, my parents had been raised during the Great Depression and the Dust Bowl days followed by World War II, when mere survival had even been questionable. Surprisingly, both sides of my family had not been *Grapes of Wrath* migrants to California during those awful social and economic times of the 1920s and 1930s. Consequently, emerging from that family history, I had been conditioned to seek a modest, simple lifestyle, unburdened as far as possible by stress and financial want. Hence, my life's objectives just naturally emerged. I don't know that I ever wrote those objectives down on paper until I wrote this book, but their concepts were always in the back of my mind, and they tempered everything I did.

In retrospect, I have been married to my wife for more than 50 years. We have three baptized believing children – two boys and a girl – all of whom completed college without debt, two of them later having achieved advanced degrees. I graduated from Harding College. The jobs I held over the years were generally better than I deserved, but I was blessed with a succession of excellent, tolerant bosses. I was financially able to take early retirement. My work also provided sufficient income so that my wife could be a stay–at–home mom. We live in Bartlesville, Oklahoma, an ideal city – small enough to serve us but close enough to Tulsa to meet our big–city needs. I served in the U.S. Army Reserve and National Guard for six years, expecting any day to be sent to Vietnam but never having had to go. I have served in leadership positions in multiple congregations, as well as having frequently taught Bible classes.

In a word, all of my life objectives have been met to a degree far exceeding my expectations or my deserving of them.

Further, incredibly, despite our inauspicious beginnings, my wife and I have visited together 39 foreign countries on five continents and all 50 states and the District of Columbia. I have ridden a camel in the shadow of the Pyramids of Giza and stared the Sphinx in the eye. We have sailed through the Bosporus and have visited the Spice Bazaar in Istanbul, and we have stood in the Amber Room in the Catherine Palace in St. Petersburg, Russia. We have witnessed Michelangelo's art on the ceiling of the Sistine Chapel in the Vatican and his statue of *David* in Florence. We climbed Notre Dame's towers before they burned. We have witnessed the weird physical phenomena associated with standing on the Equator in Ecuador. We have viewed Paris from the top of the Eiffel tower and admired *Mona Lisa* at the Louvre. I have purchased a diamond ring at a gold souk in Dubai. We have eaten haggis in

Edinburgh and poi in Honolulu, attended theatre in London and New York, and viewed Normandy's beaches and cemeteries. We have walked the streets of ancient Ephesus and Corinth and have stood atop Mars Hill in Athens in the footprints of the Apostle Paul. We have stood in the shade of the olive trees on the Mount of Olives, crossed the Kidron Valley to pray at the Wailing Wall in Jerusalem, and walked the Via Dolorosa, Jesus' path to the cross.

I have survived a plane crash. I have shaken hands with the future (Ronald Reagan), past (Gerald Ford, George H.W. Bush), and wannabe (George Romney, Jesse Jackson) presidents. And the list goes on . . . gondola rides in Venice, windmills in Holland, fjords in Norway, *The Last Supper* in Milan, and the tower of Pisa.

I speak of these things humbly, for in no case were my righteousness, intelligence, or abilities responsible for their occurrence. However, it begs a huge question – In addition to experiencing my primary objectives in life, how did all these other magnificent blessings come to pass? For them to have happened by accident would have been a mathematical impossibility, and there is no way under heaven that I could have earned or deserved them. So, then, just how did that naïve boy with the humble beginning wind up here having enjoyed all these blessings and experiences? There appears to be only one legitimate answer as to how he had arrived at this place, at this point in time, in the condition in which he found himself. There had to have been divine intervention.

"Ebenezer," I finally replied to my coffee companion.

"Huh? Explain," he said.

"Ebenezer," I replied. "Here I raise my Ebenezer, hither by Thy help I've come."

"That almost sounds Biblical," my friend said.

"It is almost Biblical. Actually, it comes from an old church hymn," I explained. I did not remember the exact Biblical text at the time. Still, I continued, "It refers to what one of the Old Testament Prophets said and did following some miraculous deliverance of the Israelites, I think."

I then went on to explain something to the effect that, despite my good intentions and a few good decisions, during my life, I have also made plenty of bad decisions – due to immaturity, lack of wisdom, and sometimes for just the wrong reasons. I learned later in life that right decisions trump good intentions. I have to believe that God has not only smiled at my right choices and actions but has also helped me through my self–created morasses, sometimes patting me on the back and occasionally whacking my knuckles, in the hope that I would eventually learn something about life and faith. I have no other explanation of how I wound up with a perfect wife, great and loving children and grandchildren, an excellent employment career, a comfortable retirement, excellent health, unbelievable worldwide experiences, and wonderful life–long Christian friends. Though I usually sought the good, my motives were sometimes impure, so my current situation certainly cannot be attributed only to my wisdom, good judgment, modest talent, or even my righteousness. I had considerable celestial help.

I explained to my friend that my entire life had been filled with frequent, beneficial, inexplicable events – some seemingly insignificant, others meaningful and life-changing. When viewed as a whole, these events can only be attributed to God's intervention in my life – His attempts to salvage one more soul – me – and, by extension, my whole family. As expected, some of the "blessings" he provided were not well received by me at the time but were viewed by me quite negatively. However, as I think back, the sum total of those interventions was an unimaginable blessing to my family and me, and I can only view them as a God thing.

My friend asked me to elaborate.

I asked him if he could sit there all day to sit there drinking coffee while I told the story. He agreed that maybe he didn't have that much time to spare on that particular day, and jokingly suggested that I write a book.

The more I thought about his comment, the more the idea of writing a book seemed to make sense. I am not arrogant enough to believe that my life is exceptional or that it is significant enough to warrant recording in a book. Instead, the way my life has unfolded, the many unexpected and unexplained events of which it is comprised, is due, I believe, to the obvious, often blatant, intervention of God in my life in both low times and in times of celebration. This chronology, and the way all the significant events over a period of more than seven decades seem to be mysteriously connected, might be of interest and some value to other struggling Christians. The story might help some understand that all of life is not smooth sailing, but some rough seas are to be encountered, endured, learned from, and overcome. Only then is the complete picture clear. With this in mind, I decided that a book might be worthwhile.

Therefore, based on my reflections on life over many years and based on my friend's reluctance to sit through a whole day of coffee–drinking listening to me drone on, I decided to write this book. I hope and pray that the reader will find it both interesting and, more importantly, helpful in negotiating life's journey.

As implied above, my life can be best characterized as a collection of anecdotes – significant events – which, I believe, have been the result of God's intervention. Consequently, rather than write the book as strictly a chronological recording of my life I have written it with some chronology but have also digressed frequently to describe a significant event that warrants its own chapter. I wanted to highlight some events in enough detail to support my thesis that they were not accidental but rather providential. Also, some of the anecdotes were not necessarily life-changing but were at least life-enhancing and interesting and often amusing. I hope you will also find them that way.

That being said, here I raise my Ebenezer; hither by Thy help, I've come.

Two

SEMINOLE (1944–1952)

"It was a dark and stormy night." I realize those are the words with which the Snoopy character in the "Peanuts" comic strip always begins the great novel he attempts to write. However, it perfectly describes my beginning. It all started for me on a dark and stormy night, 10:10 p.m., March 25, 1944. I was born that evening in Seminole, Oklahoma. At the time, my dad, William Ray "Ray" Vaughan, was serving in the Army Air Corps in the South Pacific among some of the ugliest combat of World War II. He came out uninjured, but he experienced some of the most horrible war scenes, witnessing death and destruction daily. This experience stayed with him throughout his entire life, but that is another story. He was on a ship in the middle of Pacific, heading for duty in the combat zone on October 3, 1943, his birthday. Ironically, he was in the middle of the Pacific heading back to the States on October 3, 1945, once again on his birthday. Consequently, he was still in the South Pacific on the day I was born. My mother, Cuma Brock Vaughan, was a war bride, keeping things together on the home front and eventually delivering me on that stormy night in March.

Both my dad and my Mom were from rural Oklahoma and were high school graduates. My Mom was a salutatorian at Prairie View High School near Earlsboro, which was near Seminole. My dad graduated from Mountain View High School, also near Seminole. Dad's high school's name was sort of ludicrous in that there were no real mountains near the school. Neither of my parents attended college in those days, although my dad did pick up a few college hours later in life.

When my dad returned to civilization, he found work in Seminole as a salesclerk in a department store, the C.R. Anthony Company. At the time, Anthony's was a regional competitor of the J.C. Penney Company and Montgomery Ward. Dad's boss, the manager of the store, was Edwin Marshall.

19

Dad established a good working relationship with Mr. Marshall, who, ironically, played a significant role in my life sixteen years later, in a different city. I use the words "ironic" and "ironically" frequently during this treatise. There have been so many ironic events and circumstances that have occurred during my life that I want to highlight some of them and express the belief that God loves irony in the working of His will.

It was tough for Dad to support a wife and child on a department store salesclerk's pay, so at the time, we did without some luxuries – like an automobile and a telephone. Eventually, he found better paying work driving a cement mixer truck for National Concrete Company in Seminole.

We lived in Seminole for the first seven years of my life. During that time, we lived in four different houses in the town. Our first house, on East Broadway in Seminole, did not have indoor plumbing, although it was in the city limits. We had an outhouse in the back yard. My dad was still working at C.R. Anthony's at that time, and we were still unable to afford certain luxuries – in this case, a refrigerator. I remember the iceman coming around several times per week delivering a block of ice, which was then put in our "ice box" for use. I still remember the tongs with which he handled the block of ice and the card beside the back door showing how many ice blocks we were requesting.

Since we did not have an automobile, Dad walked to work. We walked almost everywhere we went – the exceptions being when a friend or relative who had a car would occasionally drive us.

I remember one particular anecdote from our time at that house. We only lived there until I was about 3 or 4 years old. My Mom joined the Home Demonstration Club in Seminole, kind of a cross between a sewing circle and a group of master gardeners. Children were not welcome at the meetings, so it became necessary for Mom to figure out how to deal with me at the first meeting. A young girl next door did babysitting, so Mom lined her up to sit with me for a couple of hours when she attended the meeting. When she took me next door to the babysitter's house, I leaned against the door and sobbed because I didn't want to stay with the sitter. Mom left me anyway and went away in anguish to her meeting.

While she was gone, the sitter read me stories and introduced me to a Hershey's chocolate bar as she read the stories. I quickly changed my attitude and thought staying with a sitter was not such a bad idea after all. As it turned out, Mom, guilt-ridden, left the meeting early and hurried home to rescue me – expecting to see me lying on the floor wailing. Instead, when she returned, I was sitting on the sitter's lap, eating a Hershey bar, and I was in no hurry to go home. Although she was relieved that I was not suffering, she never left me with a sitter again in my life. On my account, she gave up her membership in the Home Demonstration Club after only one meeting.

When I was about four years old, we moved to a house on Highway 99 on Seminole's north side. This house was only about a block, through an orchard and up a hill, from my Great Grandpa Atkinson's house. Great Grandpa Atkinson was my Grandmother Vaughan's father, and his wife, deceased at the time, was full blood Western Cherokee. It is through that branch of my family tree that I have my Western Cherokee blood.

Great Grandpa Atkinson was also a carpenter. We were still living near the poverty line and had no money for frills like new furniture. In the meantime, I had outgrown sleeping in the floor in Mom and Dad's bedroom and needed a bed of my own. My dad built me a twin bed out of scrap lumber in Great Grandpa Atkinson's workshop, and I slept in that bed for at least 14 years, through four more houses in three cities, until I went away to college.

We moved about a mile farther north on Highway 99 to a larger house about a year later. By then, my dad was working at National Concrete, and we were a little more affluent. We had managed to buy a car, and we had indoor plumbing and a refrigerator. The car, a brand new 1949 Chevrolet, had a sticker price of less than $1000. As with most automobiles at that time, it had exactly zero options; two-door, stick-shift, 6-cylinder, two-speed windshield wipers, no power accessories, no radio. It did have a heater, for which I was grateful.

Our house on Highway 99 had a huge front yard that fronted the highway. My memories of the house also include a large sandbox in the back yard, beehives along the back fence, and the three of us sitting on a quilt in the front yard on clear nights looking at the stars and catching fireflies. It was a simple life, but I really relished those evenings in the front yard with my Mom and dad. It was so peaceful, and I was comforted by the presence of my parents, and all was well with the world.

The sandbox out back was a welcome toy and was heavily used. Also, there was a girl a couple of houses north of us by the name of Lana Merle Ellison. She was a year or two older than I, and we played a lot together – my first real opportunity to have a playmate nearby. She had a tricycle, and she would let me ride it.

Two scary events that occurred at that house stand out in my memory.

The first involved bagworms in some of our trees. In combatting the bagworms, Dad filled a large pan with boiling water and then threw the water on the worms' bag. I got a little close, and he accidentally doused me with the hot water. Fortunately, I suffered no third-degree burns, but my neck, chest, and right arm were pretty painful. In the long run, no real damage was done, and, in fact, we never even visited a doctor. But I still remember having to stay in bed for a few days as a result.

The second event involved angry bees. There were three or four active beehives along our backyard fence. Once I was in the wrong place at the wrong time, and the bees swarmed on me. I don't know how many stings I received, but I do remember my eyes swelling shut at the time. However, consistent with the times, I did not go to the hospital and apparently received no long–term injury.

We moved into our fourth and final house in Seminole at about the time I started first grade. It was located on the west side of Highway 270 near its intersection with Highway 9. Highway 270, if followed northwest, led to Shawnee and then to Oklahoma City. Highway 9, if followed west, led to Earlsboro and eventually Norman. Earlsboro was where my Mom grew up, and at the time, her mother and dad, my grandparents Brock, still lived there.

My Grandpa Ernest Brock was an oil field pumper for an oil company, Barnsdall Oil Company. Once again, another irony, since my dad wound up his working career as an oil field pumper for an oil company, Exxon. But more on that later.

Grandpa and Grandma, Jessie Whisman Brock, raised six children – five boys and a girl – in what amounted to a four-room house with no utilities except electricity and a water well. They also had a storm cellar, which was a bonus considering how often tornados visited the area each spring. I don't remember much about the house except that it was on a dirt road in the prairie, and I don't remember seeing any trees.

I do recall my Grandpa Brock taking me to work with him from time to time. He had to check the fluid levels in the oil gathering tanks and report his findings. Since electronic communications were decades in the future, at that time, the method of recording and reporting the tank fluid levels was a manual operation. It involved writing the tank levels on a piece of paper and putting the paper in what was essentially a tin can nailed to the top of a post with another, larger, tin can turned upside down over its top to protect it from wind and rain. Then periodically, someone from the oil company would come around and collect the reports. Grandpa Brock would read the tank gauges, write the fluid level on the form, and give me the form to stow in the new-fangled storage device cans. I thought I had died and gone to heaven I was so proud to be able to help.

Due to ill health, my Grandpa retired from Barnsdall Oil when I was about seven years old and moved with Grandma and their two remaining school-aged sons to Shell Knob, Missouri.

There is an interesting story regarding Grandpa Brock, me, and God;

at least I have given it considerable thought over the years, and I still don't know the answer. Grandpa Brock was my absolute hero, and I loved him dearly. His ill health had brought him near death on several occasions, and in 1953, when I was nine years old, he fell critically ill and was not expected to live. The hospital at Cassville, Missouri, the closest hospital to Shell Knob, didn't give much hope that he would ever leave the hospital. I worshipped my Grandpa, and the thought of his dying practically paralyzed me. Having been brought up in a Christian home and told about the power of prayer I prayed with all my nine-year-old might that he might live "just eleven more years." I distinctly remember praying this. I rationalized that I could better handle his death at age 20 than I could at age nine. Well, he went home from the hospital once again – in poor health, but alive, nonetheless.

Over the next several years he had other health crises much like the one in 1953 but managed to pull through each time. Finally, in 1959, six years into the illness and my prayer journey, he finally succumbed. It was a blessing to him because he had suffered so much through the years. I viewed it as a gift from God. I had prayed for 11 more years and Grandpa had been given 6 more years – more than half what I had desperately asked for. Although I was not 20 years old, I was able to deal with his passing much easier as a 15–year–old than I would have been able to as a 9–year–old. Maybe this is all just so much wishful thinking, but I cannot help but believe God gave my family and me six more years of Grandpa's life. That's how I viewed it then and still do decades later. This is probably the genesis of my belief that God really does listen to his children and will answer their prayers within His will.

My grandparents Brock had moved to Shell Knob just a few months before my family moved to our house on Highway 270, just outside of Seminole. Our life there saw significant changes in my young life. I guess with my dad's job driving the cement mixer our financial situation continued to improve, because while there, Dad traded our 1949 Chevy for a similarly–equipped, brand–new 1951 Chevrolet. Imagine, two new cars in three years.

A second change in my lifestyle occurred at this house – for the first time I got my own "room". My room was what had been a back porch that had been enclosed and turned into a small bedroom. One door from my room led outside, and another door, which had originally been the back door, opened into the kitchen. Since it was the first time I had slept alone in a room, and since it was actually a back porch with a door to the outside, and since and monsters could easily enter and carry me off, I was a little intimidated. However, when the porch had been converted to a room, the carpenters hadn't bothered to close off the window that opened from a bedroom onto the porch. Consequently, my bed was placed against the wall where the window was, and the bed in Mom and Dad's room was similarly positioned in their bedroom. The window was left open, and at night my Mom would reach through the window and hold hands with me. That comforted me and allowed me to not worry about monsters. I look back fondly on that memory.

It was while we lived in the house on Highway 270 that I started my school days. I did not attend kindergarten – I'm not sure there was such a thing as kindergarten in Seminole at that time. To get to school in Seminole I walked alone about a quarter mile beside busy Highway 270 to the school bus pickup at the intersection of Highway 270 and Highway 9. It picked me up at 7:30 each morning. I repeated the walk in reverse after school, being discharged from the bus at about 3:45. No big deal in the early 1950s, but today it would be unthinkable to allow a 6– or 7–year-old child to do that. The bus route was very long, but it seems the kids got along well and did not hassle the driver. It's just as well – in those days, the bus driver would have dealt out some retribution for misbehaving and would have been praised for doing so by both teachers and parents. Times have changed.

We had some friends that lived on the corner of the two highways where I met the school bus. They were the Hendrix family, and Clyde, the retired husband in the house, opened a small drive–up restaurant on the corner. He sold "Dixie Dogs" along with some other food items and drinks. Dixie Dogs are what we call today corn dogs, and they were delicious. We didn't have a lot of money in our family, but I can never remember having to pay Mr. Hendrix for a Dixie Dog.

I started first grade at Central Elementary School in Seminole. Central had grades one through six and consisted of two buildings side–by–side. Grades one through three were housed in one building, and grades four through six were in the second building next door. There was a very large playground with a fence down the middle that prevented crossover between the older and younger children. There was a water tank, Seminole's sole source of water supply, at the edge of the younger playground. The tank was a huge cylinder, painted silver, about 40 feet in diameter, and probably 60 feet tall. We often played dodge–ball there with our backs against the tank. We didn't even have to wear helmets and padded vests or bubble wrap to play, and no one was ever injured. I guess we were dumb and tough in those days.

My first-grade teacher was Mrs. Sullivan, who was very patient, and, therefore, wonderful. Her room was well located, being the nearest room to the cafeteria, and the cafeteria served good food in those days – or so we thought. It was also the room nearest the nurse's station where we got our immunizations with needles the size of pencil leads, so in that respect, perhaps the room was not well located.

24

SEMINOLE (1944–1952)

In second grade, I had another terrific teacher, Mrs. Thomas. We learned all the things we should – reading, cursive writing, and multiplication tables up through 12 by 12. Mrs. Thomas was firm but fair, and I really loved her. Also, in second grade I got my first crush. Her name was Marilyn Smith, and her dad was preacher at the Methodist Church. She was blonde, blue–eyed, and beautiful, and, more importantly, she also liked me.

During my first grade I became aware of but not well acquainted with a third grader by the name of David Boren. He eventually was elected as Governor of Oklahoma, served two terms as a U.S. Senator and later became president of the University of Oklahoma.

Other precious, pleasant memories of Seminole come readily to mind. Our family situation changed drastically with the acquisition of the new car. Until we got a car, we had very few options for travel or recreation outside our house. Once we got the car, the whole world seemed to open up. We were able to drive to my grandparents' house, 300 miles away in Missouri, and we were also able to take advantage of the limited recreational and social thrills available in small-town America – going to church, "going to town" and, most exciting of all, going to the drive–in movies.

Admittedly there weren't a lot of actual recreation options available in Seminole, Oklahoma, in the late 1940s and very early 1950s for a family that didn't have two extra nickels to rub together, but having bought a car, however, we could now go to the drive-in theater, which was always a great attraction. It had giant searchlights outside the theater, which were shined into the night sky, reminding everyone all over the town of the presence of the theater and guiding them to it. The searchlights were surplus equipment that was used by the Army in World War II to spot enemy aircraft at night. Drive-in theaters were always a treat, but I don't remember ever being able to stay awake through the entire movie. It's a shame that with daylight savings time nowadays delaying their showings by an hour, they have gone pretty much the way of the dodo bird.

Another recreation option was to "go to town" on Saturday night. During those days, all the downtown merchants stayed open late on Saturday night, and they would have contests to attract customers into their stores. One such favorite contest was a guessing game whereby a merchant would place a large jar in his store window and fill it with dried pinto beans or marbles and invite people to "guess how many" beans were in the jar. A person would look at the jar and formulate a guess and would go inside the store and write his guess and his name and address on a slip of paper. The one who guessed closest to the actual number of beans would receive some sort of item or discount in the store. Another way customers were attracted into stores was the presence of a simple drawing – put your name on a piece of paper, drop it in a box inside the store, and at the end of the evening, a name would be drawn out to receive a prize of some sort. As simple and as boring as these might seem in twenty-first century America, these were big drawing cards for small towns in the early 1950s. Downtown was always packed on Saturday nights, and I remember that we usually had to circle several blocks several times to find an empty parking space. We also used the opportunity to look in the store windows and to dream about what we would like to buy. Even children who had no money could dream.

Another situation that changed once we acquired the new Chevrolet was the opportunity to attend church regularly. My Mom had come from a strong religious background – her mother and her mother's family had been strong Christians and leaders in the church for decades. My dad was not a Christian at that time, but he became a Christian sometime in the late 1940s, likely due to my Mom's influence. My earliest memories of church were of the Church of Christ in Seminole, and our preacher was Brother Green. I don't remember his first name, but he was well-loved by the congregation. I specifically remember Sunday school classes and Vacation Bible School, along with the cookies and lemonade. I remember the felt boards where Bible stories were illustrated with felt cutouts, and I remember coloring books with church themes. I remember sitting in the auditorium with Larry Quinalty, a friend of mine, and fidgeting as young boys do at such times. Those days in that church formed the basis for my future Christian walk, and I will forever be grateful for them. Larry Quinalty intersects my life several years later. In Larry's case, the intersection would be a significant event.

However, unbeknownst to me, God was working in my life even at that early date. The good times in Seminole and my romance with Marilyn Smith were about to come to an end because the first great significant event in my life – what I would years later consider God's first providential, Ebenezeresque act on my behalf – was soon to occur. It had required seven years to manifest itself, but when it came, it came with a bang.

It was in December 1951, halfway through my second-grade year in elementary school in Seminole. I had fallen in love with the church there and all the activities and friends it provided. In addition I had close relatives in Seminole, and there were lots of fun things to do, even though we were poor. To my seven–year–old mind, everything was perfect. However, things were about to change dramatically. Dad came home from work one day and announced that we would be moving to Ada, Oklahoma, 37 miles from Seminole. He would begin working at a gasoline plant near there that was owned by Carter Oil Company. Given my happy young life in Seminole, that announcement crushed me.

At the time, since I was unable to look around the corner to the future, so to speak, the announcement of the job-change and the required move was met by kicking and screaming on my part. I was totally happy and satisfied by the status quo – my own room, church, the occasional drive-in movie and friends, especially Marilyn Smith. The last thing I wanted was for this situation to change. However, as always, God's providence ultimately and forever worked for not only my good but also for the good of my immediate family and for dozens, if not hundreds of others scattered across several states and decades. Also, from social and scholastic standpoints, the move to Ada brought me the best years of my life until I entered college.

Waxing philosophically later, as I matured and reflected on the great, significant events in my life, I came to realize that God used each subsequent event – frequently some sort of relocation – to build on the previous event to fully deliver and reveal His blessings. If the chain had been broken at any point, I would not be here today writing this book, and it frightens me to consider that, in that event, my wife would be who knows where, our adopted daughter would be who know where, and our sons, and subsequently, our grandchildren would never have been born. Not only that, there are several other people to whom we introduced their future spouses or led to Christ who, had the chain of events been broken, would have led entirely different lives. The power of God and his significance and influence in making silk purses out of what appear to be sows' ears in our lives is profound and wonderful. God most certainly does work for the good in all things for those who love Him.

Of course, at the time, all this was still foreign to my seven–year–old mind. I was not yet familiar with Romans 8:28, and I had experienced nothing which would give me hope for the future. So, I just wept and probably offered a child's prayer and hoped that God was listening.

THE PROVIDENCE OF GOD

Although I didn't realize it at the time, I had been the beneficiary of the following events which would positively affect my future life:

1. I became friends with Larry Quinalty who would become my roommate at Oklahoma Christian College a few years later and who would subsequently preach at the Shell Knob, Missouri, Church of Christ, home congregation of my uncle and aunt, a congregation I have visited many times over the years.

2. I was introduced to Edwin Marshall, who would provide me with two years of a part-time after-school job in Bartlesville, Oklahoma.

3. My dad changed jobs and went to work with Carter Oil Company, which necessitated my family's move to Ada, Oklahoma which, in turn, would initiate a series of beneficial events that affected the rest of my life.

Hither by His help I had come.

Three

ADA (1952–1960)

That seemingly simple event – Dad's changing jobs and our moving to Ada – would change my life forever, but not in the way I figured it would. I had been crushed and had met the announcement with kicking and screaming but in vain. No more Marilyn Smith, no more Mrs. Thomas, no more "going to town" on Saturday night, and no more incredible experiences at church. My life, as I knew it, was over.

Although I did not recognize it at the time and definitely didn't appreciate it, as time would tell, it was a critical link in my life that eventually blessed me, my family, and many, many others scattered across the country with whom I would become acquainted. It was the first of the three job changes that my Dad made during my life – birth through college graduation – which required moving to another city. I had no clue that God was working for my good and also "for the good of others that love him." As it turned out in my own personal life over the years nothing could have been more real for me than Romans 8:28.

At that time, the "blessing" of moving to Ada was not providing any hints. As it turned out, that blessing was like a seed that is planted and requires time and care before it produces a tree. Then the tree itself also involves time, watering, and nurturing before it produces its fruit. And then the fruit requires additional time and sunshine to ripen. You don't go directly from seed to mature fruit without some intervening time and pain, and effort. In this case, the seed – the move to Ada that enabled my Dad to go to work for Carter Oil Company – took years to mature and ripen.

We made a move to Ada during January of 1952. The Carter Oil Company gasoline plant where Dad was working was located near Fittstown, Oklahoma, only eight miles south of Ada. However, for many reasons, it behooved us to live in Ada rather than Fittstown – housing, shopping, church, schools, etc. Besides, the commute to work was very short and easy – just down Highway 99, ironically, the same highway we had lived on during our time in Seminole. Subsequently, we rented a house on Fifth Street in Ada.

My time in Ada spanned 3½ years of elementary school, all of junior high school, and a year of senior high school, a period of slightly more than eight years all told. Those were easily the best years of my pre-college life. The blessings I received there – church, friends, community, schooling, sports, adolescence – molded my life in ways that are still influencing me today.

During our Ada years, we lived in three different houses. Our first house in Ada was at 1018 East Fifth Street. In a recent visit, I discovered that the house is no longer there. In much of the 1000 block the houses have been removed and have been replaced by commercial businesses. Also, since that time, Fifth Street has been renamed Arlington Street. As in those days, the street remains a section of Oklahoma State Highway 1 and is heavily traveled.

We rented the house and lived there for perhaps two years. My memories of life at that house are somewhat limited, given my age at the time. However, I still have several specific memories that stand out. The first involves our next-door neighbors, the Williams'.

The Williams had one child still at home, a son by the name of Donald Ray. Donald Ray was about two years older than I, but we were great play-mates. My first fond memory – our favorite game was pretending we were pirates and having play sword fights. Two blocks west and across the busy Fifth Street was an early version of a convenience store. It sold gasoline but also stocked a good selection of groceries. One of the things they stocked was oranges from California. In those days, the oranges were shipped to grocery stores in small crates constructed of thin wooden slats – top, bottom, and sides – and about two feet long. When a crate had been emptied, the store owner would simply throw it away. From time to time, Donald Ray and I would go to the store and salvage a crate. We then took it home, removed the slats, and carved wooden swords out of the slats. We were pretty imaginative at the time, and we were also very young – both being pre-teens.

So what is wrong with this picture? Two grade-school-age boys cross-ing a heavily–traveled highway by themselves, both going to the store and returning, using sharp knives to carve up wooden slats without supervision, and then using their creations to try to whack or "stick" each other as they "fought" with swords, also unsupervised. If that had happened in today's "enclose children in bubble wrap" mindset, all of our parents would have been in jail for child neglect, and Donald Ray and I would have wound up in foster care. However, we proved that we had at least enough sense to look both ways before crossing the highway, to use a knife properly and safely, and to avoid attacking vital points on our bodies during our "fights." As far as I can remember, neither of us ever suffered any kind of injury in our playing.

A second fond memory involved Halloween trick or treating. As mentioned, I was very young at the time, and our front yard faced Fifth Street/Highway 1. Since my family was not blessed with discretionary money that could be used to buy a lot of discretionary junk like candy, it was very important that I make a huge haul trick or treating. All the houses with reputations for giving out generous treats were located across Fifth Street and generally along Sixth and Seventh Streets and the streets that intersected them. Consequently, to maximize my trick or treat haul it was necessary that I cross the highway four times on Halloween – over to collect treats and back to dump my sack of the treats and then repeat the trek to refill and dump my second sack. All the while I was doing this I was wearing a mask that impaired my vision, and I was an unaccompanied eight–year–old boy wandering the streets alone in the dark. Once again, my family and I violated all the safety rules of child-rearing. However, this only happened one evening a year for about two years – until we moved to a different house in Ada – and, admittedly, child predators and perverts were extremely rare in 1952 and 1953 in Ada, Oklahoma. I long for those good old days, but they are gone forever.

I was in the second grade when we moved into Fifth Street's house, and we stayed in that house through my third-grade year. Consequently, during that period, I had to walk to school – it's what was done in those days. Willard Elementary School was located on Ninth Street, so I had to walk four blocks south from Fifth Street to Ninth and then two blocks west on Ninth to reach the school. Once again, crossing Fifth Street/Oklahoma Highway 1 going and coming, unaccompanied. It's a miracle I lived to write this memoir. Fortunately, my mom was not a helicopter mom.

At any rate, I survived crossing Fifth Street unaccompanied hundreds of times, cutting wood with a knife, sword fights, going trick or treating alone, and then walking to and from school by myself for about two years until we moved, and all during that time I suffered no injury or trauma.

During my years at Willard Elementary I had several what I would call exceptional teachers – Mrs. Sara Lance in second grade, Mrs. Azalia Reeves in third grade, Mrs. Mabel Williamson in fourth grade, and Mrs. Louise Johnson, the school music teacher, in particular.

Since we had moved to Ada mid-year of my second grade, I was apprehensive about the new school, but Mrs. Lance welcomed me, introduced me to the class, and made me feel like I belonged from day one. I made many friends in the second-grade class, among them John Beauclair and Charles "Kit" Mohr. These two friends would make an unexpected appearance later on in my life.

31

Mrs. Reeves was also great. In her class, we started getting into the more challenging subjects – math, spelling, etc. – but she made it fun. In third grade, I met John Ramsay and Eloise Bentley.

John became one of my best friends ever. We did everything together until I moved from Ada in 1960, and even then, we managed to visit. John was the son of a doctor, grandson of a doctor, and became, guess what, a doctor – an Orthopedist like his father.

Eloise was smart, pretty, friendly, and my anguish over the loss of Marilyn Smith in Seminole gradually faded. Eloise was sort of my girlfriend at Willard School.

Then one day, when I was in the third grade, Dad came home from work and announced that he was changing jobs. I panicked when I heard the news. I thought, "Oh, no, here we go again." He announced that Humble Oil Company had bought out Carter Oil Company and that from now on he would be working for a different company. (Several years later, Humble Oil changed its corporate name to Exxon.) However, Dad said we didn't have to move because he would still be working at the same place but for a different boss. Humble Oil would take over the gasoline plant's management but would continue operating it with the existing employees. The transaction was largely transparent to our family, except that Dad got a raise in pay as a result. Given my new–found love of Ada, I breathed a huge sigh of relief.

Ironically, had my Dad not taken the job with Carter Oil in the first place —over my strong protestations at the time—he would never have later been in a position to work for Humble Oil/Exxon. As will be seen, his job with Exxon would significantly impact nearly every aspect of my future life.

Sometime in 1953, we moved exactly one block south and two blocks west from our house on Fifth Street to 826 East Sixth Street. This, I suppose, relieved my parents' angst, if any, about my having to cross Fifth Street on a daily basis, although I was totally unaware of any such angst on their part. Also, it was a shorter walk to school, particularly since I was able to cut through peoples' yards and go directly to the school rather than having to go to the end of the block on Eighth Street and then head south. In those days, people didn't have their back yards fenced and populated by Pit Bulls. As long as I didn't leave trash in their yards nor step on their flowers, they didn't complain when I used their yards as a sidewalk. How times have changed.

My fourth-grade teacher was Mrs. Mable Williamson. She was tough but very good. She challenged us and made us better, and I loved her. Her husband was Principal at Ada High School. One thing that Mrs. Williamson did that would have landed her in jail in the twenty-first century was her habit of periodically sending me out just before the noon hour to buy her lunch. I thought it was great – get out of class for a few minutes and make some brownie points with the teacher. There was a small café across Mississippi Avenue, a little over a block west of the school. Mrs. Williamson would give me 60 cents – yes, 60 cents – and send me to the restaurant to purchase a pulled pork sandwich for her lunch. Mind you, I had to cross two streets to reach the café, and Mississippi Avenue was a major artery in Ada with lots of traffic. I did this several times as a 10–year–old during the year, and, miracle of miracles, I wasn't run over by a car or kidnapped by a pervert lurking to nab the first child that appeared unaccompanied by an adult. No one thought anything of this at the time, and I was pretty much the envy of the rest of the class for getting to do so.

One of my classmates in Mrs. Williamson's room was Tom Palmore. It was during that year that he discovered and began to exploit his talent in art. In later years he attended a prestigious art school in Texas and became the resident artist in Philadelphia, Pennsylvania. During that period in his life, sometime in his 30's, he was featured in a *National Geographic Magazine* story, which highlighted his work in Philadelphia and showed many of his paintings. Tom later moved to Santa Fe, New Mexico, and became immersed in the art scene there. I last saw him at the Ada High School 50th Class Reunion of 1962 grads in 2012. Even though I did not graduate from Ada High School, I attended its reunion simply because I had made and retained a large base of close friends there. Among other things, Tom had published a coffee table book of his works, and he gave me one and autographed it for me.

Another of my classmates in Mrs. Williamson's room was Bill Peterson. We were friends throughout elementary school and into high school. I re-member hanging out with other friends at his parents' house on Northcrest Drive. Bill was the son of a doctor, but medicine was not his interest. He majored in law in college and eventually was elected District Attorney in the 22nd district in Oklahoma, which includes Pontotoc, Seminole, and Hughes counties. Ada is located in Pontotoc County.

Bill gained considerable national notoriety in two murder cases he pros-ecuted in Ada. The first was chronicled in John Grisham's only non–fiction book, *The Innocent Man*. The book told the story of the murder of a woman in Ada and Bill's prosecution and ultimate conviction of the two men thought to be responsible. The murders occurred in 1982, many years before DNA became a tool of the law to identify criminals. Sufficient circumstantial ev-idence existed to try the two suspects, and they were ultimately convicted. They were granted two additional trials, I believe, and in each case they were again convicted and sentenced to death.

Fortunately, death penalty cases go through many judicial reviews before they are carried out. During the years-long reviews of this case science had discovered DNA, and it had become a significant factor in determining the guilt or innocence of an accused. The evidence collected in the original investigation of this murder was still available. It was reexamined, and it was found to contain DNA that exonerated the two who had been convicted of the crime. Instead, it pointed to another man, ironically a key "witness" in the prosecution of the two suspects. The "witness" was subsequently charged with the crime and eventually tried and convicted, and the two men who had been imprisoned for nearly twenty years were freed at last. In Bill Peterson's defense, the evidence initially used in the prosecution of the case appeared solid, and he tried the cases in good conscience with the tools he could work with.

The second case where Bill gained notoriety was chronicled in a book entitled *Dreams of Ada*, by Robert Mayer. In this case, in 1984, a female convenience store clerk disappeared and was thought to have been kidnapped and murdered. Two suspects were identified, arrested, and brought to trial. Once again, the evidence was circumstantial, but both suspects were convicted and sentenced to life imprisonment. This was still prior to the introduction of DNA evidence, but it didn't matter at any rate because it turned out that there was no DNA to process. In this case, Bill was once again working with what evidence he had and, I think, did so in good faith. The remains of the young woman who disappeared were discovered many years later a few miles from Ada, but there was no evidence uncovered in the discovery which warranted reopening of the case. To this day many believe the two who were convicted are innocent of the crime.

I last saw Bill 1n 2012 at the 50th reunion of the Ada High School class of 1962. We pointedly did not discuss the events or the books but instead dwelt on old memories.

Of course, at the time I was attending Willard Elementary School, none of these future events was even imaginable.

Mrs. Louise Johnson taught music at Willard to all students in grades four through six. She tried in vain to coach me in the art of singing, but I was a few keys short of any visible musical prowess. Nevertheless, she persevered and produced a number of school musical plays in which I, along with those who were actually talented in music, performed. Mrs. Johnson and her husband drove an MG convertible automobile at the time, which everyone thought was super cool. She was really patient and kind with me, which I greatly appreciated.

My fifth grade was also interesting. My teacher was Miss Flora McReynolds. Miss McReynolds was not only a teacher but also a very talented artist.

She and her sister, Miss Vera McReynolds, who taught at the Washington Elementary School, also taught oil painting in their spare time. They had a small studio set up at their house, and students came once a week after school for lessons in oil painting. The cost was $1.00 per session, and the McReynolds provided easels, paint, and brushes. Students had to provide their own canvas boards. We learned a lot about oil painting techniques, even though we were young. We also had opportunities to view some of the McReynolds sisters' own oil paintings, which were great.

A very interesting event took place during my year in fifth grade involving Mrs. McReynolds and a "chalk talk." A chalk talk involved an easel similar to those used in business presentations today and the large pad of papers that are used by the presenter. Mrs. McReynolds would lightly make a pencil sketch of an outdoor scene on the large sheet of paper – trees, mountains, a stream, etc. She would then assign students to color portions of drawing and would give each student the appropriate color of chalk to use. Then all of the participants in the chalk talk would take their assigned piece of colored chalk and line up to the left of the easel. The first student would use his chalk to color his or her assigned portion of the picture. That student would then step aside and the next student would step in with chalk and color in his or her assigned area. When the last student had finished, the picture was finished. The artwork was limited, given the talent of the students and their medium, but it was fine and was an accomplishment for the students.

In those days, network TV did not broadcast during the midmorning. Instead, each station came up with its own programming, and this frequently took the form of live local general interest talk shows. To have some sort of interesting act or performance on one of those shows was golden. Not only that, color TV was just beginning to take hold. So when Mrs. McReynolds contacted the CBS affiliate in Oklahoma City and offered a live chalk talk presentation, involving children and art work in colors, the program manager jumped at it. It would provide a really interesting diversion from the usual boring conversations that filled the time on such shows – and free of charge to boot. A can't-lose proposition.

On the day of the show several cars filled with Mrs. McReynolds' students departed Ada for the 90–mile drive to Oklahoma City. We arrived at the TV station, were welcomed, and conducted our chalk talk on live color TV to everyone's delight. No one messed up, and the response from the TV audience was very kind.

I was a star. I was on TV for the first time, and it was in color.

Anyway, my fifth grade school year was memorable.

One other thing that made the year memorable was that I had my first date, and it was with Eloise Bentley. We went to the movies and afterward enjoyed fountain drinks together at the drug store next door to the theater. Since I was only 11 years old at the time and obviously couldn't drive, and since our family only had one car, still the 1951 Chevy, and since my Dad was working the day of our date and had driven the car to work, it was incumbent upon Eloise's mother to chauffeur us to the theater and back. So she picked me up for the date and then picked us up at the drug store afterward and drove me home. I was too young to be embarrassed. My allowance those days was 25 cents per week, and it cost me less than two weeks' allowance to fund the date. It cost 10 cents for each of our tickets to the movie and 10 cents for each of our fountain drinks at the drug store next door afterward—a total of 40 cents spent. The last of the big spenders. Things were a lot cheaper in those days. I think that was the only date we ever had together, but we remained good friends throughout our school days and afterward.

My sixth-grade teacher was Mrs. Edna Wallace. Her husband was Principal at Ada Junior High School. Mr. and Mrs. Wallace attended the Central Church of Christ, as did my family, and the Wallaces lived only four doors down from us on Sixth Street. As a result, we became good friends with them. Mrs. Wallace was a take–no–prisoners teacher, but she was fair and effective. Although she was tough, I never heard anyone complain about her.

I had gained a little athletic prowess during elementary school, and by the sixth grade, I had learned how to play basketball. I was short, but I was quick and could handle the ball. John Ramsay and Kit Mohr were tall for sixth graders, and all I had to do was get the ball to one of those guys, and we could pretty well count on them, scoring a basket. We played the other elementary schools in basketball games, and due to John's and Kit's presence on the court, I don't think we were ever defeated that year. It should be noted that when John was a senior at Ada High School, he was named High School Basketball Player of the Year in the state of Oklahoma by the *Tulsa World*, so obviously his basketball talents were already demonstrable by the sixth grade.

By the end of my sixth grade my life in Seminole was a distant memory. While in Ada, I had encountered a group of great teachers and had made a load of really good new friends, including Eloise Bentley. I had been exposed to a great church environment, and I had made straight A's in school. I had been able to participate in the elementary school athletics that were offered. Also, contributing to my growing appreciation of Ada was the fact that in sixth grade, I was voted Valentine King in my class, whatever that meant. These things signaled that I had been fully accepted by my classmates and friends and had completely been assimilated into the Ada environment.

I had come to believe that things couldn't get any better and that the move to Ada had indeed been a blessing rather than a curse. My previous complaints to God about the move had been long forgotten by me and had been replaced by a profound sense of gratitude – to the extent that a 12–year–old boy can feel and express real gratitude.

Sometime during my 6th-grade year my Dad bought us a new car. He traded the old 1951 two-door Chevy for a new 1956 Chevrolet Model 210, turquoise, and white in color. Apparently, to avoid forcing my mom to deal with too much new-fangled technology in her driving Dad had it equipped exactly like our 1951 Chevy. It was stick–shift, no radio, no A/C, no power steering or brakes. The sticker, which I looked at, listed absolutely zero options. Except for the model year, the only differences were that the '56 Chevy was four-door and had turn signals. Of course, both of those elements were standard equipment. However, I thought it was the most beautiful auto I had ever seen. They kept the car until 1966, ten years until I had graduated from college.

When I finished at Willard Elementary School, it was time to move on to Ada Junior High.

Two significant events occurred in our household during my seventh-grade year. First, we got our first TV, a 19–inch black–and–white model which was pretty standard in those days, and with the antenna, we were able to pick up three stations – NBC, ABC, and CBS. Secondly, my sister, Donna Drew, arrived in January of 1957, midway through my seventh-grade year. We still lived on Sixth Street at the time.

Whereas Willard School was only three blocks from our house, I was now in junior high, and that school was on the other side of town. My parents made an arrangement with the Wallaces, whereby they would give me a ride to school each morning since Mr. Wallace was going there anyway. We would drop Mrs. Wallace off at Willard and then go to the junior high. I appreciated the fact that I didn't have to walk that distance to school each day, but I was always a little apprehensive about what my schoolmates thought when I got out of the Principal's car each morning. Nothing ever came of it, however.

In the summer of 1957, we moved from Sixth Street to 1012 South Mississippi, on the south side of town. My family had always previously rented houses, but it now became possible for us to buy our own place.

The house originally had two bedrooms, but we really needed three, since we now had an infant girl in the family. At that time, Drew was about six months old. To remedy the shortage of bedrooms, my Dad, with the help of his relatives – Uncle John Atkinson, Truman Atkinson, and Billy Joe West – converted the one–car garage into a third bedroom. I helped them in the construction process by staying out of the way.

This house was quite a bit closer to the junior high school than the one on Sixth Street. I usually rode my 3–speed racing bike to school. To do so, I had to ride up the hill on Mississippi Avenue and then ride uphill on the 4–lane Highway 99 on up to Sixteenth Street. Riding west on Sixteenth, down the long hill, across the unmarked railroad crossing, and up the long hill on the other side put me within about four blocks of the junior high school. I was always totally exhausted when I reached the school. Coming home was not so bad – just the return hill up Sixteenth Street, and then when I hit Highway 99 it was downhill all the way to our driveway.

The ultimate problem, however, was not the hills. The ultimate problem was Highway 99. There were no bicycle lanes nor shoulders nor sidewalks adjacent to the 4–lane highway. Consequently, on my way to school each morning, I rode my bike up the hill on the highway among the automobile traffic until I reached Sixteenth Street

On the highway, as I neared Sixteenth Street, I would ride my bike in the middle lane of the highway, ostensibly the passing lane, since I would be turning left onto Sixteenth Street. It is a wonder that I survived the three years that I made that daily trek to school and back. I don't ever remember having any close calls, but I do remember having a minor encounter with a State Trooper. Once I was in the passing lane about two blocks short of Sixteenth Street on my way to school when a State Trooper pulled up behind me. I was aware of the vehicle, but cars would typically move to the right lane and pass by me, often offering me an obscene gesture. I accepted the gestures without complaint since the passing lane, due to the highway's curve, was a few yards shorter than having to stay in the right lane next to the curb. Anyway, the State Trooper was not willing to pass me on the right with an obscene gesture. He whooped his siren and flashed his lights to get my attention. When I looked back at him, he was shaking his finger, not obscenely, at me but very forcefully indicating that I should move out of the fast lane – which I did expeditiously. He didn't stop, but I believe I learned the lesson. I don't remember ever riding in the passing lane again, either going to or coming from the school.

Ada Junior High was truly a transition from early childhood to adolescence. I came into junior high as a popular kid in elementary school – Valentine King, etc. When I arrived at the junior high, I quickly became a very small fish in a very large pond – just another number. No incoming students from the other five elementary schools had ever heard my name. I ran for Seventh Grade Class Vice President, and most of the voters, when they heard my name, asked, "Who?" It goes without saying that I lost the election.

Consequently, I had to start at ground zero to establish my identity in the school. Doing so became very difficult because I had no social capital – small stature, relatively unathletic at that age, not particularly handsome, not from an affluent family, could not sing – anything. All I had going for me was a history of good grades, and the hope that they would continue. Fortunately, they did continue, and I was able to gain some traction from that. However, junior high remained a challenge to me to abandon elementary school attitudes and activities and adopt the more sophisticated mores of adolescence.

Over time as I grew both physically and socially things turned around somewhat. By my ninth grade year, I had grown enough and developed enough self–confidence to go out for some junior high varsity sports. I went out for the basketball team, but lacking any extraordinary size or talent at that level I did nothing but serve as fodder for the real players during practices. I made every practice session but never suited up once. It should be noted that our basketball team went undefeated that season, so it goes without saying that skill and competition on the team was fierce. The nucleus of that junior high team won a state championship as high school seniors. My good friend, John Ramsay, was the center on the team and was a beast on the court and, as mentioned, was later named the outstanding high school player of the year in Oklahoma. He wound up with a full basketball scholarship to Southern Methodist University.

I also went out for the junior high football team. As with the basketball team, I had no previous experience, no extraordinary size, and no specific skills regarding passing or catching the football. Once again, I served as fodder for the real players. Never missed a practice, but never suited up for a single game. As with the basketball team, the football team went undefeated for the season. Not only that, they went unscored upon. The players were horses, so to speak, and, as with the basketball team, competed well when they reached high school. Many went on to play at the college level.

Tennis was a different matter. My Dad had played tennis in high school, and he tutored me a little and eventually encouraged me to go out for the junior high tennis team. I was finally to achieve some athletic success in the ninth grade. I made the tennis team as the number 4 player. During the season, I played four matches against other schools – two as singles and two as doubles – and was the only player to go undefeated that year. I was awarded a letter in tennis and proudly wore it.

I was surrounded by fantastic teachers during junior high. Their collective lot in life seemed to be to instill in their students the attitudes, skills, and education that would enable them to meet life head-on. Two of my favorite teachers were Mrs. Vera Simmons and Mr. Renfro Herndon. I will always remember the notation in my yearbook by Mrs. Simmons, my Algebra I teacher.

"You are a leader," she wrote. That little statement has given me strength on innumerable occasions in the decades since. I also need to say that early on, I was totally lost in Algebra I until one day it dawned on me that "X" could be any value – depending on the equation. I can't say that math in general ever came easy to me after that, but Mrs. Simmons certainly gave me a good start. A few years later, I made 5 hours of A in a college Calculus class, one of my favorite moments, and probably attributable to Mrs. Simmons.

Mr. Herndon was exceptional in grounding the students in government, Constitution, and social studies in general. By the time I was in junior high, Mr. Herndon had not missed a day of teaching in more than 30 years.

I survived junior high and was eager to go across campus to the high school. At that time, Ada High School was located on the same campus as the junior high, just 100 yards or so to the west. I had kept my grades up in junior high, I was inducted into the National Junior Honor Society, I had made a bunch of new friends, and I had actually earned an athletic letter. I felt that I had turned a corner in my life and was ready to step into a new and more gratifying and challenging chapter. As it turned out, my expectations were confirmed, but the results were only short-lived before I was once again having a serious conversation with God.

My career at Ada High School was short but sweet. It seemed that my social skills had improved over my junior high days, and I was much more at ease with fellow students. As was the case three years earlier, however, my fellow sophomores and I were once again the new kids on the block, the rookies, so to speak. As it turned out, the upperclassmen were not cruel, and we sophomores assimilated into the high school scene reasonably easily.

One of the first blessings of my sophomore year was meeting Eddie Roark. He and his family had moved to Ada over the summer, and he would eventually become an Ada High School graduate. Eddie's Dad had decided to go back to college and had enrolled at East Central State College, the college in Ada. Eddie's family included his parents and a younger brother. The family was assigned "married student" housing at the college. The housing was wooden Army barracks that had been converted into dormitories. The married student housing was usually a two-bedroom "suite" that also included a very small kitchen and living room and one bath. It was two-stories and had a very narrow staircase that led to the bedrooms upstairs.

Eddie and I became great friends, and he and I and John Ramsay became almost like the "Three Amigos." We did everything together. There was considerable intelligence and drive among Eddie and John. Eddie eventually became a big-time lawyer in Las Vegas and John, as mentioned, became an orthopedic surgeon in South Dakota.

At some point, my family migrated from the Central Church of Christ to the Southwest Church of Christ, primarily due to the fact that there was a larger youth group at Southwest.

Another friend of mine was Mike Howard. He was a junior, and he and his family attended the Southwest church. His parents had bought him a 1959 Studebaker Silver Hawk, one of the slickest cars I had ever seen. Since he was a year older, he was one of a very few of my friends who had a driver's license, and he used to haul me everywhere. My family was close friends with his grandparents, so Mike and I were pretty thick.

Other friends of mine in Ada that I should mention are Jim Threlkeld, Steve Smethers, Joe, and Shirley Barker, Richard and Edna Osborn, Jerry Howard, and Donna and Judy Briscoe.

I became friends with Jim Threlkeld when we both entered junior high together. He and his family also attended the Southwest Church of Christ, which was probably one reason we made the move to Southwest. Years later, I was best man at Jim's wedding, and our paths crossed again, even later in Independence, Missouri.

Steve Smethers was the son of Wayne Smethers, a preacher for the Church of Christ. I got to know Steve when his father held a gospel meeting in Ada when I was 11 or 12 years old. Wayne eventually became a preacher in Ada, and during that time, Steve and I attended Ada Junior High together. After about two years Wayne and his family left Ada for another preaching situation. At the time, I didn't know where they moved to, but I would soon find out.

Joe Barker and his family attended church with us in Ada, and my parents were very good friends with them. As for Richard Osborn and his family, Richard not only worked with Dad at the gasoline plant in Fittstown but also attended church with us.

Judy Briscoe was a classmate of mine from junior high through my sophomore year at AHS. Her older sister Donna was engaged to a young man named Jerry Howard. Jerry was very talented in music and was a leader while at AHS in both the band and choir. In addition, he regularly led singing at the Southwest Church of Christ. Jerry and Donna were married in 1960, and my family and I were privileged to attend their wedding. Many years later, after I had retired, I would meet their grandson, Reese Howard, and his wife Tiffany, at church in a "small world" event, so many of which have so frequently have occurred in my life.

It should be noted that Donna Briscoe Howard appeared in the book *Dreams of Ada*, previously mentioned. At the time of the disappearance of the convenience store clerk, Donna was a teacher at the Hayes Elementary School in Ada and was a witness of some sort in the trial of the suspects.

Life goes on as usual, but some people/actors frequently appear in more than one role. It keeps things interesting. Consequently, I will cross paths with many of these friends later, along with several others in what can only be called "small world" events. However, there have been so many small world events in my life that I have to believe that they can't all be coincidental but rather the Providence of God. In each case, the small world event occurred at a critical time that either lifted my spirits, or in some other way worked to my benefit.

I made many other close friends during my one year at Ada High School that impacted my life positively, but none as close as those mentioned.

One of the early signs that my standing among my classmates had improved was the fact that I was elected to the Ada High School Student Council as a sophomore rep. I was one of 10 fellow sophs elected to the Council. My good friend John Ramsay was also among those elected to the Student Council with me.

All of the extra–curricular activities in which I participated as a sophomore were associated with politics or academics. I was elected to the National Honor Society, I was a member of the International Understanding Organization – a student organization that dealt with recognizing and appreciating different cultures around the world – and I was a member of the Latin Club, of which I was co-chairman,

I did not go out for any of the school sports. Given my lack of size and my failure to make any dents in the basketball and football teams in junior high, I figured that trying out for those teams as a high school sophomore would be an exercise in futility. What sports skills and physical dimensions I would ultimately possess were still a year or two away. I decided I could always try out for the teams later if conditions improved.

My high school classes were delightful. My favorite subjects were Plane Geometry under Mrs. Bernice Mowdy, Latin under Mrs. Cecile Smith, and Biology under Mr. Benny Floyd.

Mrs. Mowdy might have been the most effective teacher I encountered in my undergraduate career. She taught a subject that I have had opportunity to apply in my life on innumerable occasions, and she made it actually fun. She was results oriented, and she was driven to get every student in the class engaged in the subject. Her objective was to press every student not only to pass the course but to pass the course with honors if possible. In addition to her teaching acumen she also established a class seating practice that encouraged – no, demanded – that each student actively push himself or herself to obtain the highest grade in the class that was personally possible. She did this by seating all the students in order of their current grade in the class. It was her philosophy that the students with the lowest scores needed more of her attention and were therefore seated in the front row of the class. Those with the highest grade were assigned to the back row. The seats were reassigned at the beginning of each six–week grade reporting period, depending on each student's grade average at the time. A student could basically tell at any time during the year where he or she ranked in the class. The ultimate objective was to occupy the right–most seat in the back row – the seat reserved for the highest grade average in the class. To my delight and surprise, I occupied that seat for the school year's final six–week period. In today's educational environment where excellence is ignored and mediocrity is celebrated – "Everybody is equal. Don't shame the slackers. Give everyone a trophy for merely participating." – Mrs. Mowdy would have probably been fired. We need more teachers like her, I believe.

Mrs. Smith's Latin class was truly enlightening. I never had any idea how much of the English language had been derived from Latin. Over the years, it has provided me background and understanding of words that would have been otherwise unfamiliar to me. The resulting expansion of my vocabulary due to the Latin class has benefitted me greatly in my reading and writing. Although I approached the class with trepidation, I can truthfully say, regarding the class, "Veni, vidi, vici." ("I came, I saw, I conquered," to the Latin impaired readers.)

Mr. Floyd's Biology class was no picnic. He taught the subject indepth and demanded that his students be active participants. We were required to compile a Biology notebook, complete with notes and drawings of the flora and fauna, and the notebook became part of our grade. I recall spending hours, including overnight stays, with Eddie Roark in this parents' crowded college housing – the converted Army barracks – working with him to put together our notebooks and study for tests. Years later, while a student at Harding College, I took a Biology class, and the notebook I had compiled as a sophomore in high school and still retained became a source of information that was helpful as I aced the college class.

I was baptized during the fall semester, a few months shy of my 16th birthday. As was the custom in those days before internet, HBO, cell phones, and the like, most churches held two gospel meetings – "revivals" – each year, one in the spring and one in the fall. At the fall gospel meeting at the Central Church of Christ, Brother A. G. Hobbs was preaching. I believe he held a gospel meeting in Ada two or three times over the years. He was very good and very effective, a "hellfire and brimstone" preacher, and I really liked him. By age 15, I had fully realized the importance of baptism, but I had procrastinated at the regular church services and at previous gospel meetings. However, at this revival, I really felt the need to respond. That particular night several had gone forward to be baptized, but I still hesitated. In my mind, I rationalized, "If one more goes forward, I will follow." Intellectually, I was continuing to procrastinate, because we were on the last verse of the invitation song, and no one had responded for the last verse or two. I figured it would be just more wishful thinking on my part. Then God intervened. David York, a friend a year or two younger than I, stepped out into the aisle and headed toward the front. Before I knew what was happening, I stepped out and followed. I will always be grateful to David York, wherever he may be, for taking that step.

That evening sort of completed my growing up in Ada. I had moved from a reluctant elementary school kid to high school without suffering any wounds. I had made friends, kept good grades, become a Christian, and had matured into a somewhat typical teenager. While it is true that I had no regular girlfriend, I had still managed to socialize with the girls in my class, albeit somewhat clumsily since I was still too young to drive. In addition, my church life was great since several of my schoolmates attended church with me, including Mike Howard and Jim Threlkeld. All in all, I had progressed in every way possible from the geek I was in junior high to a somewhat more confident high schooler, and the prospects for improvement seemed promising.

Although I had not become well acquainted with the Ebenezer in the Bible during my years in Ada, I did give thanks to God many times for the move there, realizing that the move from Seminole had truly been a blessing.

Then it all came crashing down.

One day during the spring of 1960, my Dad came home from work and sang a very familiar song, second verse. "We are going to have to move again. I'm being transferred to Bartlesville."

At this point, I came unglued, almost to the point of apoplexy. I had this great life in Ada, and it was spiraling upward in every respect – socially, scholastically, and spiritually – and I didn't even know where Bartlesville was. I didn't recall ever even hearing of it. Although in the back of my mind, I had finally realized that the move from Seminole to Ada had turned out very well for me, I didn't see any possible way that a move to another city this late in my high school career could be of any possible value. I was crushed.

In June 1960, we made the move from Ada to Bartlesville.

THE PROVIDENCE OF GOD

It was a few years before I realized the significance of the beneficial life-changing events which God brought about as a result of our move from Seminole to Ada:

1. My Dad's new employer in Ada, Carter Oil Company, was eventually acquired by Humble Oil/Exxon. This eventually led to my Dad's being transferred by Exxon first to Bartlesville and later to Okemah, Oklahoma. Both moves would later have significant positive impacts on my life.

2. I had become acquainted with the Smethers, Barker, and Osborne families at church in Ada, all of whom would eventually move to Bartlesville, Oklahoma, and welcome me upon my arrival. Joe Barker would eventually provide a personal reference, which was very helpful to me.

3. I had become friends with Kit Mohr and John Beauclair in elementary school, both of whom would eventually move to Bartlesville.

4. I had become friends with Eddie Roark in high school and he became my dorm–mate at Oklahoma University a few years later.

5. I had become friends at church with Jerry Howard and Donna Briscoe and even attended their wedding. Their grandson, Reese Howard, and Reese's wife, Tiffany, would move to Bartlesville many years later and joined us at church there.

6. The most significant result of the move to Bartlesville was that people I met there influenced me to enroll at Harding College, which set the tone for the remainder of my life.

Hither by His help, I had come.

Four

BARTLESVILLE HIGH SCHOOL YEARS (1960–1962)

Little did I know at that time that my family's move to Bartlesville would be the key to the rest of my life. Almost every element of my entire adult life – education, employment, marriage, friends, and church – was eventually orchestrated by events and people whom I encountered in Bartlesville. Absolutely none of it would have happened if we had not first been providentially sent to Ada so that my dad could be employed first by the Carter Oil Company there and then by Exxon, resulting in our having to move yet again – to Bartlesville. The move to Bartlesville was just the beginning of a powerful and wonderful series of things to come. Eventually, I would recognize the help that God provided due to the move to Bartlesville and would raise my Ebenezer. Still, in the summer of 1960, that did not seem a possibility.

The move to Bartlesville opened my eyes to a different world, and that world would prove to be very small indeed.

Life in Seminole and Ada was very typical Oklahoman – small-town values, small businesses supporting largely agricultural and ranching activities, and a very homogenous citizenry. On the other hand, Bartlesville was a very cosmopolitan community, with an infrastructure of professional, highly–educated people demanding and receiving a well–above average income. The residents were very diverse, with people actually coming from all over the world to the city to work. The nexus of this community's unique identity was the presence of the headquarters of two major oil companies – Phillips Petroleum Company and the Cities Service Company. The city was also home to the Phillips Petroleum's R & D lab, the largest of any other oil company's research facilities at that time. Ph.D.'s and CPA's were attracted to Bartlesville like ants to picnics, resulting in a socio-economic situation uncommon to small cities in the United States.

For my family, it took some getting used to. The obstacles we had to overcome before we felt "at home" were threefold.

First, the presence of the "corporate" attitude which prevailed in Bartlesville, as opposed to the "good ole boy" attitude from which I arose, probably slowed our assimilation into the Bartlesville lifestyle.

Second, my dad worked for Exxon, and Exxon was larger than both Phillips Petroleum and Cities Service combined. However, at that time, there were more than 11,000 combined employees of Phillips and Cities Service in Bartlesville, and there was a total of eight Exxon employees. Hence, the relative overall size of the companies was irrelevant.

Third, Bartlesville's Phillips and Cities Services employees were overwhelmingly white-collar, and my dad's job was definitely blue collar.

Small world events kicked in very early in our days in Bartlesville. As mentioned previously, Wayne Smethers, our former preacher in Ada, and his family, including his son, Steve, had moved from Ada about a year before we did to, of all places, Bartlesville—an extremely small-world event. Having known the Smethers family from Ada we placed our membership in Bartlesville at the Limestone Church of Christ where Wayne now preached. Our reacquaintance with the Smethers family greatly enhanced our acceptance into the brotherhood at Limestone. It was very helpful in allowing us to quickly make good friends at the congregation.

Two other small world experiences also kicked in with our move to Bartlesville. Joe Barker, a friend of ours in Ada, had taken a job with Phillips and moved his family to Bartlesville a year or so before our moving there. And it gets better. Another friend from Ada, Richard Osborn and his family, had also moved to Bartlesville some time before our move. Ironically, Richard had also taken a job with Phillips Petroleum. As mentioned earlier, both of these families worshipped with us at the Church of Christ in Ada. It was like old home week when we attended our first Sunday at the Limestone Church of Christ.

The small world experiences did not end there. Also as mentioned previously, both John Beauclair and Kit Mohr had also moved to Bartlesville in the months prior to our move. Their parents were not associated in any way with either Exxon or Phillips Petroleum, but both sets of parents had taken new jobs in Bartlesville. Their moves were apparently strictly "coincidental" —a word with which I was beginning to become very familiar. I had known John and Kit since second grade, so I was able to meet some friendly, familiar faces upon my arrival at the high school in Bartlesville. All in all, there were three complete families and two school friends who had preceded me to Bartlesville. In retrospect, it certainly appears that God was a great help in making my transition to Bartlesville as painless as possible. And, as will be revealed, our move to Bartlesville was critical to the entirety of my life following the move.

Not long after we had gotten settled following our move yet another small world event kicked in. Even though my dad now had a better job in Bartlesville, we certainly were still not affluent by any means. We watched our money, and, although we never missed a meal and were always warm and dry in our house, we nevertheless had no spare money lying around. I received a weekly allowance, but it was basically a pittance and was truly all my family could afford. Funding dates, putting gas in my car, and buying movie tickets were difficult, although I did find 25 cents often enough to buy a quart size drink – yes, a quart – at the A&W Root Beer stand.

This latest small world event unfolded shortly before the startup of my junior year in high school. My dad happened to run into an old friend of his from his days in Seminole. Earlier in this book, while describing our life in Seminole, I mentioned a man named Edwin Marshall. He was my dad's first boss in Seminole when Dad had worked at the C. R. Anthony store there. By some miracle, Mr. Marshall had been transferred from the store in Seminole to, of all places, the store in Bartlesville, Oklahoma. Do you believe in coincidences? I think God's hand was in this.

In Dad's reunion with Mr. Marshall, he was asked about our family. When Mr. Marshall learned that there was a 16–year–old boy in the family who had plenty of spare time on his hands and a chronic lack of spending money, he asked Dad if that boy might like to pick up some part-time hours (translation: money) working in Anthony's store over the Christmas holidays. It did not take Dad long to inquire if I was interested in such an adventure, and it took even less time for me to reply positively. Clean work, no heavy lifting, inside job, and good pay for the time ($1.00 per hour). In addition, as an employee, I would be entitled to significant discounts on purchases I made in the store. The store carried quality clothing that I would be proud to wear. It was a no–brainer. So I went to work in mid–December of that year, working on weekends and also after school and in the evenings when the store started staying open late near Christmas.

This small world event could only be explained as another instance when God intervened in my life and made the move to Bartlesville a blessing to me. By this time, I had actually been exposed to Ebenezer in the song "O Thou Fount of Every Blessing" at church and had come to associate that name with help received from God. And, after reconsidering the move from Seminole to Ada and its attendant blessings I was beginning to feel that maybe the move to Bartlesville might also turn out to be a gift of God. But the jury was still out by January of 1961.

However, the job turned out to be more than just part-time at Christmas. When the following summer rolled around and school was out I worked full time until school started up again in September. I also worked the Christmas season of my senior year and some again in the following summer before heading to college, a total of about two years.

Shortly after our move to Bartlesville, I had met and made friends with the Butcher boys. Ray and Jay Butcher were twins a year younger than I, and they and their parents were also members of the Limestone Church of Christ. We became fast friends (I had a car), and we ran around constantly for the two years I spent in Bartlesville prior to college. Ray and Jay were big guys, and both were starting defensive tackles on the high school football team.

They were goofy, fun-loving, and a little rough around the edges and took no prisoners, so to speak, and I was glad for many reasons that they were my friends. Although our adventures together were never illegal or particularly dangerous, nevertheless, it seems we were always bumping up against the thin line that separated good from stupid. Miraculously, we never attracted the attention of the authorities. Two years later, sometime after I left for college, they and their parents moved to Oregon, where their family originally lived.

Classes at College High School commenced right after Labor Day in 1960, and I entered the school with no small amount of trepidation. I was in a school more than twice the size of Ada High School, and I knew exactly five people on the first day. At least I had passed my driving test and had obtained a driver's license by the time school started. In the meantime, my mom had pulled $500 out of her savings to buy me a used 1955 Ford so I could drive to school. It wasn't much of a car, but it got me to school and back. And it provided transportation for some dates when my social life kicked up a notch.

In those days, the high school in Bartlesville went by the name of College High School. There was nothing presumptuous about the name. Rather, earlier in the city's history, when the high school was built, the building also housed a Junior College in addition to the high school. Hence the genesis of the name "College High School" or "Col–Hi" as it was generally referred to.

As the city grew, a decision was made to add a second high school in the Bartlesville school district. The new high school was located on the east side of town whence most of the population growth had occurred, and it was named Sooner High School. College High retained its name at the time. Adding the second high school in Bartlesville, over time, proved to be problematic in that it basically cut in half the pool of athletes at each school. It made competing athletically against their traditional rivals difficult since the talent was now spread between two schools instead of being consolidated into a single school. In the mid–1980's the two schools were reunited into a single school, and the new name for the new school was Bartlesville High School. However, I never attended Bartlesville High School. It was still College High School while I was there.

One of the first people I got acquainted with in my new school was Ed Bailey. He was also a junior and sat beside me in my Algebra II class, and he became my closest new friend. When I was barely avoiding trouble with the Butcher boys, I would hang out with Ed. He was brilliant and majored in Physics or Engineering or something near that in college. He was also sort of shy, and that is probably why we hit it off so well. His dad worked in Research & Development at Phillips, but the difference in our social statuses did not matter in our friendship. Ed was not a large guy, but we still referred to him as "Big Ed."

An interesting "small world" situation developed involving Ed Bailey, which would not come to fruition for another year. Afternoons at home after school I enjoyed watching a TV show on KOTV, channel 6. It was entitled "The Lee and Lionel Show," and it featured Lee Woodward, a ventriloquist, and his sidekick puppet "King Lionel," a lion, who proudly took on that persona. The show included Three Stooges movies and considerable chit chat between Lee and King Lionel. The chitchat was far-ranging, frequently somewhat intellectual, and always hilarious. It also featured conversations with viewers in the form of letters Lee would receive. The letters' topics varied, and they would sometimes actually involve communications between the viewers themselves, with Lee Woodward serving as the mediator. My friend, "Big Ed," Bailey was one of those who sent letters to the show, and his comments often contributed to the script. He was simply referred to as "Big Ed" in the discourse on the show.

At one point during the summer of 1961 competition arose when another viewer, an upstart from Tulsa, chimed in proclaiming himself to be "Big Ed." My friend, Ed Bailey, responded by claiming to be the original "Big Ed" and that the interloper from Tulsa was a fraud. It was all in good fun, of course. As with the "Big Ed" from Bartlesville, the actual identity of the "Big Ed" from Tulsa was never revealed. The verbal jousting occurred primarily during that summer and seemed to fade during the fall. Then, the next summer, the letters from Tulsa commenced once again and continued until late that summer. Ed Bailey and I assumed that the pretender had either surrendered to reality or, more likely, was no longer watching the show. Eventually, the rivalry was forgotten, and Ed and I moved on to bigger things, such as our upcoming freshman year in college.

However, as will be discussed later, the "second Big Ed" appears in another of those wonderful small world events that have so frequently enhanced my life. Stay tuned.

Overall, my time at College High was solid but not particularly remarkable. I made some friends, kept my grades up, and stayed out of trouble. I made the Honor Roll every semester, retained membership in the National Honor Society, and was actually named a National Merit Scholarship Semi-Finalist – with my photo on the local newspaper's front page. However, no one asked me for my autograph, so it was apparently no big deal. I wound up graduating number 12 in a class of 426 seniors. The track coach wanted me to join the track team and run the high hurdles. I was quick, but I would never have been able to compete with the large school track stars in the high hurdles. I did have had some excellent teachers at Col–Hi. Mrs. Hilda Downey in Social Studies and Mr. Cliff Pattison in English Lit come to mind.

I made my first and only "C" in high school as a first semester junior in Mr. Pattison's English Lit class. Being new and still feeling a little awkward, I did not generally join in the class discussions regarding our reading assignments. I did well on the tests but did not frequently opine during class. At some point, I learned – too late to salvage my first semester grade – that Mr. Pattison encouraged and rewarded class participation. Having learned my lesson, during the second semester, I always had my hand up and had something to say – not always worthwhile, but Mr. Pattison did not grade on the quality of one's comments. He just encouraged discussion and added points to your grade.

One hilarious discussion that I remember was a time when we were philosophizing on the relationship between heredity and the environment. Most of the students had bought into the evolutionary theory that "environment determines heredity." It was necessary, according to this theory, for an animal to physically change – evolve – as its environment changed if it were to survive. The evolution from amoeba to simple water creature to fish to amphibian to a mammal, etc., progressed as the animal's environment changed. For example, polar bears lived in the Arctic environment, and they had to evolve heavy, white, warm coats of fur. Camels lived in the desert, and their heredity had "evolved," allowing them to grow large internal sacs in which they could store water, which was necessary for them to survive in the desert. Alligators lived in swamps, and their required evolution had allowed them to survive on fish and to hold their breaths for long periods, even though they did not have gills. And so on.

During the discussion on evolution versus heredity I piped up and made the bold statement that I felt it was the other way around, that heredity actually determined environment. The groans among the students were palpable. People were rolling their eyes and wouldn't look at me. I simply made the case that polar bears did not grow fur because they lived in the Arctic. They were already hirsute (I love that word. It means "hairy."), and it made their life intolerable in the south. Therefore, they migrated to the Arctic "because" they had fur and needed relief from the heat. I also pointed out that although their fur coats were too warm for anything south of the Arctic that in winter, the extremely frigid weather in the Arctic and the scarcity of food required that they hibernate, even with their warm fur.

I also used the example of birds – generally, they flew to warm weather, either north or south, depending on which hemisphere they found themselves at the time. Their heredity was definitely determining the environment in which they lived.

Eventually, my logic got trite, and I even mentioned that geriatrics retire to Florida and Arizona – to environments they can tolerate when their skin gets thinner as they age. At that point, it got out of hand.

The resulting discussion did not get ugly, but it did raise a lot of questions and many comments. I spent most of that hour defending my thesis. The result was that even with occasionally inane comments, I was not hesitant to participate in class discussions after that. As a result, I receive an "A" in the class for the second semester.

The remainder of my high school career was pretty routine. My social life was adequate, and I did make a number of casual friends. I attended the football and basketball games, I kept my grades in good shape, mostly as A's with the occasional B, and I miraculously made an A in Typing.

At the time, the Exxon Corporation, in an effort to keep the pipeline flowing with new Mechanical and Petroleum Engineers into their company, offered full-ride scholarships to Tulane University to employees' children who could pass muster. Tulane was and remains a great Engineering school, among other curricula. To determine who received scholarships, those administering the program viewed the student's high school transcript, looking not only at GPA but the courses completed to achieve that GPA. Sometime early in my final semester of high school, my transcript was thrown into the pool of candidates. It didn't take the administrators to long to determine that I was science– and math–light in my classes, so I was courteously declined. At the time, I was not upset because, as has been mentioned, I was very naïve about college anyway, and it didn't seem like such a big deal. However, in retrospect, had I been accepted, my entire life from that time forward would have been dramatically different.

During my two years in Bartlesville, most everything was basically a blur, but three events stand out in my memory. One was life-threatening, one was an incredible honor, and one was life-changing. Had the first event turned out a little differently, none of the subsequent events would have ever happened.

The first memorable event occurred in late summer 1961, shortly before beginning my senior year. Ed Bailey was as much of a sports nut as I was, and we learned that the Dallas Cowboys were playing the Baltimore Colts in an exhibition football game in Norman at Owen Field, home of the University of Oklahoma football team. The Colts were my favorite professional team, and Johnny Unitas, their quarterback, was my favorite player. We obtained tickets and planned to attend the game. The drive from Bartlesville to Norman took about three hours. The game started at 8:30, so we figured to leave Bartlesville at about 4:30 p.m., make a leisurely drive, stop someplace for a quick dinner, and arrive at the game by the kickoff. The most obvious route to Norman from Bartlesville was through Tulsa, onto the Turner Turnpike to I–35 at Oklahoma City, and then south on I–35 to Norman. A piece of cake.

Ed was driving, and as it turns out, he completely drove past the intersection with the Turner Turnpike, and we wound up someplace in the country south of Tulsa on a highway that was definitely not the Turnpike. At least we had enough sense to head west on this unknown highway, realizing that it would eventually have to intersect the Turnpike. As we were heading west on this secondary road, Ed was trying to make up for lost time, and he was fudging a little on the speed limit. He also, at one point, took a curve to the left side of the double yellow line. Much to his surprise, there was an automobile coming our way also to the left of the double yellow line. Of course, the on-coming auto was in its proper lane. I thought we were dead. Somehow Ed managed to yank our car back into the proper lane without colliding head-on with the other car and without turning us over or sending us into a herd of cattle grazing in a field on the right side of the highway. That was the closest I have ever been to what would have been a fatal accident (but it wouldn't be the last – stay tuned). Ed avoided a head-on collision by less than one second.

We eventually found the Turnpike and made our way to Norman. We were still breathing.

The Cowboys upset the Colts, which was disappointing, but we made the trip back to Bartlesville without incident. On the way home, Ed drove below the speed limit and stayed in his lane.

The second memorable event was merely an honor at the time, but years later, it was treasured in my memory. It had been announced that a Hollywood actor and political activist was coming to Bartlesville in late February

1962 to give a speech, and the public was invited. The speech was to be held in the Phillips Petroleum gymnasium, the largest venue in Bartlesville. When chairs were added to the gym floor, it would seat several thousand people. For some reason that I don't recall, eight College High seniors were selected as special guests, and they would be given front–row seats and would be permitted to greet the speaker following the speech and shake his hand. For some reason, God only knows, I was among those eight students selected to sit down front.

The speaker's name was Ronald Reagan.

At the event, Mr. Reagan gave a politically inspiring speech entitled "Losing Freedom in Installments," which warned of the threat of communism. Although I was aware of whom Mr. Reagan was – he was, after all, the host of the *Death Valley Days* TV show and had played in many movies – the significance of the moment escaped me at the time. Following the speech he gathered with us students, shook hands with each, and asked our names. He was super friendly and seemed very genuine. I got him to autograph my program – which is still framed and hanging on my den wall.

In 1968 Mr. Reagan ran for President but was defeated by Richard Nixon in the Republican primary election. Some years later, Mr. Reagan was elected to two terms as Governor of California and eventually two terms as President of the United States of America. History will also reveal that he was one of our greatest and most effective Presidents.

Often we stand, unaware, in the presence of greatness, and that was one of those times. I didn't fully appreciate or understand it at the time, but it has become one of my most endearing memories.

The third event that stands out in my memory actually began prior to my near misadventure attending the football game in Norman. Still, it was ongoing throughout my two years in high school in Bartlesville. It started at some point during my junior year. It was the habit of the local Churches of Christ to sponsor youth rallies so that the kids from all the local churches could mix and mingle. One such rally involved the Limestone Church of Christ youth and the Bartlesville Sixth and Dewey Church of Christ youth. The rally encompassed all the usual things that went on at such events – refreshments, mix–and–mingle, games, and a devotional. This particular event was really my first exposure to the Sixth and Dewey youth. Their youth group was slightly larger than that of Limestone.

Some of the games required partners, and in one game I was partnered with a girl by the name of Kay Spearman. It was an understatement to say that she was beautiful. It was also useless to pursue her for any other reason than just as a friend, because she was betrothed, but not formally engaged, to a guy who lived and worked in Tulsa. He was a little older than she and had graduated, so to speak, from youth rallies. Anyway, he was in Tulsa, 50 miles away, and he could not be with her at every church or social event. She was also a junior at Col–Hi, although at that point, I had never met her on campus, but we became friends.

In the course of our conversations over the next few months, we discussed college plans. As juniors, it was incumbent upon us to get some college applications in the works. When she asked me where I planned to attend college, my response was, "I have no idea." At that point, East Central State College, the college in Ada, remained a possibility as did Oklahoma University, but everything remained nebulous. Since none of my direct ancestors on either side of my family had, to my knowledge, ever graduated college, I had absolutely no assistance from parents or relatives. That being said, my parents were adamant about breaking that history and were encouraging me to go to college. They just had no advice or experience to bestow on me on the issue. Further, I had no idea what I would study.

One of the young men from Limestone happened to be attending Harding College, and he was not impressed with the college. I remember he gave a short report from the pulpit at a church service during Christmas break, and he said (and I quote like it was yesterday), "At Harding, they roll up the sidewalks at dusk." That statement at the time was pretty off-putting regarding any desire to attend Harding. At that point, I crossed Harding off my list of possibilities as well, as by association, any church-related colleges.

As it turns out, it was a good thing I had an eraser on my pencil when I crossed church-related colleges off my list of potential places to attend.

My new friend Kay Spearman had told me that she and another Sixth and Dewey girl, Janice Durrill, were planning to attend Oklahoma Christian College. Historically, Oklahoma Christian had started out in Bartlesville in the 1950s as a junior college and, in recent years, had migrated to its current campus in Oklahoma City. That, alone, was sort of a drawing card. The more we talked, the more inviting OCC became, and it eventually seemed that applying at OCC might be the thing to do.

Following my conversations with Kay, I decided to check out the campus of OCC. The Butcher boys and I dutifully visited the campus on High School day in the spring of 1962. It was a beautiful campus, all the buildings were new, and I was very favorably impressed by everything I saw. I remember one of the events held on campus on High School day was an old fashioned spelling bee. I entered and figured to at least be competitive. The first word I was given was "gauge," like a gas gauge.

Easy peasy, a piece of cake. "G–U–A–G–E," I replied.

Oops, I immediately recognized my mistake, but too late. You don't get do-overs in spelling bees. I was invited to sit down and was embarrassed to the max. I sat around for a while, taking in some more of the spelling bee. When I finally left, they were contesting over five– and six-syllable words, and I had flopped on one–syllable "gauge."

The disaster in the spelling bee did not dissuade me, for ultimately, I did apply to OCC, was accepted, and was awarded a small scholarship.

This third significant event – my meeting Kay Spearman and being influenced by her to attend Oklahoma Christian College – wound up being the pivotal point in my life. As it turned out, my entire life – marriage, career, even Christianity – was the result of that friendship and Kay's influence

Before I could actually start my college career, however, I had to first graduate from high school, and as it turned out, the graduation ceremony would be memorable. The ceremony was held in very late May at the high school football stadium. The evening was pleasant for that time of year – not too hot and no rain in sight. In those days, the graduation ceremony included a Baccalaureate address. This speech was traditionally a sermon delivered by a local preacher, and it usually contained a lot of praise for the graduates and a lot of good moral advice. Our Baccalaureate speaker that year was Sidney Roper, preacher for the Sixth and Dewey Church of Christ. Sidney was a Bible scholar with, apparently, a photographic memory. He also, traditionally, preached lengthy sermons in the pulpit. I knew Sidney – his son, Sidney Jr., was a good friend of mine – and I thought it was neat that "one of ours" was going to deliver the Baccalaureate.

Sidney spoke for about 35 minutes – not a record for a Baccalaureate address – but probably close. During the entire 35 minutes, he did not utter a single personal word. His entire address was quoted from scripture and was cleverly woven together into what I thought was a masterpiece lesson. He touched on the things that tempted all high school students and would only worsen when they were away at college on their own. I felt his sermon was absolutely appropriate for the occasion and a stunning success. How wrong I was.

As early as the next day both students and their parents started nipping and complaining about the sermon. The common theme of the complaints of the parents was, "My children would not engage in such activities." The graduates were generally asking, "Who was he talking about?"

I had to roll my eyes and shake my head. I had lived with these students for the past two years, got to know many them personally, and got to know a lot of others by reputation. Of course, they participated in the things Sidney spoke of, and in some instances, I am ashamed to admit, so did I.

At any rate, due to the uproar it caused, that was the last Baccalaureate address ever held in conjunction with Bartlesville High School graduations. The administration summarily discontinued future Baccalaureate addresses. However, I was proud to have been in attendance that evening.

Following graduation, I worked a lot of hours at C. R. Anthony's that summer and come Labor Day; it was time to head to college.

Fate had to have one last whack at me prior to actually departing Bartlesville. As my car was loaded and ready to go, my parents took the time to take photographs of my departure. It's a good thing they didn't have a movie camera because what happened next would have made a good segment on "America's Funniest Home Videos" TV show.

After the photograph and the kisses and hugs I got into the car, and it would not start. The motor would turn over, but the engine would not kick in. Dad was there, and he suggested that he push the car. In those days, it was common to push a car to get it running when all else failed. So, he got in his car, carefully touched his front bumper to my rear bumper and pushed and, hallelujah, my car started. I drove away with a sigh of relief. But fate was not finished with me just yet.

I made it as far as downtown Bartlesville. I pulled into the Phillips 66 station on Cherokee Avenue to fill it with gas. When the tank was filled, and I attempted to start the car to continue my journey, it once again would not start. At that point, I realized I was the recipient of three tremendously good breaks: (1) I had broken down on the driveway of a station which had a service bay, (2) another friend of mine, Nolen Goff, worked there as a mechanic, and (3) I had a little money in my pocket. This was many years prior to the advent of credit cards. Was this a God thing? I suspect so, but it didn't engender any prayers of thanksgiving at the time.

Nolen had the car pushed into the garage, and he looked it over. He determined that the carburetor was deceased. He proceeded to install a new carburetor, set the timing, and adjusted the points and fuel flow, and when we fired it up, it started. The bill for the new carburetor and labor came to $37, and I had $55 in my billfold. I have to think that God has a sense of humor.

At any rate, I paid the bill. I headed for Oklahoma City, driving through Pawhuska and Ponca City to intersect with Interstate 35, which delivered me within two miles of the OCC campus. I chose that route on that day because the other logical route, the Turner Turnpike between Tulsa and Oklahoma City, carried a toll of $1.40 for the privilege of using the road, and I was already cash poor. Another reason for this choice was because I remembered my previous odyssey through Tulsa on the way to Norman for the football game that almost ended in disaster.

I arrived safely on the Oklahoma Christian College campus, picked up my dorm key without further impediment, and went to my home for the next nine months to unpack.

Looking ahead as only He can do, God's Providence determined that it would be beneficial for me to have credible help in determining my future education solution. Due perhaps to my slow uptake on frequently obvious clues, God gave me an oracle that I could absolutely not miss – the beautiful young woman, Kay Spearman – to persuade me to give a Christian college serious consideration. And it worked.

THE PROVIDENCE OF GOD

I was beginning to think that maybe Ebenezer and I would get reacquainted. As with the move from Seminole to Ada, which had eventually blossomed greatly, the move from Ada to Bartlesville was beginning to show promise. Each move had provided a basis for blessings in subsequent moves. The move to Bartlesville had specifically blessed me as follows:

1. My family's move to Bartlesville was cushioned by my many friends and acquaintances that had moved there from Ada and Seminole.

2. I did not receive a scholarship offer from Tulane University, which made possible my eventual attendance at Harding.

3. I made new lifelong friends in the church in Bartlesville, and their presence would influence my decision to seek employment in Bartlesville a few years later.

4. I met new high school friends at church who persuaded me to attend Oklahoma Christian College. Attending Oklahoma Christian College would introduce me to the blessings found at a Christian college and would eventually influence my decision to enroll at Harding College.

Hither by His help, I had come, but what I did not realize was that by the fall of 1962 my Bartlesville experience was far from finished with providing blessings in both the near future and in the long–term. Stay tuned. Ebenezer lives!

Five

OKLAHOMA CHRISTIAN COLLEGE (1962–1963)

The small world was about to strike again. I arrived on the campus of Oklahoma Christian College in early September 1962. After having picked up my dorm room key, I went to the dormitory to get settled. At that time, OCC had two men's dorms – Old Dorm and New Dorm. Clever names. I was assigned to "New Dorm," second floor. It was motel style, with a door leading to the outside and a balcony that ran the building's length with stairs down to the ground level. The college had just that year transitioned from a junior college to a four–year college, and they had admitted more students that year than they had anticipated. Student housing was therefore crowded, and I was assigned a room with two other roommates. As a result, there were three beds in the room. Other housing options were on the drawing board, but it was still a year or two away.

I was the second to arrive at the room, so I got to choose my bed from the remaining two available. I chose the upper bunk, and that left a regular bunk for whoever showed up next.

At that time, a small world chose to occur once more. My roommate introduced himself, and it was Larry Quinalty – my friend from elementary school days in Seminole ten years earlier. I didn't recognize him at first, but we got reacquainted quickly. He now lived in Pawhuska, only 20 miles from Bartlesville. I had driven within six blocks of his house earlier that day on my way to OCC. We spent some time reflecting on our school days in Seminole and our times at the church there.

However, incredibly, the small world was not finished for the day. It had only just begun. While Larry and I were talking, our third roommate arrived, a young man named Ronnie Stumpff. Upon meeting him, I told him that the Stumpff name was pretty familiar to me. I told him that I had run across some Stumpffs over in Missouri and also that there were two or three Stumpffs in Bartlesville. The Stumpffs in Bartlesville ran a barbershop, had an insurance agency, and a funeral home, among some other businesses. I asked him where he was from and if he was kin to any of the Bartlesville Stumpffs.

When he told me he was from Cato, Missouri, a small town near Cassville, Missouri, I nearly dropped my teeth. I knew then why the Stumpff name sounded familiar. My great–grandparents, grandparents, and some uncles had known the Stumpff family for decades. The Stumpffs were all Cassville High School graduates, as were two of my uncles, and the family worshipped frequently at the Cassville Church of Christ. My great–grandparents and some other relatives were leaders in that congregation. On my family's frequent visits over the years to Shell Knob, Missouri, only 20 miles from Cassville, I had spent considerable time in Cassville and had worshipped at the Cassville Church of Christ a few times. That was where I had heard the Stumpff name but had never actually met any of them.

But the small world wasn't finished yet. Ronnie then told me that the Stumpffs in Bartlesville were his brothers. It turned out that one of the brothers, Paul, attended the Sixth and Dewey Church of Christ. At that point, I had never met him, but I was familiar with their businesses in Bartlesville. It was turning out to be an old home week, and we hadn't even unpacked our things in the dorm room yet.

Ronnie and I reminisced over the things to be found in and around Cassville – the Triangle Café in Cassville, the bus station where I frequently visited to buy comic books and ice cream when I was in Cassville. We also talked Flat Creek, which ran through the town and was anything but flat during heavy rains. We spoke of times each of us had spent at Roaring River State Park, about 7 miles from Cassville. Roaring River's source was a huge spring that poured thousands of gallons of ice-cold water hourly from the depths of the earth. The water was so cold that it was virtually unswimmable for several miles downstream from the spring, but the trout fishing was fantastic. Also, it turns out that his family also regularly bought groceries at Whisman's Super Market in Cassville, which was owned and operated by my great uncle Charlie Whisman. We had a grand old time catching up on everyday things.

It now appeared that, in addition to Ada and Seminole, people from southwestern Missouri were also migrating to northeastern Oklahoma in great numbers.

So, as fate would have it, both of my roommates were from my past, which made my transition to college life just that much easier.

We got unpacked and stored our clothing and supplies away and then decided to meet our neighbors in the dormitory. We walked next door to see who and what might be inhabiting that room. The occupants of that room were both upperclassmen and, I guess, qualified for a 2–person room. At any rate, there were only two occupants of the room next door.

One was a guy named Paul Wood from Elk City, Oklahoma, several miles to the west of Oklahoma City. His roommate was a giant of a fellow named Ed Davidson. "Big Ed" Davidson of Tulsa, Oklahoma. Does that sound familiar?

The small world was relentless. At that point, the small world chose to kick in once more, and with emphasis, and I had not been on the OCC campus an hour yet.

It turned out that Ed was a senior, a big guy, a weight man on the track team. He tossed the discus, and the shot put. He was also an intellectual, majoring in Engineering, I believe, and an outstanding chess player. He and I enjoyed many good chess games that year.

In talking with Ed, I was astonished to learn that he was from Tulsa and was known as "Big Ed." It seemed far-fetched, but I asked anyway if he had ever watched "The Lee and Lionel Show" on KOTV. He said he had been a regular viewer each summer when he was at home in Tulsa. I told him that I was also a regular viewer, and I asked him if he could possibly be the contentious guy who sent letters to the show and claimed to be the real "Big Ed." He proudly owned up to the claim and was curious about who the other guy who claimed to be "Big Ed" might be. I told him the other "Big Ed" was a friend of mine and was currently a freshman at Oklahoma State University. It is indeed a small world.

Ed was not what you think of when you think of a large weight man on the track team. He was remarkably fast on his feet. Once, carrying a trash can half full of water, he chased me across the dorm balcony, down the stairs, across the lawn to the other dorm, up the stairs to the balcony on that dorm, caught me, and dumped the whole load of water on my head. It should be noted that I deserved the soaking due to an unfortunate decision I had made earlier in a dorm water fight.

Ed was also an outstanding table tennis player. One of the traditions at OCC at that time was table tennis. There were two table tennis tables set up in the Student Union, and they were continually in use. Several times during the year spontaneous single-elimination tournaments were held – no prizes, just the satisfaction received in playing well. The two best table tennis players at OCC at that time were Ed Davidson and Stanley Morris. Ed was a smasher with great wrist action. He would stand near the end of the table, and, without moving his feet, return everything sent his way with a lot more speed than it came with. Stanley was a defensive player. He would stand 5 or 6 feet beyond the end of the table and return everything that came his way, usually winning the point when his opponent finally made a mistake.

I think Ed and Stanley, between them, won almost all of the tournaments during the year. My best finish was a single semi-final, in which Ed finished me off without breaking a sweat. I probably played 200 or more table tennis matches that year and finally got pretty good. Not Ed Davidson good, but way above average. As I would find out later, that table tennis experience would prove to be a blessing.

My time at Oklahoma Christian had started on a very positive note, what with the small world events that greeted me upon arrival. I felt comfortable right away and certainly didn't feel like a stranger. Kay Spearman and Janice Durrill from Bartlesville also added to my social comfort, as well as Archie Wright, a girl I had known in Ada and with whom I had attended church there. My small world experiences were starting to get ridiculous. Can anyone believe they were accidental?

I was still somewhat intimidated, however. As mentioned, none of my immediate family had ever attended college, so they could not give me any advice as to what to expect. Also, all my closest friends at OCC were college rookies, so they were still in the same learning curve as I. What compounded my feelings of intimidation was the fear that my scholastic capabilities would not be sufficient to handle college classes. As I look back, the fears proved to be unfounded, but they were daunting at the time.

The enrollment process did nothing to assuage my fears. I was placed in New Testament Survey, Chemistry I, and Advanced English, plus three less stress-inducing classes – 15 credit hours.

In addition to enrollment and the start of classes, another thing we as freshmen had to endure at OCC was "Fish Week" – "fish" being the slang term applied to all lowly freshmen. Many humbling acts were traditionally required of the freshmen by all upperclassmen for a full week, but two requirements stood out.

First, freshmen were required, at all times, to carry chewing gum to be given to any upperclassman who demanded it. At first, we carried Juicy Fruit and Spearmint sticks. However, as a group, we decided early on that those brands were too expensive, given the daily demands. We felt the upperclassmen were not necessarily worthy of the premium gum. So, we started carrying Chiclets, less expensive, small candy-coated tablets of gum. Then someone got a bright idea. At that time, there was a laxative brand on the market whose tablets were the same size, shape, and color of the Chiclets gum tablets.

We bought the laxative tablets, substituted them in the Chiclets packages for the gum, and distributed them upon demand. The laxative tablets were pleasant tasting and chewable, and by the time the "victim" realized it was not a Chiclet, it was too late. It took about a day for the upperclassmen to quit soliciting gum from the freshmen.

The second thing the freshmen had to deal with during Fish Week was a frequent "air raid" warning. When an upperclassman yelled "air raid," all freshmen within hearing had to hit the ground and cover their head. Mercifully it did not rain during Fish Week, but we still ate a lot of dirt, and we managed to survive the week.

Following Fish Week was social club "rush" week. Oklahoma Christian did not have Greek fraternities and sororities. Instead, it permitted social clubs without any national affiliation. The social clubs were co-ed and contributed considerably to a new student's social integration into college life.

The clubs had many similarities, but they also had their individual emphases. Some were top-heavy in music students, some were populated with Bible majors, etc. I joined the Olympians social club primarily because it had an excellent athletic persona. Perhaps its name gave away its secret. Several members were good athletes across a number of sports. It was particularly promising in intramural football and intramural basketball. It also had excellent social assets, so it was far more diverse than just sports. In the end, it was a good choice for me.

That fall I had the privilege of playing on probably the only intramural football team in history to go undefeated and still not win the championship. In those days, games tied at the end of the game stayed that way – tied. The Olympians played six games, won 3 and tied 3. The team that won the championship won 5 games and tied 1 – us. On a personal note, I started the season on the bench but wound up the season starting in the defensive backfield.

The Olympian basketball team was the real deal. We blew through the schedule undefeated, virtually unchallenged. The only close game was against the Faculty, which also fielded an intramural team. They had some coaches and ex–varsity players on their roster, so they were pretty salty, but we edged them out. On another personal note, I was not a starter but got plenty of playing time off the bench since so many of our games were blow-out victories.

I enjoyed the Olympians, and the club did help me adjust to college life and instilled in me a feeling of belonging.

Following Fish Week and "rush" week, we concentrated our attention on the reason we were here – classes. It turns out I was not the only freshman who was scholastically intimidated. However, we eventually figured out that the geniuses in high school would be geniuses in college. The rest of us would seek and find our individual academic level, and that the level would not likely be much different from that which we attained in high school. Of course, classes would be more challenging, and study would be more critical, but we came to accept that and to adjust. After all, we were supposedly much more mature in every way as college freshmen than we were as lowly high school seniors.

Of course, it took some getting used to. Mr. James Skaggs taught my Advanced English class. Mr. Skaggs was only about 23 years old. He was a prodigy and had graduated from college at about age 20. This was not even his first year to teach college English. The good news was that at his age he related to us 18–year–olds. The bad news was that he felt the need to establish his authority in the classroom. I will give him great credit for being able to do so effectively.

He established that authority early and with a bang. Our first assignment was to write a short essay on dorm life. Mine was a parody entitled "Dorm Life is Fun." In the essay I went about dispelling such a notion as pure fantasy. When he returned my paper he had noted that content was acceptable and even interesting, but everything else – grammar, verb tense, sentence structure – was sadly lacking. I received a D– on my first effort at advanced college English. I think that grade was therapeutic in that it introduced me to reality at the college level and inspired me to take my studies very seriously. I recovered from that initial blow and eventually received grades of B in both semesters. I actually enjoyed Mr. Skaggs' classes and learned a lot.

My Chemistry class under Mr. Eugene Bailey was fantastic. Having not taken chemistry in high school, the class terrified me at first. However, Mr. Bailey was an excellent teacher and made chemistry relatively understandable and even enjoyable. I achieved B's in both semesters. There was one admonishment that Mr. Bailey gave us concerned working safely in the lab. He told us that if anyone did anything careless that required anyone to have to use the shower in the lab to flush off toxic chemicals that the perpetrator would receive an automatic F for the semester. We took his warning to heart, and no one had to flush themselves in the shower the whole year.

I liked Mr. Bailey so well that I took a giant leap and enrolled in his Calculus class in the spring semester. I had had excellent math teachers in high school, and their efforts paid off. I made 5 hours of A in the Calculus class, which I consider one of my highest academic achievements in college. Miracles continued to visit my life.

A third class that had me worried the first semester was New Testament Survey. It sounds harmless enough, but the legendary Dr. Hugo McCord taught the class. Dr. McCord was a giant in the brotherhood of the Churches of Christ, a great teacher, and a preacher, and a genuine Bible scholar. Also, he was a Vice President of OCC. It was rumored that he had memorized the Torah and was working on memorizing the New Testament. I was concerned that someone of his intellectual and spiritual stature would include teaching so far above my head that I would be lost by the time we reached Matthew chapter two.

What galvanized my fear and supported the idea that he had memorized so much of the Bible came through my observation of him as he taught. We would be studying, for instance, the book of Hebrews, which is near the end of the Bible, and he would be "reading" a scripture from that book, but the Bible he was "reading" from was opened to somewhere near Daniel in the Old Testament, near the middle of the Bible. In other words, he wasn't actually reading scripture. He was quoting scripture from memory, and he was just using the Bible as a prop. He just didn't want to waste time thumbing through the Bible to locate the scripture he was dealing with. I managed to survive and earned an A in New Testament Survey in the fall and another A in Old Testament Survey in the spring.

There was another side of Dr. McCord that is worth mentioning. Dr. McCord was stately, proper, and dignified and was not known for pulling pranks. He taught New Testament Survey in the main auditorium. Probably half the freshman students were in that session of the course. One day, "coincidentally" during Fish Week, he asked us all to stand. This was not unusual, because we would frequently stand for prayer or a hymn. When we were all standing, he looked us over, a smile spread across his face, and he yelled, "air raid." Of course, all of us freshmen experienced a knee–jerk reaction and hit the floor. Dr. McCord got a chuckle out of that. However, we freshmen gained a new respect for the Doctor after that.

Student life at OCC was enjoyable, and I made many good friends. Two in particular were Jim Duggar and Richard Lawson.

Jim was my next-door neighbor during the spring semester when I moved into the Old Dorm, and we hung out a lot together. He visited my home in Bartlesville once or twice on weekends during the year. He had run for freshman class president and lost, but in the spring he ran for sophomore class president and won. He also drove a Triumph Herald convertible, which I envied, and which came into play a little later on in the year.

Richard also became a good friend. Richard was a freak in that he was a math genius and an excellent tennis player. With tennis being the only sport in which I had lettered in school, I stupidly agreed to play him in tennis a few times that fall. He beat me like a rented mule, smiling all the time. He tried out for the college tennis team and had no trouble making the cut. Not unexpectedly, he wound up being the number one player.

Two interesting things about Richard. He was from Wichita, Kansas, and I went home with him one weekend. On Saturday morning the breakfast his mother served was cold pizza and Pepsi. It may have been both the most unusual and most delicious breakfast I ever tasted.

There was one other interesting tidbit about Richard. As mentioned, he was a math genius and went on to establish Lawson Software and became the company CEO. Richard is also a member of the Oklahoma Christian University Board of Trustees and has donated generously in time and money over the years to Oklahoma Christian.

Richard ran for sophomore class vice president at the time Jim Duggar ran for president, and Richard, likewise, was elected to the office.

One of my classmates was Martha "Marty" Mitchell. She was also a freshman, and we sat next to each other in chapel. Marty was dynamic, and I think all the guys, both freshmen, and upperclassmen, had their eyes on her. However, she was down to earth and friendly, and we got to know one another. One time I had the nerve to ask her for a date, and she accepted. Now what? I was driving a semi–operable 1955 Ford, which was not suitable for dates. We had planned to attend the 1962 version of the movie "Mutiny on the Bounty," starring Marlon Brando. The movie was playing at a downtown Oklahoma City theater, and I needed something other than my old beater Ford to drive us there. Remember Jim Duggar's Triumph Herald convertible? Jim graciously allowed me to borrow his car that night for the date.

Marty and I became good friends that year. She eventually married another friend of mine, Terry Johnson. Terry later became president of Oklahoma Christian. Terry was also a preacher, and in yet another small world event, I ran into him one Sunday many years later at the Church of Christ in Shell Knob, Missouri. Shell Knob was the small town (population 52) where my grandparents lived, and they worshipped at the Church of Christ there. Terry would preach there from time to time when he was in the area. Shell Knob is so small that it is not even shown on many Missouri maps, but I believe God put us together in that tiny, remote town in another small world situation to my blessing and wonderment.

Terry was also an athlete. He played shortstop on the Eagles baseball team.

I had not played organized baseball since Little League in Ada, but while in high school in Bartlesville several of us would gather on Sunday afternoons and play pick–up games. Ed Bailey played as did Steve Smethers. Steve was a pitcher and eventually pitched for the Col–Hi Wildcats baseball team. Even

Steve's dad, Wayne Smethers, would join us from time to time. Apparently, Wayne was a good baseball player in his youth and retained his skill set very well. He was in his early 40's when he joined us for our games. He could pitch and still had a wicked curveball. Some pretty good players participated, including some high school varsity players, so this was not pitty-pat baseball. At any rate, the sum total of my baseball experiences between Little League in the eighth grade in Ada and my freshman year in college were these Sunday afternoon games.

However, at OCC, I decided to try out for the varsity baseball team on a lark. I had been pretty successful on Sunday afternoons in Bartlesville. I understood the game and thought I might be able to make the team. However, I had two serious shortcomings. First, my glove had been stolen the previous summer, and I had not replaced it. Besides, I didn't have any spikes. So I tried out for the team sans glove and spikes.

I wore sneakers to the tryouts, and someone was kind enough to lend me his glove while I was there. Even though I hit the ball pretty well in the batting portion of the tryout, my lack of equipment plus the availability of plenty of other qualified athletes who had equipment made my potential contributions to the team moot. I did not make the cut, and I cannot fault the coach in any way. However, I have often wondered if I had had the proper equipment if I would have been given a second look.

The reason I mention this baseball anecdote is that later on when I was at Harding, I played "Major" class intramural baseball for three springs (1964, 1965, and 1966), was on the championship team two of those years, and made the all-star team all three years. There were some pretty salty players in the Major class, almost all whom had played high school baseball. In addition, during summer break in 1965, I played for the Okemah Indians Summer League team. In those days, college baseball schedules did not encompass half of the summer as they can do now, and many college players would join local city teams that played in Summer Leagues to keep their skills sharp for fall baseball. I competed well in the summer league, playing every inning of every game. This will be revisited in a later chapter in this book. It still makes me wonder if I had the goods to play at OCC if I had had the proper equipment.

In retrospect, however, I feel strongly that the hand of God was on the tiller, and He was providentially guiding me. Had I made the OCC team, the balance of my entire life would likely have changed. For one thing, making the team would probably have influenced me to stay at OCC for at least another year, and, as will be seen, it was critical that I leave OCC after only one year.

One of the guys who did make the team was Bill Goodwin, a fellow freshman. In another ultra-small world event, more than 30 years later, we ran into each other at a Harding football game. His son and both my sons played for the Bison, and we just happened to have seats next to each other at that game. We recognized one another after all those years and had a good visit. How do those things happen without celestial help? It keeps life interesting.

Another fellow freshman who earned a spot as a catcher on the varsity baseball teams was Perry Dalby. In yet another small world event, I ran into him at Fort Dix, New Jersey, in the spring of 1967, when we were both in advanced infantry training.

As noted earlier, my family was not exactly affluent. In order to have some consistent spending money at college it became incumbent on me to find a part-time job. One or two of my friends worked at a Humpty Dumpty Super Market not too far from campus. Early in the spring semester, I applied there and was hired, and I began earning a salary of $1.00 per hour. I was scheduled to work about three, sometimes four evenings per week plus some weekends, about four hours each shift. I was attempting to balance work hours with study time, and this worked out pretty well. I worked the job pretty much to the end of the school year.

As luck would have it, come Spring Break, I was scheduled to work most evenings that week. Since I was low man on the totem pole seniority–wise at the store, I could not get the week off. So I stayed in the dorm that week and picked up as many hours at the supermarket that I could. Jim Duggar also stayed on campus that week. The drive to his home in northern Illinois was very long and really wasn't worth the effort for the little amount of time he would be able to spend there. About a half dozen other boys had to stay on campus for one reason or another.

This plethora of guys soon drained the Coke machines in both of the men's dorms dry, and the Coke supplier did not attempt to refill the machine during the week when ostensibly no one was there and when there would apparently be no sales of cans of Coca–Cola. When the machines became empty, they would be empty until the next week.

Then one of the guys had a bright idea. I had begun to become leery of brilliant ideas, but I listened anyway. There was not a single girl staying on campus over Spring Break. Consequently, it was highly likely that the Coke machine in the girls' dorm was still loaded with product. The girls' dorm was constructed similarly to that of the men's Old Dorm in that it had a covered atrium, an open space, among the rooms on the second floor, and that was where their Coke machine was located. That was the good news. The bad news was that a 7–foot wooden fence surrounded the entire dorm, apparently to keep feisty girls in and feisty boys out. However, at that time, there were no girls present, so the fence was moot.

The brilliant idea was that we would merely scale the fence at some point, go to the second floor and buy cans of Coke and return. No harm, no foul. However, the fly in the ointment was that although no girls were present in the dorm, the house parents were present in the dorm. And their dining room window looked directly toward the men's Old Dorm, with no part of the fence to block their view. Unfortunately, one of our guys failed to take that factor into consideration.

We found a place far away from the house parents' window, scaled the fence, went upstairs, and each of us bought a can of Coke. We looked around a bit since none of us had ever been in this particular geographical location before. Then we went to our entrance point and hopped over the wall to return to our dorm. Once again, no harm, no foul. However, one of the guys went temporarily brain dead. Instead of climbing the fence, he thought it would be easier just to jump down the 10 feet from the balcony, which overhung the fence. Do you see where this is heading? In doing so, he jumped down immediately outside the house parents' dining room window with a loud "thump" as they were enjoying their lunch. You could hear the thump all the way back to where we were scaling the wall. Of course, from their front-row seat, the house parents witnessed the guy fall from the sky, so to speak, and heard the loud thump when he landed. And our expedition to buy Cokes went into the toilet in a nanosecond.

The house dad ran outside, belying his age, and grabbed the knucklehead who had jumped over the railing. About that time, the rest of us came around the fence, and he nabbed all of us. Busted! We explained that our Coke machine was empty, and with no girls around, we felt it was OK to buy sodas at their machine. The house dad disagreed. He took all of our names and promised that we would be hearing from Mr. William Kirk, Dean of Students. This kind of put a damper on the remainder of Spring Break.

Classes started up again the following Monday, and each of us received an invitation from Dean Kirk to visit his office at 11:00 that morning. It didn't take long for the wheels of justice to act. None of us were troublemakers, and none of us had ever been inside the Dean's office before. Jim Duggar was among our group – the president-elect of the upcoming sophomore class. I still remember Dean Kirk's words. "If it had been anyone else! I just can't believe you guys did this." He didn't know whether to smile or frown.

Due to our clean record and the fact that we had done no real damage and there were no girls present at the time, we were not disciplined except that we had to keep our collective noses clean for the foreseeable future. If any other incidents occurred, this issue would become a factor in any actions taken by the administration. He explained in tactful terms how stupid our actions were and reminded us that the house dad would probably have gladly allowed us to buy sodas. If only we had asked rather than breaking and entering. Actually, just entering—we didn't break anything. Anyway, this became another fond memory from my freshman year at OCC.

Another remarkable fond memory, actually an outright miracle, manifested itself that spring. The story is almost unbelievable on two or three levels, but it must be told.

Since I did not work every weekend at the Humpty Dumpty Super Market, and since my laundry needed washing and ironing regularly, I made a weekend trip back home to Bartlesville as often as was practical. Usually, Kay Spearman would ride with me on the trips. And since the journey to and from Bartlesville went through Pawhuska, Larry Quinalty, who was from Pawhuska, frequently hitched a ride. The practice was to head to Bartlesville Friday afternoon after the last class and return to Oklahoma City after a home-cooked dinner on Sunday evening. The trip was about 2 ½ hours. My old Ford usually handled the trip acceptably.

However, this time on the way back to Oklahoma City it conked out somewhere south of Guthrie on Interstate 35. We were driving along, and it just quit. It was about 8:00 p.m. on a Sunday night. I decided I would try to hitch a ride to some fantasy land where I had the idiotic thought that some auto repair shop had stayed open on a Sunday evening and could bring a tow truck and get us going again. I was grasping at straws. There was likely no auto repair shop in the entire state of Oklahoma that was open on a Sunday night. But I had to give it a try.

Larry and Kay were with me at the time, so that made it doubly stressful and embarrassing. Dutifully I stepped out of the car and hung out my thumb in the hopes of enticing someone to stop in the dead of the night and give a stranger a ride to who knows where. The cars that came by zipped past so fast that the wind they generated almost knocked me down. After about 15 minutes and no nibbles, I got back in the car to discuss our meager/nonexistent options with Kay and Larry. As mentioned earlier, Kay was stunningly beautiful. That particular evening she was wearing a white top and white shorts – it had to have been by the grace of God. Anyway, Kay said, "Let me try."

While Larry and I remained in the car, Kay got out, stood beside the highway, and hung out her thumb. The first car that approached us laid probably a hundred feet of rubber stopping. It backed up and stopped beside Kay, and the passenger rolled down his window and asked what the problem was. Kay briefly explained that we were stranded and needed a ride at least to the next town to see what could be done about our situation. The car that stopped did not have room for three more passengers, so it was agreed that I would ride with them, and Larry and Kay would remain in my car until I was able to come back to rescue them. The driver was mightily disappointed that, instead of Kay, I would be riding with them, but he agreed to help.

I got in the back seat, and we headed south. About two miles south, we came upon an Oklahoma Highway Patrolman parked beside the road writing a ticket. The driver suggested that it might be a good idea to get the patrolman to help, and I agreed. So he stopped and let me out, and I walked over and explained my dilemma to the patrolman when he had finished writing the ticket.

This wasn't the patrolman's first rodeo. The first thing he said was that there was, miraculously, an auto garage back up the highway in Guthrie that stayed open very late, even on weekends, and it had a tow truck. He offered to take me to the garage, and I readily agreed.

He drove on further south a mile or so until he came upon a crossover, made a U-turn, and headed back north toward Guthrie. We passed my car sitting beside the road on the other side of the highway, and I waved to Kay and Larry. About a mile north of my car, we met an auto going nearly 100 miles an hour heading south. The patrolman explained that he had some business to attend to and would I mind a slight delay in my trip to Guthrie. Before I could answer, he found another crossover, made a fast U-turn and headed south again at a little over 100 miles an hour, lights flashing, in pursuit of the speeding car. We passed my car again, and again I waved at Kay and Larry. The driver of the other car soon noticed the patrol car's flashing lights and slowed down and pulled over. The patrolman issued a ticket, and we headed south once again in search of a crossover. The patrolman once again made a U-turn, heading north, once again, toward Guthrie. As we passed my car for the third time, I dutifully waved to Kay and Larry for the third time.

We came to the Guthrie exit very shortly, and the patrolman dropped me off at the all-night garage. I thanked him, and he bade me good night.

I explained my dilemma to the mechanic at the garage, he fired up his tow truck, and I accompanied him down the highway to my car, which was still there, as were Kay and Larry. He hooked up my car, towed it back to Guthrie, and went to work. He determined that the generator (in those days cars had generators instead of alternators) was dead, and the only alternative was to replace it. With considerable dread, I asked how much the charge would be. Insurance would pay for the towing, but I still had to pay for the parts and labor associated with the repair. At that time, credit cards were unheard of, and among the three of us, we had a little over $50 in cash. He told me parts and labor came to $37 and some change (remember, this was 1963). I gathered that amount from my friends and myself, and I paid the bill. And I thanked the mechanic profusely.

This was the second time my car had laid down on me in about six months, and the repair bill came to $37. It turns out that there was something magical about a $37 auto repair bill. In my entire life, I have had an auto serviced on the road exactly four times, and every time the bill came to $37 and some change. In 1971 near Mount Airy, North Carolina, the power steering hose became detached on my Chevrolet Malibu, and all the power steering fluid leaked out, making it very difficult to turn my steering wheel. I pulled into a service station in Mount Airy, and the attendant reattached the hose and refilled the power steering fluid. The charge was $37, and some change. In 1986, while in Orlando, Florida, visiting Disney World, the differential on my Ford station wagon began roaring. I pulled into a service station, and the attendant discovered that the differential was very low on grease. He refilled it and sent me on my way. The charge, $37 and change. Weird. I suspect if I ever have another breakdown, the cost will be exponentially more than $37.

Following the generator's replacement on my Ford, we drove on to the campus and were only about an hour behind our scheduled arrival time.

All in all, that was a memorable evening. I can only believe that, once again, God had a hand in salvaging our trip back to OCC. What are the odds that we would find an all-night garage nearby, receive a thrilling ride to the garage, and once again have only a $37 repair bill – an amount we were able to pay? None of those factors were reasonably likely to happen. There are no odds. It had to be a miracle.

During the year, I made many good friends. They enriched my freshman college experience, and I crossed paths with several of them in small world events later in my life. Gary Ellis, a fellow freshman, and an excellent musician, in an astonishing small world event, moved to – guess where – Bartlesville many years later. The small world event, in and of itself, was not the astonishing part. That he was eventually selected as an elder was the astonishing part. (Only kidding, Gary.) Gary and I played a lot of lousy golf during the time he lived in Bartlesville. We grew closer in Bartlesville than we did during my year at OCC.

In a continuing small world event Ronnie Stumpff, after college, moved to, yes, Bartlesville to participate in the Stumpff clan's business enterprises. He opened a florist shop which complemented his brother's funeral home.

Everything considered, my freshman year in college was great. I made friends, and I made the honor roll, I enjoyed a good social life, and, due to the people I was around every day, I am convinced that I began to mature spiritually. And I had some very memorable experiences.

However, as autumn turned into spring, I began some serious thinking about my future. When I had entered OCC, I had no idea what course of study I would follow. During the spring semester, I took an Introduction to Business class. I found the class very interesting and decided to major in Business Administration. As mentioned earlier, OCC was transitioning from a junior college to a four-year college, and, frankly, its upper-level business classes there were still in their infancy. I made the tough decision to transfer next fall to a school with a stronger Business department. I finally settled on Oklahoma University. Accordingly, I made an application to the University. My GPA's in both high school and my freshman year in college were good, so I was accepted.

By this time, I believed that I had made appropriate, legitimate plans regarding my future. I had decided on a college major, and I had decided on the University, which would provide that study. At that point, I had felt very confident and comfortable and that things were finally sorting themselves out. At the time, I prematurely lit up a metaphorical cigar to celebrate.

Another issue, not within a light-year of my sight at the time, was the fact that the year at OCC had exposed me to the blessings and benefits not only of a smaller student body but to life on a Christian college campus. I did not realize that until much later.

Meanwhile, self–satisfied and full of confidence, I headed home to Bartlesville for the summer.

THE PROVIDENCE OF GOD

The year had been fantastic in every way, and the disappointments of moving first to Ada and then to Bartlesville had faded from sight. Blessings He showered on me during the year included:

1. My entry into OCC was cushioned not only by my friends from Bartlesville, who were attending but also by my old friend Larry Quinalty who was miraculously assigned as my roommate.

2. The first semester, my other roommate was Ron Stumpff, whose family in southwestern Missouri I was already familiar with. Ron would move to Bartlesville a few years later, where we were reunited.

3. OCC gently introduced me to the college experience and greatly relieved the uncertainty and tension I had felt upon entering college. I had also succeeded academically, which gave me confidence in my ability to deal with college going forward.

4. I had been exposed to a Christian college environment that had been pleasant in every way and which eliminated any misgivings I might have had about attending Harding later on.

Hither by His help, I had come.

Six

BARTLESVILLE (SUMMER 1963)

I returned to Bartlesville for the summer following my very enjoyable year at OCC. My future had already allegedly been planned – the next three years at Oklahoma University, eventual graduation with a degree in Business Administration, followed by a good job in that discipline in some attractive city. However, unbeknownst to me, the summer of 1963 was going to be a pivotal point in my life, eventually turning my whole world upside down. As it turned out, everything that I am today – my education, my family, my career, my home, even my spiritual life – is ultimately a product of my summer of 1963 in Bartlesville, Oklahoma.

The summer started with a bang. I had planned to work during the summer, and I had expected it to be at the C. R. Anthony store again for $1.00 per hour, $40.00 per week, around $175.00 per month. However, my dad had arranged for me to go big time. As mentioned earlier, he now worked for the Exxon Corporation in a producing oil field near Bartlesville. Each summer, Exxon hired a summer roustabout to work in that oil field with a job title of "Maintenance Man B." The summer employee was always a college student who could physically handle pretty strenuous labor. My dad was able to procure the Maintenance Man B job at Bartlesville that summer for me. It was an hourly position, of course, but it paid $3.25 per hour, around $550.00 per month – a huge salary for a summer employee. Certainly, a huge step up from Anthony's work. Truth be known, it was slightly more than what I earned in my first full–time job following college graduation three years later. Not only that, I lived at home – no rent, no food costs, free laundry. I was living the dream.

It did not take me long to learn that the job also benefitted me in another way – physically. The job was very physically demanding, and I was usually involved in digging out and repairing or replacing pipelines which had sprung leaks. The job also entailed a lot of lifting and working with heavy tools. And, of course, the job was performed entirely out of doors in Oklahoma's June–through–August summer heat. It actually reached 110 degrees three consecutive days in August – midweek, of course, when I was working, as opposed to a weekend when I could have soaked in a pool. At any rate, I gained physical strength on that job that summer, and I developed a suntan for the ages. As will be seen, that suntan, I believe, may have played a significant role in everything that happened to me for the rest of my life.

As in the previous summers, I hung out with the Butcher boys and Ed Bailey, and I played some pickup baseball games on Sunday afternoons. Nothing out of the ordinary. However, that changed relatively early in the summer on a Wednesday night.

As was customary, our church met on Wednesday evenings. One Wednesday, the Butcher boys and I decided to attend the service at the Sixth and Dewey congregation in Bartlesville. No particular reason other than just to catch up with some of the Sixth and Dewey youth. After all, I knew Kay Spearman and Janice Durrill, so we wouldn't be complete strangers.

In consideration of the suntan I had developed from my work, I dressed in a white t-shirt with an OCC logo. Not only that, I had already toned up from my work in the oil field. I thought I looked fairly good, and who knows, I might meet a new girl. I didn't know very many of the Sixth and Dewey youth at that time. Also, I had a car and a little cash in my pocket from my first paycheck from Exxon. So I picked up Ray and Jay, and off we went.

The service that evening consisted of speakers and singing – no classes. In the auditorium, the Butcher boys and I sat down directly behind Kay Spearman. She happened to be sitting beside a girl by the name of Martha Koger. Although Martha had also been a student at College High, I had never met her. It turned out that Martha was a senior, having just graduated from Col–Hi. In a later conversation with her, I learned that their graduation ceremony did not include a Baccalaureate address, so it appeared that the school administration was holding fast to its decision to outlaw the Baccalaureate addresses due to Sidney Roper's "incendiary" remarks the previous year.

Prior to the beginning of the Wednesday evening service, all of us were chatting, and as we talked, it became rather obvious that I had begun to pay a lot of attention to Martha. I was then and still am on the introverted side of ego, but I did manage to engage Martha in conversation. Eventually, before the evening was over, I clumsily managed to ask her for a date, and to my surprise, she accepted. I don't know if my tan and toning had anything to do with her acceptance of the date, but it didn't hurt.

As a result, over the rest of the summer, we dated frequently. The usual things – movies, Sunset Lake for swimming, the occasional church youth rally. Along the way, we talked about future plans, and I learned that Martha had enrolled at Harding College for the fall. Remembering the words of the Harding student who spoke at the Limestone Church the previous summer – "At Harding, they roll up the sidewalks at dusk." – I sort of teased her about her decision. I was strutting around blowing and going about my anticipated career at Oklahoma University and all the benefits and fun it provided, not the least of which was a championship football team. However, all my bluster did not influence Martha's decision.

As we continued to date and discuss our college plans, I started to consider that maybe Harding deserved a closer look. I am sure that my attraction to Martha had some influence on that thinking. Still, I remembered the enjoyable year I had spent at Oklahoma Christian, a sister Christian college to Harding, and the more I dwelled on it, the more I became conflicted regarding my decision to attend OU. Of course, by that time, it was too late to change plans for the fall semester of college. But I might consider enrolling at Harding for the spring semester. By all indications, Harding was an excellent educational institution and had the reputation of having a superior Business School. Unbeknownst to me at the time, that reputation would be proven in spades just a couple of years down the road.

In our conversations, Martha did not once actually encourage me to transfer to Harding. I think I just assumed that she would want me to, given the good times we had enjoyed together that summer. At that time, I believe she was OK with whatever I decided, but she was not pushing for a decision either way. I mistakenly took her silence on the matter as encouragement.

However, the very enjoyable summer came to an end, and it was time to say our goodbyes. We headed in different directions to college and promised to write. It was terribly bittersweet, at least for me. The summer had been amazing – as perfect as any summer could be. I had an excellent summer job with great pay and what I thought was a summer romance that perhaps held promise for something bigger later on.

THE PROVIDENCE OF GOD

I was still in a state of uncertainty regarding long–term college plans, but I was getting some new ideas, and the thought of seeing Martha on a regular basis was very appealing. I most certainly raised my Ebenezer at summer's end due to the following:

1. I had enjoyed and profited physically and financially from the summer job with Exxon.

2. I had met Martha Koger, who unintentionally influenced me to eventually enroll at Harding.

What I did not realize was that although God had indeed blessed me unbelievably that summer with regard to my future, I had totally misread the signs. In just a few months, I would question whether or not God was still holding my hand. It will turn out that He was still in my corner, but I first had to go through a trial or two.

Seven

OKLAHOMA UNIVERSITY (FALL 1963)

Oklahoma University promised to be an unforgettable experience.
In the first place, I was no longer sure that I even wanted to be there. This feeling had nothing to do with disappointment in the University, per se. After all, the University had an outstanding academic reputation. My professors, as I would later discover – with a couple of exceptions – were excellent. I found the food at the cafeteria fair, and there was a pretty good football team on campus to root for. A student season ticket for the five home games with a reserved seat at Owen field cost only $8.00, or $1.60 per game. What a bargain. You can't even buy a hamburger at the stadium for that price anymore. Also, as I would learn, I already had several friends attending OU. The uncertainty I felt stemmed from the events of the immediate past summer vacation.

As chronicled earlier, during the summer break, I had met a young lady, Martha Koger, who was planning to attend Harding College in the fall. Not only had the two of us experienced an enjoyable summer but I had also learned from her considerably more about Harding – all of it favorable. It was not a place that "rolled up the sidewalks at dusk," as I had previously heard. Instead, it was a vibrant college, had an excellent academic rating, and offered outstanding opportunities for engaging personal experiences – social, academic, and spiritual. Also, a Christian atmosphere permeated Harding as it did Oklahoma Christian, and the small enrollment – compared to OU – made it less likely that I would be "lost in the crowd." Enrollment at Harding at the time was approximately 1150 students as opposed to 14,000 on campus at OU. I would be more than just a number at Harding. All of these things appealed to me, and I was "at sea," so to speak, concerning my immediate college future.

Additionally, as a Christian, some of the anticipated aspects of life on the OU campus troubled me. I had no idea what to expect in the classes at OU. I knew the teachers would not necessarily be those I ran into at church during Sunday morning. I suspected that the students would have different priorities in every aspect of life than the students I typically rubbed elbows with at OCC. Despite these misgivings, I decided to suck it up and give the University of Oklahoma my best shot, at least for the time being. Of course, at that late date, I had no choice.

However, the seed of change had been planted, and I was willing to feed it and water it and watch it grow, and see exactly what type of fruit it produced.

I arrived on the campus of Oklahoma University in early September 1963. I had enrolled in 14 hours, and I had been assigned to the Buchanan House dormitory.

When I moved into my dorm room, "small world" struck again with a bang. The first person I ran into as I entered the dorm was Eddie Roark, one of my very best friends from Ada. He was also living in the dorm. At the time, there were approximately 7,000 male students on campus scattered across dozens of dormitories and fraternity houses, and one of my best friends in the world winds up in my dorm. It was like my experience at Oklahoma Christian encore une fois. What are the odds? The Providence of God ignores the odds.

Eddie, like myself, was a sophomore, and he was majoring in Math. As mentioned in the story of my time in Ada, he ended up as a lawyer in Las Vegas, Nevada. I'm not sure how that transition came about, but at the time, it was not an issue. He greatly helped me navigate the uncertain waters of campus life at OU. This was another of the "small world" blessings that I have received and enjoyed during my life. To the non–believer, it was obviously just another freak, near–mathematically–impossible accident.

Another of my good friends was enrolled at OU – Mike Howard, also from Ada. Mike and I had attended church and run around together a lot in our years in Ada. Mike was a member of the Lambda Chi Alpha fraternity, and he made me feel welcome on the campus by inviting me to a Lambda Chi "rush" dinner. The guys in the fraternity were amiable, and it was an enjoyable experience. Since Mike was the immediate past president of that chapter of Lambda Chi, I had a pretty good chance of being invited to join. However, I really wasn't in a frame of mind to join if invited.

First of all, fraternities were expensive, and my parents did not have the financial resources to absorb that extra cost each year easily. Secondly, I was still bothered by the fact that I was in Norman, Oklahoma, rather than in

Searcy, Arkansas, 350 miles away. I had already begun to consider plans to leave OU for Harding, so even if the finances had been available, I would likely have been a short–time fraternity member. I thanked Mike for the invitation but did not pursue membership.

My classes included Accounting 101, Air Force ROTC, Economics 10, Speech 101, and Government 101. As it turned out, the only "routine" class among them was Air Force ROTC, and even that was "iffy" given that the war in Vietnam was escalating. Every other one of my classes had some level of drama that made them interesting.

One of my most exciting and apocalyptic classes at the University was Accounting 101. Two issues made it memorable, one of which adversely affected my overall college GPA. The event in the class that sank my boat concerning achieving an "A" in the course occurred immediately before Christmas break in 1963. The class met Monday–Wednesday–Friday at 8:00 a.m. Christmas break that year started at the close of classes on Wednesday, December 18, and commenced again on Monday, January 6 – I still remember the dates like they were yesterday. During the class on Monday, December 16 – two days before Christmas break– the professor announced that we would have an exam on Wednesday, January 8, the second class following our return from Christmas break.

On Tuesday, December 17, one day before the start of Christmas break, a blizzard hit Oklahoma with heavy snow and ice everywhere. My dad thought it wise that he come pick me up rather than having me drive to Bartlesville on the ice-packed highways. So that afternoon, he picked me up at my dormitory, and we crept back to Bartlesville safely. By the next morning, Wednesday, December 18, Norman, Oklahoma, looked like the North Pole. However, the University did not cancel classes, and the Accounting 101 class met as if nothing had happened. Of course, I was not there because, by that time, I was in Bartlesville inside my warm house. I was not the only Accounting student who cut class that day. I later learned that only four students actually showed up for class, the remainder already at home for the holidays or staying away from class due to the blizzard. At any rate, the professor was miffed. He told the four that bothered to come to class that since it was obvious that everyone who had cut class already knew the subject and didn't need further instruction, he was rescheduling the exam FROM Wednesday, January 8, TO Monday, January 6, which would be our first morning back on campus after Christmas, an 8:00 a.m. class. There was no notice given of the change other than that given verbally to the four stalwarts, obviously Norman residents, who attended the last class before Christmas.

When we walked into class that Monday morning, January 6, after not cracking a book for almost three weeks, we totally expected another lesson, perhaps a review before the test. Instead, the professor passed out tests, and everyone took the exam cold turkey except for the four who had received the heads–up during the last class before Christmas. I made a 78 on the exam, and, seriously, if I had had a half hour to review my notes beforehand, I would have made at least a 90, perhaps higher. Almost everyone got bit by the test, but the 78 eventually knocked my semester average down to 89, which was a B.

This was significant because my final GPA at graduation from Harding, including the B in Accounting 101 at Oklahoma University, was 3.48. Had I made an A, my final GPA would have been 3.50. I am still troubled by what I perceive as pettiness on the part of the professor, ignoring the actual safety issues the blizzard presented. However, I probably received an unwarranted higher grade somewhere along the line, so it has probably all evened out.

The other interesting situation that I encountered in the Accounting class was the presence of Joe Don Looney in the class. Joe Don was an All–American for Bud Wilkinson's University of Oklahoma football team in 1962, and he was expected to repeat that performance in 1963. However, Fate sometimes just doesn't play fair. He was handsome, huge, and fast as a gazelle – the perfect running back. With his looks and build, he could have been a movie star ala The Rock (Dwayne Johnson). Joe Don sat one row behind and two seats over to the left from me in the class. He could barely fit into the desk.

In the second football game that fall OU played Southern Cal in the Coliseum in Los Angeles on national TV. Joe Don was a running back, and he showcased his talents in the game. OU won the game 17–12. Although it was truly a team effort, Joe Don played no small part in the victory. The opponents simply could not contain him. He averaged more than 5 yards per carry and returned a punt 52 yards. In addition, he was the team's punter. He looked every bit like the world's best football player against a very good team. After the game, the TV announcers interviewed Joe Don and Bud Wilkinson, congratulating them on such a great game. On TV, Joe Don grinned and played the humble card during the interview. He was perfect, and he was famous from coast to coast among football fans. That was Saturday.

On the basis of that game, the Oklahoma Sooner football team rose to the Number 1 ranking among college teams at that time.

On Monday, he was in the Accounting class, grinning from ear to ear, and rightfully so. Everyone patted him on the back and told him, "Way to go." Our professor singled him out and said, "Congratulations on a great performance, Mr. Looney." If nothing else, it showed that the professor wasn't totally out of touch.

The Texas game, the annual Red River Shootout, was scheduled in two weeks. For decades the Oklahoma football team has scheduled a "bye" week just ahead of the Texas game because the game is always tough, and extra preparation time was warranted. Accordingly, there was no football game the next Saturday as they used the extra time to practice. So following the Southern Cal game, Joe Don was in class on Monday, Wednesday, Friday, and then the following Monday and Wednesday, prior to the Texas game on Saturday, continuing to soak up the accolades and "atta boys" that he really did deserve. He came across as a really good guy, and it was actually an honor to be rubbing elbows with him.

He was not in class the Friday before the Texas game since the football team always traveled to Dallas on Friday before the game on Saturday.

I need to digress for a moment for some additional background on the weekend.

My friend, Eddie Roark, and I had tickets to the game. Both of us being basically destitute financially, our good friend John Ramsay, now a starter on the Southern Methodist University basketball team, arranged for us to stay free of charge Friday night in an SMU men's dormitory. Our student tickets to the game cost $5.00, so basically, our only other cost was gasoline, which in those days was about 27 cents a gallon. We drove down to Dallas in my car. We were going to be able to witness one of the football classics for less than $10.00 each. That was the good news.

The bad news was that our seats were far apart. There were 75,000 people in attendance at the Cotton Bowl that day – the usual turnout for this game. The Cotton Bowl stadium is located on the Texas State Fairgrounds, which was also occurring the same weekend as the OU-Texas football game. The Texas State Fairgrounds' dominant feature was "Big Tex," a statue positioned roughly in the middle of the fairgrounds that stood about 50 feet tall. There were probably another 15,000 people at the fairgrounds that day in addition to the football fans – people everywhere, half wearing red and half wearing orange. My agreement with Eddie was that we would meet "at the foot" of Big Tex after the game so we wouldn't have to wander around the grounds for an hour trying to find one another. Cell phones were still more than 40 years in the future. Our strategy apparently was not unique. I am serious when I say that more than 10,000 other people that day had made the same arrangement to meet at the foot of Big Tex. The crowd, at least 20 deep, entirely circled Big Tex's cowboy boots. We finally ran into each other, but not quickly.

That was the digression – now back to Joe Don Looney and the football game.

Sad to say, Texas beat OU every way possible that day, holding Joe Don, if I remember correctly, to less than 10 yards rushing. The final score was Texas 28, Oklahoma 7. Needless to say, OU lost its Number 1 ranking in the football poll the next week, falling to number 6. Also, needless to say, there were no TV interviews that day with Bud Wilkinson and Joe Don. Darrel Royal, the Texas coach, got all the air time.

The following Monday, Joe Don was not in the Accounting class. His star had fallen after only two weeks. He never showed up again in Accounting and left the football team and OU shortly after that. A story with a sad ending, but it was still a thrill to be in class with him, if only for a semester. Truly, for many reasons, that Accounting 101 class was etched into my memory forever.

My Economics 10 was a basic economics course taught by a Graduate Assistant who was state chairman of the Students for a Democratic Society, and it was a wild ride.

According to Wikipedia, "Students for a Democratic Society (SDS) was a national student activist organization in the United States that was one of the main representations of the New Left. Founded in 1960, the organization developed and expanded rapidly in the mid–1960s, with over 300 chapters recorded nationwide by its last convention in 1969. Though various organizations have been formed in subsequent years as proposed national networks for left-wing student organizing, none has approached the scale of SDS, and most have lasted a few years at best."

And the state chairman of the SDS was, of all things, my Economics teacher. Talk about a mismatch. Needless to say, I had to keep on my toes for the entire semester to attempt to filter fact from ideology in the class. At that time, students were more pragmatic than they are today, and there was a considerable vigorous debate for the entire semester. I remember the teacher attempting to enlighten us on how the government was funded and that increased taxation, particularly on the wealthy, was the only way to pay the bills. There was little mention of the fact that higher tax rates usually depress motivation to earn and, as a result, even eventually have a negative effect on profits, wages, and, ultimately, tax collections. I always referred to this course as Socialism 101. My final grade there was a B, which was probably another miracle.

Speech 101 under Professor Ressler was a delight. One time he challenged the students to prepare and deliver a speech defending the "unpopular" side of some current socio-economic issue – Anti PC would be how it was labeled today. Some students advocated for the death penalty; others condemned the execution as a "cruel and unusual" punishment. Some spoke on male-female issues. One person lambasted President Kennedy, and so on. I chose to speak regarding a highly publicized incident of a black man publicly beating an American white man senseless in Ibadan, Nigeria, only a few weeks earlier in August. In my speech, I insinuated that I was aghast that the black man was not arrested and prosecuted. After all, not only did the police not interfere with the beating, but they simply stood by watching and actually cheering, and there were more than 10,000 witnesses also cheering for the black thug. I also pointed out that there was no international uproar regarding the incident and that the press (even then!) chose to slant their stories rather than report the truth. I stated that I felt the white man was unjustifiably assaulted and would have a great case if he brought charges against the black man.

I received an "A" on my speech and was congratulated by several for being courageous in taking the opposite side of such an explosive incident. At that point in history, black-white relations were tenuous at best in the nation. What I failed to mention in my speech was that the event was a professional boxing match, the black "thug" was Dick Tiger, reigning world middleweight boxing champion at the time, and he was defending his crown against Gene Fullmer, a white man. I also did not mention that the bout was fully sanctioned by the WBA (World Boxing Association), and there were 11,600 paying fans in the stands rooting for their hometown hero. I just shook my head. No one challenged the speech, which had been a totally biased and misleading piece of journalism, totally ignoring critical facts. As I think back, I believe my speech was an early manifestation of press practices today – half-truths seasoned with a basketful of "spin." Then, as now, it is unclear to me as to whether people just don't know or just don't care.

My Government 101 class turned out to be a classic, a memorable time in my life that I still recall as if it were yesterday.

The class met at 1:00 p.m. on Mondays, Wednesdays, and Fridays. The Monday and Wednesday classes consisted of lectures in a large auditorium with 200 students, and on Fridays, the class broke up into groups of 20 students each that met in smaller classrooms on campus. The purpose of the Friday class was to give the students a forum in which to discuss the topics presented on Monday and Wednesday. In addition, other issues not presented in the earlier lectures were fair game for discussion. The discussion held in my class at 1:00 p.m. on Friday, November 22, 1963, was historic.

At about 12:15, I returned to my room from lunch in the cafeteria and prepared to head to the Friday government class. As usual, I had the radio in my room turned on and tuned to KTOK, my favorite radio station – a station that played the hit songs of the time. At 12:35, the radio announcer broke into the music and said, "President Kennedy has been shot."

Those were his exact words, and I will remember them forever.

Needless to say, I was stunned, thinking that it was some sort of bizarre practical joke. Ironically, earlier that morning, listening to KTOK, I had heard the Kingston Trio's rendition of the song "Big Ball in Boston," which contained the lyrics,

> *"The folks who come from Boston are said to be quite dated. So whadda ya have to say, my friend? Well, uh, Bobby and uh Teddy and I made it."*

The song obviously refers to the Kennedy clan – Bobby, Ted, and John – all of whom had been elected to political office, and the "response' to the question posed in the song was obviously an imitation of how John Kennedy spoke and would have answered. I thought it was ironic that the lyrics to that song suddenly came into my mind. I wondered if that song would ever be played again on the radio.

I gathered my notes from the lectures earlier in the week and headed to my government class. I suspected the topic for the day would not be related to the week's lectures, and it turned out to be true. As I walked to class, many students who had heard the news were weeping, and others were as yet unaware of the news.

The discussion coordinator was a Graduate Assistant, but he did a fine job keeping the class calm and under control. Many students were suspecting the Russians were behind the assassination due to their embarrassment over the Cuban Missile Crisis. Others thought the Mafia had taken the President out due to Robert Kennedy's efforts to prosecute Mafia leaders. Finally, some believed Vice President Johnson had a hand in the assassination. It was no secret that Kennedy and Johnson were not friends, and Kennedy had only added Johnson to the ticket in the 1960 election in order to secure the Texas electoral votes. It was also no secret that Johnson would have liked to have been President.

In the end, everyone was shocked, and there was no consensus, as is still the case today, as to who or what was behind the assassination.

That is the only Government 101 class I recall from that semester, and I recall it like it was yesterday.

Intramural sports at OU were little more than an afterthought, especially compared to my experience the previous year at Oklahoma Christian and my as–yet–unknown experiences at Harding. Admittedly, with 14,000 students on campus, not to mention all the other attractive activities, intramurals were not a significant item in most of the students' agenda. However, there was an intramural football tournament among the men's student dormitories. Each dorm that wanted to participate signed up and formed a flag football team.

My dorm, Buchanan House, dutifully formed a team and even practiced once. The main function of the practice session was to determine who could play what positions. I was selected as a pass receiver. There is not much to report regarding our season. We won no games, and I scored the only touchdown we made all season. We won no trophies.

All in all, my classes and activities during my one semester at Oklahoma University were memorable in every way.

As time passed, however, it became apparent that a transfer to Harding at semester was inevitable. My social life at OU was non–existent, and I was still infatuated by Martha and her odyssey at Harding. I was wasting away at OU, and Harding appeared to be the end of the rainbow. This feeling was fueled by the correspondence that took place between Martha and myself. We exchanged letters on a pretty regular basis. I told her what was happening at OU, and she told me what was happening at Harding. Her letters were much more interesting than mine.

She told me that she had joined a social club on campus. There were no formal fraternities or sororities at Harding due to, among other things, the "entertainment" that was usually associated with the Greek houses. Instead, as at Oklahoma Christian, social clubs were available to allow the students to join other like-minded students in dinners, outings, sports, scholastic and theatrical activities.

Martha had a wonderful alto singing voice, so it did not surprise me when she told me that she had auditioned for and had been selected to join the Harding Acapella Chorus, the professional-quality choir on the Harding campus.

About that time, I got to thinking that a weekend trip to Harding would be a great experience. I would get to spend some time with Martha and get a preview of the campus. A visit seemed like a no–brainer. The question was how to accomplish it.

At about midterm, I ran into an OU student who was from Little Rock. I asked him if he had ever heard of Harding College. He said he understood that it was a fine college, but not a very exciting place – somewhat echoing the sentiment that they rolled up the sidewalks at dusk. Although he wasn't a wild animal, he had a little different attitude towards behavior than was prevalent at Harding.

I then moved on to my real motive for asking the questions. I asked him if he was going to go back home at any time during the semester. He told me he was, and I asked if I could hitch a ride to Searcy if I paid for half the gas. He said he would enjoy the company.

We found a convenient weekend for the trip and made plans. I wrote Martha and told her I was coming for a visit. In retrospect, she didn't sound too thrilled, but she invited me to come on ahead.

When the Friday of our trip finally arrived, my friend and I headed east following our afternoon classes. The plan was to drop me off in Searcy, and then he would go on down to his home in Little Rock, about an extra 50 miles of driving for him. This was before I–40 was completed between Oklahoma City and Little Rock, and it was two-lane all the way compounded by mountains once we hit Arkansas.

I arrived on campus that Friday evening at about 11:00 p.m. Martha had made arrangements for me to stay in the Armstrong Hall dorm room of Phil Dixon, also a freshman and an Acapella Chorus member. I was able to find my way to Armstrong Hall and located Phil's room. His roommate was Steve Thornton, also a freshman. They had been awaiting my arrival.

The guys were very friendly and welcoming and were most hospitable. We visited awhile, and then we hit the sack.

On Saturday, I found Martha, and we spent the day touring the campus and just hanging out. This visit was in October, and the campus was beyond gorgeous – almost idyllic. Large trees with unbelievable colors. I fell in love with the campus at first sight. I noticed that Martha seemed a little detached, but I thought nothing of it at the time

Sunday, we attended worship service at the College Church, near campus, where most of the student body attended. After the service, we ate lunch together, and then it was time to say goodbye. I noticed that Martha was pretty cool during my departure, much like her demeanor on Saturday. However, I once again shrugged it off as meaning nothing. My friend picked me up at the entrance to the campus, and we headed back to Norman.

After I visited Harding, Martha's letters became less frequent and less personal. As mentioned, Martha had joined the Acapella Chorus. In her correspondence, she mentioned that membership in the Chorus, due to its stature, was taking up a lot of time. Rehearsals were frequent and sometimes lengthy, and sometimes ad hoc. She also said the Chorus periodically made short day trips to area schools and churches to perform and that they also made longer, multi-state tours each year. The Chorus was well–known and very well received wherever it appeared. She brought up the fact that the time required for regular classes and study plus the Chorus time constraints were seriously eating into her spare time. She hinted that her letters would likely continue to be more infrequent due to her extremely full schedule. I told her I understood fully. That turned out to be untrue. I totally misunderstood because I failed to read "between the lines," which, in retrospect, were as clear as an Arizona day. I think I was in a severe state of denial.

I failed to consider that, as a pretty freshman girl on a relatively small campus, she was understandably attracting a lot of attention and was in serious demand. As it turns out, one of those giving her attention was a sophomore football player by the name of Randy Crider.

True to her word, Martha's letters became rarer and rarer as the semester drew to a close. I noticed the increased elapsed time between letters, and I also noticed that she was subtly attempting to dissuade me from transferring to Harding.

However, the die had been cast by that time. I had already contacted Harding regarding applying for admission there for the spring semester, I had been accepted, and they had even offered me some scholarship money. At this point, there was no turning back, whether or not I would be welcomed there by Martha.

When I ran these plans past my parents, they were pretty upset.

Dad was upset because the tuition at OU at that time was $7.00 per semester hour, and Harding's tuition was $21.00 per hour. (Yes, I understand that those tuition rates were ridiculously low, but that was then, and this is now.) This would increase the cost to attend Harding by about $200 per semester, given that housing and food costs were comparable between the two colleges. When I told Dad that Harding was giving me a $200 per semester scholarship, he was less upset, but he was still not sold on the transfer.

Mom was a little more perceptive. She realized that I had dated Martha for the summer, and Mom "did" read between the lines on my motive to transfer. I remember as clear as day when discussing this with Mom. She said, "You won't be at Harding a month before you and Martha break up." My mother assumed that Martha and I were actually "going together," which was only half true. As it turned out, Mom's ESP was alive and well.

At any rate, Mom and Dad finally consented to the transfer, and plans were set in place to make the move.

When I notified Martha of the situation, she was absolutely not thrilled – I don't know any more powerful way to express that. However, she was diplomatic about it all.

These conversations and decisions occurred in November. Christmas break promised to be interesting. During the break, I picked up some hours and a few dollars working at C.R. Anthony's. Martha came home, and during the break, we saw one another and had a few dates. I thought she seemed pretty indifferent, but I figured it was just my imagination. Once again, I was illiterate regarding reading between the lines.

Christmas came and went, the blizzard that plagued us at the start of

Christmas break had abated, Martha returned to Harding, and I returned to the campus at OU. The first class I attended upon returning to OU was my Accounting I class, and I got hit squarely in the face with the surprise test my professor afflicted us with. At that time, it strongly reaffirmed my decision to leave because had I enrolled at OU for the spring semester, I would have had the same professor as my Accounting II teacher.

I finished out the semester, which concluded in early January. I earned a 3.21 GPA for the semester, making an A in speech and B's in everything else. It would have been a 3.42 had I and the other students not been blindsided by my Accounting professor.

I packed up my things in my car and headed home to Bartlesville, and prepared for the next step in life. There is no way I could have known at the time, but the decision to transfer to Harding College actually determined the entirety of the rest of my life.

THE PROVIDENCE OF GOD

I wasn't necessarily thinking of an Ebenezer during my semester at Oklahoma University since I had so many other things on my mind. However, certain beneficial events that semester – probably God–inspired – not only contributed to my well–being for the semester at OU, but they also set me up for my life-changing experience at Harding.

1. To cushion my move to Oklahoma University, I was pleased to be greeted by my old friend Eddie Roark as I move into my dormitory.

2. I reunited with another close friend, Mike Howard, and enjoyed some positive interaction with his fraternity.

3. Martha Koger and I corresponded regularly, describing in her letters the joys she was experiencing at Harding, which influenced my decision to enroll at Harding later.

4. My experience at OU was completely different from that at OCC – lost in the crowd, missing Martha, missing the church and Christian environment. The contrast between OCC and OU was glaring, and it cemented my desire to get back into the Christian college environment and, thanks to Martha, Harding was the target.

Hither by His help, I had come.

Eight

HARDING COLLEGE (SPRING 1964)

After arriving in Bartlesville at the conclusion of the fall semester at OU, I had very little turn–around time before I had to head to Harding. I don't recall Martha coming home to Bartlesville during the semester break, so that made things a little less hectic. My parents were still not sold on the idea, although it was too late in the game to change things. As sort of an admonition for my making the decision to transfer to Harding without family consensus, my dad told me that I could not take my car to Searcy. He did not give a reason, but I was sure it was to show that he still retained fatherly authority. I was hoping that the sanction would be temporary and that I would have wheels at Harding at some point.

It was ironic in a way because, in order to transport me to Searcy, we loaded up my 1955 Ford – now nine years old in an era when people bought new cars every three years – and headed to Arkansas. Mom and Dad drove me to campus, unloaded, and then drove back to Bartlesville, all in one day. I think that experience was not lost on them. At some point during that semester, I was able to catch a ride home to Bartlesville, after which I was allowed to take my car back to campus. Their experience of making the round trip in one day with the knowledge that it would have to be repeated periodically was probably a factor in that decision.

Unbeknownst to me at the time, every significant event that had occurred in my life had led to this moment – my arrival on the campus of Harding College. My dad's safe return from World War II, all of the new jobs for my dad, all of the family moves, all of the encounters with friends in Bartlesville, even the year at OCC had "worked together" to lead me to Harding College in the spring of 1964. The stage had been set. Now I had to fasten my seat belt for a wild ride that I would experience over the next several decades.

When we arrived on campus, I got my key and my dorm assignment, and we went to unload. I was assigned to Armstrong Hall. Armstrong Hall was famous for having a railroad track located on its south side, directly across the street. A very noisy, whistling train ran past the dorm every morning at 6:00 a.m. It would have served as a very effective alarm clock if I had chosen to get up at 6 o'clock. However, as it was, it was a real nuisance.

As a side note, many years later, the tracks were rerouted away from campus, and the old tracks were removed. David Underwood, a friend of mine at Harding, had been aware of the travail the train visited upon me while I lived in that room, and several years ago, he presented me with a spike that had been removed from the track when it had been taken up. I still have that filthy spike in my memento cabinet. I had the last laugh on the train.

Aside from the nuisance of the train, my room in Armstrong Hall was quite pleasant. The rooms in Armstrong were actually a part of a two-room suite that shared a single bathroom, which was really handy. And, unlike my moving into my dormitories at both Oklahoma Christian and Oklahoma University, which had been kind of like old home week, none of the guys in the suite were friends from my previous home towns. My roommate was Ron French, a junior Business Education major from Liberal, Kansas. However, in another small world event, I was already acquainted with the two guys in the other room in the suite. They were Phil Dixon from Newport, Arkansas, and Steve Thornton, from Thermopolis, Wyoming, whom I had stayed with during my visit to Harding during the last semester. That made three colleges in a row where, upon arrival, I was placed in a dorm that included people I already knew. Just another coincidence, I'm sure.

In keeping with the serendipitous occurrences which have populated my life, Phil, Steve, and I were involved in one another's marriages some years later. I was Steve's best man at his wedding, and Phil was the best man at mine.

My first priority upon getting settled was to find Martha and get reacquainted. When we met, she gave me a tour of the campus and showed me where the Administration Building was located so I could complete my enrollment and pick up my textbook list. Following that, I visited the bookstore and paid what seemed a fortune for books.

Classes started, and I began to settle into my new routine, which was, of course, light years distant from my days at the University of Oklahoma. As I concentrated on becoming acclimated to the Harding scene, I was reminded that one of the critical aspects of any college experience is the cafeteria, and at Harding, that took a little getting used to.

HARDING COLLEGE (SPRING 1964)

At that time, the cafeteria at Harding was probably unique in the entire college world. The cafeteria was in the basement of Pattie Cobb Hall, the oldest girls' dormitory on campus. Due to limited space and a growing student population, the meal service had to be carefully managed. There were two cafeteria-style serving lines where the students were able to make limited selections of food. As a student exited the serving line carrying his tray, he was directed by a hostess to a specific table. Each table had six chairs, and the student was expected to occupy one of the empty chairs at the table indicated by the hostess. When the six chairs were filled, the hostess directed the next student to another empty table and repeated the process until that table was fully occupied. If you entered the cafeteria with a friend or a group of friends, there was no guarantee that you would be able to sit together as you dined. There were only a limited number of seats available to accommodate the meal–time onslaught of the student body, and random, uncontrolled seating would have resulted in some level of chaos as students wandered about the dining room carrying trays of food searching for a place to sit. It sounds silly, but it really was the most efficient way to get all the students seated in the crowded dining room.

At that time, I also learned that the southern hospitality practiced at Harding implied that no one should leave the table until all at the table had finished their meal. It was amusing when a young belle was seated at a table with five football players. Typically the football players would gulp down their food without chewing and would be finished before the young belle had finished buttering her biscuit. But they would patiently wait until she was finished, and I never heard anyone complain. It was just the way things were done.

At that time the food was not great, but it was OK. I never went hungry, and most students managed to put on their "Freshman 15" pounds while dining there. At one Sunday evening meal, my friend Steve Thornton convinced me that the meat on the sandwich was goat meat and persuaded me to give it to him. But ordinarily, the food was recognizable, and he never attempted that ploy successfully again.

During the first few days on campus, Martha and I spent only a nominal amount of time together. I was aware that Martha had never been particularly excited about the prospect of my enrolling at Harding, but I had never really given it much thought as to why. I had been on campus for about a week when certain things came into sharp focus. Following a Sunday evening church service which we attended together, as we were walking back to campus, Martha told me she had been seriously dating a guy named Randy Crider and that we must stop seeing one another. She said they had been dating for several weeks. At that time, everything became crystal clear. It suddenly made sense as to why her letters to me at OU had become less personal and less frequent and why she had not been thrilled at the prospect of my attending Harding. I was, perhaps for the first time in my life, speechless. However, with nothing left to say, we civilly parted ways, and each of us began the next segment of our life.

I did realize that life had not ended. In the short time I had been on campus, I had already started making some friends, many of whom I am still close with today. Following the last awkward conversation I had with Martha, I received lots of support from my new friends. I think many of them had seen this coming because they were aware that Martha and Randy had been dating for some time. Also, it is only natural for a pretty girl and a nice guy to find each other on a small campus and then take the acquaintance to a higher level, and one of those giving her attention was Randy Crider. Martha and Randy were married a year or two later and have now celebrated more than 50 years together. They made good choices.

As a side note, I need to mention that Randy was a stand–up guy, really nice, smart, and a fine Christian man. In later years he served in the Army, established a successful business, and became an elder in the church. Under the circumstances, the fact that they were attracted to each other should not have been surprising.

Martha had tried to spare my feelings by subtly discouraging me from transferring, but I had been too blind to see. However, by this time, and due to this event, I was becoming somewhat adept at reading tea leaves and had decided that dwelling on the breakup would be counterproductive. Although I didn't realize it at the time, this very painful event – much like the move from Seminole to Ada and then the move from Ada to Bartlesville – would eventually turn out to be worth the pain involved. Ultimately a series of unbelievably coordinated steps, seemingly providential, had led me to Harding. And as this book will reveal, the blessings resulting from those moves would ultimately and exponentially and, in some cases, indirectly satisfy all of my life's priorities.

So, I moved on from the breakup and concentrated on both my classes and the extraordinary intramural sports program that Harding provided. I also decided to pledge a social club.

I had enrolled in 17 credit hours for the spring semester, so it's probably a good thing I wasn't distracted by dating regularly. A welcome relief was Dr. James Hedrick, my Accounting II teacher. He was an exceptional accountant, an exceptional human being, and he never double-crossed the students on the test schedule. Although I personally didn't ever sit for the CPA exam,

Dr. Hedrick had a reputation for turning out accounting graduates who routinely passed all four parts of the CPA exam on their first attempt.

Another of my teachers during the semester was Jerry Starr, an Assistant Professor of Economics. At that time, the only experience I had in the field of Economics at the college level was my Graduate Assistant teacher at Oklahoma University, who was also the president of the Oklahoma chapter of the Students for a Democratic Society. To say that Mr. Starr's perspective on the field of Economics and capitalism digressed from the views of my previous Economics teacher would be a gross understatement. Their views were somewhere around 180 degrees apart. I found Mr. Starr's Economic philosophy logical, sound, and, frankly, comforting. Before I graduated, I would have Mr. Starr in three more classes. And I would eventually become acquainted with his brother, Kenneth Starr, who, years later, made the national news every day for months. He was the prosecutor in the impeachment of President Bill Clinton.

Even with the heavy load, the new environment, and the disappointing beginning on campus, I nevertheless managed a 3.18 GPA for the semester. All things considered, I was satisfied with the results.

The social clubs at Harding were similar to those at Oklahoma Christian, except they were not co-ed. The club I chose was the TNT social club. It was a veteran club, having been on campus for decades. Its two faculty sponsors were Dr. Joseph Pryor, Dean of the College, and Virgil Lawyer, Dean of Students. Also, it was populated with a variety of upstanding students — Bible majors, athletes, music majors, class officers, and Alpha Chi members, to name a few. Alpha Chi is the Harding equivalent of Phi Beta Kappa. With that makeup of sponsors and fellow students, it was very attractive to me. TNT ostensibly stood for its motto, "Trustworthiness, Noble Ideals and Tact." However, I suspect that at some point in the past, the motto had been devised to coincide with its name. At any rate, it was a superior social club, true to its motto, and is still functioning at a high level all these years later.

I notified the club leadership of my intent to seek membership, and plans were set in place to subject me to the pledging process. Steve Thornton, one of my new friends, also decided to pledge TNT at the same time that I did.

Being accepted into the club required two steps. The first step involved an applicant's making his intentions publicly known. For TNT, this was accomplished by the applicant's wearing around campus, during pledge week, a fake firecracker constructed of a toilet paper cardboard cylinder painted red and strapped to the top of his head. By the way, members of other clubs achieved status in their clubs by stealing the fake firecrackers worn by the TNT pledges. Consequently, TNT pledges embedded needles in their headgear, clearly visible, so that if someone attempted to grab one off his head, he was rewarded with a fistful of needles. Potentially, very painful, I am told. This practice was well known on campus, and as a result, no TNT pledge's firecracker had been ripped from his head in years.

Also, it should be noted that most pledging took place in the fall semester when there were hundreds of pledges of the various social clubs wearing weird costumes, roaming the campus at any given moment. Unfortunately, Steve and I were pledging during the spring semester and were uniquely conspicuous to the entire student body during that week.

The second step to being accepted into the club involved avoiding being blackballed when the club convened to vote on the pledges. All it took was one single "no" vote to keep a pledge from being accepted into the club. To make things worse, the pledges were told that the club would meet for an overnight campout at Red Bluff, a remote wilderness location near Searcy, to conduct the voting and the subsequent initiation of the successful pledges. All the pledges were required to attend the meeting and spend the night with the club, win or lose.

As mentioned, Dr. Joseph Pryor was one of the TNT faculty sponsors. Tall, stately, dignified – wisdom and integrity personified, a preacher, a teacher, Dean of the College and Vice President of the college. He was one of the Godliest men I have ever met, and he was thought to not engage in cheap frivolity. At each pledge induction ceremony, it was his duty to call the pledges to stand before him one at a time in the wilderness, in the darkness, faces lighted by only a campfire, and pronounce judgment. On campus, when Dr. Pryor spoke, EVERYONE listened. When I was called before him that night, he simply said, "Steve Thornton was accepted, but you will not be invited to join the club. I am sorry." I was stunned. It took my breath away, and I thought I had died after all this work and humiliation. Dr. Pryor didn't lie. I couldn't believe it, and I couldn't speak. I simply stumbled away from Dr. Pryor and disappeared into the darkness to recover my dignity. With the disappointment of the breakup with Martha still weighing heavily on my mind, I momentarily rued the fact that I had ever heard of Harding College.

As I was leaving the campfire area, Dr. Pryor called out to me and said. "I'm sorry. I have made a mistake. Actually, you were voted in. I just misread the note." Apparently, he did occasionally descend into cheap frivolity.

I almost broke down. That nanosecond turn of events was almost more than I could handle. I still couldn't breathe, still couldn't talk. At that point, all the members rushed forward and patted me on the back, and welcomed me to the club.

Of course, it was all a sham. The club's body had met two weeks earlier and voted on whom to accept as new members. Essentially, everyone who was accepted as a pledge would be offered membership. The frightening rejection by Dr. Pryor was just a traditional part of the initiation ceremony. I will always remember that moment, and I will always be grateful that I joined that club.

I have always enjoyed sports. I attended three colleges during my college career, and neither of the other two came close to matching Harding's intramural program. The program was set up so that every student enrolled – male or female – who was physically able could participate. There was a myriad of events for the students, both individual and team. The men's team sports menu included flag football, baseball, basketball, volleyball, tennis doubles, and handball doubles. At that time, racquetball was still in its infancy and had not yet been introduced at Harding. The men's individual sports menu included tennis and handball singles, cross country, wall–climbing, baseball throw, football throw, football punt, baseball base running, and the pursuit race.

No one, regardless of his skill level, was excluded. For instance, the baseball and basketball programs had been set up so that the more experienced/talented players could participate in a "major class" league with a higher level of competition, and the lesser experienced or new–to–the–sports players could compete against one another in the "minor class" at a lower skill level. This assured that everyone would get playing time against similarly talented athletes. Tryouts were not part of the process to determine which level a student would choose. Rather, when signing up to play, each student chose for himself which level he would participate in. Naturally, some overestimated their talent and signed up for the higher league and wound up gathering a lot of bench time.

To encourage intramural participation, points were awarded to each participant just for playing, even if they or their team finished dead last. Additional points were awarded on the basis of the team's or individual's results in the competition. The higher the team or individual finished in the competition, the more points the participant received. In each team sport, excluding tennis and handball doubles, all-star teams were selected by a vote of the participants, and those who were voted to the all-star teams received additional points. Points were accumulated, and at year's end, Harding Intramural Athletic letters were awarded to the top ten individuals in points earned. In addition, a "Sports Skill" champion trophy was awarded to the individual who had earned the most points in individual events – singles tennis, cross country, football punt, etc. Finally, the Intramural Director selected an "Intramural Athlete of the Year," and a trophy was awarded for that honor also.

In the spring semester, I participated in baseball, volleyball, tennis doubles, and handball doubles team sports and every single individual event. I was on the championship "major" baseball team and was voted to the all-star team. Having participated only during the spring semester, I did not accumulate enough points to earn an Intramural letter that year.

I was not a varsity quality athlete in any sport, so I did not try out for any of the varsity teams. However, I remained a rabid sports fan and closely followed the Harding varsity athletics. Harding fielded a variety of varsity intercollegiate sports teams, including football, basketball, track, cross country, tennis, and even intercollegiate bowling. Harding competed in the Arkansas Intercollegiate Conference – the AIC. Excluding the University of Arkansas, at that time, most of the other colleges in the state of Arkansas were members of the AIC. The AIC itself was a member of a larger body, the NAIA, the National Association of Intercollegiate Athletics. The large colleges such as the Universities of Oklahoma, Arkansas, Alabama, Ohio State, etc., belonged to conferences which were part of the NCAA, National Collegiate Athletic Association – the big boys who played in the Rose Bowl and such. Just below that level was the NCAA II, larger colleges that did not field powerful football and basketball teams. The next tier down at that time was the NAIA.

Harding's varsity athletic teams were known as the Bison. It took me a while to learn that the word "Bison" is both singular and plural – hence "Bison" could be grammatically correctly applied when describing a single Bison athlete or a group of Bison. While it is true that Harding did not possess varsity teams that could compete with those at the University of Oklahoma, nevertheless, the Bison teams were able to compete well against their peers, both those in Arkansas and those in other states who were also members of NAIA.

I had arrived on campus in January 1964 and, therefore, was not witness to the Harding football season just completed. The team was 1–8 for the season. I did get on campus in time to watch the basketball team play the last half of its season, and it fared better, going 14–12. The sparkplug on the team was 5'8" Ned Boaz. He was a playmaker, and he was as quick as a hiccup. He was named to the all-conference second team in the AIC. The leading scorer for the Bison and for the conference was Vernon Rogers, who was accorded first-team all-conference honors.

Harding's real competitive athletic strength in those days was its track stars, particularly its cross country team. The cross country team dominated the AIC that year, winning every meet they entered, including the AIC championship. A key member of the team that year was Cliff Clark, a sophomore from Shelter Island, New York – a town on Long Island. He would eventually earn All–American honors.

The baseball team compiled a 7–11 record that year. The track and tennis teams were competitive but did not win any championships. Ironically, the Bison bowling won the AIC and competed on the national level. Harding and the AIC were some of the very few institutions that competed in intercollegiate bowling. A member of the bowling team was a friend by the name of Rob Barber. His reappearance in my life a few years after graduation would have a dynamic impact on my future.

I did not participate in any other activities for the remainder of the semester except for intramural athletics and the TNT social club. Consequently, the rest of the year passed pretty routinely. I continued to make friends and dated several young women, but no romances evolved.

However, three issues were unfolding on the home front.

In the first issue, my family continued its gypsy odyssey. About halfway through the semester, my dad received a promotion by Exxon Corporation and was transferred to Okemah, Oklahoma, a small town right in the middle of the state. He was promoted from "roustabout" to "pumper," the same type of job my Grandfather Brock had held so many years ago with the Barnsdall Oil Company. A pumper is responsible for managing the production in the oil fields. Each oil field – indeed, each individual oil well in an oil field – is managed as to the amount of oil it pumps from the ground on a daily basis. In addition, if an oil well broke down or needed service, the pumper had to take the necessary steps to return it to operation. If the maintenance was something minor, he would perform the service himself. If it involved a serious issue, he would call in an oil well service company that could service a well from the top of its boom all the way to the pump at the bottom of the hole, including all the pipes, sucker rods, motors, and equipment in between. When my dad determined that a service company was required, the Landers Oil Well Service, based in Okemah, was usually called. As will be seen a little later, Landers Oil Well Service played a role in my life.

The second issue involved the church in Okemah. Upon their move to Okemah, my parents placed their membership at the Okemah Church of Christ. The congregation was not large but was populated with wonderful, friendly people. It did not take long for my parents to feel right at home among the members.

One of the members of the church was a man by the name of Tommy Hall. Mr. Hall was actually 1Sgt. Hall, a First Sergeant in the Oklahoma Army National Guard, the famous 45th Infantry Division Thunderbirds who had fought so gallantly in both World War II and Korea. One of the heroic achievements of the 45th in World War II was its liberation of the concentration camp at Dachau. Col. Cotton Smith (Ret), who had been a combat battalion commander in Korea, was also a member of the congregation, as were his two sons, Jerry and Mack Smith, who were currently officers in the outfit.

My parents' move to Okemah and their subsequent acquaintance with Tommy Hall and the Thunderbirds would come into play significantly in my life two years down the road. In addition, my dad's association with the Landers Oil Well Service would take on meaning in only a matter of weeks. God things just kept on happening.

The third issue was unfolding from a long distance, Kansas City, Missouri, in fact. At the time, two of my mother's brothers lived in the Kansas City area, and one of them, my Uncle Howard, had a brother–in–law who built houses in metro Kansas City. Uncle Howard had been encouraging me to come to Kansas City for the summer, live with them, and work in construction for his brother–in–law. It sounded wonderful to me. The Exxon job in Bartlesville was not renewable since my dad no longer worked in the oil field there, and I had no solid summer job prospects, so the thought of living in Kansas City for the summer, the big city, going to baseball games, etc. sounded great. Dad thought that I could get work with the Landers Oil Well Service with my experience in the Exxon oil field the previous summer. I could live at home, and it would be an uncomplicated situation. I lobbied for the Kansas City job, however, and finally, Mom and Dad consented to allow me to travel to Kansas City for the summer.

When late May came, I packed up and headed to our new home in Okemah and stayed just long enough to unpack, repack and head to Kansas City. Little did I know what lay in store for me.

THE PROVIDENCE OF GOD

I don't know if I raised an Ebenezer or not for God's Providence in blessing my first semester at Harding. If I didn't, I should have. Among the blessings I received:

1. I had been welcomed by students and faculty, had succeeded academically and socially, and had appreciated and enjoyed the semester's experience to the extent that ever transferring to another college was completely out of the question.

2. I had broken up with Martha, which left me available to search for my true love, the woman I would eventually marry.

3. During the semester, my parents had been transferred from Bartlesville

to Okemah, Oklahoma, a move that would eventually determine my military service.

Hither by His help I had come. Now it was off to see what Kansas City had in store for me.

Nine

KANSAS CITY HERE I COME - AND GO (SUMMER 1964)

"Everything's up to date in Kansas City . . ." Being an Oklahoman, I have heard that song from the musical "Oklahoma" sung a thousand times at least.

I had been to Kansas City a few times over the years to visit my uncles, aunts, and cousins, and I always enjoyed the trip. One exceptional trip stands out in my mind. It happened to be another of those small world events which seem to follow me everywhere. We had a friend from Ada, Jerry Walker, who was a pitcher for the Baltimore Orioles baseball team, and while we were in Kansas City in the summer of 1960, the Orioles happened to be in town to play the Kansas City A's. My family and I had actually attended Jerry's wedding at the church while we still lived in Ada. Jerry was somewhat of a celebrity in that he had been the winning pitcher for the American League all-stars in the Major-League All-Star Game the previous year.

Since we were friends, my dad called the hotel where the Orioles were staying and talked to Jerry for a bit, and Jerry offered him complimentary tickets to the baseball game that evening. We went to the game. Jerry did not pitch that night, but he did talk to us and gave me an autographed photo, which I still have. Not all my trips to Kansas City were that thrilling, but it was always fun.

When I arrived in Kansas City in the summer of 1964, two of my uncles, two of my aunts, and ten of my cousins lived in the metro area. My uncle Kermit and his family had moved to Portland, Oregon, a few years earlier, or otherwise, I would have had thirteen cousins in the area. My cousins and I had always been pretty tight knit. During the years of my Grandpa Brock's declining health, we were with them frequently at my grandparents' home in Shell Knob, Missouri. Now I would have the opportunity to be with them for what I anticipated would be an extended visit – maybe nearly three months if all went right. At any rate, spending time with close relatives, going to major league baseball games, playing miniature golf at Crestview, a good job at a good wage working in construction – it seemed like maybe my luck was indeed changing. However, as will be seen, my personally developed plans frequently have a way of going awry.

My Uncle Howard lived in Independence, Missouri, a suburb just east of Kansas City. I arrived at his house very early in June, ready to get settled in and go to work. I greeted Uncle Howard, Aunt Mae, and all their kids – Pat, Sam, Anita, Bob, Sarah, Sally, and Peggy. Yep, seven kids in the household. Uncle Howard's house had three bedrooms, a basement, and 1½ baths, but we made it work.

Shortly after I had unpacked, Uncle Howard broke the bad news. New construction in the metro had pretty well dried up for the time, and his brother–in–law, the builder, currently had no houses under construction. Further, he had had to lay off almost all of his workforce. No good job with good pay was waiting for me. This situation had developed rather quickly, and Uncle Howard really had not had time to inform me of the situation.

However, Uncle Howard told me there were probably a lot of summer jobs available in the area, and I was welcome to stay with them while I looked for work, and after I found a job. I accepted his offer not only because I wanted to spend the summer in Kansas City but also because I was ashamed to have to tell my parents that the great summer plans in Kansas City had imploded.

I checked the newspaper and discovered that Clark Oil was seeking service station attendants. The next day I visited the Clark office in downtown Kansas City and applied for a job. I remembered my previous summer job with Exxon that paid $3.25 per hour. In the interview, I brought up my experience working for an oil company and casually mentioned the pay. The Clark personnel rep explained that there was a great difference between the type of work I had done the previous summer and the work that I would be doing this summer if hired. I quickly crawfished and told him I would be happy with whatever the duty was and whatever the pay might be. He told me that I would be pumping gas, cleaning windshields, selling cans of oil, and selling packs of cigarettes. And the pay would be $1.10 per hour. He also told me that I could expect a pay raise within two weeks of starting work if my work was acceptable. He offered me the job, and I accepted.

I was assigned to the Clark station at the very busy corner of Charlotte Avenue and Truman Road. Clark attempted to keep its service station operations very basic. The only things they sold in those days besides gasoline were two grades of oil by the quart and several brands of two types of cigarettes – filter and non–filter – by the pack. Filter cigarettes were 29 cents per pack, and non–filter cigarettes were 26 cents per pack. How times have changed.

Clark also kept its gasoline program remarkably simple. They advertised that they sold "Only One Grade – The Very Best." That meant that they only sold high octane gasoline – ethyl, as it was known in those days. They did not market regular octane gasoline. Those who drove a VW Beetle or Chevrolet Impala 409 and pulled into a Clark station bought exactly the same gasoline.

Also, in those days self–service was still decades in the future. Every gallon of gasoline that was sold on this busy street corner was personally introduced into the customer's gas tank by an attendant. And, it should be noted that this station had twelve pumps. For an attendant on solo duty, which I frequently was, it got very hectic at times.

One thing more – credit cards were still years away from coming into use, so all transactions were in cash: no credit cards, no checks. However, with the limited inventory of items to sell, most transactions were fairly simple.

I trained on the day shift but was soon assigned the 4:00 p.m. to midnight shift. And, true to their word, I received my promised raise two weeks later – 10 cents an hour all the way up to my new pay rate of $1.20 per hour.

However, it only took me a month to determine that the job was not working out very well. One evening the midnight shift attendant did not bother to show up, and I wound up working from 4:00 p.m. until 8:00 the next morning. Not only that, this was the 1960's, a time of growing national unrest, sit-ins, and sometimes violent social protests. Further, while I had expected the summer in Kansas City to be a financial bonanza working on a construction crew, I had only about $50 in my pocket to show for a month of work. Given my pay, my work situation, and the potential personal safety issues associated with my work location, I made the decision to eat crow and head back to Okemah for the remainder of the summer. While in KC, I had indeed sampled its pleasures – major league baseball games, miniature golf, lots of games and such with my cousins and Aunt Mae's fine cooking. I had suffered another bust, and after one month, it was time to head for home.

Overall, it had been a bad decision to go to Kansas City that summer. I should have confirmed the potential job before I ever headed to KC, but I was so eager to sample the big city life that I ignored any possible problems that could arise and headed north full steam ahead.

I now packed up and headed for Okemah with my tail between my legs, dreading to have to face my dad and hoping God would mitigate the consequences. As usual, God did not disappoint.

Dad did not chide me in any way for what had happened – he didn't need to – and neither did he waste any time. I arrived home in Okemah on Saturday and went to work for Landers Oil Well Service very early Monday morning. Admittedly, I had earlier given Dad a heads–up phone call that I was coming home, so without even hanging up the phone, he called Landers and asked if they could use some summer help. I think he already knew the answer, but he was just getting the ball rolling.

I attended church Sunday morning after I got into town and became reacquainted with some of the members that I had met on weekends at home during the spring semester at Harding, including Tommy Hall and the Smith family of the 45th Infantry Division Thunderbirds. Almost exactly two years later, I would get to know those men up close and personal.

Monday morning, I got up early and made it to the Landers office by 7:00 a.m. I filled out and signed all the necessary paperwork and climbed onto a pulling unit. The pay was better – $1.75 per hour plus time and a half for overtime – significantly better than the $1.20 per hour I was pulling down at the Clark station. In addition, I had a daily commute of eight blocks each way instead of 20 miles each way, as I had had with Clark. My gasoline purchases plummeted in addition to the better wage. I wasn't going to get rich, but I was going to do considerably better.

The Landers' work vehicles were called pulling units. Their primary purpose was repairing anything and everything that was below ground at an oil well – sucker rods, pipes (called casings), and pumps. The pumps were suspended at the bottom of a string of steel sucker rods, and the sucker rods and pump were encased in a pipe that reached to the bottom of the well. When an oil well suffered a breakdown, it was almost every time due to a problem someplace below ground. Either a malfunction of the pump at the bottom of the well, or a "parted" (broken) sucker rod down the hole someplace, or a leak in the pipe encasing the sucker rods and the pump. In order to repair any of these problems, it was necessary to "pull" the broken equipment out of the ground for repair or replacement. Hence, the name "pulling unit." A pulling unit crew was made up of two or three roustabouts and an Operator. The Operator was the boss.

On my very first day on the job, one of the roustabouts nearly got killed. Had I been in his place, I would most certainly have died. OSHA rules had not been enacted in those days, so while workplace safety was encouraged, the Federal Government had not yet addressed it. I was not wearing a steel helmet that day, and the operator reminded me that I needed one. I told him I would have one by tomorrow. Under today's OSHA rules, I would not have been allowed to work that job that day.

There was a leak in the casing on this particular job, so it was necessary to pull the pump and all of the sucker rods out of the casing and then pull out all the casing itself. This is the hardest and most time-consuming type of repair we performed. Essentially, we had to nearly empty the hole to make the repair. A winch with a cable was used to pull out the equipment from the hole, and attached to the end of the cable was a set of tongs that were used to "grab" the sucker rods and lengths of the casing and pull them up from the hole.

We had extracted the sucker rods and pump and were pulling out the casing. The tongs slipped and allowed a 20–foot long, 3–inch diameter length of casing to come crashing down on the side of the roustabout's head. Fortunately, he was wearing a steel helmet. It stunned him, and he wobbled around a bit, but in a short time, he was back in working order. The only apparent damage was a huge dent in his hard hat and a headache. However, had I been standing there instead of him, it would have killed me instantly. I have to believe God used that as a teaching moment. As this book will document, I have dodged several bullets in my life. Needless to say, I was very careful for the rest of the day and had acquired a steel helmet by the end of the day.

The rest of the summer in the oil field was uneventful, which is exactly as we liked it—just hot, hard, dirty work. We occasionally endured an oil shower, but it was all part of the job. In fact, the rest of the summer was pretty routine. Not only that, I had earned decent money working with Landers Oil Well Service without incurring any living expenses, so the summer ended far better than it started.

Unlike the beginning of the previous semester, I was not exactly chomping at the bit to be heading back to Harding. True, the semester there had been satisfying, despite the collapse of my love life, and I had enjoyed a good academic and social life. However, my wounds of the spring semester had not yet completely healed. That being said; nevertheless, I never gave a second thought to transferring. I was just not all revved up to head for Searcy like I had been the previous January.

I had come to love the small Christian college environment, and I felt that, despite my disappointment during the first semester there, Harding was going to be able to provide the true education and spiritual enhancement I needed and wanted. So come early September I loaded up my car and headed back to Searcy, but filled with some uncertainty following the events of the spring semester.

THE PROVIDENCE OF GOD

The more I thought about it, particularly some time later when I was able to look at things objectively, I came to believe that the spring semester at Harding, followed closely by the summer misadventure in Kansas City, constituted a 5–month long "come to Jesus" moment. Consequently, I eventually raised an Ebenezer in honor of that period of personal maturity and education. And, in retrospect, the summer escapade was not a total bust. After all:

1. I spent a month working in Kansas City, living with family, and this would later have a significant influence on my decision to accept employment with Phillips Petroleum at their Kansas City office upon graduation.

2. The time in Kansas City had given me an opportunity to become acquainted with the metro area and would make my move there two years later much easier and with a better idea of where to seek housing.

3. My work in the oil fields during the summer kept me in shape physically and gave me a little more insight into the petroleum industry, in which I would eventually make my career.

4. I spent those last two months of summer in Okemah rubbing elbows with leaders in the Oklahoma Army National Guard, the 45th Infantry Division, the famed "Thunderbirds" of World War II, and Korea. This introduction to these leaders paved the way for me to enlist in the National Guard there following my college graduation.

The school of hard knocks is never easy and comes at a price, but even a bad experience can sometimes pay off in the long run. In time I learned that the school of hard knocks, which I attended during the early summer of 1964, was indeed a great education. It brings to mind a quote from Louis L'Amour:

"Good judgment comes from experience, and a lot of that comes from bad judgment."

I feel that this applied to me in spades in the summer of 1964. My bad judgment did not sink my boat but rather developed some level of good judgment in me. However, being a slow learner, I would go through another uncomfortable experience a few years later, but, once again, my discomfort would lead to eventual good judgment—more on that a little later.

Meanwhile, I hung up my hard hat and headed for Searcy and chapter 2 of my Harding College adventure.

Hither by His help, I had come.

Ten

JUNIOR YEAR - THE BLESSINGS BEGIN (1964–1965)

The 1964–1965 school year would prove to be a transitional period in my college career. It was almost like a fresh start. The uncertainties of a college major and the institution where I would obtain it would finally be settled. I would make a whole set of new, long–term friends, and I would begin to establish myself as a legitimate, as opposed to a nomadic student, and I would spread my wings and get involved in many substantial student activities. My failed previous romance, the primary reason I transferred to Harding in the first place, now rested in the dustbin of history. I was primed for a new beginning, and there would be no better place to start than at Harding College in Searcy, Arkansas.

To begin with, I had a new roommate and a new room. As had been arranged near the end of the previous semester, I would be rooming with Kyle Smock, a fellow TNT member, and we would be in Graduate Dorm. It was a slight misnomer, for it was not reserved for graduate students. I'm not sure how it came by its name, but it is irrelevant. What was really important was that it was a half-block from the railroad track, and the 6:00 a.m. train whistle no longer had any effect on my sleep.

I had arrived on campus that fall with no particular expectations other than to make some more new friends and to keep my grades up. I hoped to find romance, but given the fact that my last effort at romance had crashed and burned, I decided to tread lightly in any new relationships. Beyond that, I looked forward to a full academic year at Harding and planned to increase my participation in extracurricular events such as intramural sports and per- haps some student organizations. I had enrolled in 15 credit hours for the fall semester, including another Economics course under Jerry Starr and what would turn out to be a very dynamic Biology course under Dr. Robert T. Clark.

Dr. Clark taught Biology 101 and 102, among other courses. Earlier in his life, he had worked in the U.S. Space program and had also taught at the University of Oklahoma. In his class, he touched on all forms of biology, both flora, and fauna, but he focused on human anatomy. He introduced his students to DNA and RNA in 1964, more than 30 years before they became household words. His tests were beasts, but if you took good notes and crammed for two days before the test, you could be rewarded with a good grade. It also helped that his lectures were extremely interesting. I put in more study time for his course than any I took in my college career, and I actually learned the subject beyond just studying for the tests. Also, he had the ability to draw illustrations on the board with both hands at the same time. It was uncanny. In his "spare" time, he coached the college cross–country team.

As will be revealed later, Dr. Clark's teaching played a very significant role in my military career in the summer of 1968. It was another one of those God things.

During the course of the year, I met a new, dynamic faculty member, Billy Ray Cox. Mr. Cox had been vice president of Dallas Ceramics Corporation, headquartered in Dallas, and had taken leave of that position to join the Harding faculty. He was a CPA and taught a variety of strategic Business courses. He would eventually rise to the Vice Presidency at Harding. During my junior year, my interactions with Mr. Cox were casual, but his impact on my senior year was more than just significant.

As I settled in during the semester, I began to venture beyond my comfort zone and became more involved in campus life. Of course, it was a given that I would dive into intramural sports with both feet and that I would participate to the limit in my social club. I dated several young women during the year, but none seriously. However, I did join some campus student organizations – particularly the American Studies group, Student Circle K, and the Young Republicans.

This was the autumn of 1964. President Kennedy had been dead almost a year, and Lyndon Johnson was seeking election to President. Vietnam was just becoming a front-burner issue, although it had not yet flared to daily front-page news. Barry Goldwater was the Republican candidate, and, despite his geopolitical savvy, he was destined to go down to defeat in the election. The Young Republicans on campus were pretty well hamstrung as far as making any impact on the outcome of either national or state and local elections. We basically met and moaned.

JUNIOR YEAR - THE BLESSINGS BEGIN (1964–1965)

The Young Democrats, although a relatively insignificant minority on campus, were feeling their oats and pounding their chests as the November elections delivered their inevitable results. LBJ was elected to a full term, and Congress was safely in Democrat hands. Ironically, one member of the campus Young Democrats was strangely misaligned with his club brothers and sisters. His name was Kenneth Starr and, as previously noted, was the younger brother of Professor Jerry Starr. In later years Kenneth he became a justifiable thorn in the Democrat sides, particularly those of one Bill Clinton.

Kenneth was a freshman during the fall semester and quickly became well–known and heavily involved in campus activities. He was the Freshman Favorite male student, a member of the Young Democrats, and was a staff writer for the Harding Bison, the student newspaper. I attempted to recruit him to pledge the TNT social club, but he decided instead to pledge Lambda Sigma. Our loss, their gain. Lambda Sigma was a good club, populated with a lot of brainpower. Of course, Kenneth eventually was a significant player in the national political arena and remains a force to this day. One of my greatest disappointments was my failure to recruit him to TNT.

The American Studies group was perhaps the single most valuable organization I ever joined during college. The group was comprised of social science majors – Business, Accounting, History, Political Science, etc. One of its great benefits was that each semester the group toured a major American city and visited historical, political, and business sites and organizations located there. The tours were open to all junior and senior American Studies students who had a current GPA of 3.00 or higher, and the tours were cost-free to those students. We traveled on a college bus, and all lodging, food, and admissions were paid for by the college. I was accepted into membership during the fall semester. During the four semesters of my eligibility, the group toured Cincinnati, St. Louis, Dallas, and Chicago. This first semester we toured St. Louis.

At the time, Dr. Clifton Ganus, Jr., was Vice President of the college, and he was also the faculty sponsor of the American Studies group. As such, he accompanied the group on all the tours that year. I was aware of Dr. Ganus's presence and status on campus, but the American Studies program was my first opportunity to interact with him. Over the years, we became good friends, and I even spent some nights at his residence. Dr. Ganus was a large man. In his book, *Contempt*, Kenneth Starr referred to Dr. Ganus as "a mountain of a man." That might have been a slight overstatement, but he was tall and strong and regularly participated with the faculty in the intramural sports teams they fielded. There was a faculty intramural basketball team, and when Dr. Ganus drove the lane in a basketball game, you didn't want to get in his way. Dr. Ganus passed away in 2019 at the age of 97. He was old and full of years and had a crown with many stars. I miss him greatly when I visit the Harding campus.

The American Studies group toured St. Louis in the fall of 1964. We visited Grant's Farm, Purina Mills, and attended a St. Louis Hawks basketball game, among other things. The Gateway Arch was still under construction at the time, so we didn't get to visit it. This was my first American Studies tour, and it confirmed the validity of my decision to transfer to Harding.

When the second semester rolled around, I signed up for 17 credit hours. Three classes were especially memorable – Jerry Starr for Business Statistics, Mrs. Ermal Tucker for Business Communications, and Coach John Prock for PE.

In the spirit of demonstrating the use of statistics, Mr. Starr announced at the beginning of the semester that each student would be able to determine his or her own final grade for the course by using statistics principles to his or her advantage. It would be simple enough. There would be five exams during the semester, including the final, and each would be weighted the same. At the end of the semester, students could choose either their "mean" (average) score for the five exams, or their "median" (middle) score of the five exams, or the "mode" (most frequent) score – among the five scores. As in most classes, 90–100 was "A," 80–89 was "B," 70–79 was "C," and 60–69 was a "D." Below 60 was, of course, failure. Mean, median, and mode are statistical values frequently used by statisticians to prove or disprove a case, depending on which value suits their purpose.

By the grace of God, I scored 92 on each of the first two exams. On the third exam, I made an 86. At that point, I had cinched a "B" for the course because with only two exams remaining, even if I scored zero on both, the 86 would be no worse than the "median" or "middle" score for the five exams. At that point, I was happy that I would achieve a good grade at worst but kept in mind the fact that the two 92's presently constituted a "mode" and could possibly render an "A." On my fourth exam, I made an 84. My four exam scores at that point were 92, 92, 86, and 84. However, the thought crossed my mind that if I repeated either an 86 or an 84 on the final that my 92's would no longer constitute a unique "mode" score, and I would consequently earn in a "B," the 86 remaining the median score. Receiving an "A" seemed like a worthy and achievable goal.

I decided to employ a radical strategy. I intentionally tanked on the final exam, scoring a 72. However, in so doing, I preserved an "A" in the course by means of the "mode" option, with my 92's constituting the mode.

I received an "A" for the course with no castigation from Mr. Starr. After all, I had played by the rules and, once again, benefited from an event that defied the odds. My grade was a perfect example of the beneficial use of mathematical statistics and also an example of how statistics can lie.

Mrs. Tucker taught Business Communications, the art of writing business letters, and business reports. She was one of the toughest teachers I ever encountered at any level of education, but she was up front and fair. In those days, computers and word processing software were not even on the horizon. All business letters were hand-typed, usually on a manual typewriter. Mrs. Tucker demanded perfection in every letter the student turned in. By perfection, I mean there could be no evidence of any typos on the document. When she looked at a paper for grading, she first held it up to the light to determine if any erasures were present or if a "white-out" solution had been used to correct any typing errors, or if there were any strikeovers. Then, as she read the paper, she ferreted out any misspellings. If any of those conditions existed on a paper, it earned an automatic F, regardless of how exquisite the content may have been. That sounds very harsh, but she was upfront with it, so there were no surprises. It sometimes required retyping a business letter several times to get it to letter-perfect. This forced the students to pay very close attention to their output because, as I later learned in business life, a letter can either make or break a project or a contract.

During the semester, in addition to assignments composing business letters to fictional addressees, we had a project which required our contacting actual national corporations and soliciting general information concerning their business. In some cases, it required several letters to the business to ask and answer questions. I contacted HIS, a leading manufacturer of men's clothing at the time. They apparently liked my letters, for they sent me several pieces of company information and advertisements.

One of my very good friends, who shall remain nameless, contacted a company that manufactured light bulbs – perhaps GE. He used the words "incandescent" and "fluorescent" many times in his letters to them. In each case, however, the words were misspelled "incandescant" and "flourescant." The first misspelling occurred on the title page and on virtually every other page in the project pack, and, consequently, it did not take Mrs. Tucker long to assign a grade of "F" to the project. That grade reduced my friend's overall semester grade to a "C." It seemed overkill at the time, but it was a lesson learned, and my friend went on to a very successful business career. It was a college class, and expectations were somewhat higher than those of high school. The situation actually elevated my appreciation of Mrs. Tucker's integrity.

If your paper was "clean" of misspellings or corrections, Mrs. Tucker then read and graded the grammar and content related to the assignment. She gave excellent advice on letter construction – things like getting the subject of the letter before the recipient early in the letter and then reinforcing your thesis with appropriate facts and figures. In the end, I actually made an A in the class.

The knowledge I brought from this class was crucial during my entire business career, and I have had many bosses along the way to compliment me on the letters I have written to them or on their behalf. I will always owe a debt of gratitude to Mrs. Tucker.

Coach John Prock's PE class was Volleyball and Table Tennis. In the volleyball portion of the class, we were taught to set, dig, serve, and spike the ball. Pretty much everyone learned to master those movements well enough, depending on how tall or agile they were.

In the table tennis portion of the class, we were taught the serve, the kill shot, and a variety of return shots. We were taught how to use both the sandpaper and the rubber–face paddles. Also, a significant portion of our grade in the table tennis portion of the class was based on how well we competed with fellow classmates. The more often you won, the better your table tennis grade would be. Do you see where I am going with this? Do you remember my mentioning the table tennis mania at Oklahoma Christian and the fact that Big Ed Davidson, among others, tutored me pretty well in the skill of table tennis? My muscles retained their table tennis memory from a couple of years earlier, and I went undefeated in table tennis during the semester. As a result, I earned an A in that PE class. It turns out that all that time I spent playing table tennis at OCC had not been wasted after all.

Of course, my interest in athletics continued unabated.

On the varsity level, the Bison football team progressed somewhat from the previous season, doubling its number of wins. They posted a 2–8 record for the 1964 football season.

The Bison basketball team was competitive, but victories were harder to come by due to the graduation of some key players, including Vernon Rogers. The team earned an 11–17 record for the season. However, Ned Boaz was still dazzling with his ball-handling and shooting and provided real leadership on the court. At 5'8", Ned led the team in rebounding and scoring.

As usual, the cross country team was exceptional, winning every meet during the year except the first one. Cliff Clark once again anchored the team.

New varsity sports were added by Harding for the school year – swimming and tennis. Also, varsity golf was just getting off the ground at Harding at that time.

JUNIOR YEAR - THE BLESSINGS BEGIN (1964–1965)

As for my participation in intramurals during the year, I played every team sport and entered every sports skill event. During the year, I played flag football, major division basketball, and major division baseball. My baseball team won the championship, and I was voted to both the football and baseball All-Star teams. I also teamed up with Dennis Manuel, a varsity football player, to win the intramural doubles tennis championship. It was a very good year, intramural–wise, and by placing in the top ten in intramural points, I was awarded an intramural letter for the year.

The TNT social club also was very competitive in club sports. We played for the championship in club football and basketball but suffered close losses in both games. In club fastpitch softball, however, we blew everyone away. Dan Smith, a new club brother, a transfer from York College, was THE pitcher on campus and, as such, was virtually unhittable. We won every game in the tournament without breaking a sweat.

Club track and field was interesting. For some reason, I was named captain of the TNT track and field team. We already had some pretty good athletes in the club, but the new pledges brought in some additional help. Among them were some who could run fast, jump high, and throw the shot. By some miracle, we won the Club Track and Field Championship by a single point. Little did we know that a year later, that one–point victory would seem like a landslide.

Athletics aside, the American Studies group spring tour that year was Cincinnati, Ohio. It turned out to be a remarkable experience on several levels. One morning about 50 of us left campus on the school's bus heading for Cincinnati, and we stopped in Paducah, Kentucky, for lunch. The restaurant was cafeteria-style, and every individual item on the foodservice line was individually priced ala carte. Although a new dining hall at Harding was under construction, it would still be months before I could transfer from the Pattie Cobb Hall cafeteria. And, although the Pattie Cobb cafeteria was acceptable, it was not by any means a 5–star restaurant. This cafeteria at Paducah was my first opportunity in weeks to chow down as I saw fit. I loaded up with roast beef and all the trimmings plus several vegetables and pieces of bread. I didn't want to appear a pig, so I bypassed a serving of salad and, instead, took two desserts. The only mistake I made was sitting down beside Dr. Ganus at the table.

"You know, we can feed three students at Harding for a full day for what your lunch cost," he said. He wasn't being sarcastic or critical. He was merely stating a fact and teaching a gentle lesson – don't take advantage of someone's generosity just because you can. I still remember and appreciate and laugh about that lesson today decades later.

The other lesson I learned from that experience was not to sit beside Dr. Ganus at meals on tour.

We arrived in Cincinnati and, over the next four days, toured several businesses and interesting institutions. Two events come to mind – a steel mill tour and attending a Cincinnati Red baseball game one evening.

I don't remember the name of the steel mill we toured, but it was one of the country's leading steel manufacturers. During the tour, I remember watching a man operate a small enclosed cab–like vehicle that ran on a short railroad track above large containers of molten steel. His job was to grasp vats of molten steel and dump them into the containers below. There were four or five containers, and the man piloted the vehicle back and forth on the track above them, loading his vats with red–hot liquid and then positioning them over the proper container and then dumping them.

I remember asking our tour guide how long the vehicle operator could endure the heat generated by the molten steel before taking a break. He told me the man could run an entire eight–hour shift without a problem because the vehicle was air-conditioned.

He then went on to say that a hundred years ago, the vehicle was not air-conditioned, and because of the heat, it required two operators to do the job, with them swapping off every hour. The vehicle was air-conditioned at some point, and two operators were no longer needed to combat the heat. However, the union would not agree to eliminate the second job, so there were still two operators, even though the heat was no longer a factor. That was my first lesson in union-management negotiations and how unreasonable some demands could be.

The baseball game was an event to remember. Several of us decided to attend the game one evening, and the Reds were playing the Atlanta Braves. The name of the Reds' baseball stadium at the time was Crosley Field, named after the Crosley family that owned the team. As we approached the field to buy our tickets, we were met by a complete stranger who offered to give us his tickets. He offered us eight tickets. To say that we were suspicious would be a gross understatement. However, we looked at the tickets, and they looked genuine. In addition, he was not asking for any money. Further, the young man was dressed in a manner that suggested he was not only not poor but was likely pretty affluent. We figured we had nothing to lose, so we accepted the tickets.

Nevertheless, we approached the gate with some trepidation. When we gave the ticket taker our tickets, he looked at them and told us the Crosley box seats were directly behind the Reds' dugout. We were stunned and speechless. We had received free gratis the Crosley family box seats for the game. Apparently, the Crosley's were unable to attend. So, we put our chins in the air and headed toward our seats. Needless to say, we were very courteously received by the stadium staff as they directed us to our seats.

This event alone made the evening memorable. A second thing made the game even more memorable. We got to see a young Pete Rose play in what was just his second year in the Majors.

We returned to campus on Saturday, and my second American Studies tour was in the books, and it remains very memorable.

I had had a great year at Harding academically, socially, and athletically, far better than I had anticipated the previous September. No potential romances, but a host of good friends, and I was no longer a stranger on the campus. My intentional involvement in campus life had introduced me to a host of new friends, across a myriad of interests and activities, and a sizeable portion of the faculty and staff. It had truly been a good and unexpectedly valuable school year.

However, as spring arrived and the school year wound down, it was time to plan for the summer. I loaded up my car and headed back to Okemah and another anticipated summer working in the oil fields. However, I felt that something had changed.

THE PROVIDENCE OF GOD

The school year had been very good to me in every way, and it erased any reservations I had had about returning to Harding the previous fall. It is possible that my meatiest and most intense college classes occurred during this, my junior year at Harding. As noted below, my learning was certainly not just limited to business knowledge. Whether or not I raised an Ebenezer, I was nevertheless very thankful for the experience and gave God the glory. Significant blessings I had received during the year:

1. Dr. R. T. Clark's Biology 101 and 102 classes provided instruction that was directly responsible for my passing an Army Medic qualification test several years later, which, in turn, enabled me to retain my status as an Army Medic.

2. Mrs. Ermal Tucker's Business Communication class was directly responsible for my perceived success in writing business letters, reports, and company procedures in my career over the years.

3. Mr. Billy Ray Cox's Business classes and my informal interactions with him both while at Harding and in the years afterward provided an invaluable positive impact on my career at Phillips Petroleum.

4. The American Studies tours greatly enhanced my understanding of corporate America and life in the big city.

Hither by His help, I had come.

Eleven

SUMMER (1965)

I did not particularly look forward to the summer of 1965. It promised to be basically a repeat of the summer of 1964, except with a month's head start on the hot, grimy, sweaty work that I endured during July and August of the previous year when I returned from Kansas City with my tail between my legs. There were positives, however. I would make decent money with absolutely no living expenses, and I would tone up and develop a tan to die for. The thought crossed my mind that developing that appearance would not be a bad thing heading back to college, where the girl/boy ratio was close to 1:1.

As expected, I was rehired for the summer by Landers Oil Well Service and reported to work at 7:00 a.m. my first Monday back in town. Since I had arrived back in Okemah the previous Friday evening, it did not give me much time for R&R.

However, on the Sunday between my arrival back in town and my reporting for work on Monday, I attended church and renewed a number of acquaintances. There were several youths at or near my age, and we were able to establish some loose plans to get together during the summer. My dad made it a point to have me shake hands with Tommy Hall and every one of the Smith guys – Cotton, Jerry, and Mack. Although this gesture meant little to me at the time, it would turn out to be a significant event only one year later.

Monday morning at the Landers Oil Well Service, I was teamed up with the same crew I had worked with the previous summer. However, this time I remembered to bring my hard hat on the first day.

Basically, my summer employment was very routine – no injuries, no accidents, just hot, hard, sweaty work. And, as I had done the previous summer, I achieved somewhat the look of a southern California beach lifeguard. I

123

hoped that would work to my benefit as I returned to Harding for my senior year.

Two things made my summer interesting and provided valuable diversions from the regular 5– and sometimes 6–day work week grind.

First, I met Clint Clay, a friend of my parents, who owned a butcher shop in Okemah and also was a huge baseball fan. He fed his enthusiasm for baseball by sponsoring a local summer baseball team, the Okemah Indians. As mentioned in a previous chapter, in those days, many college players would join local city teams that played in Summer Leagues to keep their skills sharp for fall baseball. Mr. Clay asked if I played baseball. When I told him that baseball was probably my best sport, he asked what position I played. I told him second base was the best fit for me. I had a good glove but maybe not a strong enough arm to play shortstop or the outfield against the competition we would be facing.

Mr. Clay subsequently gave me a uniform and penciled me in at second base in the next game. He had me batting eighth since he had absolutely no idea of how I could handle the college pitchers I would be facing. I have never been a power hitter, but in my first at-bat, I hit a long fly to left field that the outfielder caught against the fence. Had it not been caught, it would have been a home run. It raised some eyebrows in the dugout, and I think the other players maybe thought I belonged. In the next game and for the rest of the season, I batted second in the lineup. I had a pretty good summer. Although I never did hit a home run, I played every inning of every game and wound up batting .295 against the best pitching I had ever seen. I only struck out four times the whole summer. In addition, I stole 12 bases in 14 attempts and did not ground into a single, double play. Even yet, I wonder if I had the goods to play at OCC two years earlier if I had had the proper equipment.

The games were always evening games or weekend games so that the players could participate without having to take time off from work. We played 19 games, including a year-end tournament, from early June until early August. By that time, all the college players had begun the process of preparing to return to school. It was a great experience for me, and it was the highest level of baseball competition I ever experienced.

The second interesting diversion I experienced during the summer was a surprise visit from Bob Adams, a good friend of mine and who would be my roommate at Harding in the fall. Bob hailed from Homestead, Florida, a city SOUTH of Miami, basically on the highway to Key West. Homestead was, metaphorically speaking, just short of a million miles from Okemah, Oklahoma.

It was probably around 8:00 p.m. on a weeknight in early August, and I was half asleep on the couch watching television. My reverie was interrupted by a knock on the door. I opened the door, and there stood Bob. He was on his way to Chama, New Mexico, a small town in the extreme northern part of the state just south of the Colorado state line. He was on his way to visit David Lee, a junior at Harding and a friend of ours. David's father managed a dude ranch in the Rockies just over the New Mexico state line in southern Colorado. David had arranged for us to spend a night or two on the dude ranch on the house – an offer that could not be refused. Meanwhile, Bob had driven almost 2000 miles from Homestead to Okemah over the past three days and still had about 1000 miles to go. Bob wanted to know if I wanted to join the party. By joining the party, he meant getting back on the road immediately and driving all night.

The next day was a workday at Landers, so it was a tough decision. However, for a 21–year–old, the temptation was too great to pass up. Mom and Dad were not too thrilled with what was happening, but they didn't stand in the way. After all, I had gone to work the first Monday after I arrived home from Harding and had not had anything resembling a vacation or time off at that time. It was not difficult to take a day off at Landers. The Lander's work schedule was not so full that this put them in a tight spot. My dad agreed to call Landers the next morning and explain that I would not be at work for the rest of the week.

So, I packed up, and we headed out. We took turns driving and drove all night and arrived at Chama at about dinner time the next afternoon. The next morning we headed to the ranch. Upon arrival, David took us on a jeep tour of the mountains, and we saw mountain lakes and primitive forests that were magnificent. Returning to the ranch, David's father grilled us some of the best steaks I have ever tasted. We spent the night at the ranch and headed back for civilization the next morning. If I remember right, we drove straight through to Okemah. Bob spent the night with us and then continued his journey back to Florida.

Oh, to be young and foolish again. Overall, we drove about 2000 miles round trip, and we spent only two nights in a bed. But it was a great experience and well worth it. We saw some spectacular scenery I had never seen, and I enjoyed a great time with a friend. It was just the respite I needed to get me through the rest of the summer and prepare my mind for Harding's upcoming fall semester. It also gave Bob and me a great chance to get to know one another better, given the fact that we would be rooming together at Harding in a matter of weeks.

Following the trip to New Mexico and Colorado, I had about two weeks to get my act together and head back to Searcy. I did not know what to expect once I arrived there. I had experienced a great junior year there and had become a solid member of the Harding student body. However, I had no relationship with any girl to go back to, and, I guess, "senior panic" was in the back of my mind. In addition, I still had to finish my degree, seek employment, and deal with the escalating situation in Vietnam and the potential military issues associated with that. I had a lot on my mind as I headed east toward Arkansas.

THE PROVIDENCE OF GOD

The competitive baseball experience and the trip to Colorado made my summer unforgettable. With the money I earned with the oil well service and the physical condition that it brought about, I really could not have wished for more. Once again, I don't remember raising an Ebenezer, but I was truly thankful for what had come my way.

1. The summer was stress–free, and the baseball team and the trip to New Mexico enabled me to fully enjoy the summer break.

2. I had experienced a short vacation in some spectacular scenery which I had never seen before.

3. I had had a good summer job that provided me more benefit than just a paycheck.

4. I maintained my relationship with the Oklahoma National Guard leaders, unaware that they would soon determine my military service.

Hither by His help, I had come.

Twelve

BLESSINGS CONTINUE (FALL 1965)

I arrived on the campus of Harding College in the fall of 1965 full of hope that my long-established goals—a happy marriage with children, a quality college education, a career consistent with my abilities and interests, an opportunity to honorably serve my country and, perhaps most importantly, a maturing Christianity—might be effectively addressed during the nine months remaining in my college career. While it is true that I had by this time established myself as a legitimate student and classmate, nevertheless, as I arrived back in Searcy, only a college education and Christian growth seemed to be on track. The three remaining biggies – marriage, career, military service – remained absolutely nebulous at that point.

I got my room key and set about unloading my things. My new roommate, Bob Adams, was already there. He had apparently survived the long drive back to South Florida following our sojourn to New Mexico and Colorado just a few weeks earlier.

After I got moved into the dorm, it was time to get a class schedule and buy books. In 1966 Harding required completion of a minimum of 128 class hours to graduate. I entered the fall semester with 94 hours completed, which means I had to successfully pass another 34 hours during the next two semesters. As I was to learn later, this was complicated because the 128 hours had to include a number of "required" courses and a minimum number of "upper level" hours. At the fall enrollment, I did not give this much thought, for 34 hours in two semesters in not an unusual load. I enrolled in 18 hours for the fall semester, and that would only leave me 16 hours to take in the spring semester, with graduation to follow. Easy, peasy, right? Not so fast.

127

As it turned out, I had painted myself into a corner because, as I would learn to my chagrin at spring semester enrollment, I still had some hoops to jump through on both counts – "required" courses and "upper level" hours. As will be related a little later in this document, my expectation of skating through my final semester at Harding would blow up in my face come enrollment for the spring semester.

My courses for the fall semester included:

- Money and Banking 322
- Business Law 315
- Industrial Management 254
- Personnel Management 365
- Principles of Marketing 330
- History and Analysis of Religious Music 331

All were upper-level classes, and all were 3–hour courses, 18 hours in all. One course – Money and Banking – was taught by Jerry Starr. Two courses – Industrial Management and Business Law 315 – were taught by the dynamic Billy Ray Cox. Overall, the course load looked both interesting and manageable.

The one class that provoked the most fear in me was Business Law 315. I imagined a very dry, fact-filled class that would struggle to retain my attention. I could not have been more wrong. As it turned out, the class, along with its second half – Business Law 316 in the next semester – were among the most dynamic and interesting classes I ever sat for. Mr. Cox taught the class not from the perspective of an attorney but rather from the perspective of the businessman. He taught us how to navigate an enterprise within the law rather than how to litigate. As the former business executive, he spoke from experience, which enhanced his credibility as a teacher exponentially.

The class was by no means easy, however. It was very tough. In fact, even Mr. Cox acknowledged that fact when, approaching the semester final exam, he told us we could use every resource available "except your neighbor's paper" to complete the final exam. We could use the textbook and all the notes we had taken. Kind of like a law office, he explained, where all sorts of reference books and papers were available to prepare for a case.

That announcement was like a breath of fresh air. In preparation for the exam, I reviewed the text, organized my notes, and even indexed them for quick referral during the exam. It resulted in the most thorough study I had ever engaged in while preparing for an exam. I was loaded for bear the day of the exam. As he was passing out the exam papers, Mr. Cox reiterated what he had said about using notes, text, etc., to help us on the exam. Then he dropped the other shoe. "However," he said, "if you have to take the time to look up the answers in your textbook and notes, you will never finish the exam."

He was right, of course. The exam was just short of toxic, but I was so well prepared that I aced it. I earned an "A" for the semester in what I had anticipated being the toughest course I would take in college. I was actually looking forward to Business Law 316 next semester.

All in all, the fall semester proved to be the most satisfying academic experience of my entire college career. Of the 18 hours taken, I pulled 15 hours of "A" for a semester GPA of 3.833 – the best I would ever achieve.

Academics aside, I continued to be very involved in campus life. During my senior year, I decided to expand my horizons a little further. I added two new endeavors – Chorale and the *Bison* (school newspaper) staff.

The Chorale was a singing group much like the Acapella Chorus, except that auditions for acceptance were not required. Basically, a large group of students wanted to participate in a choir/chorus but were either not talented enough to join the Acapella Chorus or who did not have the extra time required of Acapella members for rehearsals, trips, etc. A lot of the Chorale members fell into the latter category, and, consequently, there were a large number of very talented singers in the group. Then there was me.

At the time, I was not only atonal, but I was basically amusical (if that is a word). My roommate, Bob Adams, was a member of the Acapella Chorus and was tremendously musically talented. He was glad I had joined the Chorale, but he was dismayed at my lack of musical ability. He coached me and prodded me and tried to help me to a better understanding of music. He introduced me to scales, clefs, notes, harmony, sharps, flats, keys, and the like. At one point, he took me to the office of Dr. Earl Moore, Chairman of the Music Department, for an informal evaluation. The evaluation consisted mainly of Dr. Moore playing a note on a piano and then asking me to emulate the note with my voice. I rarely hit the note he played, but, ironically, I would usually sound out a harmonious note. Dr. Moore's evaluation was that, at the very least, my music "ear" recognized harmony, and that was a good step toward actually hitting the notes that were written in the music. He also said that I would be able, with practice, to sing the bass line in a song in harmony with the other parts. As a result, neither Bob nor I were discouraged by my performance with Dr. Moore, and it actually encouraged my participation in the Chorale. Dr. Eddie Baggett was director of the Chorale. With his coaching and the influence of the musical people around me in the Chorale, I was able to grow in knowledge and understanding of music and actually begin to carry a tune. I will always appreciate Bob Adams and Dr. Baggett's efforts to teach me music, and the result has made me much more appreciative and much more participatory in the Christian music I am exposed to every week.

The second activity I embarked upon as a senior was as a staff writer for the *Bison*, the school newspaper. It will come as a surprise to nobody that I signed on as a sports reporter. My duty was to report varsity, intramural and intra–club sports events, and write an occasional sports feature story. I was not the only sports reporter. Also, since the campus was rife with sports activities from Monday through Saturday, the sports desk had plenty of fodder to deal with almost every week.

The priority for the sports staff was varsity sports reporting. It was incumbent upon us to write up every basketball, football, and baseball game with the occasional tennis, swimming, track, cross–country and varsity bowling events thrown in when possible.

For the record, the football team posted a 5–3–1 record that fall, a vast improvement over the 2–8 record the previous season. The team beat Millsaps College 14–0 in the Homecoming game. The basketball team, unable to fully fill the shoes of the graduated Ned Boaz, went 11–18, but it was buoyed by the play of future stars Harold Alexander and Ronnie Brown. Ronnie set a school scoring record of 47 points against Arkansas Tech. The baseball team went 10–9, and the bowling team won the AIC before being eliminated from the District tournament.

As usual, the track and cross–country teams shined. The track team entered nine meets during the season, winning six and finishing second twice and third once – a superior season. One of the meets the team won was the AIC Championship. The cross–country team continued its dominating efforts. During the season, it participated in ten meets prior to the National Championships. In those ten meets, the team won eight times and finished second the other two times. In the National Championships, the team finished seventh, capping a truly remarkable year. As usual, Cliff Clark was the leader of the team, but this year he had been joined by a prodigy, Jim Crawford, who was more than able to pick up the baton after Cliff graduated.

Harding had started a men's swimming team the previous year, and that program was still in its infancy. My major contribution to the swim team results' reporting was to ignore the school sports team name, "Bison," and to dub the swim team the "Water Buffalos." Not unexpectedly, the nickname became popular, and the swim team gained some notoriety as a result.

During the year, I wrote several columns reporting results of the Bison football and basketball teams. Among the columns, I wrote for the *Bison* that fall was the reporting of the Harding Homecoming football game and a sports feature that spotlighted Ronnie Brown, the spectacular sophomore Harding basketball player. More will be revealed regarding those two articles a little later in the book.

With regard to intramural sports, I participated in all the team, individual, and club sports in the fall, competitively in some and as a blocking dummy, so to speak, in others. Dave Fouss, a fellow TNT member in team sports, and I won the Handball Doubles crown. It was mostly due to Dave's playing, however. He also won the Handball Singles crown in individual sports, slicing and dicing me up along the way.

Intramural flag football was a story unto itself on several levels. I do not presume that there is much interest in flag football among those who read this, but I mention my experiences in this activity at Harding simply to relate what I believe to be a series of nearly impossible, against–all–odds events which occurred on the flag football fields there. The events were not likely the Providence of God but are just examples of more of the remarkable, often bizarre events I have experienced during my life. It seems like my life has been fraught with unusual events, and flag football at Harding provided a few more. So, please bear with me as I tell the story.

When one signed up for an intramural football team at Harding, he also specified what positions he could play. I signed up as a pass receiver and defensive back. Someone who signed up to play "cornerback" was accidentally interpreted by the Intramural Director as "quarterback" and was assigned to my team as a quarterback. When our team assembled for its first practice session, no one stepped forward as the quarterback. For some reason, and I will never know why the team elected me as the quarterback. Since I knew how to throw a football and had had some experience playing intramural football at both Oklahoma Christian and Oklahoma University, I reluctantly accepted the challenge. I warned the team, however, not to expect miracles.

We discovered early on, however, that fate might be viewing our team kindly, as we won the first game in miraculous fashion. Late in the game, with the score tied, we faced third down and a mile, deep in our own territory. I called a long pass play that could if successful, at least earn us a first down. When the ball was snapped, I faded back to pass, and we were so deep in our end of the field that I was forced into the end zone to set up for the pass. The other team blitzed when the ball was snapped. I was toast. They were going to tackle me for sure and score a safety and win the game. To avoid the safety, I heaved the ball as far as I could down the middle of the field to no one in particular. I was just throwing the ball away to avoid the safety. Seemingly out of nowhere, Jim Miller, one of our pass receivers, ran under the ball and caught it and outran the defenders for a very long touchdown. You could have knocked me over with a feather because that outcome was totally outside anything I could have imagined. We went on to win the game.

That sort of set the stage for the rest of the year. We did not go undefeated, but we did win our division and qualified for the championship game.

The championship game proved to be another miracle, it seems. With less than two minutes left in the game, my team was trailing 14–12. The opposition had the ball with a second down and one yard to go for a first down. My team was out of timeouts, so we had no way to stop the clock. All the opponents had to do was gain one yard on the next two plays to earn a first down and then run out the clock.

Since getting the ball on a turnover was out of the question, our team realized that the only way we had any chance was to allow the opponents to score quickly and prevent them from adding any points after touchdown. If that happened, they would lead by a score of 20–12 with approximately a minute or so left in the game. If miracles happened, we could score a TD in the remaining time and then add a two-point conversion to tie the game and send it into overtime. And maybe pigs could fly, also.

So, on the next play, the opponents ran the football, and our team looked like the Three Stooges, and the Keystone Kops combined as we clumsily and intentionally failed to grab any flags, and the opposing player ran for 41 yards and a touchdown. If the opposing player had given any thought to the situation, he would have gained the first down and then taken a knee. In so doing, he and his team could have run out the clock without ever touching the ball again. However, human nature apparently intervened, and the runner could see his name in lights, so to speak, for scoring the clinching TD. It turned out to be a bad decision on his part.

Following the TD, we were able to prevent the opponents from adding a PAT, so part one of our strategy – the easy part – had worked, and the score stood at 20–12. Now, all we had to do was score eight more points in 1 minute and 31 seconds with no timeouts.

We received the kickoff and were immediately penalized for an illegal block in the back. That forced us to start our drive on our own 5–yard line. Obviously, we had to throw the ball if we were to have any chance. Once again, as in our first game of the season, I found myself forced back into the end zone to pass. This time, however, my pass protection was better. I remember George Holcomb, a big guy from Mobile, Alabama, taking out two pass rushers with a single block, and I was able to complete a pass downfield. I don't know how many plays it took, including both completed and incomplete passes, but we scored a touchdown with 4 seconds remaining in the game. That made the score 20–18. Miraculously we scored a 2–point conversion to tie the score at 20–20.

We kicked off with four seconds remaining, and the opponents were unable to do anything in that short amount of time.

The overtime rules were not "sudden death," whereby the first team to score was the winner. Instead, overtime was a 5–minute period to be played like a regular part of the game.

We received the kickoff and marched down the field in about 2 minutes, and scored a TD, but we could not add the PAT. We led 26–20 with about 3 minutes remaining. We kicked off, and the opponents now had to score a TD, and pretty quickly. They decided that passing was the way to get that done. They were pretty successful and drove deep into our territory. However, we intercepted one of their passes, and we took over the ball with a little over a minute remaining in the game.

With so little time remaining, we decided to keep the ball on the ground and run out the clock. I opted for a quarterback keeper right up the middle. Once again, fate smiled on me. I ran basically untouched for 70 yards until I simultaneously ran out of gas and out of bounds. I had, I think, Larry Griffith to replace me at quarterback, and he ran another keeper and went in for another touchdown, basically as time expired. We won the championship by a score of 32–20 in overtime. Pigs, as it turns out, can occasionally fly.

I was reluctant to even mention something as insignificant as an intramural football game because I don't think God deals in deciding the outcome of such things. However, this is just another of the very special events that have so frequently occurred in my life and that have enriched it so very much.

Also, I realize that intramural flag football at Harding is not varsity football, but almost every intramural player played high school football, and a few had also previously played varsity football at Harding. The point being that the intramural players were by no means amateurs. Rather they were talented, intent, tough, and competitive. Not surprisingly, several injuries occurred during the year in this "non–contact" sport. One injury which stands out in my mind is the injury sustained by Ken Johnson. Ken was a TNT member, an Alpha Chi member, and was a very fast runner. He went down with a knee injury early in the season, and it knocked him out of football for the rest of the year. It was especially troubling because, although he was not a member of my intramural team, he had been counted on to be a significant force on the TNT club football team a little later on, plus the annual club Track and Field Meet in the spring.

Club football began following the intramural season. TNT was one of three clubs that had a very competitive football team. The other two were

Sub–T, and Mohican. Both of those teams had members who had played varsity football at Harding but had used up their eligibility.

TNT at the time had no ex–varsity players of any kind. Three of the class presidents were members of TNT, but that fact was insignificant on the football field. Not only that, we did not have Ken Johnson as a running back due to his injury.

Club intramural football that fall was a downer. TNT lost to Sub–T in a close game and then lost to Mohican in another nail–biter. Two things stand out in my memory in the Mohican game. First, one of the Mohican players had a front tooth knocked out during the game, but the tooth was not difficult to locate. It was imbedded under the skin in the forehead of my good buddy Steve Thornton. The second thing that I remember about the game is that Roy McGee, one of my favorite bigger–than–life characters of all time and who had been a four–year letterman on the Bison football team, scored the winning touchdown at my expense. I was playing defensive safety, and he was a pass receiver, the position he had played on the Bison football team. When the ball was snapped, I made a move to cover him, but he put a move on me that faked me out of my underclothes, so to speak, and caught a TD pass that sealed Mohican's victory. All I could do was shake his hand.

The only club athletic activity in the fall that was uplifting was club fastpitch softball. TNT repeated as champions, with Dan Smith once again blowing everyone away at the plate. He was virtually unhittable.

In the fall of 1965, Mr. Billy Ray Cox began to play a huge role in my career at Harding. The two classes of his that I was taking in the fall – Business Law and Industrial Management – had already introduced me to his business acumen, but those were only precursors to what was to come in the spring semester. However, in addition to those courses and others, he was teaching, Mr. Cox had taken on yet another job during this fall semester – director of the American Studies Program. Dr. Clifton Ganus, Jr. had been promoted to president of Harding, and Mr. Cox had assumed Dr. Ganus' duties within the American Studies Program. As mentioned earlier, Mr. Cox had been a Vice President at Dallas Ceramics, a huge tile manufacturer headquartered in Dallas, Texas. He had taken leave of that post the previous year and had come to Harding to join the faculty, and he would eventually rise to Vice President at the college. As a result of his position at Dallas Ceramics, however, he was a prominent citizen in Dallas with many contacts among the area's business leaders. He was also a huge Dallas Cowboys fan.

Not surprisingly, the first American Studies trip he scheduled in his new role was a trip to Dallas in October.

There were many highlights of the Dallas trip. To begin with, we were housed in the Adolphus Hotel, a historic, landmark hotel for more than a century. In addition, we enjoyed lunch in a restaurant atop one of the tallest buildings in Dallas, we toured Texas Stadium, the home of the Dallas Cowboys (Mr. Cox, the Cowboy fan, pulled some strings to make that happen), and we visited Dealey Plaza – the President Kennedy assassination site. However, the most memorable event of the trip was a luncheon meeting with H. L. Hunt.

Haroldson Lafayette Hunt Jr., known throughout his life as H. L. Hunt, was a Texas oil tycoon. By trading poker winnings for oil rights, he ultimately secured title to much of the East Texas Oil Field, one of the world's largest oil deposits. From it and his other acquisitions, he accrued a fortune that was among the world's largest. At the time of his death in 1979, he was reputed to have the highest net worth of any individual in the world.

With this background information, the American Studies students were as a group pretty overwhelmed and subdued as we entered the luncheon with Mr. Hunt.

It did not turn out as any of us had imagined. First, Mr. Hunt shook hands with and personally greeted each of the approximately 50 American Studies students. My recollection is that he had the softest hands of anyone I had ever met. He was 76 years old at the time, and his responses to the questions we would ask left no doubt that his mind was as sharp as ever. He politely fielded a few questions, and then he turned the tables on us. He began asking us questions – about the trip, about the American Studies Program, about our plans for the future – and he carefully listened to our responses. The interviewee had become the interviewer. In so doing, he put us totally at ease, and we learned the lesson that an incredibly rich, powerful, and famous person isn't necessarily arrogant or unapproachable. Over my life, I have been privileged to personally meet several other business, and political people, including Ronald Reagan. Mr. Reagan was the only other one that gave off the same vibes as H. L. Hunt. Even prominent people are really just regular people thrust into a very visible role, and the way they respond to that role is based on their character rather than their prominence.

The trip to Dallas remains one of the highlights of my life. It was my third American Studies tour, following the trips to St. Louis and Cincinnati the previous school year. By this time, I had come to realize that the education obtained at college, particularly at Harding, was not limited to the classroom and lab. For a Harding Business or Social Science major, Dallas, St. Louis, Cincinnati, and Chicago – come spring – were intense classrooms and labs which exposed the students to non–theoretical, non–book–learning environments. These were experiences with real-life businesses and organizations, including rubbing elbows with the principals in those businesses and organizations and getting an up-close view of the real world. The lessons learned under those circumstances were invaluable, and I will always be grateful to Harding for providing them.

Academically and socially, the fall semester was the best of my college career to that point. I had achieved the highest GPA that I would manage in four years of college, and all the courses for the semester had been upper level. I had made more new friends and had participated enthusiastically in a number of campus organizations, Chorale and the *Bison*, being the latest. I still had no romantic prospects on my radar, although I had dated some very great young women in the fall. Also, it was still a little early to begin serious job hunting. Harding had a great reputation for hosting corporate head hunters, including those seeking candidates for jobs in the business arena. The word was that recruiters would start showing up on campus relatively early in the second semester, so there was no reason to get nervous this early. However, of growing concern were the unknowns associated with my future military service obligation.

The war in Vietnam was escalating, and, due to the unpopularity of the war, the number of voluntary enlistments was plummeting. Heretofore, all young men attending college, trade school, or graduate school, as well as all married men, were granted draft deferments. Once an unmarried young man left school for whatever reason he was fresh meat for the draft. Only married men were still untouchable for the draft. As voluntary enlistments fell off drastically, it became necessary for the Selective Service System to take additional steps to fill its quota of soldiers, primarily for the Army and the Marines. Consequently, it decided to declare all married men eligible for the draft except those with children. Those married men who had previously been deferred under the previous rules were "grandfathered" and remained deferred from the draft. Generally speaking, if a man was a daddy, he was safe from the draft. It was beginning to look more and more like I would graduate from college and then be snapped up by the draft. Not only that, another factor was complicating my future – companies were routinely eliminating draft-eligible young men from their recruiting. Few companies were willing to offer a man a job and then have to wait for him to complete two years of military service before beginning work. It wasn't time yet to start worrying about my military obligation, but it was certainly time to start factoring it into my long-range plans.

With no sweetheart on the horizon at that point, and realizing the value of advanced education, I had also decided to apply for entrance into graduate school in the school of Business. At that time, Harding did not offer advanced degrees in Business. I applied to Oklahoma University, Oklahoma State University, and Arkansas University. By applying for admission this early, I hoped to hear from them early in the second semester. I figured they would await my first-semester final grades before making offers if any. If so, it would still give me plenty of time to make a final decision as to whether or not to attend grad school.

I headed into my final semester at Harding with anticipation and trepidation, with excitement and uncertainty, as several critical questions regarding my future – marriage, job, and military service – remained unanswered.

THE PROVIDENCE OF GOD

With the personal successes and blessings I enjoyed during the fall semester, I do remember giving God the glory – gratefully raising an Ebenezer. Blessings He providentially provided included:

1. I had finally found my footing and had excelled – for me, at least – academically and socially. I had expanded my horizons by joining in several campus activities and had begun thinking seriously about the next step in my life – graduation – and what followed with respect to marriage, career, and military service.

2. I had attended great and significant classes and had made my best semester GPA ever, 3.833.

3. With no sweetheart on the scene during the semester, I was able to fully concentrate on the classes and activities at hand.

4. It was the richest time I had ever experienced in college. What I didn't know at the time was the next semester would eclipse this one.

Hither by His help, I had come a long way in a short amount of time.

13

PREPARING FOR GRADUATION
(SPRING 1966)

Despite the joy and optimism I enjoyed the fall semester, nevertheless, my final semester at Harding College began "not with a bang but a whimper," with apologies to T. S. Eliot. As things began to unfold, I didn't feel that it was exactly the end of the world, but from my perspective, you could see it from where I was standing. I entered my final semester almost exactly like I entered my first semester in college at Oklahoma Christian – totally at sea, so to speak. Nothing significant in my life had really jelled by this time, and time was running out. I had no prospects in sight for marriage, even though I had attended the "marriage factory" – Harding College – for two years. At this point, I had had no job interviews scheduled and was both concerned and uncertain about my career. Not only that, the war in Vietnam was escalating, and I was currently a prime candidate for the draft immediately following my graduation. I had concluded that the war and my draft status would trump any plans I might otherwise make.

As satisfying as the first semester had been, it ended on a down note. My roommate for the first semester had been my good friend Bob Adams. Bob and I had been thick as thieves for the past two years, but he had decided to drop out of Harding at the end of the fall semester. This was not a problem I had expected to encounter going into my final lap in college. He never fully explained his decision to me, and I never pressed him about it. We have remained friends over the years and still exchange birthday and Christmas cards. Years later, he moved from Florida to southwestern Oklahoma – he had some relatives in the area – and strangely enough, he was later elected mayor of the small town of Cordell. During his time in Cordell, he and I would meet periodically in Oklahoma City and have lunch together. Larry Griffith, a fellow TNT member, became my roommate for the second semester. Larry was also very musical and was a member of the Acapella. Years later he became director of the Lipscomb University Acapella Chorus in Nashville, Tennessee.

On a positive note, however, I had completed 112 hours of college credit at this point in my college career, and ostensibly I needed only 16 more credit hours to reach 128 hours, which was the minimum requirement for graduation. A 16–hour semester is usually an easily manageable load. However, keeping in tune with all the other discouraging factors I was encountering entering my last semester, I soon discovered, much to my chagrin, that qualifying for graduation was going to be a little more complicated than merely signing up for 16 credit hours.

True, the fall semester had been very good – new activities, more new friends, great grades, social and athletic successes – but the lifelong issues as mentioned above were still unsettled with, at this point, no solutions on the horizon. Not surprisingly, I entered the final semester with anticipation and trepidation, excitement, and uncertainty.

As it turned out, I could not have been more wrong.

All the worrying and potential ulcers turned out to be a waste of time and effort. As usual, God provided in His own unique and superior way. When the spring semester finally came to an end, I realized that words were inadequate to describe what a blessing it had been to live on the Harding campus from early January 1966 until late May that year. Even the year "66", as will be seen, held a special meaning.

Everything dear to me – marriage, job, military service, and growth as a Christian – came together in a glorious concert during those five months. During the semester, I would meet an intriguing young woman by the name of Shirley Swayne, who would eventually play a very big role in my life, but those details will be revealed in later chapters. I was also the recipient of several significant campus honors, during that time, including two appearances on television, which could only have occurred at Harding. At the conclusion of the semester, actually, with tears in my eyes, I reflected on the remarkable events in my life that had brought me this far. I gratefully raised my Ebenezer, as it were – truly, "Here I raise my Ebenezer, hither by Thy help I've come." God's Providence, against which I had often complained and grumbled while it was being unfolded, had been manifested fully. And as described previously in this book, the absence of even one of those events would have canceled everything that would follow.

However, as the semester was getting ready to start, and not being capable of knowing what was in store for me in the upcoming months, I simply enrolled, bought my books, picked up my cafeteria card, and headed to my room. I had kept the same room as I had lived in the previous semester, and I had managed to recruit my good friend Larry Griffith as my new roommate. At that point, however, I was like a rudderless boat drifting on the sea, at the mercy of fickle winds, staying afloat while hoping for the best.

Unexpectedly, the enrollment process for the spring semester created even more angst for me that was not actually resolved until I completed the final exam in my English History 402 class in early May. As a Business major, why was I even taking an upper-level English History class in the final semester of my college career? Was it a death wish? As I entered the enrollment process with my faculty advisor, I believed that I simply lacked 16 hours to complete my minimum required 128 hours for graduation. But there was a hitch.

I did not realize that I was one history course short of the history class required for graduation, and it could be any history course that I had not yet taken. However, to complicate matters, I was also three hours short of the minimum number of "upper level" hours required for graduation. It presented a dilemma for me. To graduate, I would, therefore, not only have to complete a history course, but it would also have to be an upper-level history course. The only upper-level history course being offered that semester was English History 402.

My faculty advisor is the one that came up with a solution – the only possible solution, as it turned out – and it basically scared me to death. He suggested that enrolling in English History 402 would kill three birds with one stone – gain the history course needed for graduation, meet the minimum upper-level hour requirement (English History 402 being a 3–hour course gave me another 18–hour semester – oh joy!), and fulfill the minimum 128–hour graduation requirement with a couple of hours to spare. He failed to mention, but I correctly surmised, that the English History would be populated with junior and senior History majors. I could picture myself failing that course in the presence of all the future History Ph.D.'s and thereby not graduating in May. Reluctantly I crossed my fingers and signed up for the class as it was my only alternative.

After launching my academic future on a wing and a prayer, so to speak, I went about preparing for the unknown.

The classes I enrolled in for the semester were:

- Church and Young People 334
- Corporate Finance 343

- Personal Finance 320
- Business Law 316
- English History 402
- Independent Research 450

Each was a 3–hour course, each an upper-level course, 18 hours in all. Quite a load for any semester and there was a certain amount of pressure involved since it was incumbent that I successfully complete each of the courses in order to graduate on time.

I only mention these courses because three of them are indelibly etched in my personal memory.

Business Law 316 was the second-semester continuation of Business Law 315. All the conditions that existed in Business Law 315 continued unabated into Business Law 316. Same teacher, same intensity of study, same rules regarding taking the final exam. And miracle of miracles, I made the same grade, "A," as I did in the first course. Six hours of "A" in Business Law is remarkable for anyone, especially me. One of my proudest moments

Oh yes, regarding the English History class. It was taught by Raymond Muncy, one of my favorite professors – he had taught my Contemporary History course the previous year. He had a tremendous sense of humor and used it frequently to augment or complement a point he was making. And, as I suspected, the English History class was indeed populated by history sages, and it was a struggle for me to compete with them. However, Mr. Muncy was such a great teacher and kept the class so interesting I miraculously maintained an "A" in the class until the final exam. I made just low enough of a grade on the final to pull my grade down to "B+." I considered it a victory then and still do to this day. I had managed to fulfill my history and upper-level course requirements somewhat in an unexpected style.

My Independent Research 450 course is a whole story unto itself and almost dominates my final semester's narrative at Harding. The class, comprised of only six students, was unique in that it was essentially a full semester of studying, analyzing, and applying business principles not against a textbook but rather against 39 other colleges in an intercollegiate scholastic competition. The story is so compelling and remarkable that it deserves a narration of its own and is discussed at length in the next chapter.

Of the 18 credit hours I took during the semester, I Made 12 hours of "A" and 6 hours of "B" for a semester GPA of 3.67. This brought my overall college GPA to 3.48. The "B" I made in Accounting 101 at Oklahoma University due to the teacher's petty shenanigans cost me a 3.50 GPA. Not that it matters, but it still gnaws at me after all these years.

PREPARING FOR GRADUATION (SPRING 1966)

My grades for the semester were just the icing on the cake, given all the other significant beneficial life events that occurred during that spring.

THE PROVIDENCE OF GOD

This particular semester, as it began, was fraught with academic uncertainties for me. As mentioned, I had to meet several criteria in order to graduate on time, and as will be seen in the chapters to follow, there were other severe pressures I had to deal with besides academia – future employment, military obligation, and marriage possibilities, to name a few. In the meantime, God had smiled on me in the area of academia, and I was very grateful:

1. I had almost miraculously been able to fulfill my history, upper-level hours, and required hours for graduation through a single class – English History 402– taught by one of my favorite professors.

2. In what had to be considered a Class One miracle, I had made a B+ in the English History course.

3. I had achieved the second highest semester GPA of my college career while taking 18 hours of upper-level courses, including English History 402. If you still don't believe in miracles, I don't know what to say.

Hither by His help, I had come.

Fourteen

NATIONAL CHAMPIONS

The previous year Harding had been invited to participate in the National Intercollegiate Marketing Competition sponsored by Michigan State University. The competition involved forty colleges and universities scattered from coast to coast participating in a simulated business enterprise. Each school's team was comprised of six Business or Accounting majors hand-picked by its school. In a controversial finish to the previous year's competition, Harding, the smallest school in the competition, was named runner–up, but the perception among the gathering at MSU was that Harding should have won. In the spring of 1966, the competition was again sponsored by Michigan State University, and Harding was once again invited to participate and determined to right the wrong of the previous year.

The forty teams were divided into five groups or "Industries," with eight teams per Industry. Harding was placed in Industry #1 along with Dyke University (name changed to David N. Myers College in 1995), Texas A&M, Western Michigan, Rochester University, Marquette, Xavier, and Virginia Tech – not exactly a group of losers. Notable teams placed in the other four Industries included:

South Carolina	Kent State
Notre Dame	Dayton
Temple	Kansas State
Mississippi	Northern Illinois
Southern Illinois	Bowling Green
Wisconsin	Massachusetts

Valparaiso	Bradley
Arkansas	Evansville

With these heavyweights in the field, it was a given that competition would be high level and intense. At first glance, it would seem that Harding was grossly overmatched, but remember that David was also grossly overmatched, and you might recall how that turned out.

As they had been in the 1965 competition, Mr. Billy Ray Cox and Mr. Jerry Starr were the Harding advisors to the 1966 team. The team they assembled for the upcoming competition consisted of Robley Barber, Larry Yurcho, Dean Bond, Ken Johnson, Don Johnson – no kin to Ken - and myself. Ken was the only holdover from the 1965 team. I was the token Business Administration major, all the others being Accounting majors. It probably explains why I was selected for the team – they wanted to demonstrate diversity, even in 1966. The competition, its preparation, and participation constituted the entirety of the Independent Research 450 course mentioned in the previous chapter, and we were the only six students in the course. Our grade for the course depended on how well we applied the principles we had learned in Harding's schools of Business and Accounting to the task at hand – the Marketing Competition. We were not required to win the competition, but we were expected to compete intelligently and effectively.

The contest required each college team to make "corporate" decisions regarding production, pricing, inventory management, marketing, R&D, quality control, etc. – the essential issues faced by any significant manufacturing enterprise – while operating a hypothetical manufacturing company. The competition would run for eight simulated quarters – two simulated years. Each team initially competed only against the seven other teams in its Industry for those eight quarters, and at the end of that part of that competition, the winners in each Industry would convene at MSU and duke it out for the national championship.

Beginning very early in the spring semester the teams met each Saturday at their respective colleges, formulated a strategy for a quarter, and transmitted its decisions to the Michigan State University computer. The MSU computer would then analyze the results of each team's strategy against both the competitive strategies of the other teams in its industry and against a simulated business environment, and they would then transmit those results back to each team. Over the next week, each team would then review its strategy and the results it had achieved and tweak its strategy as needed for the next quarter. They would then meet again on Saturday and transmit those decisions to MSU.

This continued for eight weeks, at the end of which a winner in each Industry would be announced by MSU. The five Industries' overall winners were then required to defend their strategy in a live presentation before a panel of business leaders and MSU faculty on the MSU campus. All the other participating teams were also invited to the campus to view the presentation and to celebrate the competition. After viewing the presentations of the five Industry winners, the panel would then declare a winner. The championship trophy would be presented to the winning team by Michigan Governor George Romney, the same George Romney who would challenge Richard Nixon for the Republican Presidential nomination in 1968 and the father of Mitt Romney who would challenge Barak Obama for the Presidency in 2012.

In the preliminary competition, Harding was declared the winner in Industry #1. This was exactly what had happened the previous year – Harding had won the preliminary competition but had been stymied in the finals. However, buoyed by our success thus far and filled with confidence, the eight of us – the team members and our advisors – set out in a van heading for Michigan.

The final competition was to take place on Saturday, April 23. Upon our arrival in East Lansing, we got settled in and prepared for the finals event. When our big moment came, Ken Johnson delivered the Harding presentation, defending our positions and strategy brilliantly, and he basically blew away the competition. The outcome was known by everyone in the auditorium well before the decision was announced. To no one's surprise, Harding was declared the winner.

At the 1966 National Intercollegiate Marketing Competition Harding College, David, in the presence of 39 Goliaths, was crowned National Champion.

Harding College. National Champions. That had a nice ring to it.

We shook hands with Gov. Romney, posed for pictures, and celebrated at lunch with all the other teams. We didn't realize it at the time, but our notoriety as members of the Harding team was just getting started. Also, I suspected that each member of our team would earn an "A" in our Independent Research course, and that suspicion was confirmed a few weeks later.

Another amazing thing occurred following our victory dance. One of the industry executives that had attended the final presentations – I don't know if he was a judge or not – verbally offered Ken Johnson a position in his company that would guarantee to make Ken a millionaire. It should also be noted that Ken was married and had been married long enough to be ineligible for the draft, so he was an extremely valuable commodity. His value was enhanced by the fact that he was a Summa Cum Laude Accounting major.

Although Ken was a senior and would be seeking work in a few weeks, he nevertheless declined the offer for whatever reason. In 1966 a million dollars was big bucks.

Following the closing ceremonies at MSU, our conquering team boarded the van and headed for Chicago. Chicago was the site of our American Studies tour for the spring semester, and it had been scheduled to commence immediately after the conclusion of the Business Games finals at Michigan State.

THE PROVIDENCE OF GOD

In the most unlikely of scenarios imaginable, a very small college in the middle of Arkansas had taken on a group of prestigious universities –Texas A&M, Virginia Tech, UMass, Kansas State, and Notre Dame, among others – in an intellectual and academic competition and had slain the giants. This particular event was the crowning academic moment in my entire college career. We had sat at the feet of outstanding professors, they had taught us a considerable amount of scholastic and practical business acumen, and we had applied what we had learned in a situation where it counted. I received many other blessings during the spring semester of my senior year at Harding, but this event warranted its own chapter.

1. I had been a member of the team of Harding Business and Accounting students who had won the national championship in the National Intercollegiate Marketing Competition.

2. Then–Governor George Romney of Michigan had presented us with the trophy.

I realize that all these "blessings" were simply temporal honors, and in the eternal scheme of things, they are meaningless. However, at the time, they really felt good. I also would like to point out that the group of guys on the team were all pretty mature and level–headed, and as far as I can recall, none of them allowed the situation to inflate his ego. On a personal level, in order to graduate on time, I still had to make a passing grade in English History 402 and contend with Business Law 316, where no prisoners were taken. But it was a pretty great time, and as subsequent chapters will attest, there were still a lot of good things to come before the end of the semester.

Unbelievably, however, hither by His help, I had come.

Fifteen

CHICAGO

When we arrived in Chicago, we checked in to the Allerton Hotel, awaiting the American Studies group's arrival the next day. Mr. Cox knew his hotels. The Allerton, like the Adolphus in Dallas, was and remains a fine and historic hotel.

The next day, while the American Studies group was still in route, the eight of us attended a Chicago Cubs baseball game. This was 1966, and lights had not yet been installed at Wrigley Field, so the game was played in the afternoon. We rode the El to and from our hotel, a new experience for all of us. In 1966 the Cubs were still perennial losers, and seats at the stadium were cheap and plentiful. We got seats directly behind home plate.

Technology had apparently not yet reached Wrigley Field. In the first place, lights still had not yet been installed at the stadium, so night games had never been played there. In addition, to announce the starting lineups, an ancient gentleman in a long overcoat – it was April 25 and still cold in Chicago that time of year – stood at home plate and read the names of the players while holding a corded microphone. It was almost like being in a time warp, and the feeling was priceless.

The San Francisco Giants were playing the Cubs that day. I don't remember who won the game, but Juan Marichal, a future Hall of Famer, pitched for the Giants.

Later that day, the American Studies group arrived and checked into the Allerton.

My one memory of the stay at the hotel involved Delmar O'Dell, a TNT brother, and an American Studies member. He and I were rooming together, and our rooms were on the 7th floor of the hotel. In the lobby, we got into a discussion as to whether the ancient elevators in the hotel were any faster than just walking the stairs. Delmar made a bet that he could reach the 7th floor faster than the elevator. As the rest of us entered the elevator in the lobby, Delmar hit the stairs. The elevator did not stop between the lobby and the 7th floor, and as we exited the elevator on the 7th floor, Delmar came racing around the corner from the stairwell into the elevator lobby – totally wiped out. The race ended in a tie. However, it did encourage us to use the elevator for the balance of our stay there.

Our Chicago American Studies tour was, to my mind, the best tour of the four I participated in. We were exposed to a wide variety of significant experiences.

Once again, we got to rub elbows with a national figure – Chicago Mayor Richard J. Daley. Mayor Daley served several terms as mayor of Chicago, and his son, also named Richard Daley, followed in his footsteps many years later. Mayor Daley was a very powerful politician but was courteous to us and answered a lot of questions. He also left a lot of unasked questions unanswered regarding Chicago politics and high-profile murders in the city over the years, particularly mob activities, the Valentine's Day massacre in 1929, and the assassination of John Dillinger outside the Biograph Theater in 1934. Admittedly all of those events occurred years before Mr. Daley was elected mayor, but many suspected that he was not totally unaware of the circumstances surrounding each of them.

The "Stormy, husky, brawling, City of the Big Shoulders," from Carl Sandberg's poem "Chicago," describes the city not only in Sandberg's day but still also today. I have visited Chicago many times over the years, sometimes for extended periods. I have always loved being there, but I have never wanted to live there. The city is far too intense for my psyche. Our visit with Mayor Daley will always remain in my memory.

Chicago is very versatile and offers many interesting diversions, many of which our group got to experience.

One morning we got up early to visit the Chicago Stock Exchange. The Exchange officially opened, I believe, at 8:30 a.m., and we wanted to be there when the bell rang for the opening. We arrived about 15 minutes before the opening, and the scene was calm and quiet. The traders were talking mutedly with one another and drinking coffee, and supposedly just quietly visiting. Suddenly the bell rang and all Hell – pardon my French – seemed to break loose. There was shouting and waving of hands and all kinds of action. The trading day had begun, and the buying and selling was off to a roaring start.

It was a lesson we Business majors learned up close and personal.

During our stay in Chicago, we also took a boat ride out on Lake Michigan, and we drove up Lakeshore Drive – probably the premier high dollar high rise complex in the country at the time and may still be. It was housing, unlike anything we Okies and Arkies had ever seen. We also visited the Museum of Science and Industry, a remarkable museum.

Finally, one afternoon while we were there, the whole group got to go to another Cubs game. This time they were playing the Dodgers, and future Hall of Famer Don Drysdale was pitching for the Dodgers. I don't remember who won that game either. What I remember was that our group sat in the center field bleachers, front row, and carried on a non–vulgar trash-talking conversation with the Dodger center fielder for the whole game. He was probably glad when the game was over.

Then it was time to return to Searcy and reality.

THE PROVIDENCE OF GOD

It seems that the semester just kept getting better and better. I was running out of stones for the Ebenezers I kept raising. The trip to Chicago was both educational and fun. An additional blessing I received as a result of the trip was that many years later, I made numerous business trips to Chicago, and the experiences gained from the American Studies trip were of great assistance in my making the business trips more efficient and enjoyable. As for the specific, timely blessings I received as a result of the trip to Chicago:

1. All the tensions associated with upcoming graduation, potential graduate school, career, military obligation, and the pressures associated with preparing for and then participating in the Marketing Competition were temporarily forgotten upon our arrival in Chicago.

2. Winning the National Championship not only elated all of us to near giddiness but also provided a valuable item to include in our future resumes.

3. The activities in Chicago – visiting the Chicago Stock Exchange and the Museum of Science and Industry, meeting Mayor Richard Daley, and even the boat ride on Lake Michigan – were extremely educational experiences.

4. Riding the El for the first time and witnessing two baseball games in historic Wrigley Field will always be remembered.

5. Even better, I would shortly be reunited with Shirley Swayne upon our return to Searcy, and I was anxious to see where that adventure would lead us.

Truly, hither by His help, I had come.

Sixteen

HONORS AND GLORY

After we returned from the Marketing Competition in Michigan and the American Studies tour of Chicago, it was late April. We had a little time to relax and kick back before our final push toward graduation. Several intramural and club sports events and some social activities such as the Junior-Senior Banquet and club banquets were still to occur before year-end. There were also several years–end awards and honors events that held special significance. One club sports event stands out in my mind in particular.

As mentioned earlier, my friend Ken Johnson – a fellow TNT brother, a brilliant student, and also an excellent athlete – had suffered a knee injury during a fall intramural football game. He subsequently had been lost to TNT in the club football tournament, and I feared that his services would not be available for the Club Track and Field Meet in the spring. Knee injuries such as his require considerable time to heal correctly.

At Harding, each full-time student must attend daily Monday–Friday chapel services in the college auditorium. Since attendance is mandatory, students are assigned specific seats, and attendance is recorded. Perhaps due to the will of God or perhaps due to another cosmic, against–all–odds accident (there were about 1700 seats in the auditorium at that time), Ken Johnson and I were assigned seats next to one another. Consequently, we had the opportunity for a short visit each time chapel convened.

In January, about two months following Ken's knee injury, I had started casually questioning him almost every day at the chapel as to how the knee was progressing, how rehab was going, etc. In the back of my mind was the fact that Club Track and Field Day was about three months away, sometime in late April or early May. I had once again been appointed captain of the TNT track team, and I was hoping against hope that Ken would be healed enough to participate in the event. The previous year TNT had won the track meet, with Ken's participation, by a single point over the second-place team. This year a victory would be very difficult if our premier sprinter was unable to run in the dashes.

Early on in my pre–chapel quizzes, he would be very non–committal in his comments due to the fact that the healing process was still ongoing. I would mention the upcoming track meet, and he would generally give me a discouraging statement along the lines of, "Well, I sure wish I hadn't hurt my knee. It still hurts."

For the next three months, I prodded him, cajoled him, playfully "dissed" him, encouraged him, and generally planted the seed in his mind that he would be fully healed by the date of the track meet and that he could outrun most everyone on one leg anyway. I sensed that his resolve was gradually melting, and about a month before the track meet, he said he might be able to run after all. It was impossible to turn handsprings in the confines of the auditorium seats, but I turned virtual handsprings in my mind. I briefly considered changing my major from Business to Psychology. My constant badgering of him had paid off.

Club Track and Field Day arrived, and TNT was once again locked in a tight contest for the trophy. The TNT tracksters whom we expected to win or place in their events had done so, but we still needed to pick up some un-expected points in other events to repeat as champions.

If you will recall, in a previous chapter, I mentioned that during my senior year, the College High School track coach wanted me to run high hur-dles. I declined because I was not nearly fast enough to compete effectively against the athletes I would face in the track meets. However, in the present situation, TNT did not have anyone to run the high hurdles at the Club Track meet, so, as team captain, I felt I had nothing to lose by filling that slot. The first four places received points in all the track events – the fourth-place finisher receiving one point.

Long story short, the high hurdle's finals were to be run in two heats, and the four fastest runners in each heat would be timed with a stopwatch. There were only 12 contestants, so eight ran in the first heat and 4 in the second heat. I ran in the second heat. In that heat, I finished dead last – fourth – but my time was faster than any of the runners in the first heat, so I was awarded fourth place, and TNT was awarded one single point for my effort. Unbe-knownst to me at the time, as the meet continued, that single point would become very significant. Miracles would continue to happen.

A little later in the meet, Ken Johnson, who had not done any serious training ahead of the track meet, ran in the 100-yard dash and the 220-yard dash. He finished second in the 100 and fourth in the 220 for a total of four points. Really, really good for a guy who was probably out of shape and still had an unsure knee. At the end of the day, TNT won the track championship by ½ point. There was nothing more to say, given that the team had received five totally unexpected miracle points from Ken Johnson and me.

With that "decisive" victory by TNT on Club Track and Field Day, I believed I had used up my quota of miracles for the year.

However, God's quota of providential gifts had apparently not yet been fulfilled at that point, and several other blessings awaited me before graduation. By this time, I had met and fallen in love with a girl by the name of Shirley Swayne – miracles continued to happen! – and we managed to make the end–of–year banquet circuit. Our story will be revealed in the next chapter, but there are other providential events that occurred prior to the end of the year that warrants mentioning.

First, upon returning from the National Intercollegiate Marketing Competition at Michigan State University, our championship team was honored during a chapel service. We were called up onto the stage and introduced, although most of the students already knew all of us. Our hands were shaken, and our backs were patted, and we enjoyed our moment in the sun. What made the time so special was that our little college – enrollment of about 1600 by the time – had taken on the giants and defeated them. The championship was not a victory by six students. It was a victory by and for an entire student body, and it gave it a tremendous sense of pride.

Our championship resonated beyond the campus. The story was picked up by the *Arkansas Gazette,* Little Rock's newspaper, and lo and behold; our pictures appeared in the newspaper along with a cover story.

Not to be outdone, two of the Little Rock TV stations jumped on the bandwagon and invited us to their studios for live interviews. We weren't exactly rock stars, but the Michigan State adventure had put Harding solidly on the map. In many ways, it appeared that the entire state was proud of Harding.

On April 25, while I was still in Chicago with the American Studies group, the Arkansas Collegiate Press Association, the association of all the college newspapers in the state, held its annual awards banquet. At the banquet, the Harding *Bison,* as usual, received numerous awards, including best Arkansas college newspaper (again), and several of the reporters also won awards, including myself. Among the columns I wrote for the *Bison* that year were the Harding Homecoming football game's reporting and a sports feature entitled "He Came to Play," which spotlighted Ronnie Brown, the star sophomore Harding basketball player. I was awarded by the ACPA a first place in "sports story" for the Harding Homecoming football game column and a second place in "sports feature" for the story about basketball player Ronnie Brown.

Later, back on campus Dennis Organ, the *Bison* editor, while presenting the awards to the *Bison* staff, remarked that it was ironic that the only "rookie" reporter on the *Bison* staff won two awards, and no one else won more than one. Among the staff writers was my friend Kenneth Starr who would eventually become a household name across America. In the back of my mind, I was thanking Mr. James Skaggs, my OCC English teacher, for his efforts to teach me the language and how to use it.

Two more honors came my way late in the semester.

The intramural sports program at Harding was superior to any that I had witnessed at my two previous colleges. The objective of the college was to encourage as many students as possible to participate in intramural sports. One of the perks associated with intramural participation was the awarding of Intramural Letters – much like a varsity letter, but with the word "Intramural" on the letter itself. Every year the top ten individual point-getters in intramural sports were awarded the Letters. As mentioned earlier, students earned at least one point for merely entering an event, such as intramural Cross Country. For instance, I entered that particular race and finished about 50th place, but I had earned a point or two in doing so. The higher the finish, the more the points earned. Points were also earned in the team sports, and additional points were awarded for being selected to an All-Star team.

Not only were Intramural Letters awarded but also trophies for "Sports Skill Champion" and "Intramural Athlete of the Year" were awarded. The Sports Skill Champion was the student that had earned the most points in individual events – Cross Country Run, Football Punt, Peg Board Climb (a killer), Baseball Base Running, etc. The Intramural Athlete of the Year was the student that earned the most points overall – combined individual sports skill events and team events

Every spring, at the conclusion of intramural athletics for the year, the Intramural Sports awards were handed out, and, as was the custom, the awards were announced in a chapel service. Since I had participated in every single intramural event – team and individual – during the school year and had played on two intramural champion teams and made an All-Star team or two, I was confident that I would win an Intramural Letter

In Harding's chapel service, freshmen were assigned the first several rows in the auditorium, sophomores the next several rows, and so on. As a senior, my seat, next to Ken Johnson, was six rows from the top of the balcony. It was literally a five–minute walk from my seat down the stairs to the stage. Having won an Intramural letter the previous year, I was pretty sure I had earned a second Intramural Letter this year. Since all those receiving awards were called to the stage to receive their award, I thought I should attempt to get a little closer to the stage in case my name was called. I decided on the perfect solution.

By this time, Shirley Swayne and I were going steady. Since she was still a freshman, she was sitting in the middle of a row just a few rows from the stage. I persuaded the girl in the seat next to Shirley to give me her seat for chapel that day. With her seat being occupied, she would not be counted absent. She consented and gave me her seat.

Mr. Cecil Beck, the Intramural Director, started calling the names of those who had won Letters, and sure enough, he called my name. I made my way from the freshman section to the stage, stepping on everyone's feet in the row along the way. After all 10 of the awardees had received their Letters, I made the return trip to my seat, bruising a few more feet as I went.

Then Mr. Beck announced the Sports Skill Champion. He once again called my name. I was stunned. However, I once again stumbled my way to the stage and back, much to the consternation of those sitting near me.

Now it was time to announce the Intramural Athlete of the Year. I was just getting comfortable in my seat, and those on whose feet I had stepped were finally breathing a sigh of relief, and then Mr. Beck called my name again. I had been named Intramural Athlete of the Year. It was almost more than I could handle, and, to tell the truth, those sitting near me were getting a little tired of my trips to the stage. However, I mangled their feet one last time and went to the stage to receive the award. I had never before in my life and never since been the sole honoree, in any event, not to mention before a crowd of 1600 or so peers. I was humbled in a manner that was indescribable, and at the same time, I was very, very proud. My award was not so much due to my athletic skill but was rather to my persistence and my willingness to give it my best shot even in things I wasn't very good at. I discovered in later life that giving your best shot under all circumstances is a good strategy.

In true Harding tradition, the photos of all the winners of Intramural Athlete of the Year from the 1950s until the current year are permanently displayed on a TV monitor on a wall in the Ganus Athletic Center. It should be noted that my cousin, Jerry Brock, was named Intramural Athlete of the Year at Harding three years later.

Except for my trophy wife–to–be, that concluded the honors and awards

I received during the semester. It was an unbelievably rich and rewarding period of time, one over which I still shake my head in disbelief.

THE PROVIDENCE OF GOD

Once again, I raised an Ebenezer for the blessings I had received during the semester – indeed, for the entire school year. These honors and awards were very humbling and made me extremely grateful for their receipt. I have never claimed that I deserved any of them, but rather give the glory to God for the manner in which they provided a very positive and lasting impact on my life. I still lean toward introversion, but I have come to believe that hard work, the presence of talented friends, and the grace of God can work wonders, even for people who aren't superstars. In review, here are the unwarranted blessings I received through God's grace:

1. I was appointed captain of the TNT club track team and "coached" it to victory by the overwhelming margin of ½ point over the second-place club.

2. Perhaps prompted by my constant badgering, Ken Johnson ultimately decided he was physically able to participate in the club track meet, did so, and earned four points in two races.

3. I finished dead last in a hurdles race and yet was awarded one point, which, with Ken Johnson's improbable performance, enabled TNT to win the championship trophy by the aforementioned ½ point.

4. As a rookie reporter, I unbelievably won two newspaper writing awards in the presence of so many others who were veterans at the craft across the entire state of Arkansas.

5. Along with my Marketing Teammates, I was interviewed on two television stations, and I managed to avoid tripping over my tongue or otherwise making a fool of myself during the interviews.

6. I won the two biggest Intramural sports awards at Harding in the face of tremendous competition.

7. Best of all, I had won the heart of Shirley Swayne.

I continue after all these years to shake my head in disbelief at these things that occurred. Hither by His help, I had come, unbelievably far beyond my expectations. And God was not finished yet.

Seventeen

AT LONG LAST—LOVE

Amazing and unexpected blessings continued to follow me during the spring semester, almost like God was just toying with me.

While my academic, athletic, and campus social lives were blossoming far beyond my expectations during my last semester at college, the more important aspects of my future – marriage, career, and military service were still dangling. When March arrived, none of the corporate recruiters had shown up on campus, and I still had not received replies from Oklahoma State, the University of Arkansas, or Oklahoma University regarding my application for graduate school. Military service opportunities had not even begun to manifest themselves, and there was no serious young woman on my horizon. Nothing had jelled, and I was beginning to feel pretty uneasy. I had become firmly ensconced on several fronts in a condition they call at Harding "senior panic."

Then, almost overnight, everything changed. The most dramatic and important blessing of my life, save my baptism, had its inception in mid-March. It all started at church on a Wednesday evening service.

I was very regular in my attendance at the College Church of Christ in Searcy, seldom missing Sunday or Wednesday services. I regularly sat near the front of the auditorium on the right-hand side at those services, where most of the other students sat. However, by the grace of God, one Wednesday night in March, I was attending with Phil Dixon, and we got there a little later than usual. Consequently, we sat on the right side but had to sit near the back. I noticed this beautiful girl I had never seen before sitting two rows in front of us during the service. I asked Phil if he knew who she was, and he said he didn't. However, he said he knew the guy she was with. I asked, no, pleaded with him to find out her name, and he said he would.

A couple of days later, Phil told me that her name was Shirley Swayne, she was a freshman, and she lived in the Cathcart Hall Dormitory. However, he also told me that her date that Wednesday night was not planning to ask her out any more. I asked why, and he said the guy, who was also a freshman, had discovered that Shirley was somewhat older than he. He had learned that Shirley had worked for two and a half years following her high school graduation and was entering Harding as a 20-year-old freshman. She had subsequently turned down his request for another date with him. As we all did, he had assumed that it was because she didn't want to date someone younger than she. At the time, I was very encouraged by the news, but I later discovered the hard way that that was a very, very bad assumption.

However, at the time, after giving that assumption consideration, I jumped to the conclusion that it could work to my benefit. If she didn't want to date younger guys, that would disqualify half the guys on campus—freshmen and sophomores—as potential dates for her and would therefore thin my competition by at least half. After all, she was both beautiful and obviously had logical discernment regarding whom she would date. Even though it would prove to be a very difficult and tricky courtship, except for my decision to be baptized, deciding to pursue Shirley Swayne was the single best and most important decision I ever made in my life.

Having learned Shirley's name and campus address, I did not waste any time making my move. I was in the lobby of Cathcart Hall the afternoon following my learning of her name and where she lived. As per procedure, the women's dorms always had a receptionist in the lobby to chase away loitering guys or to inform the residents via intercom of visitors. I asked the receptionist to page Shirley Swayne. Shortly Shirley appeared in the lobby and looked around for someone she recognized. The only person in the lobby, aside from the receptionist, was me, and she looked a little puzzled to see only me.

I will always remember my first words to her. They were, "You don't know me from Adam, but my name is Johnny Vaughan." And it was true she had never seen me nor heard my name before that day in March. However, I mentioned that I had seen her at church and wondered if she would consider a date with me at church the coming Sunday morning. It was a lame introduction, I admit, but at that point, it was all I had. Although for all she knew I could have been an ax murderer, but she bravely consented, and we made plans for her to meet me in the lobby of Cathcart Sunday morning.

So, we had our first date, appropriately enough a church date. As I pursued her for additional dates, she consented but hesitantly. As it turned out, Shirley was a really hard sell, but as they say, "nothing good comes easy." As mentioned earlier, the assumption that she didn't want to date younger guys had been a huge miscalculation on my part. Rather, early on, she told me that she wasn't really interested in entering into a serious relationship with anyone, including me. She said she came to Harding with one thing in mind to get a college education and that serious dating for the foreseeable future was off the table. When I learned this, rather than throwing in the towel, I went into scramble mode, and my devious mind desperately came up with a ridiculously brilliant idea. After some careful thought and scheming on my part, I suggested to Shirley that she and I make a pact, a very strange pact. This is the gospel truth.

Our pact was that since neither of us, supposedly, wanted to enter into a serious relationship anytime soon that we would take ourselves off the market, so to speak, and date each other exclusively. As for the pact, I was, metaphorically, blowing smoke, but Shirley, the trusting soul that she is, bought into it. By "dating" in this manner, we could enjoy each other's companionship with the understanding that we would not get emotionally involved, and we would also possibly eliminate heartbreak for some unsuspecting soul who might actually want to date either of us more seriously. We just wouldn't be available to date others, and, supposedly, our dating each other would be strictly platonic.

The pact was a "Hail Mary" effort on my part. Since I had become really smitten with Shirley and desperately didn't want to lose her, I felt the only way to accomplish that was for us to somehow date long enough for her to possibly change her mind. So, I concocted the ploy to convince her that I, too, was not interested in taking our relationship beyond casual dating. The excuse I offered to support my agreement to our pact was to tell her, truthfully, that I had suffered a failure in three relationships over the past four years.

During Christmas break of my senior year in high school, a girl named Judy from Albuquerque, New Mexico, came to Bartlesville to visit her uncle and aunt, who were members of our church. She was a beautiful blue-eyed soprano. We struck up a great relationship while she was in town. She was able to visit Bartlesville once more the following summer, and I eventually visited Albuquerque twice myself. In addition, during this time, we exchanged letters several times each week. Due likely to the long distance between us, things just didn't work out, and she gave me the pink slip, ironically, on Thanksgiving Day in 1962, during my last trip to Albuquerque. It made the 544-mile drive back to OCC in Oklahoma City pretty somber. Long-distance romances are very difficult.

The following summer was the summer of Martha Koger, a beautiful, blue-eyed alto. That episode has already been discussed earlier in this treatise.

As described, I was stuck at Oklahoma University while she was an exceptional, unattached girl on Harding's campus who was probably the target of half the male student body there. She could not be ignored, and she wasn't, and the rest is history.

During my junior year at Harding, I met and had a brief relationship with another Judy, also a beautiful, blue-eyed soprano. It seems that I had a bent for musically talented blue-eyed girls. It should be noted that while Shirley is a musically talented soprano, she is brown-eyed. Judy and I dated for a while, and then she became ill and had to drop out of school. Although she eventually returned to Harding, the romance by then had basically died on the vine. Once again, absence from one another – my third long-distance relationship – was likely a factor in that outcome.

But God apparently decided to change the dynamics. For one thing, He stopped placing beautiful blue-eyed women in my path and changed that particular dynamic to a beautiful brown-eyed woman.

Since I had previously whiffed on a romance with three great girls, I decided that I was going to subject Shirley to a full-court press, but somehow do it subtly. Thus, the birth of the ploy to take ourselves off the social market and date each other exclusively but "not seriously."

As a result, we did begin to date, at first informally, and then regularly – every church service and eventually on every other possible social occasion. Suddenly Shirley and I were together basically every day. She dined in the Pattie Cobb cafeteria, and I dined in the new Heritage cafeteria, but I would let her use my meal ticket at the Heritage at times when I had accumulated surplus funds on the ticket. Consequently, we even had informal dinner dates occasionally.

Over time her attitude gradually changed, and she began to enjoy my company more than she had anticipated. I think at some undetermined point, she stopped "liking" me and actually started loving me. Of course, I had already been at that stage with her for quite some time – probably from the first date. However, I am ashamed to say that even after she had begun to show a genuine interest in me, I still intentionally acted a little standoffish with her – I wanted to sink the hook really deeply, given my relationships with past girlfriends. It broke my heart to appear indifferent in the face of her changing attitude, but I stuck to my guns for a little while longer. At some point, my true feelings would become overwhelmingly evident.

That point occurred in early May.

In the process of getting to know one another, Shirley told me about her home and family life. Her parents lived near Yellville, Arkansas, on a farm. She was the ninth of ten children, and eight of the ten were brothers.

Consequently, she was considerably younger than her older brothers, and her parents were considerably older than mine. Her parents were products of the Great Depression and the Dust Bowl days and had lived in both Kansas and Arkansas. They were not poverty-stricken, but they were poor. This was 1966, and their home still had no utilities except electricity and propane for the cookstove. They still fetched water for drinking, washing, and bathing from a nearby spring, but the water was very good. The house was heated by a single wood stove. Her father had worked in sawmills but was now basically retired. They produced most of their own food in a garden and with their livestock. This situation was not foreign to me, as my grandparents had lived under similar conditions near Shell Knob, Missouri, only a few years earlier. Consequently, none of what she told me shocked me.

On the contrary, I felt a little relieved because, given her home life to this point, her expectations of me as a husband and provider could not have been very high and should be well within my reach. My biggest fear was facing her seven older brothers and winning their acceptance. Here was this city dude trying to take advantage of their little sister. However, I faced another, potentially more serious, challenge – her dad.

Shirley was still living at home when she had announced late in the previous fall that she intended to go to college come January. At that time, her dad told her that if she was going there to get an education, that was fine and dandy, but she should forget it if she was going there for any other reason. She should just keep her good job at Baxter Laboratories instead. She assured him that she was going there for an education. Now, here it was only four months into her college career, and she was, by this time, heavily involved with a guy.

Eventually, in early May, Shirley invited me to go home with her for the weekend. When we arrived, I discovered that her parents were saints, and they made me feel totally at home from the get-go. It turned out that her dad was a St. Louis Cardinal fan, as was I, so in that respect, we hit it off from the very beginning. None of Shirley's brothers were particularly sports fans, so I was almost like the son her dad had never had. Her only younger sibling, her brother Dennis, was still in high school at the time, and I also gained his respect.

On Sunday morning that weekend, it was time to go to church with the family. They attended a very small, old congregation located deep in the hills by the name of the Freck Church of Christ. Freck had been a small village in years past but had long since died. However, there was still a large cemetery located there along with the church. The cemetery was still maintained and was still being used for burials. The church building was old but still functional, and the congregation consisted of about 50 people. The church served Christians who lived in the rural areas of Marion County and had, in fact, served the current members' families for generations. Those in attendance included all age groups, including some small children. Sunday School classes were held, followed by the worship service. Morale was high, and the fellowship was genuine. The small congregation presented an amazing spirit for a church that, by all rights, should have died decades earlier.

Following the church service, we returned to Shirley's house for Sunday dinner, and then it was time to head back to Searcy.

By that time, we had been together almost continuously for two months, and I had also finally made it known that I was in it for the long haul – my pretense of indifference had totally collapsed by that time. I was dating her with the serious intent of taking this relationship to the next level – marriage. Although we had not spoken of it, the subject had become the elephant in the room – impossible to ignore, but as yet not openly discussed. Also, we had just successfully crossed a significant threshold – I had met not only her parents but also her little brother and had apparently passed the test with flying colors. In our journey back to campus from Yellville, the subject of marriage was finally broached, albeit gently. I could not get down on one knee to ask for her hand while driving through the mountains, and as yet, I had not purchased a ring. But by the time we arrived back on campus, the issue had been settled – we would get married sometime after graduation. We eventually settled on September 3. Hopefully, that would allow me time to get settled in my job, providing the military didn't have other ideas, and it would give Shirley time to make all the plans and preparations.

At that point, it became incumbent upon us to notify our fellow students of the upcoming joyous occasion, and that announcement was best accomplished by the presence of a diamond on a young lady's left–hand ring finger. We had good intentions, but there was a problem – I had no idea how much diamond rings cost, and it didn't matter much anyway since I was essentially broke. Someone told me that I could probably get a bank loan, so I visited a Searcy bank, and they were happy to lend me $200 for an engagement ring. Being a Searcy bank just a few blocks from the Harding marriage factory, I don't believe this was the bank's first rodeo.

Phil Dixon recommended a jewelry store in Little Rock, and one Saturday morning, Shirley and I violated a Harding rule – no off-campus single–dating by automobile – by setting out in my car for Little Rock to buy a little rock. We found the jewelry store and were able to acquire a ¼ carat diamond ring for $200. The stone was tiny, but it was worth a million dollars to me.

Upon our leaving the jewelry store, things immediately got complicated. I don't know why things like what happened at that time keep happening to me. I keep complaining that the world is very small and there are only so many possibilities, but I seem to continually beat the odds in such situations – like running into people I know at awkward times. I can only believe that God has a sense of humor and likes to keep people – especially me, it seems – off-balance from time to time. Bear in mind that Shirley and I were at that moment openly flouting the Harding no–single–dating by automobile rule.

As we walked out of the door of the jewelry store that morning, of all things, Dr. Clifton Ganus Jr., president of the college, and Mr. Virgil Lawyer, Harding's Dean of Students, were sitting in an automobile stopped at a red light at the corner. Their car was directly in front of the door from which Shirley and I exited, and both of them got an up-close and personal view of our indiscretion. Of course, they recognized us – I was actually a pretty good friend of Dr. Ganus by that time, and Dean Lawyer was one of the sponsors of the TNT social club. They both limply waved at us, and then Dr. Ganus shook his finger at us and offered a crooked smile while doing so. Dean Lawyer had the reputation of being fair but firm in his adjudication of campus rules violations. I thought we were dead and that I would be sent home only two weeks short of graduation, and my life was, for all practical purposes, over. They didn't linger but drove on when the light turned green. How and why do things like this continue to haunt me?

That was Saturday, and I dreaded Monday with a fear worse than death. I had expected to find a note in my campus mailbox summoning me to some sort of inquisition, but there was no note. So, I decided to man up and go to Dean Lawyer's office without being summoned. However, as an insurance policy, I took Shirley with me in the hope that her presence would inspire leniency on Dean Lawyer's part. It did not hurt that she was beautiful, had a clean record to that point, and was sporting a diamond. When we entered Dean Lawyer's office, he looked at us and was grinning from ear to ear. I suspected he was really enjoying the moment, having caught two students red-handed arrogantly ignoring the rules. However, I was entirely mistaken. Shirley showed him the ring, and he congratulated us on the engagement, wishing us well. My head was spinning, but I thanked him for his mercy. I don't even remember him mentioning the "meeting" in Little Rock. I think maybe even God got a chuckle at my expense. We later visited briefly with Dr. Ganus and got much the same reaction from him.

It had been a struggle from the beginning – the "non–dating" dating, having no money to buy a ring, getting busted in Little Rock, and the uncertainty of a visit to Dean Lawyer's office. But in the end, it was worth all the tension and uncertainty that came with it. We were married less than four months later, on September 3, 1966. But that is another story.

THE PROVIDENCE OF GOD

I have thanked God probably a million times for providentially placing me in that particular seat in the church auditorium on that particular evening and for placing Phil Dixon there to help usher me into the most significant secular event in my life. Unexpected events and situations that occurred during that last semester at Harding, which I feel were blessed by God include:

1. I was late for church on a Wednesday evening, which providentially placed me in a seat where I saw Shirley Swayne for the first time.

2. Shirley's obvious indifference to serious dating drove off potential suitors – until she met one who was not above employing chicanery to achieve his ambitions.

3. Time spent years earlier with my grandparents in their rural Missouri home enabled me to feel very comfortable when I was in Shirley's parents' rural home.

4. Shirley's upbringing and home life prepared her to be a perfect match for me.

5. I was readily accepted by Shirley's parents and siblings.

6. The fact that her dad was an avid St. Louis Cardinals fan provided the two of us with a lot of common ground and things to talk about.

7. Miraculously, Shirley didn't dump me before I managed to initiate my deceptive ploy.

8. Miraculously, Shirley accepted my proposal for marriage.

9. I was able to fund a modest engagement ring with a ¼ carat diamond, which Shirley eventually proudly wore for 48 years before receiving something better.

10. Miraculously, the two of us did not get sent home on the spot for violating the no–single car dating rule.

In review, I obviously had a lot of help along the way to discovering and pursuing Shirley. I have raised a thousand Ebenezers over the years in thanks for this series of events. Truly, truly, hither by His help I had come.

18

AFTER GRADUATION - WHAT NEXT?

The critically important aspects of my future – marriage, career, and military service – were still dangling in in mid–April. At that point I had not yet proposed to Shirley, and although I had interviewed with several corporate recruiters and received some job offers, I had not yet decided to accept any offers that I had received. I had still not made a decision regarding graduate school, and I was still very uncertain as to what form my military service might take.

The graduate school acceptance notices arrived during early March, but I had not immediately responded. I had been offered admission to graduate school at Oklahoma State and Arkansas, including a fellowship stipend at each. I had not been accepted at Oklahoma University. Its reason for their declining my application was that they were only accepting Oklahoma University graduates into their graduate Business school at that time. I grudgingly accepted that their decision was probably due to the university's popularity, its Business school's excellent reputation, and the overwhelming number of OU graduates who likely applied due to the change in the Selective Service System's deferment criteria. I decided to await further developments on the marriage, employment, and military service issues before deciding. Graduate school would have deferred my being drafted for the duration of graduate school, but it would only have delayed the inevitable.

As for my potential military career, in early March, I had gone to Little Rock Air Force Base and had taken a physical as a hedge against being drafted into the Army. My dad had been in the Army Air Corps (early version of the Air Force) in World War II, and he had told me that Air Force life was much better than Army life. I had passed the physical with flying colors, and they told me my eyesight was 20/15 in both eyes – exceptional vision. I was a perfect fit for a fighter pilot.

There is an interesting anecdote associated with my Air Force physical. The Air Force doctor had told me that I needed to bring a friend with me to the Air Force Base on the day of the physical, who could drive me back to the Harding campus. As the physical was scheduled for a Saturday, a great many of my friends had deserted the campus for the weekend, and I did not have a readily available friend to accompany me to the physical. Being of a relatively healthy body (but apparently not of sound mind), I decided that I did not need a chauffeur to and from the Air Force Base and that I could drive myself. Did I mention that I was to undergo an eye exam? The first thing they do in an eye exam is to dilate your pupils. I came out of the exam with my pupils the size of nickels, and there was not a cloud in the very sunny afternoon sky. I could see virtually nothing. And the pupils were not going to return to their normal function for hours. Under these conditions, I could not possibly drive myself safely back to the campus.

But a memory from my past saved the day. In the mid-1950s, there was a TV show entitled *Sgt. Preston of the Yukon*, a series about a fictional Canadian Mountie. I watched the show faithfully. Quaker Oats sponsored the show and as part of the publicity Sgt. Preston was periodically featured on their cereal boxes. One box contained a description and a drawing of a "snow mask" that Sgt. Preston used when working in bright sunlight in the snow when the brightness overwhelmed his eyes. In such conditions, the pupils of the eyes can only with great difficulty reduce in size small enough to permit decent vision. The mask was nothing more than a cardboard mask with extensions to fit over the ears and containing two very narrow slits through which the user would peer. The slits admitted very little light, emulating the reduction in the user's pupils' size, thus allowing the user to see reasonably well under the circumstances.

As I sat in my car that afternoon following the physical, I could see virtually nothing – it was like looking into a floodlight. Still, the dilation would not allow my pupils to reduce to normal size anytime soon. By the grace of God, I recalled Sgt. Preston and his snow mask from the Quaker Oats cereal box of 10 years earlier. I happened to have some papers in the car. I took an ordinary sheet of typing paper, and using my car key, I gouged two narrow slits in the paper, spaced roughly to coincide with the spacing between my eyes. With my left hand I held the paper in front of my eyes, started the car, and, peering through the two narrow slits, headed back to Searcy. Thankfully my old car had an automatic transmission, so I did not have to use my left hand on the drive back. I drove slowly and carefully and reached my dorm safely.

As with so many of the events of my life I have often wondered if my intrigue with both Sgt. Preston and Quaker Oats was not one of those little "miracles" – a seemingly innocuous hint given by God that was manifested years later by saving my bacon, so to speak. As I have mentioned, I have experienced too many such unexplained happenings in my life to believe they are simply coincidence.

But back to my story. By mid–April, I still had heard nothing regarding any Air Force enlistment options.

Most of the corporate recruiters had started showing up in early March. There were a dozen or more corporate recruiters that arrived on campus seeking Business Administration graduates. Still, I eventually selected only four to interview with – Phillips Petroleum Company, J.C. Penney Company, Firestone, and Fidelity Union Life Insurance Company. The insurance company was a late arrival, coming to the campus to conduct interviews in late April. They specifically requested that of all the senior members of our National Championship Marketing team agree to interviews, which we all did. However, the jobs they were offering were life insurance salesmen jobs, and that was not a career path I was cut out for. Ultimately, they offered jobs to all four seniors on the Marketing team, but none accepted.

Phillips Petroleum sought to fill Finance–related job openings in its Credit Card Center in Kansas City, Missouri. J.C. Penney and Firestone were offering jobs as Manager Trainees at locations to be determined.

My interviews with Phillips, Penney's, and Firestone went very well, and all three of the companies were encouraging and told me they would get back to me very soon. A few days later, five of us Business Administration students were contacted by Firestone asking if they could speak with us further at their Memphis, Tennessee, office. One morning the five of us all piled into a car and made the 110-mile drive to Memphis for the interviews.

Those interviews also went well, and as I remember, all of us were offered jobs on the spot. We would start as Manager Trainees with the intent of eventually managing a Firestone store. We were told that almost all of the company's upper management had begun their careers as Manager Trainees. They offered good benefits and a competitive starting salary. Those of who had made the trek to Memphis thanked them for their courtesy and job offers and promised that we would give a firm reply within a week or so. None of us wanted to make a commitment until we had heard from the other recruiters.

Early in April, I had received written offers from both Phillips Petroleum and J.C. Penney to go along with the Firestone offer. Fidelity Union Life

Insurance Company had still not arrived on campus. The Phillips job was financially oriented, while the Penney's job would involve managing a department in a Penney's store – essentially sales-oriented and managing people – with the hope of advancing into store management. As mentioned, the location of the Phillips job was Kansas City, where I had a ton of close relatives, but neither Penney's nor Firestone could specify the location of the store I would start out in. In addition, the Phillips job offered higher starting pay than either Firestone or Penney's. Phillips Petroleum held all the cards – type of work, pay, location – so I decided to notify Firestone and Penney's that I appreciated their offers but would have to respectfully decline.

However, I could not yet formally accept the Phillips job because their offer came with a caveat – I had to be draft resistant. That is, my pending military obligation could not include the possibility of being drafted and thus delaying my career at Phillips for two years or more. They could not hold that job open for two years in the hope that I would return.

So here I was in limbo. I had turned down two good job offers that had no military service caveat, but I had not yet received anything from the Air Force and didn't feel that I could accept the Philips offer in my present state. In addition, the graduate school offers from Arkansas and Oklahoma State were still hanging out there.

About this time, I started getting good vibes from the Oklahoma National Guard – the Thunderbirds – that they likely had some openings. Not guaranteed, but likely.

What to do? I decided to roll the dice and accept the Phillips job and cross my fingers and pray that the National Guard had a slot for me. I declined the graduate school offers, and when I accepted the Phillips job, I was a little ambiguous about my military obligation. At that time, they asked no further military-related questions, but my Phillips career would have ended very abruptly had I received a draft notice after accepting employment with them. I would have been toast. However, when all the smoke cleared, I was scheduled to begin my employment in Kansas City on Thursday, June 9, 1966.

I took a short trip to Bartlesville to visit with the draft board there about this time, mid–May, having not yet received any positive word from either the Air Force or the National Guard. Bartlesville is where I had registered for the draft when I turned 18 years old. The draft board man looked at me like I was prime steak and told me I would not last the summer before being drafted. Not what I wanted to hear.

My trip back to campus was a little somber. However, during the remainder of the month, I finished my course work, got engaged to Shirley, nearly got kicked out of school when I bought the engagement ring, and on Thursday, June 2, I graduated Cum Laude from Harding College.

Then things got a little complicated immediately following the graduation ceremony. My good friend Steve Thornton was getting married, and I had been asked to be best man in the wedding.

The wedding and the reception were scheduled to take place on Saturday afternoon, June 4, in Lubbock, Texas, only two days following my graduation. What complicated matters even further was that the wedding rehearsal and dinner were scheduled for the evening of June 3, only one day following graduation. That allowed only about 24 hours to travel the 715 miles from Searcy to Lubbock to be on time for the Friday evening festivities.

My plan was to drive to Lubbock following the graduation ceremony, bringing along with me Shirley and my cousin, Jerry Brock, who was also in the wedding party. Then, following the wedding and all the post-wedding activities, the three of us would pile into my car and head back north. I would stop in Okemah and pick up some clothing to wear at my new job in Kansas City, drop off Jerry at his home in Tulsa, deliver Shirley to her home in Yellville, and still arrive in Kansas City a day or so ahead of my start–to–work date of June 9. This compressed time frame with what would encompass almost 1700 miles of driving in my old Ford – including the last 263 miles from Yellville to Kansas City – all within seven days, was going to make for very interesting time and travel logistics. Needless to say, it would take some careful planning and precise execution of those plans, plus no small amount of good luck, to get everyone where they needed to be when they needed to be there.

My parents had attended the graduation in Searcy, so they had loaded up my things into their car and headed for Okemah. Jerry's parents had attended the graduation and had taken his things back to Tulsa. Shirley, however, was not going directly to Yellville. She was going with me to the wedding, and then, following the wedding, I would deliver her to her home. Consequently, in addition to the three of us in my car, we also had to carry Shirley's clothes and things with us on the trip to Lubbock. Shortly after I received my diploma, we loaded up and headed southwest to Lubbock.

We drove all afternoon and night, arriving in Lubbock early the next morning. We found the hotel where Steve was staying and caught a few winks before the rehearsal and dinner. Then the following day, we got spiffed up and went to the wedding in the early afternoon.

The wedding was routine, thankfully, and then the craziness resumed. Following the wedding, we immediately headed back to civilization. I had to first drive to Okemah, 414 miles from Lubbock, to pick up my clothes. From there, I had to drive to Tulsa, 71 more miles, to drop off Jerry at his home. Following that, I had to drive from Tulsa to Yellville, another 208 miles, to take Shirley home, a total of 693 miles – Lubbock to Yellville – in basically one stretch following the wedding reception late the afternoon of June 4.

However, the last leg of this journey – from Tulsa to Yellville – was not without incident. My old 1955 Ford beater had been a faithful car and had served me well and now had 115,000 miles on it, but somewhere between Tulsa and Yellville, it announced its impending retirement. During that drive, the tailpipe drooped and began dragging on the highway, leaving a trail of sparks. I had some bailing wire in the trunk by some stroke of luck, so I pulled over beside the highway and using the wire reattached the tailpipe to the frame so at least it was no longer dragging. That seemed to temporarily resolve the problem. We finally made it to Shirley's house arriving there sometime in the evening on June 5, absolutely dead tired.

I spent two nights at Shirley's house, and then on June 7, I headed for Kansas City and my career. However, my old Ford had given me a foreboding of things to come, and I was a little apprehensive as I set out on the 263-mile drive north to Kansas City. And not without reason, but that is a story for the next chapter where the phrase "impulse purchase" would be redefined.

THE PROVIDENCE OF GOD

What with the engagement, the job offer and the hopeful resolution of the military service issue I metaphorically raised a huge pile of stones named Ebenezer and thanked God for His help to this point. A few of the blessings I had received during my last semester at Harding included:

1. I had been the recipient of a number of honors and awards – academic, athletic, personal and on a national scale – that erased from my memory all the bumps and bruises I had allegedly sustained over my first 22 years of my life.
2. Under unusual circumstances I had met Shirley Swayne, and under additional unusual circumstances had persuaded her to marry me.
3. I had driven back to campus safely from the Air Force Base while essentially blind.
4. By the grace of God I had received multiple offers of employment, graduate school and military service which gave me the opportunity of making choices about my future.
5. Over a five–day period I had safely logged almost 1700 highway miles

from Searcy to Lubbock to Yellville to Kansas City, which in itself is remarkable, if not a miracle.

6. My personal walk with God was strengthened, and I was blessed with making new lifelong friends.

My experiences in 2½ years at Harding ultimately had defined and set in motion the goals and aspirations that would influence the remainder of my life as they pertained to the objectives I had established. It seems that they all came to a head in the spring of 1966. Harding College had been a catalyst by providing life opportunities that I doubt I could have found elsewhere. I certainly would not have found my wife anywhere else. The Providence of God continued to insert itself into my life, and I continued to raise Ebenezers.

What next?

Nineteen

GETTING SETTLED IN
INDEPENDENCE (SUMMER 1966)

As mentioned earlier, my Uncle Howard and his family lived in Independence, Missouri, a suburb on the east side of Kansas City, so it was there that I was actually headed when I left Shirley's house. Unbeknownst to me, when my faithful 1955 Ford Fairlane had dropped its tailpipe two days earlier on the highway between Tulsa and Yellville, it had begun a death spiral. Being ignorant of what the car was actually telling me, it was my intent to limp into Independence and then call on my uncles – Uncle Howard and Uncle Don Ray – to help me replace the worn-out tailpipe. My uncles were very adept at working on automobiles. In fact, my Uncle Don Ray worked at the local Ford factory. Fate, however, had a different idea.

After I had left Shirley's house and was traveling north on Highway 71 toward the Kansas City metro, somewhere north of Nevada, Missouri, not only the tailpipe but also the muffler began dragging, creating a potentially dangerous Fourth of July display under my car. Once again, I pulled over and reattached what I felt was the car's complete exhaust system. When I started the car up to resume my journey, the starter hesitated, likely indicating a weak battery. I had already had one memorable episode with a dead battery on I–35 on my way back to Oklahoma Christian three years earlier, and I was no longer in a mood to be forgiving to the car.

At that moment, I made the irreversible impulse decision to stop at the next Chevrolet dealer I encountered on the way to Independence and trade what was left of my Ford for a new Chevy. I was in no mood for further dramatics involving my car. Never mind that I had less than $100 in my pocket and still did not actually hold a job. My mind was made up.

175

I have to believe that God took pity on me because there was, providentially, a Chevrolet dealer located in Harrisonville, Missouri, on Highway 71 Bypass – the highway that eventually led directly to Independence. Without hesitation, I pulled into the dealership and asked to look at a new Chevy. The salesman looked over my car – I did not mention the problem with the exhaust system – and said he had someone in mind that might want my car. At any rate, they took my car as a down payment and sold me a new Chevrolet Impala 2–door hardtop, V–8, power everything, and a radio. No air conditioning. I financed $3450, including interest, at $95.83 per month for 36 months and continued my journey to Independence, arriving there with no further hassles.

As a side note, the car salesman was apparently not blowing smoke when he told me he had someone in mind who might want to buy my old Ford. I took the new Impala back to the Harrisonville dealer a few months later for an oil change, and I saw my old car, all shined up, driving down a street in Harrisonville. They had probably replaced the muffler and tailpipe by that time.

When I arrived at Uncle Howard's house, I showed my new car to him and his family and then settled in and prepared to go to work two days later with Phillips Petroleum Company. I would start looking for an apartment in a few days.

However, as of June 7, I still had received no word from either the Air Force or the Oklahoma National Guard, and I was beginning to get sweaty palms.

Miracles continued to follow me. The second evening I was at Uncle Howard's – the day before I actually started my job with Phillips – I received a phone call from my dad informing me that I would be accepted into the Oklahoma National Guard if I could be in Okemah for the enlistment and swearing-in at 6:00 a.m. on June 11. I told him I would be at their house late the evening of June 10, leaving Kansas City immediately after work that day.

I made the trek to Okemah and officially joined the Oklahoma National Guard, finally bringing closure to the uncertainties that I had been dealing with for the past year. I still had not heard from the Air Force, but at that point, the issue was moot.

June 11, 1966, the official beginning of my future. What next?

In retrospect, if I had not been the best man at Steve Thornton's wedding, I would likely have begun my career with Phillips on Monday, June 6, 1966, and in so doing would have made Phillips history. On June 6, 1966, you see is 6/6/66 date–wise, which is a holy date at Phillips. In the Phillips monthly news publication, *Philnews*, I later saw that five people actually had

176

gone to work for Phillips that day, and their picture was in the publication. Ah, me. Opportunity wasted.

My Uncle Howard's house had three bedrooms with 1 ½ baths plus an unfinished basement. Uncle Howard had a wife and seven – yes, seven – children living at home at the time, so I made occupant number ten in the house. However, they didn't seem to notice my presence so much since I represented only a very small increase percentage-wise in the number of people living there. I got unpacked the next day and prepared myself for my new life.

The Phillips Credit Card Center was located south of downtown Kansas City about 15 miles or so as the crow flies from my Uncle's house, somewhat farther by auto. Office hours were 8:00 a.m. to 4:30 p.m. with a half-hour off for lunch. I didn't know how long it would take to make the drive to the office since I was totally unfamiliar with the distance, the route, and the potential traffic, so I left my Uncle's house at 6:00 a.m. on my first day of work. At that hour, the highways and streets were basically deserted, and I arrived at the office at 6:20. The doors were still locked, and there weren't even any lights on at that time. So, I took a short, nervous nap in my car and then approached the office at about 7:45 and began what was a very happy and satisfying career at Phillips Petroleum – served strangely enough in three different stints. However, those details will be revealed a little later on. The following morning I waited until 7:15 to leave for the office and arrived with time to spare.

As mentioned earlier, I had to make a fast, unexpected trip to Okemah after work on Friday to enlist in the Oklahoma National Guard and then return to Independence very late the following Sunday night.

Shirley and I were to be married on September 3, so it was incumbent upon me to find an apartment that would be suitable for a young single-income married couple. I started searching for lodging the next week and located a duplex at 1424 West Waldo, on Independence's west side. The duplex was located about six blocks from President Harry Truman's mansion. The rent on the duplex was $87.50 per month, and I was to take possession on July 1. My Uncle had to put up with me for another couple of weeks.

The apartment was typical – one bedroom, one bath, kitchen, and living/dining room. It had a hookup for a washing machine, but at that time, I had absolutely no furnishings of any kind. I made the decision to buy some inexpensive, rudimentary furniture so I could "live" there until the wedding. There was an outlet store in Independence named "Wild Woody's," which sold closeout and surplus merchandise at deep discounts. I bought a cheap bedroom set and a very cheap living room set at Wild Woody's, and my parents gave me an old dining table with chairs. Living in those conditions would not be great, but I knew things would get better relatively soon.

Finally, on July 19, I received notice from the Air Force informing me that I had been accepted into the Air Force. They offered me Officer Training School, followed by Fighter Pilot Training. I still have their letter. I was to either report to Lackland Air Force Base, Texas, on November 1, or notify them of my decision to decline the offer. I was pleased with the offer, but my military future had been settled by that time, and I gracefully declined their offer.

The rest of the summer passed without incident. I made my required every–fourth–weekend drills plus a two–week summer camp with the Oklahoma National Guard, spent a few weekends with Shirley in Yellville, and waited until September.

Our wedding was scheduled for September 3, 1966, the Saturday before Labor Day. We scheduled it for that date so that I would have a 3–day weekend, not yet being eligible for a vacation with Phillips.

It was still hot in northern Arkansas at that time, and a day earlier, the air conditioner at the church had gone on the blink. Consequently, the Yellville Church of Christ was pretty uncomfortable when the wedding began in the afternoon. Shirley was miserable under her veil, and sweat was dripping off her face. I suspect the long dress didn't help any, either.

Phil Dixon was my best man, and the other guys in the wedding were Kyle Smock, my former roommate at Harding, and Jerry Brock, my cousin. The minister was Shirley's former principal at her high school, Doyle Davenport. The soloist was Lee Ellen Hendrix, one of my friends from Harding. One of the songs she sang was "You'll Never Walk Alone," which was and remains one of my all-time favorites. It perfectly states my promise to Shirley, that she would never have to walk alone through the storms of life, and I would always be at her side. I realize this may sound a little corny, but it is a promise that is very dear to my heart.

I think every one of the Missouri uncles on my mother's side showed up at the wedding with all their children. My grandmother Brock was also there. It was quite a wonderful family gathering.

Following the wedding, we held a reception at the local electric company's lunchroom, and fortunately, the air conditioning was working at the electric company facility. I will never know how we obtained access free of charge to the electric company facilities, but I didn't ask any questions.

Shirley's parents were in no financial position to pay for a wedding, so I applied some of the financial principles I had learned at work to pay for the wedding, and Shirley borrowed her best friend's wedding dress and veil. Fortunately, both women were of the same size. The church was free, the minister was free, and our use of the electric company's facility was somehow free. The only out–of–pocket expense we incurred was the wedding cake and some decorations. If I remember right, the wedding cost a total of $150.00, and the marriage is now at 50+ years and counting. The lesson here is that the cost of the wedding is irrelevant to the success of the marriage – or at least it should be.

My best man decided it would be clever to chain a cowbell to the back bumper of my new car. When we left the reception, amidst cheers and thrown rice, I heard a really ugly clanging sound coming from the rear of my new car. Outside of town, I pulled off the roadway and discovered the cowbell chained to the bumper, and it had been secured with a combination lock. I didn't happen to be carrying a bolt cutter or a hacksaw on my honeymoon, and there was no way I could pry it loose. I was about to decide to return to Yellville and accost my best man when, to my surprise, he drove up behind me in his car. He parked behind my car, got out and calmly opened the lock. I don't remember any words we exchanged at that moment, but they probably jeopardized our friendship if there were any.

Shirley and I stopped in Eureka Springs, Arkansas, for an abbreviated honeymoon.

The next morning, Sunday, we drove on to Cassville, Missouri, and attended church at the Cassville Church of Christ. I was looking for some of the Stumpff clan, but there were none present that day. However, my grandmother was there, having returned from the wedding. She wasn't expecting to see us, and we didn't think we would see her. When she found us at church, she invited us home for Sunday dinner. Unbeknownst to Shirley and me, my Uncle Don and Aunt Myra and their three children were also having Sunday dinner with Grandma Brock. They had stopped off in Cassville on their way back to Kansas City following the wedding. However, two more unexpected extra mouths to feed made no difference to Grandma. As usual, she had made enough food to feed an army, including three types of meat – fried chicken, roast beef, and baked ham along with all the trimmings – and she apologized for not having anything to serve us. We were amazed, but she did it without effort. I suspect she always had a refrigerator full of goodies just in case someone came to visit. She was great.

Later that afternoon, we made our way to Independence and to our duplex. Our duplex was an upper/lower arrangement, and we had the lower floor. It took us all of 15 minutes to discover that there was a small child living above us that had a very squeaky walker and that he roamed the house at all hours of the day and into the night. It seemed like there was a constant squeaking emanating from our ceiling. However, we lived through it with no damage.

I went to work every day, and Shirley was a homemaker. After a month or so, she inquired as to whether they might have a job for her at the Phillips office. I told her she ought to apply. At the time, I thought it was a slam dunk – here was a beautiful, nice girl with some college that anyone would want to hire. I was right. She was offered a job on the spot when she applied.

We didn't work in the same area of the office, but we commuted together, and we had lunch together, so it was perfect. What we didn't know at the time was her job was another gift from God because two months later, I would be called to Army basic training, and her job would be our only real source of income for about five months. Another coincidence? I don't think so.

THE PROVIDENCE OF GOD

The Providence of God continued to bless me while we settled into life in Independence:

1. I was gently introduced to career, financial, marriage, and family responsibilities by close family members and newly found colleagues at my workplace.

2. Shirley landed a very timely job early on, which carried us through what would have been a financial crisis just a few months later.

It had seemed that God always seemed to put me in the right place at the right time to enrich my life. Continuing, hither by His help, I had come.

Twenty

MILITARY SERVICE (1966–1972)

$\mathbf{M}$y military service spanned a total of six years and overlapped two separate periods of employment with Phillips Petroleum, plus one with Hallmark Cards. Rather than fit the military service anecdotes piecemeal into the overall narrative, it seems more appropriate to describe it in a single chapter, with the realization that the whole drama stretches from June 1966 through June 1972. Here goes.

In early June 1966, I had moved to Independence, Missouri, and had begun my initial employment with Phillips Petroleum. As mentioned earlier, I had also been sworn into the Oklahoma National Guard the same week that I began my employment. Shortly after my being sworn into the National Guard, my unit was sent for its two weeks Army summer training at Fort Chaffee, an Army post near Fort Smith, Arkansas.

The Oklahoma National Guard was an infantry unit and was classified as a "Standby Ready Force" or "SRF." In 1966 the war in Vietnam was heating up, and SRF units were subjected to special treatment by the Department of the Army. SRF units were required to train with the same intensity and with the same purpose as active Army units. Of course, the only difference was that the SRF units weren't stationed at Army posts and could not train daily. Instead, the SRF units met on weekends every four weeks plus two weeks in the summer and underwent typical active army training – field exercises, firing range, etc. The purpose of the special attention paid to SRF units was that they were basically "on call," to be called to active duty at a moment's notice and thereby bypass the extensive training required to bring a non–SRF unit up to combat readiness. Basically, an SRF unit could be sent into battle in a matter of a very few weeks as opposed to several months of training required by other Reserve and National Guard units. Not only that, the Oklahoma National Guard Thunderbirds had served heroically in both World War II and Korea, and everyone assumed that they would eventually be called to serve in Vietnam.

Despite the mosquitos and heat, I had managed to survive my two weeks' summer camp and returned to Kansas City and my job. The albatross hanging over my head during this time was my impending call to basic and advanced military training. Whether active Army or National Guard and Reserves, every new soldier had to undergo roughly three months of basic training followed immediately by another three months of advanced training. When you are called up for the training in the National Guard and Reserves, you are for the most part separated from your family – and job – for up to six consecutive months. The date of my entry into training was uncertain, but everyone figured it would be prior to the end of 1966.

However, awaiting my call–up, throughout the summer and into the fall, I continued to meet for weekend drills at Okemah every four weeks. Bear in mind that I was living in Independence, Missouri, at the time and working in the Phillips Petroleum office in Kansas City. To make the 6:00 a.m. roll call on the Saturday mornings of the drills every four weeks, I had to drive from Independence to Okemah on Friday afternoon after work, arriving at Okemah sometime after midnight, and then be up bright-eyed and bushy-tailed, shaven and spit-shined, so to speak, at the armory at 6:00 a.m. I would then return to Independence each Sunday evening following the conclusion of the drill, arriving home well after midnight.

Come Thanksgiving, I still had not received my call to basic training. Shirley and I had planned to spend the Thanksgiving holidays with her parents in Yellville. Bill Dye, my friend from Harding, who also worked in the Phillips office in Kansas City, was also heading to his parents' home for the holiday. His parents still lived in Little Rock, Arkansas, and since he had to drive near Yellville on the way to and from Little Rock, he offered to take Shirley and me with him and drop us off in Yellville. He would then pick us up on the way back to Kansas City the following Sunday afternoon. That sounded like a good idea to us, and we all left Kansas City early Wednesday afternoon, the day before Thanksgiving.

The best-laid plans of mice and men . . .

As usual the unusual happened, as has been a frequent occurrence over my life. It was exactly at that time that the Army chose to call me up for basic training, and it was exactly at that time that I had chosen chose to go off the grid, so to speak. It would be very difficult for anyone to contact me at the Swayne's very rural house given that they had no telephone - but who would be trying to contact me over Thanksgiving anyway? When we arrived in Yellville later that Wednesday evening, I was basically incommunicado.

As was its practice, the Department of the Army, when it wanted something done, it wanted it done yesterday. The Army had decided, apparently on the Wednesday before Thanksgiving, that I was to report for basic training the following Monday. The Army notified my National Guard commanding officer of this information, and my Commanding Officer dutifully called my house in Independence later that afternoon to notify me. By that time, Shirley and I were halfway to Arkansas in Bill Dye's car.

My Commanding Officer, Lt. Kenneth Clark, however, was resourceful and contacted my parents, who still lived in Okemah, to see if there was any way to reach me. My parents were aware that Shirley and I were at her parents' house for the weekend but also knew they had no phone. They made a few calls and learned that a man named Burleigh Baker owned a rural grocery store near Shirley's parents' house and gave Lt. Clark Mr. Baker's phone number. By now, it was Thursday, Thanksgiving Day, and Mr. Baker's store was closed.

Lt. Clark waited until Friday morning to contact Mr. Baker to request that he deliver a message to me at the Swayne household, of which Mr. Baker was familiar. Mid-morning on Friday, Mr. Baker showed up at the Swayne house with a note for me to call a Lt. Clark in Okemah, Oklahoma. I immediately knew it was one of two things – either I was being called to basic training, or, worse, our unit was being activated for Vietnam. I crossed my fingers and went to Mr. Baker's store to make the call.

Lt. Clark informed me that I must be in Oklahoma City by Monday afternoon to catch a flight to some place called Fort Ord, California, near Monterey. How I got to Oklahoma City was going to be my problem because I was ostensibly an Okemah, Oklahoma, area resident in the Oklahoma National Guard and was expected to be readily available when things like this happened.

On Sunday morning, Shirley's brother took me to a bus station in Harrison, Arkansas. I bought a ticket to Okemah, arriving there late Sunday evening, spending the night with my parents. Okemah was only 70 miles from Oklahoma City, so my parents planned to take me on to OKC the following morning.

Shirley's mother was very reluctant to let her go back to Independence alone, so she packed her bags to return there with her. When Bill Dye showed up at the Swayne house on Sunday afternoon to take Shirley and me back to

Independence, he was surprised to learn that Shirley had swapped me for her mother.

There were five of the Okemah soldiers who were to report to Fort Ord at that time. We all met at Will Rogers International Airport in Oklahoma City, boarded a plane, and began our active military odyssey. Getting to this point had not been easy, and it had been unusual – which seemed to be becoming the norm.

There are some Fort Ord anecdotes that were interesting.

Fort Ord is located near Monterey, California, overlooking Monterey Bay – absolutely beautiful scenery, absolutely prime real estate. Neighboring communities are Salinas and Carmel, and the Pebble Beach Golf Course. Cannery Row and all its seafood restaurants are right there. The Monterey area is the setting for most of John Steinbeck's novels, and his writings accurately capture the nature of the culture there.

Upon arriving at the fort, I was issued uniforms, and I was inoculated, oriented, and had my head shaved and moved into my barracks.

Some years earlier, there had been a meningitis outbreak at Fort Ord, so extraordinary precautions were still in place to prevent a recurrence. For one thing, every trainee wore a white patch above his name tag on his uniform shirt. That white tag meant that you could not venture beyond your barracks without appropriate accompaniment by an officer or an NCO. No going to the PX alone, not that you had the time to do so anyway.

One other thing was explained to us as we settled into the barracks. We were told that we were guaranteed eight hours of sleep every night. That was not entirely true. They actually meant that the barracks lights were turned out every evening at 9:00 p.m. and remained off until 5:00 a.m. the next morning – eight hours. What they didn't tell us was that we had to do a lot of things after the lights were turned off, and we were regularly awakened well before 5:00 a.m. You can do a lot of things in the dark of the early morning. You can get dressed and groomed – the latrine lights remained on all the time. You could form up your platoon outside because the outdoor lighting was always on from dusk to dawn and provided enough light for you to come to attention and to "dress and cover." And the moon usually provided enough light at that time for you to march in formation to the drill area and police up the cigarette butts and other trash. That left plenty of time to march back to the barracks and stand at attention until Reveille was sounded, ostensibly to wake us up, and despite the fact that we had already been up and around for about two hours. As a side note – Reveille was intended to wake the troops up, not call us to attention in formation outside in the dark. But that is an argument for another day. Anyway, we would sometimes get in more than an hour of activity before the barracks lights came on in the morning. Ah, I miss those days.

One great thing about Fort Ord, however, was the chow in the mess hall. The fort was located very near portions of California's Central Valley, where more than half the fruits, vegetables, and nuts in the United States were grown. Consequently, the produce was very fresh, delivered daily, and the cooks were pretty good. Not only that, but there were dairies in the area, and we had all the chocolate and white milk we could drink.

The food was far superior to the food I partook of at Fort Dix, New Jersey, where I was stationed following my time at Fort Ord. In fact, there were only two meals during my nine weeks at Fort Ord, which I remember being duds. One was an attempted slight–of–hand by the cooks. We marched into the mess hall one day and were greeted with what appeared to be some very delicious–looking steaks, and everyone asked for a big one. When we sat down to eat, we discovered that the "steaks" were actually liver, which almost no one liked. Much to the dismay of the cooks and the brass, the garbage cans, where we dumped leftovers from our trays, overfilled very rapidly.

The only other bad meal was just an unintentional SNAFU. We had field exercises scheduled for very early one morning, so our breakfast was to be only cold cereal and milk. The only problem was that the milk dispensers that early in the morning had not been serviced yet, and the only milk available was chocolate milk. So I ate my Wheaties with chocolate milk, and it would have done no good to have complained.

I should also mention that our Company cadre was very professional. Many of the officers and NCO's had already served in Vietnam, and they relied on knowledge and experience rather than theory when commanding a trainee company. They knew how to handle soldiers, and consequently, we had no leader/trainee incidents in my time there that I was aware of.

A few days after we had gotten settled in, I was again confronted by what I term a small miracle – my experience at Harding as a writer for the *Bison* paid off almost immediately. Fort Ord, like all Army posts, published a weekly newspaper. Company commanders were encouraged to submit interesting tidbits concerning their soldiers for publication in the fort newspaper. Also, company commanders typically review the dossiers, as it were, of all incoming trainees to see what they might have in their backgrounds and training that might be useful during their time in their units. My company commander picked up on the fact that I had been a writer for my college newspaper. He called me into his office and told me that if I would agree to write one short article each week about someone in the company – a group of nearly 250 soldiers – that I would be exempt from KP for the duration of

basic training. It took me less than one second to agree to his offer. I dutifully turned in a short article each week, two of which were published in the post
newspaper. One article spoke of one of my buddies in the Okemah unit, David Rhoades, who had been a major league prospect as a pitcher until he hurt
his arm. The other story, which was published, told of a soldier from Kansas
City who had played semi-pro football – but just not quite good enough to
make the big time. No KP for me. It seemed that Harding's experience just
kept on paying dividends.

We had hardly gotten accustomed to military life when we had an opportunity to leave for a while. Although I began my basic training after Thanksgiving, the Army granted two weeks' leave to everyone at Christmas. We
were able to leave the fort mid–December but had to be back in the barracks
by 1700 hours (5:00 p.m.) on January 1. The only hitch was that we were
on our own to get home and then get back to Fort Ord on time. The Army
would transport us to San Francisco International Airport (SFO) on busses,
but we had to pay for our own airline tickets. The only other alternative was
to remain on base in the barracks for the two-week period and to eat Army
chow. No one to my recollection exercised that option.

By the time of Christmas leave, I had not even been on active duty long
enough to draw any pay, so I was basically broke. When I learned of the opportunity to come home for a few days, I asked Shirley to send me my final
Phillips check, which had paid me through the Thanksgiving holiday. We
got paid at Phillips twice per month, so I had been paid for what amounted
to one week of work – from November 16 through Thanksgiving. She sent
the check to me, and it was for $102 and some change.

When we were released for Christmas leave, I got on the bus, not knowing if the trip to SFO would be one–way or round trip. I had no idea at that
point, the cost of a plane ticket back to Kansas City, and if it was more than
$102, I would be returning to the fort for the holidays. I was sweating bullets
when I approached the airline counter and asked about a ticket to KC. At
that point, I fully believe God was watching me, and once again handing me
a little miracle. The ticket agent said the fare to Kansas City was $98 one–
way, and he cashed my check, giving me about $4.00 in change – enough to
buy a little food in the airport. I don't know how one defines miracles, but I
believe that was one.

And God was not done yet. An even more remarkable miracle would
occur a few days later on my return to Fort Ord.

While at home for the holiday in Independence, I decided to visit the
Phillips Credit Card Center one day and say hello to all my co-workers there.
One of those I visited with was my friend and practical joker, George Bayless.

I distinctly remember when I showed up in the office that morning, he asked me, "Oh, have you been gone?"

But the thing I most remember about George was the miracle he made possible. We were talking, and it got around to basic training and Fort Ord. He wasn't sure where Fort Ord was, so I told him that it was near Monterey and Salinas. He asked me when I was returning, and I replied that I had to be back on the fort on New Year's afternoon. However, at that time, I had no idea as to how I would return.

Then the miracle occurred.

He said he had a friend who was a school teacher from Salinas (of all places) who was visiting Kansas City (of all places) during the holidays (of all times), and he asked if I might like to ride back to California with her when she headed back home after Christmas (of all times). He said she was driving her car and could probably use some relief along the way. How could this have just been a random coincidence? All this seems so improbable, but if I am lying, I am dying.

At that point, I was stunned. This was against all odds. Things like this just don't happen. This was against all the odds. I was broke and had no legitimate way to get back to the fort, and here was a ride back timely and free of cost dumped into my lap.

I accepted gratefully, arrangements were made, and at 6:00 a.m. on December 31, the lady showed up at my house in Independence, and we set out for California. Thirty–six hours later, she dropped me off at my barracks at 1600 hours (4:00 p.m.) California time, one hour ahead of the deadline. There is no way in the world this was merely a coincidence.

Once we returned from Christmas leave the training got serious. It became very intense since the objective of the training was to ultimately prepare the soldiers for combat in Vietnam. We engaged in physical fitness and hand–to–hand combat exercises plus training on the various weapons, particularly the M14 rifle, the bayonet, hand grenades, and the M79 grenade launcher. During the M79 grenade launcher training, I experienced an event that was at first frightening but turned to be almost hilarious.

Visually, the M79 grenade launcher resembles a large bore, break–action, sawed-off shotgun. The front sight is a typical fixed blade, but the launcher is also equipped with a fold-up rear sight that must be visually aligned with the front sight when targeting something. Since the ammunition is not a bullet but rather a bulky grenade, it is not fired on a straight line like a rifle. Instead, it is lobbed at the target, hence the need for the special type of sights. The rear sight can be adjusted for ranges from 75 to 375 meters, the effective range of the grenade launcher. The grenade itself is shaped like a large, fat bullet, is about 1½ inches in diameter, and weighs about a half-pound. The procedure is to estimate the distance to the target, set the rear sight to that range, align both sights, and fire away. The arc of the grenade's path requires 3 or 4 seconds to reach a target 175 meters away. The grenade explodes on impact, much like a small bomb.

During the training, a soldier is issued a launcher loaded with a live grenade and is told the estimated distance to the target. During my training session, the target was approximately 175 meters distant. I took the launcher, lay down prone on the ground, set the fold-up sight to 175 meters, aligned it with the front sight, and pulled the trigger.

In less than one second, the grenade hit the ground only about 50 meters in front of the firing line, startling everyone on the line and making a crater more than 100 meters short of the intended target. About one second later, one of the sergeants confronted me, yanked me to my feet, called me a few choice names, and asked me if I was trying to kill everyone. I said, "I think the rear sight is defective."

"Gimme that launcher," he said and jerked it out of my hands.

He reloaded the launcher, lay down, adjusted the rear sight to 175 meters, sighted in on the target, and pulled the trigger. Less than one second later, his grenade landed in the same crater I had created and exploded, once again startling everyone on the firing line.

He calmly got up, carefully avoiding looking me in the eye, handed the grenade launcher to one of the officers, and he said, and I quote, "I think the rear sight is defective, sir." He then walked away with nary another word to me. I was issued another launcher, sighted in, fired, and hit pretty close to the target at 175 meters. I know the sergeant was embarrassed.

In keeping with my history of out–of–the–ordinary events, my unit was selected for a grand experiment by the Army. The experiment involved our rifle qualifying session. Basically, after several days of rifle orientation and firing practice at the firing range, it is necessary to determine if the trainees had actually learned how to use a rifle – in our case, the M–14 rifle. To accomplish this, the soldiers were taken to the test range for firing at something other than a stationary bullseye.

The targets at the test range were "pop up" human-shaped targets, which would pop up randomly in the soldier's field of fire. They would remain stationary for no more than 5 seconds, at which time they would disappear again. The field of fire was more than 200 meters deep and about 25 meters wide, and the targets could and would pop up one at a time randomly anyplace in the field of fire – much like an enemy combatant. It was the responsibility of the soldier to locate a target, take aim, and fire. If the bullet hit the target, it would knock it down, and another target would pop up elsewhere within a few seconds, and the procedure was repeated. It was very clear which targets had been knocked down and which had merely disappeared when the 5 seconds expired. A member of the company's cadre – usually a Corporal or a Sergeant – observed the soldier's firing and would keep score as to how many targets were hit.

At the time, at Fort Ord, there were two test ranges – one facing south and one facing east. The practice had been to conduct firing tests on the south-facing range in the morning when the sun was in the eastern sky and conduct firing tests on the east-facing range in the afternoon when the sun moved to the southern sky. The point of all this was to prevent the soldiers from looking directly into the sun to locate and fire on the targets. Since the war in Vietnam was escalating, the Army decided to try this new tactic to put more soldiers through the qualifying than was possible under the current scenario. Our company was chosen as the guinea pig. Yea, for us!

The new protocol was to basically ignore the position of the sun during the firing tests and to use both test ranges simultaneously – theoretically doubling the number of soldiers who could be put through the firing tests in the same amount of time. We guinea pigs were selected to fire on the east-facing range relatively early in the morning. At that hour of the day in midwinter, the sun was barely over the eastern horizon, and as a result, the pupils in our eyes were constricted to about the size of pinpoints. In other words, our vision was severely impaired. Bear in mind that many of the targets were 200 meters out, and those targets were difficult to spot even under optimum light conditions.

The firing test consisted of 40 rounds of ammunition issued to each soldier, and the results of a soldier's firing test fell into one of four categories – "Expert," "Sharpshooter," "Marksman," and "bolo." To qualify as Expert, the soldier had to hit 36 or more targets out of the 40, as Sharpshooter 30–35 out of 40, and as Marksman at least 23. Below 23 was a bolo, and a visit with the C.O. Vision was so badly impaired shooting into the sun that out of approximately 250 soldiers in our company that took the firing test that day, there were exactly zero who qualified Expert, only three qualified as Sharpshooter and everyone else who eventually qualified earned a Marksman rating. The test protocol was a disaster.

I earned a Marksman badge, and it did not come easily. After 39 shots, I had hit exactly 22 targets. I had to hit the last target or face the C.O. with a bolo. Of course, the final target was the farthest out on the left side, about 200 meters away. By a miracle, I spotted it and cut loose with a round, and by another miracle, the round hit the target, and I qualified – barely.

In addition to being tested in their ability to fire weapons, soldiers also had to go through physical fitness tests and agility tests. Among these was the PCPT test – the Physical Combat Proficiency Test – which all soldiers had to endure and pass – or else have another opportunity to bolo. The test consisted of five events: low crawl, horizontal ladder bars, grenade throw, 'run, dodge and jump' (agility drill), and a 1–mile run. While completing the test, soldiers were required to wear their combat uniform (sans jacket) and boots.

Once again, my time at Harding had paid off. Participating extensively in the intramural sports at Harding had left me in pretty good shape come basic training. I was able to score the maximum (100 points) on every event except the mile run. To score 100 points, the mile had to be run in 6 minutes or less. I could probably have made it in less than 6 minutes if I hadn't had to wear combat boots and fatigues (long pants). As it was, I ran the mile in 6:09, and the 9 seconds over 6 minutes cost me 9 points. For the PCPT, I scored 491 of a possible 500 points. Those who scored over 450 were given a special table at mess (meals) for the duration of the training.

The remainder of my time at Fort Ord was pretty routine. In mid–February, I was sent to Fort Dix, New Jersey, for my advanced training. Three of my fellow Oklahoma National Guard trainees at Fort Ord were also sent to Fort Dix, so at least I had some people I knew at my new assignment. We flew from San Francisco International Airport to Philadelphia. It was 72 degrees in San Francisco when we left and minus 4 degrees in Philadelphia when we arrived there. There were some serious adjustments to be made over the next few weeks. As it turned out, we were issued legitimate cold weather clothing at Ford Dix, so once we had received the winter gear, we were not overly burdened by the colder weather.

When my fellow Okies and I arrived at Fort Dix, we were made aware that there were 237 soldiers in our Company, including 231 regular Army (draftees and voluntary enlistees) and only six, yes six, National Guardsmen. We four Okies and two other National Guardsmen, were the only "reservists" in the company. On top of that, all of the 231 regular Army soldiers were Officer Candidate School trainees, which generally implied they were gung–ho soldiers.

The regular Army soldiers learned very soon who the six reservists were, and this created mixed emotions among the regulars as to how we would be accepted. On the one hand, the regulars were incensed that the reservists would be going back home in eight weeks while the regulars would all probably be eventually sent to Vietnam. On the other hand, we were somewhat envied for those very same reasons. In the end, we were tolerated and managed to coexist without incident.

190

I was trained on the use of the 81–millimeter mortar and qualified Expert in its use. We were not subjected to any squirrely new experimental procedures at Fort Dix in the mortar training and qualification. I also a qualified expert in the use of the .45 caliber pistol while at Fort Dix. That gave me two Expert badges plus the Marksman badge I had earned at Fort Ord.

Overall, the training at Fort Dix was manageable, and we were allowed much more personal freedom during advanced training than we had experienced during basic training. During the eight weeks I spent at Fort Dix, I managed to get five-weekend leaves. I visited New York two weekends and Baltimore, Philadelphia, and Washington D.C. one weekend each.

As mentioned earlier, while at Fort Dix, I ran into Perry Dalby, one of my former classmates at Oklahoma Christian College. Perry was in another unit but was also an Officer Candidate. Ultimately, he had a very distinguished military career and eventually retired as a 2–star General.

My mother's cousin, Col. Darwin Brock, US Army (Ret.), lived in Temple Hills, Maryland, a suburb of Washington D.C. He had been a tank commander in World War II under General Patton. When I visited him, I didn't know whether to salute him or hug him – so I did both. He gave me a VIP tour of D.C. that weekend, and we were able to talk about family and home at length.

My final memory of my time at Fort Dix concerns our processing out. Processing out is the procedure by which those being discharged from active duty are officially turned loose and sent home. Before a soldier leaves the fort, however, he has to go through a final physical, and then he is given an airline ticket home. We were to receive our physical exam in the morning and be on an airplane back home by evening.

We, six reservists, made our way to the dispensary along with soldiers from other companies who were either processing out or who were scheduled for physical exams for one reason or another. There were a hundred or more of us lined up at the dispensary, and we were lined up in alphabetical order by last name. The name of the soldier immediately in front of me in the line was Vanover – just ahead of Vaughan. He was not a member of my company, so I don't know whether he was a reservist or regular Army just being discharged. At any rate, he had apparently had enough of whatever Army service he had been a part of and had decided to get in some last licks on his perceived tormenters as he exited from active duty.

An important point to remember is that all the medical personnel conducting the exams were regular Army, in for the long haul, and not going home anytime soon. As we approached the entrance to the dispensary, Private Vanover began with his trash-talking, reminding all the regulars that he

191

would be eating good food and sleeping on a soft bed before the day was over. They would all still be wearing green canvas uniforms and eating Army chow. And on and on and on. I tapped him on the shoulder, and, quoting a very prophetic line Harrison Ford would utter in the movie "Witness" nineteen years later, I said simply, "You are making a mistake." I advised him to keep it down until he was actually out the gate. However, he ignored me and kept mouthing off.

Long story short, the medics had some "trouble" drawing his blood and had to stick him several times. Then they fouled up his paperwork, and there was an unscheduled prostate exam. The medical staff's effort in this charade was so well choreographed that it was obvious this wasn't their first rodeo. As I was leaving the dispensary, having completed my exam and clutching my airline ticket, Private Vanover was being escorted back inside due to still another problem. As he passed me on the way back inside, he told me he should have listened to me and that his discharge was being delayed at least one day and maybe more. It reminded me of an old adage my dad once told me: "Never, ever insult the alligators until you are out of the swamp."

I left Fort Dix and returned to Independence without further incident.

I reported back to work at Phillips, and life resumed basically as it had been before my being called to active duty.

However, I still had to go to Okemah every four weeks for training, so I began to seek a transfer to a National Guard or Reserve unit closer to Kansas City. I was eventually able to transfer into the 110th Combat Engineers Battalion of the Missouri National Guard sometime late in 1967. Combat Engineers pretty aptly describes their role – they perform engineering work such as building roads and bridges, constructing buildings, etc., under combat conditions. They proudly carried both a shovel and a rifle while on duty. When I transferred to the 110th, I was placed in the medical unit. And, as with the Oklahoma National Guard, the 110th was also an SRF unit.

Three memorable events come to mind when I recall my time with the 110th. The first event involved the 110th's activities in the aftermath of the assassination of Dr. Martin Luther King, Jr. on April 4, 1968. Those activities will be described in a later chapter.

The second significant event transpired several months after my transfer into the medical unit when I was required to formally qualify for my new Method of Service (MOS) as a combat medic. At that point, my official MOS was an infantryman with a mortar specialty, MOS 11c, but the Combat Engineers unit had conditionally accepted my transfer into the unit pending my demonstrated ability to actually function as a combat medic, MOS 91b. It was one thing to train me on how to give shots and apply bandages, but it was an entirely different thing to prove that I knew medical terminology, medical equipment usage, and how to treat injuries. Hence, a written test was administered to certify my qualification. I viewed this as potentially problematic in that I had not undergone medic training while on active duty. In my previous formal training, I had learned how to drop a mortar round into a trash can from a quarter mile away, but I had learned nothing about triage, for instance.

It was scary because if I failed the test, one of two things would likely happen – either I would be discharged from the unit and placed back in the pool of eligible draftees, or I would be sent back to the Oklahoma National Guard if they still had a slot for me, which was doubtful. Needless to say, I was sweating blood when I showed up for the exam. However, I actually passed the test and qualified as a combat medic. I attributed this directly to Dr. Robert T. Clark's Biology 101 and 102 classes at Harding and how he stressed practical anatomy and physiology over flora and fauna. It seems that Harding just kept on giving and giving.

The third memorable event occurred at Fort Leonard Wood in Missouri in 1968 at the 110th's annual summer camp. It is one thing to be labeled a medical unit, but it is an entirely different thing to actually be able to practice medicine. The medical unit of the 110th contained NCO qualified medics and, per regulations, a fully licensed physician. Captain Lambert, M.D., was our physician. The ranking NCO in the medical unit was Sgt. Larry Swanson. Sgt. Swanson had a sebaceous cyst on his right forearm – a small lump. Such cysts are not dangerous but are mostly just a nuisance, always getting bumped or scraped. Sgt. Swanson had scraped his cyst during the exercises one day and was complaining about it. We were sitting in the barracks that evening shooting the breeze, listening to Larry complain when Captain Lambert happened to walk in. The Captain looked at the injury and asked Larry if he would like the cyst removed. The doctor said it was a piece of cake, and he could handle it that evening in the barracks if Larry wanted him to. What, no sterile environment with nurses running everywhere? It sounded like a death wish.

The very title "Combat Engineers Battalion" implies that the unit was trained to perform its duties under combat conditions. Consequently, the expectation was that a medical unit attached to Combat Engineers Battalion would be able to treat wounds in the forest, in a ditch, in a rainstorm, in combat – wherever it was when the wounded needed treatment. Typically, an army field hospital was a large tent. Therefore, a simple surgical procedure in an army barracks was indeed a piece of cake when compared to the conditions under which we were expected to be able to work.

Sgt. Swanson readily agreed to the surgery. Captain Lambert and two of the other medics donned gloves and masks, and the surgery began. It was a simple operation – local anesthesia, a small incision, tying off a small blood supply to the cyst, popping the cyst out, and using about three or four stitches to close the wound. It really was a piece of cake. The doctor applied a bandage, and we all went back to whatever we were doing before the operation. Very routine. If nothing else, it proved that our medical unit was legitimate and knew what it was doing. It also gave us something to talk about for a while. Given our duties in the medical unit when placed in context with the escalating war in Vietnam at the time, there was never a dull moment.

About two years after the operation in the barracks at Ft. Leonard Wood, my military career took another turn. As will be discussed in future chapters, in early1970, I wound up working for Phillips Petroleum (again), this time in Bartlesville, Oklahoma (where else?). Since I still had two years of military obligation to complete, it seemed prudent for me to hook up with another Army unit close to Bartlesville. If I could find such a unit, it would eliminate my need to travel back to Kansas City every four weeks for drills with the 110th Combat Engineers.

After the dust had settled following my move to Bartlesville, I checked around and discovered that there was indeed an Army Reserve unit actually headquartered in Bartlesville. It was an Artillery unit, but that in itself did not disqualify me from transferring into it. There were plenty of service specialties in military units that overlapped from unit to unit, and with my education and military background, I figured that I could fit in somewhere.

Before I had actually taken steps to seek the transfer, another "small world" event occurred. As mentioned in an earlier chapter, I had a friend in Bartlesville named Joe Barker, a member of our church, who had lived in Ada when my family lived there and moved to Bartlesville shortly before my dad had been transferred there. We had known the Barkers well in Ada and had renewed our friendship when my family moved to Bartlesville in 1960. When Shirley and I arrived in Bartlesville in 1970 from Kansas City, I was once again reunited with the Barkers. It turns out that Joe had been an officer in the Army Reserve Artillery unit in Bartlesville and still maintained contact with the leadership there. When I mentioned my desire to possibly transfer into the unit, he promised to call them and put in a good word for me.

True to his word, a few days later, I received a call from the Chief Warrant Officer Kirby of the Artillery unit. Chief Warrant Officers are never referred to as "Sir" or "Sergeant." Rather, they are addressed as "Mister." I never did learn what Mr. Kirby's first name was.

Mr. Kirby told me that I would indeed be able to transfer in and that the paperwork should be completed by the time of their next weekend drill, which was to occur two weekends hence. He told me to show up at 6:00 a.m. the Saturday morning of the drill, ready to go. Since I already had uniforms, it was not necessary to obtain new uniforms from the Artillery unit. Actually, all was needed was for new insignia shoulder patches to be issued and sewn on my existing shirts and field jacket. I thanked him and told him I was eager to join the unit.

Then a strange scenario developed. In retrospect, I should not have been surprised since I had been a participant in so many strange scenarios over the years. At this point, Phillips Petroleum Company was interested in employee health and provided many recreational activities to promote good employee health – one of which was an employee basketball league. The games were usually played on weeknights at the Phillips Petroleum gym. Employees formed their own teams – some were loaded with ex–varsity players and some were just ordinary guys looking for a little exercise in an enjoyable environment. Given my interest in athletics and a reasonable ability to play basketball, I eagerly joined a team that was being formed. Jim Phillips, a friend of mine from my employment in Kansas City and who had also been transferred to Bartlesville, was on my team. Our team was comprised mostly of ordinary guys looking for a little exercise – no super players, but no duds either.

One Tuesday evening, very shortly after my transfer to Bartlesville, we were playing against a team made up of very good players. We played man–to–man defense, and I drew a guy named Dean Nixon. He was two inches taller and at least thirty pounds heavier than I, and there was no fat. He was a very experienced player, and during the game, he drove me nuts. He was very good at subtly grabbing my jersey, gaining a position with a gentle elbow shove, and frequently sending me in a different direction with a little hip thrust. None of these activities warranted a foul. They are just part of the game and are very effective when employed by an experienced player. As a result of all these factors, he totally dominated me during the game. Nearing the end of the game, I had been called for four fouls (five fouls and you are out of the game), and I was totally frustrated and losing my cool. We were losing badly, so I decided to get in a good lick if I could.

The opportunity presented itself with about a minute left in the game. Dean was making a powerful drive along the baseline toward the basket, and I was between him and the basket. I saw Jim Phillips go airborne in his wake, and Dean was bearing down on me at full speed. As he arrived, I pivoted, and using his momentum and a healthy nudge by my hip, I redirected him and sent him flying over the baseline and crashing into the wall behind the basket. Dean was not hurt in any way, and I figured that I had fouled out, but at least

I got in my licks. As it turns out, just before my collision with Dean, he had fouled Jim Phillips when he sent him flying, so my foul didn't count. Dean gathered himself and walked over to me and said, "Well played." He was not angry; he was not injured; it was just part of the game—no harm, no foul, so to speak.

That game was on Tuesday evening. Fast forward to Saturday, my first drill with my new Artillery unit. I showed up all spit-shined at 6:00 a.m. and met with Mr. Kirby in the office. He introduced me to the First Sergeant, John Bond. 1SGT Bond welcomed me to the unit and showed me my work area. I was going to be the "Radar O'Reilly" of the unit, the company clerk. 1SGT Bond then told me he wanted to introduce me to the company commanding officer.

He led me down to the CO's office and knocked on the door. When we heard "Enter," we walked in. I immediately came to attention and saluted, and then I looked at the individual behind the desk. It was none other than Captain Dean Nixon. He looked at me, obviously recognizing me from the basketball game, said, "At ease, soldier," and then he chuckled. We briefly discussed the game. Thank God there were no hard feelings. In the end, he said, "I am glad to have soldiers with spunk." He then dismissed me. I saluted, left his office, and tried not to faint.

But, amazing as it was, the story does not end there. Since the weekend drills lasted all day Saturday and all day Sunday, I did not have an opportunity to attend church on Sunday on drill weekends. My next opportunity would come the following Wednesday evening when the church met for mid-week services. I showed up at the church building that evening with absolutely no thought of the previous weekend. As I enter the building, the first person I see is Captain Dean Nixon. I once again nearly fainted. He had probably been at most of the services I had attended after moving to Bartlesville but, without the terror of seeing him with Captain's bars on his shirt, I had not recognized nor remembered him. He shook my hand, and we chatted briefly regarding basketball and Army. Another incredible small–world event that defies all logic.

Dean was transferred by Phillips Petroleum a few months later, and I never ran into him again. However, my unusual experiences with him remain locked in my memory. And I will always owe a debt of gratitude to him for his handling of our initial "meeting" and my subsequent participation in the Artillery unit in Bartlesville.

However, the whole episode – the Barkers, the available opening in the Artillery unit at Bartlesville, Captain Dean Nixon – when combined with our family's initial association with the Smith and Hall families and the National

Guard unit in Okemah, appeared to have had the hand of God involved. Solving my military obligation was central to the rest of my life. As with other unusual events in my life, this episode was so much against the odds that there had to be a greater power intimately involved – God.

My military service concluded on June 30, 1972, and I was honorably discharged with a rank of Specialist 4th Class.

At the time, I still lived, temporarily, in Bartlesville, temporarily in the employment of Phillips Petroleum.

All in all, my military experience was very satisfying and very complementary to my married and professional life. Even the things that got potentially crossways – my miraculous return to Fort Ord following Christmas leave, for example – worked themselves out without adverse consequences. I had honorably fulfilled my military obligation, exposing myself to likely duty in Vietnam due to the SRF status of the units I belonged to. Still, even that worked out well in the end.

THE PROVIDENCE OF GOD

It has to go without saying that the military segment of my life was fraught with examples of the hand of God. When I considered each of these events later and then looked at them as a whole, it became obvious that God's Providence had to have been involved, and I raised an Ebenezer.

1. Friends from Okemah helped usher me into the Oklahoma National Guard – friends whom I would never have met had my dad not been transferred by his company to Okemah.

2. At Christmas, while at Fort Ord, half a continent away from my wife, I received a $102 paycheck on an extremely timely basis, and it paid for my plane ticket from San Francisco to Kansas City – the best Christmas present I ever received.

3. A spur of the moment visit with George Bayless resulted in my being able to return to Fort Ord on a timely basis and without cost.

4. Dr. Clark's Biology class at Harding had given me the knowledge to pass the combat medic MOS test, which enabled me to keep my slot in the 110th Combat Engineers' medical unit.

5. The presence of Joe Barker, an old friend from Ada, and his influence with the Army Reserve Artillery Unit in Bartlesville, enabled me to transfer into that unit with a minimum of hassle. That would have never occurred had he not moved to Bartlesville.

197

6. My introduction to the Artillery Unit commanding officer is a story for the ages.

If any one of these events had not occurred, my military life and, by extension, my married life and career and my entire life would have turned out entirely differently and most likely much less pleasant. Were these accidents or celestial Providence? When these events are stacked up with the myriad of other "accidents" in my life, I feel that the answer is obvious. These could only have been due to the hand of God.

Twenty-One

PHILLIPS PETROLEUM – PART 1 (1966–1968)

When I reported for work that first day, June 9, 1966, I was welcomed to the team and was placed in Gil Baumgart's section. Jerry Martin, a member of Gil's group, was assigned as my mentor for the next several weeks until I got the hang of things. My friend Bill Dye from Harding went to work in the same office on the same day, so, once again – as at Bartlesville, Oklahoma Christian, Oklahoma University and later at Harding – I was welcomed into a new environment by a familiar face. This was beginning to become a familiar tune, and I liked it very much.

The Phillips Petroleum credit card operations were state of the art and were likely most efficient of all the oil company credit card operations at the time. In 1966 VISA and MasterCard were still about five years from being widely introduced. American Express, Diner's Club, and Carte Blanch credit cards were available but were used primarily for dining, travel, and hotel charges. By that time, however, the major oil companies – Phillips 66, Exxon, Texaco, Amoco, etc. – had discovered that an effective means of promoting sales of their products and enhancing brand loyalty was the introduction of their own branded credit cards – what were known as "proprietary" credit cards. In most cases, an oil company credit card could be used only at a branded, or proprietary, location – a gasoline station bearing the same brand as the credit card. However, there were a few exceptions as the Phillips 66 credit card could also be used to charge lodging at Best Eastern and Best Western motels.

The primary functions of the Phillips Petroleum Credit Card Center were to provide no-fee Phillips 66 credit cards to financially qualified applicants, to bill credit card charges, to resolve customer service issues, to process payments, and, finally, to manage all the credit card accounts. My job was to manage credit card accounts and answer customer questions when needed.

Managing the accounts primarily involved monitoring accounts receivable (credit card charges) and taking action to assist customers who were in a financial bind in paying their balances and, when necessary, canceling credit card accounts that were past due and in danger of default. I am convinced that this job was given to me by God. In the time I served Phillips in this capacity, I learned enough about the discipline of personal finance – how to live within my means and to remain debt-free – that I have been able to live financially stress–free for my entire life in spite of never becoming anywhere near what I would call affluent. I witnessed in real-time the dilemmas people placed themselves in when being reckless about their finances and how such a condition can adversely affect an entire life, including one's marriage. In my time at that job, I felt that I had heard every non–payment excuse and dealt with every type of poor money management and scam known to man, and I learned from it. I could never have taken a job that better prepared me to face the financial stresses and struggles of family life.

In later years, based not only on my college education but also on my experience at that job, I actually taught adjunct Personal Finance and Basic Accounting classes at Bartlesville Wesleyan College (now Oklahoma Wesleyan University), and also several such Bible-related classes at church.

The job was an education, and a lot of that education can be attributed to Gil Baumgart, Jerry Martin, and Chuck Berven.

There was one guy who worked there, George M. Bayless, with whom I verbally jousted good-naturedly for my entire time in that office. Early on, one day, when I came back from lunch, he had left a note on my desk that Mr. Bear had called and needed to talk to me. I called the number he gave to me, and the person who answered said, "Good afternoon. Kansas City Zoo." I quickly hung up and accosted "Gumby." George's initials are GMB, so I naturally called him Gumby. There was a lot of good-natured trash talk among the people I worked with.

As was mentioned in the previous chapter describing my military service, I was called to Army Basic Training over the Thanksgiving holiday less than six months after I had gone to work in the Credit Card Center. The call–up had been anticipated to be within six months of my enlistment, and that had proven to be true. Credit Card management was aware that the call–up was impending and had pre-approved it.

Shirley's mother came to stay with her for a while during my absence, so that helped, and she took on a co-worker as a roommate a little later to help share the rent and utility expenses. I returned home from my active duty military training in mid–April 1967 and went back to work at the office.

When I returned from the Army, I was assigned the same type of work but in a different section. I would now be working for Chuck Berven, another nice guy and a very good supervisor. My work resumed with no additional learning curves required to bring me back up to speed.

Shortly after my return from the Army, Shirley and I decided to try to find a little bigger place to live. We located one at 9207 9th Street, a little further west but still in Independence. We rented one U–Haul trailer and moved all our things to the new lodging, which was a two-bedroom duplex with air conditioning and a garage. It was in a super location – closer to work (Shirley was still working at Phillips also) and, we discovered, much to our delight, was only one block from the Winner Road Church of Christ. We would be able to walk to services.

We had been attending the East Independence Church of Christ while living in the Waldo Street duplex, which was where my Uncle Howard and his family attended. It was natural that we would transfer our membership to the much closer Winner Road church.

At that point, "small world" struck again in a big way. When we entered the foyer at the church that first Sunday, the first person to greet us was an old friend, Mack Craft, the preacher. Mack and I had graduated from Harding together. This was beginning to get eerie – it seems like every time I moved, I was running into someone I knew, particularly at church. First, Wayne Smethers in my high school years in Bartlesville and now Mack Craft here in Independence. And, as will be revealed later, it did not stop here.

Thanks to Mack and his wife, we were assimilated into the new congregation quickly and smoothly. First thing you know, we were teaching classes.

The remainder of 1967 was pretty routine and enjoyable until early December. By then, I had been working in the Credit Card Center for about 18 months, I had earned my keep and had received good marks for my work – a critical factor in my future but unbeknownst to me at the time. However, in early December, my life dramatically changed again. Hallmark Cards came calling.

THE PROVIDENCE OF GOD

The raising of an Ebenezer for the blessings I received during this stint with Phillips Petroleum was deferred until sometime later when I realized their manifestation. The at–the–time unrealized blessings I received included:

201

1. I learned from real-life certain financial issues that would be of extreme personal value to me in later years. While at my job in Credit Card Center, I observed firsthand the woes families can find themselves in through careless, poor money management. The critical principles I learned in that job still guide me in my financial decisions even today.

2. I had been effective at my job and had made allies with management, which would later be of extreme benefit to my career.

3. My wife had been employed in the Credit Card Center. She proved to be a valuable and affable employee whom they wanted to retain, particularly when Phillips Petroleum moved the Credit Card Center to Bartlesville a few years later.

4. My wife was given a job in the Credit Card Center at a critical time, which enabled us to survive while my pay was reduced to $101.50 per month during the five months I was on active duty with the Army. That is what a PVT E–2 earned in 1966 and 1967.

All things considered, hither by His help we had come, making it through some rough seas.

Twenty-Two

HALLMARK CARDS (1968–1969)

One day in December 1967, I learned that Hallmark Cards, whose head-quarters were located in Kansas City, Missouri, was looking for some new supervisors. On a lark, I went in for an interview – Hallmark's offices were only a few blocks from the Phillips Petroleum offices in Kansas City. Much to my surprise and delight, I was offered a job a few days later. The job was to be a supervisor in the Season Order department, and it and entailed supervising shipping operations on an evening shift. My starting salary at Hallmark essentially matched my pay at Phillips. I understood at the time that I was not making the change for the money, but rather I viewed it as an opportunity to gain some management experience. Although I was doing very well in my work at Phillips, I did not anticipate any opportunities in the near future to actually move into management. I felt that the path to a dynamic career involved moving into management. The sooner, the better. So I resigned at Phillips early in January 1968 and went to work for Hallmark with considerable excitement.

As it would turn out, this move was another in a long list of events in my life that at the time seemed routine and logical but, by the grace of God, eventually had a profound positive effect on the rest of my life and that of my family.

J. C. Hall, the founder of Hallmark Cards, was a legend in Kansas City. I met him once, and he was an extraordinary gentleman. Mr. Hall had the practice of inviting his employees in the Kansas City complex to briefly pass through his office at Christmas for a handshake and a personal greeting. In addition, J. C. Hall was a long–time friend of Walt Disney. Disney moved to Kansas City in 1919, and in 1931 the Hall Brothers, later Hallmark Cards, signed a licensing agreement with Disney to produce greeting cards of all kinds. This personal relationship lasted until 1955. Not only was Hallmark the leader in the greeting card industry, but it also seemed to assume the personality of its founder, J. C. Hall. Its reputation as a "family" company appealed to me. By "family," I mean that pay was decent, they had an excellent profit-sharing program, and employees were treated less like employees and more like family – Mr. Hall's personal greeting of employees was an excellent example.

Other perks of employment included the ability to buy all the Hallmark products at half price in the Hallmark store in the headquarters. Even better, Hallmark subsidized employees' purchase of tickets to the Kansas City Chiefs football games. I purchased two 1969 season tickets for the seven home games (NFL teams played a 14–game season in those days) for a total out of pocket cost of $49. I got to see Joe Namath and O.J. Simpson, among other stars, play in person in Kansas City that fall.

Hallmark also sponsored departmental basketball and softball teams, which fit right in my wheelhouse. The Season Order department fielded both types of teams. We were able to use guys from both the day and evening shifts for our teams. There were some studs in Season Order, and we ran the table against our opponents in both sports. Softball was unusual in that it was fastpitch softball, but pitching was overhand rather than underhand. One of the guys on my shift was a big guy who could hurl the softball somewhere near 90 miles per hour. I'm not sure any of our opponents scored on us that season.

The opportunity to join Hallmark was exciting, and I jumped at the chance.

There were to be complications with my job change, however. I would now be working evenings 4:30 p.m. – 1:00 a.m., and Shirley was still working her day job at Phillips Petroleum. That made for a very awkward arrangement since we had only one car. That was resolved by Shirley catching a ride to work with a co-worker. However, it also meant that we got to see each other basically on weekends – during the week when I got home from work, she was fast asleep, and when she left for work, I was asleep, and then I left for work again before she got home in the afternoon. What made it even more complicated was that I attempted to be awake on the weekends, which made for a very short night Friday night. The result was that we didn't do very much on weekends, and I apparently caught some serious naps in church on Sunday.

We complicated our life in one other respect during that time – we decided to buy a house. We had been living in a very nice duplex, but we realized the benefits of home ownership, so we dived into the process. We bought a new, modest house in Independence, 1220 McHenry Avenue, not long after I had gone to work for Hallmark. It was located on the extreme east side of Independence in the Lake City Gardens addition. Of course, home ownership brought on other issues such as lawn, maintenance, and the like, and, a short time later, a near-disastrous decision to construct a concrete patio in the back yard. More on that later.

Nevertheless, I reported for duty at Hallmark. After several weeks of training with the day shift Season Order department shipping operations, I was promoted to the evening shift supervisor. Hallmark's product line generally fell into two categories – "Every day" and "Season." "Every day" included cards – birthday, anniversary, graduation, sympathy and get well – and also candles, puzzles, books, and all sorts of gift items unrelated to a particular season. "Season" included everything associated with all the holidays – Valentine's Day, St. Pat's Day, Halloween, Thanksgiving, Christmas, etc.

The shipping process was pretty simple. The order filling personnel filled boxes with the merchandise ordered, labeled the boxes with the recipient's address, and placed them on a conveyor belt. My crew included about a dozen young men. Our job was to receive the boxes, add packing paper as necessary, tape them and then assemble completed orders for shipping via commercial carriers. I had a good crew, and it was pleasant enough work. We had no labor problems or personality clashes among the crew while I was there.

There was one interesting thing about the Season Order department. Due to the number of customers around the 50 states, and probably some overseas, it was necessary to start filling and shipping Christmas orders in June – six full months before Christmas. I always thought it odd to be filling orders for Christmas cards in July.

The evening shift's lunch period was scheduled for 10:30 p.m. True to its corporate character, Hallmark provided a nifty perk for all its shipping floor employees. During their lunch period, be it at noon during the day shift or at 10:30 p.m., the lunchroom's soda machines were turned on, and employees could obtain fountain drinks free of charge.

My time in Season Order was not totally routine. One dramatic nationwide event occurred shortly after my move to Hallmark. About three months into my job Martin Luther King, Jr. was assassinated in Memphis, and civil unrest and riots erupted coast to coast. The country was already experiencing such problems due to the unpopularity of the war in Vietnam, and Dr. King's murder was the last straw. By that time, I had transferred into the 110th

Combat Engineers Battalion, a Missouri National Guard unit, and National Guard units all over the country were being activated to quell the riots.

When I went to work, I always parked my car in the parking lot on the roof of the Hallmark complex. One day arriving at about 4:00 p.m. I got out of my car and noticed smoke rising from somewhere north of the office. I knew what was happening and what was about to happen next. I went downstairs and told my boss I was leaving because I was certain our Army unit would be activated, and I had to report for duty. I told my shift leader he would be in charge until further notice, and I drove back home.

At home, I climbed into my Army uniform and headed for the armory. Sure enough, by the time I arrived at the armory, the call had gone out, and we were being activated for duty.

We were activated for about five days. There were showers and bunks and food at the armory, so it was not necessary to go home for those things. However, sometime in the middle of the event, we were allowed to go home to change clothing. One evening I left the armory, which was on South Main Street in Kansas City, and drove the 25 miles east to my house in Independence. During that round trip, I drove on Main Street, Interstate 70, and Highway 71 Bypass, a major highway through Independence. I left the armory at about 7:30 p.m., drove home, showered, changed clothes, and returned via the same route to the armory at about 9:00. Curfews from dusk to dawn were in effect at the time, and during the 50–mile round trip, I did not encounter another vehicle of any type on any of those streets and highways. It was like I was living in an episode of the Twilight Zone. Very eerie.

My main duty during the activation was to stand guard duty at General Hospital in Kansas City, where all those injured during the riots were brought for treatment. I did not get involved in any law enforcement activities, but I witnessed plenty of the results of those activities when they arrived at the hospital.

After a few days, things quieted down, and life returned to near normal, and I returned to work at Hallmark.

A few months later, another life-changing event occurred – I was offered a job in the Systems Analysis Department at Hallmark. The new job was to be a day job, same pay, and I jumped at it when offered. I had spent about nine months as a shipping supervisor and had gained some valuable experience both in a production environment and in the management of people. The move to Systems Analysis would provide me additional critical training in two areas – a giant corporation's overall operations and an introduction to computers. The event would also ultimately prove to be life-changing in two respects. Not only would the experience I gained in Systems Analysis benefit me in future employment but, more importantly, it would enable Shirley and me to resume a normal marriage. Not only that, I would sleep a lot less in church. The benefit provided in "future employment" would be realized in about another year when my employment odyssey took another turn. But that is a story to be told in a later chapter.

My life changed dramatically with the new job. Of course, very significant was the fact that it was a day job, and I actually got to see my wife seven days per week – not just on weekends. On top of that, in my new job, I fell in with five other men – Scottie Linscott, Chuck Gomer, Jerry Taylor, Don Buffon, and Robert Sawyer – who provided a good mix of education and experience, and I learned a lot. Among us, we effectively tackled and resolved a number of issues that lent themselves to either automation or enhancement of existing automation.

Don Buffon was an accountant who was eventually promoted to an Accounting Manager slot at Hallmark. One day while we were still working together, I was boasting about the very large tax refund I had received. Don was not impressed and told me that he, ideally, would like to either receive a tax refund of $25 or less or pay a tax bill of $25 or less – in other words, totally balance his withholding against his anticipated year-end tax bill. I thought he was nuts at the time, but I eventually realized he was onto something. It makes total sense for a taxpayer to manage his withholding so that the taxpayer – not the government – gets to utilize that money during the year. If I received a $5000 refund, I could have increased my take-home pay by more than $400 per month while reducing my withholding by that amount and still have received a small refund at year-end. In the meanwhile, I could have spent and/or invested the $400 per month rather than allowing the government to use it interest–free. As good as the personal finance lessons I received in the Phillips Credit Card Center were, I also learned a gem about the subject at Hallmark.

I had my first up-close and personal introduction to the world of computers at that time. Bear in mind this was late 1968, and the computer revolution had still not hit its stride. I began to understand better that computers weren't super brains – that they actually had no reasoning intelligence but could basically only do what they were told to do, but at a much faster rate and with fewer errors. They were really good at answering "yes" or "no" questions based on the criteria they were required to evaluate. While in this job, I also learned a little about how to communicate with computers, although I did not actually get into programming languages. Also, I was much more comfortable in this job than in the supervisory position, and I received good marks from my boss.

The move to Hallmark's System Analysis department gave me some specific training that had a positive effect on my future employment with, you guessed it, Phillips Petroleum. I often think back on this event and wonder if God endorsed this move because He had better things in mind for me down the road or if he merely tolerated the move because, as scripture says, He worked for my good since I loved Him. In either case, He worked wonders on my behalf. As I think over other events of my life, which will be chronicled later in this book, I sometimes get the feeling that God would sigh and say, "Well, he's done it again. What magic will I have to perform to pull him through this time?" As the saying goes, God made a silk purse out of a sow's ear over and over throughout my life. I am so thankful for His patience with me.

However, shortly after I began my work at Hallmark as a Systems Analyst, things were beginning to happen at the Phillips Petroleum Credit Card Center in Kansas City. Actually, what was about to happen in Kansas City was the result of things happening in Bartlesville, Oklahoma. Bartlesville was not only the home of Phillips Petroleum headquarters, but the city also hosted a significant presence of Cities Service Oil employees. Earlier in 1969, Cities Service had made the decision to relocate its Bartlesville office to Tulsa, about 50 miles away. The result would be the loss of hundreds of Cites Service jobs in Bartlesville, and the sudden, significant negative economic impact on the community could be devastating. In an effort to economize its own operations, and mitigate the economic impact on Bartlesville, Phillips management was considering moving the Phillips Credit Card Center from Kansas City to Bartlesville. Rumors were flying.

Then, two events occurred almost simultaneously in mid–1969 that had an immediate and profound effect on my life.

In the first event, Shirley quit her job in the Phillips Credit Card Center to give birth to our first child, Brent, born on September 27, 1969. As will be revealed in a later chapter, the birth was remarkable, if not miraculous, given certain physical issues Shirley had to deal with.

Becoming a parent changed the dynamics of our family life dramatically. For instance, Shirley's quitting her job cut our family income by about forty percent, which required a drastic readjustment in attitudes and priorities. An example: Hallmark paid its salaried employees only once per month, on the 25th of each month. When I received my paycheck two days before Brent was born, I deposited the check, kept some cash for groceries, diapers, and some miscellaneous small spending for the month, and wrote checks to pay the bills and mortgage. When I finished writing my checks, my checkbook balance, which had to last me for another month, was $7.00. Yep, $7.00. Somehow, we made it, but I still don't know-how.

But, I digress. There is an amusing anecdote associated with Brent's birth.

We did not own a camera at that time, but we felt it incumbent that we get some photographs of our new son. We decided that a Polaroid camera was our best option because we could view the pictures immediately rather than having to fill up a roll of film and then later take it to be developed. Consequently, we went in search of a Polaroid camera and found one at a full-service drug store, much like CVS or Walgreen's today. The camera was about $45, which was a tidy sum in those days. Bear in mind that at that time, we had exactly $7.00 in our checking account and very little discretionary cash in my billfold. But we had a plan. We would charge the camera on our new credit card and would not have to pay for it until we received the credit card bill in about a month.

This was 1969, the very early days of general use (bank-issued) credit cards – what we think of as VISA and MasterCard today. We had previously applied for and obtained a BankAmericard – the father of the modern VISA credit card – and I had the card in my billfold when we went camera shopping. I still have the card among my souvenirs. We went into the store on a Saturday and selected a camera and handed the clerk the BankAmericard. However, making a purchase using a bank-issued credit card was more complicated in those days. At the time, there was no internet to immediately validate a credit card, and for purchases exceeding a very low limit – probably $10.00 – the proprietor had to manually call the office of the credit card to get the charge approved. Once again, no problem, I thought. However, this was a Saturday, and the credit card office – the bank – was closed, and approval could not be made until the following Monday. Bummer!

The clerk said she would make the call on Monday and we could pick up the camera at that time – which she did, and which we did. The things we take for granted these days were sometimes pretty clumsy and slow in times past. Instant gratification in 1969 was still a phrase that had not been introduced to the dictionary.

At any rate, we picked up the camera and took a package (not a roll) of film and showed the pictures to everyone we knew. In a number of ways, that event changed our lives and for the better.

The second life-changing event that occurred had already become a foregone conclusion by that time. Phillips Petroleum formally announced that it was indeed relocating its Credit Card Center from Kansas City to Bartlesville. Phillips Petroleum had been a solid citizen of the city of Bartlesville since 1917, when the company was incorporated and located there. Therefore, it was no surprise that Phillips was concerned about the future of the city with the Cities Service withdrawal, so the company seized on an opportunity to both benefit the city and streamline its own operations with this move of the office. Unsurprisingly, in a few months, this would become a significant event in my life.

It was not unexpected that the employees' general attitude at the Credit Card Center was somewhat negative. Most were accustomed to life in metro Kansas City and all it had to offer – shopping, sports, theater, museums, all the stuff which enhances life in the big city – and they were not thrilled at the prospect of moving to the small city of Bartlesville, population 35,000. It was anticipated that attrition of the Credit Card Center employees would be close to 50%.

All of these things happening at the same time made my head spin.

It suddenly occurred to me that this might be a huge opportunity for me – Phillips would be losing a number of key employees due to the move. I had picked up both supervisory and Systems Analysis experience at Hallmark, which could conceivably be utilized in a Phillips job, and I knew Bartlesville like the back of my hand. On a personal note, I still had many friends in Bartlesville from my high school years. I learned as a youth never to burn bridges, and I had maintained bridges with executives in the Credit Card Center following my resignation there 18 months earlier. I decided to attempt to make another nomadic move in my career. I was not disappointed with Hallmark, but there could be some exciting possibilities career-wise if I rejoined Phillips Petroleum.

I approached Credit Card management and made my pitch. They were all familiar with me, and I had earned really good ratings in my earlier employment there. In addition, my wife had been a very popular employee at the office there, and she had indicated that she might go back to work in the Credit Card Center in Bartlesville if I were offered a job. One thing led to another, and I was hired back for my second tour of duty with Phillips in November of 1969.

As I had hoped, I was hired back at a more responsible position than what I had held when I was previously employed. I was brought back on board as a Methods Analyst, a very similar job to the Systems Analyst experience I had gained at Hallmark, and there was a substantial pay increase included in the deal.

When I resigned at Hallmark, they attempted to change my mind, but the promise that Phillips and Bartlesville held was more than they could offer. My tenure at Hallmark Cards had been a little less than two years, and it had been enjoyable and had been educational, and beneficial in shaping and enhancing my future with Phillips. I will always be grateful to Hallmark for the opportunity they gave me.

HALLMARK CARDS (1968–1969)

Were the jobs I had performed at Hallmark a God thing? Considering all the beneficial "coincidences" that had occurred in my life up to that point, I had to believe God had a hand in providing me those experiences ahead of the new Phillips opportunity. Had I never left Phillips in the first place, I would still be moving with the company to Bartlesville but in a much less responsible job. It appeared to me to definitely be the Providence of God, and I remember thanking God for the new opportunity – tantamount to raising my Ebenezer.

THE PROVIDENCE OF GOD

In a period of 22 months at Hallmark, I gained both supervisory and systems analysis/computer experience, which would greatly enhance and advance my future career at Phillips Petroleum.

1. I would be filling a critical position in my new job at Phillips at a time when they were losing key personnel due to the move.

2. The fact that I had been a resident in Bartlesville was viewed as valuable by Phillips management as they planned and coordinated the move of operations and personnel to, in the view of most of the employees transferring, what was a strange, new, small town.

Once again, coincidences, some initiated unknowingly by me and some initiated by my employers, worked to my great benefit. I didn't think it was possible for such unusual things to continue to happen to me, but, not surprisingly, I would be wrong. Hither by His help, I had come and was still moving forward.

Twenty-Three

TWO MIRACLES ON McHENRY (1968–1969)

Before diving back into the next chapter of my Phillips Petroleum career, I feel the need to relate two events – two miracles; I believe – that occurred while we were living on McHenry Avenue. The central premises of this entire book involve the Providence of God and the belief that in all things God works for the good of those who love Him. I feel that those two issues are irrefutably connected and occur with regularity among his children. First, however, let me provide some background on our life on McHenry.

As was discussed in the previous chapter, in 1968, we bought a house on McHenry Avenue in Independence. At that time, we could no longer move all of our stuff in a single U–Haul trailer. Instead, it now required a whole U–Haul truck to move our belongings. Since McHenry Avenue was entirely on the east side of Independence, and since the 39th Street Church of Christ was considerably closer to our new house than the Winner Road Church of Christ, we began attending the 39th Street congregation a few months after our move. At that point, "small world" struck once again. The first Sunday we attended, we were greeted in the foyer by the preacher, another old friend, Charles Clark. I had known Charles at Harding. He was a year behind me and had recently graduated and taken the preacher job at the 39th Street church. This was now beyond weird. It was almost like God was continually placing people in my life to keep me on the straight and narrow – which was probably a very good idea. However, as will be related a little later, "small world" and Charles Clark would team up again unexpectedly, and I would once again be amazed at the Providence of God.

It should also be noted that my Ada, Oklahoma, the connection just kept on giving. After we had moved into our new house, my good friend Jim Threlkeld and his wife, Martha, moved to the Kansas City area. Jim had earned a Master's degree in Engineering and had taken a job with the Bendix Corporation in Kansas City. Jim and I were high school classmates and church friends while I lived in Ada, and I had served as his best man at his wedding. It seems like everywhere I went, my past kept following me in an unbelievable series of small world events.

But the mysterious blessings did not cease with our being reunited with old friends after our move to McHenry Avenue. Two events, which I can only term as miracles, occurred just a few months apart. I will describe the second miracle first.

As mentioned, Shirley gave birth to our first child, a boy we named Brent, on September 27, 1969. "Why was this considered a miracle?" you might ask. In the first place, I have always considered the birth of a child a miracle, but this one was a little more special. Shirley and I had been trying for a child for more than a year. She had had a couple of episodes during that time that led us to believe she was pregnant, but it came to nothing in each case. There was nothing more disappointing than to see Shirley come out of Dr. Jonas' office each time and say, "No, not yet."

Finally, in the spring of 1969, she visited Dr. Jonas and came bounding out of the office with a smile as wide as the Missouri River, which flowed near our house. "We are going to have a baby, and it will arrive in September," she said, with tears in her eyes.

You might still think, "So what? This happens all the time." And you would be correct – to a point. At the time of this announcement, we had been married almost three years, and for all that time, and in fact, since she had reached puberty, Shirley's menstrual cycles had been more than just uncomfortable – they had been extraordinarily painful. She was diagnosed at age 16 with endometriosis, a condition whereby uterine inner lining tissue develops outside the uterus. It has two significant symptoms – extremely painful menstrual periods and infertility. The symptoms persisted, so following our second son's birth, Greg, several years later, Shirley had had enough and underwent a hysterectomy by Dr. Oliver in Bartlesville. The doctor told her it was unusual for someone in her condition to deliver one healthy baby, and it was almost a miracle to deliver two due to the discomfort and likely infertility involved. That being said, I have considered the birth of our son Brent in Independence a miracle and the birth of our second son Greg in Bartlesville likewise. However, as will be revealed a little later in this book, this ultimately led to another God–sponsored miracle involving a baby in 1980.

The second miracle on McHenry, which, as mentioned, actually took place prior to the first one, occurred in the spring of 1968, shortly after we had moved into our new house. It still has me baffled to this day.

Our house was brand new but was very basic – three bedrooms, one bath, a basement (which was the norm in that part of Missouri), no brick or stone, no air conditioning, and no patio. We could not do much about the first several items on our budget, but we thought we could build a patio pretty inexpensively, that is if we did the work. I had never mixed or poured even a quart of concrete, and Shirley's dad, who was visiting with us at the time, was 67 years old. That might have been a good team for concreting in a new mailbox out front, but it hardly seemed qualified to form up, install reinforcing wire and pour and finish a large concrete patio. Nevertheless, undaunted, we forged ahead. I was working the evening shift at Hallmark, so Shirley's dad and I decided to prepare the site one morning before I left for work in late afternoon and then pour the patio the next morning, once again completing our task in time for me to head to work. A piece of cake, it seemed.

However, to complicate matters, our back yard sloped away from the house, and there was no driveway or alley behind the house. The patio was to be 12 feet deep by 30 feet wide, 360 square feet in all. Due to the slope away from the house, the depth of the concrete at the outer edge was right at 12 inches. Where it attached to the house, it would only be 6 inches deep, and we calculated the average depth to be 8 inches. If our math was good, we figured it would take just less than nine cubic yards of concrete to fill the form. We formed it up and lay in the reinforcing wire and ordered the concrete. A little later, much to our chagrin, we discovered that that was a lot of wet concrete.

We had on hand some extra 2x4's for striking off the concrete and some trowels for finishing it. Since there was no discernable roadway behind the house, the concrete truck had to drive down the fence line that separated the back yard from a field. From the front of the house and either side, there was no indication of what was happening in the back yard. We could have been hosting a rock concert back there, and nobody in front of the house would have been any the wiser. This is an important factor in this miracle.

The truck started dumping its load, and Shirley's aged dad and I started spreading concrete as fast as we could. Finally, the form filled up and actually started to overflow a little. The truck driver recognized our ineptitude and slowed the concrete flow, which helped a lot. However, I was totally inexperienced, and Shirley's dad was running out of gas. We were not only having trouble striking it off, but we had not even begun the troweling of 360 square feet of wet concrete. The truck driver was helpless to do anything except control the concrete flow, which he did skillfully and mercifully. I believe he had hoped that Shirley's dad and I would have been a little more competent.

Just as we were gasping and about to crater, two young men walked down between my house and the one next door, and one of them said, "Looks like you could use some help." Sweeter words have never been spoken.

We did have an extra trowel, and the two guys dived in, leveled off the wet concrete, and then started in with the troweling. They were surprisingly adept at finishing concrete. In just a few minutes, the situation was brought under control, and the two young men disappeared, without a word, as quickly as they had appeared, never to be seen nor heard from again.

This event has been on my heart now for more than 50 years. I confess that I have no other explanation for what happened except to believe that it was a miracle. But what would lead me to believe this?

First, our neighborhood was well off the beaten path, and our house was well back in the corner of the neighborhood – we seldom had non–resident vehicle traffic. Second, there were no sidewalks in the neighborhood, so pedestrian traffic was virtually non–existent. Third, the house blocked the view from the street of anything that might be happening in the back yard. Fourth, there was no street or road behind the house where a vehicle might accidentally wander. Fifth, those two young men were not from our neighborhood – I had never seen them before and never saw them afterward.

It begs the celestial question – How in the world did two absolute strangers, physically fit, adept at concrete work, just happen to be strolling through our neighborhood in the middle of the morning in the middle of the week at that exact time, and how did they recognize the chaos that was occurring in the back yard?

The scripture found in Hebrews 13:2 says, "Be not forgetful to entertain strangers, for thereby some have entertained angels unaware (KJV)."

This scripture implies that angels might still frequent the earth and that they did not necessarily disappear when the last Apostles died. Why else would scripture say that? I am convinced that those young were "angels unaware" and that this was another miracle wherein all things God was working for the good of those that love Him. I have no other logical explanation.

There were two miracles on McHenry – the miraculous birth of a son and the miraculous visit by two strangers.

Shirley's father and I raised a sort of an Ebenezer when the concrete had been properly poured and finished – not a stone of help but a concrete slab of help. To this day, I am still scratching my head, trying to figure that event out.

TWO MIRACLES ON McHENRY (1968–1969)

THE PROVIDENCE OF GOD

As far as I am concerned, two miracles occurred while we lived on McHenry Avenue:

1. Our son, Brent, was born without incident in the face of both potential conception difficulties and delivery problems.

2. I received totally unexpected help from two total strangers, skilled in concrete work, who just "happened" to be, against all odds and inconceivably, strolling down my street without sidewalks in the middle of the day in the middle of the week.

When I look back to those incidents, I have felt that I should have headed for Las Vegas immediately while I was on a roll. However, I am not sure God blesses cards and dice, so it is probably a good thing that I didn't do so at the time.

Twenty-Four

PHILLIPS PETROLEUM – PART 2 (1969–1973)

In November 1969, I began my second tour of duty with Phillips Petroleum in its Credit Card Center in Kansas City. A little earlier, as discussions of my prospective return to Phillips seemed to be bearing fruit, Shirley had returned to work there. She was experienced in the Credit Card Center and would be a tremendous asset given the many current employees who would be leaving the company. Most of them would be reluctant to abandon their long–time homes in the Kansas City metro. Rehiring Shirley was a no–brainer.

My new job in the Credit Card Center would be what was called a Methods Analyst at Phillips but was generally referred to elsewhere as a Systems Analyst. Does that sound familiar? It was much the same as my last job at Hallmark but with more of an emphasis on keeping a multi-million-dollar computerized financial system – Credit Card operations – up and humming.

In my new job at Phillips, I would no longer be interacting with customers but would rather be dealing primarily with automated processes. In 1969, there were approximately 2 million Phillips credit card accounts across the country in all 50 states, and an average of $2.5 million in credit card charges and another $2.5 million in payments were received in the office each business day. The volume and dollar value of the transactions involved dictated that they be processed daily, with the charges and payments applied to the appropriate customer accounts and bank deposits made ASAP. It was, therefore, incumbent to keep the systems running optimally and to implement improvements when possible.

There was no internet in those days, so all credit card charges were recorded at the time of purchase on paper charge slips manually imprinted at stations around the country and mailed in batches to the Credit Card Center for processing. In addition, all payments were made by check or money order. No paying via computer or cell phone – just via snail mail. When the payments and charge slips were received in the office, all the documents were first sorted by computer and then recorded and applied to the appropriate customer accounts. Ultimately a monthly paper statement/bill showing charges made and payments received since the last statement was created and mailed to each customer. Any hiccups which occurred in the system could incur a huge cost, given the dollars involved. My new job as a Methods Analyst would be seeking, developing, and assisting in implementing efficiencies in these operations and heading off any potential hiccups.

The Systems Analysis experience I had gained while at Hallmark had providentially placed me in a position to be rehired by Phillips Petroleum and enabled me to move pretty easily into a critical position within the company. With that experience, I was able to become productive quickly, with no additional training necessary.

My new supervisor at Phillips Petroleum was Lewis "Woody" Woods. Although he was a long–time employee in the Credit Card Center, I had not made his acquaintance during my first stint there. He had worked on a different floor of the building and worked closely with the computer personnel. Woody's boss was Ted Lockin, the Credit Card Center's Assistant Manager, and the Credit Card Center manager was Riley Montgomery. I have never worked with finer people.

When I began my new job at Phillips, the Credit Card Center's immediate objectives were twofold: keeping the financial systems running and moving the office to Bartlesville.

The dynamics of the move of the office to Bartlesville weighed heavily on management's minds. The problem was how to move a "living" process 300 miles away into a different state without shutting it down during the move. The Credit Card computers ran day and night processing charges, monthly statements, and payments. If the computers were simply unplugged one day, put on a truck, and shipped to Bartlesville, it would still require several days – weeks, maybe – before they were properly up and running again. Given the unmanageable backlog of transactions that would accumulate and the cost of money in failing to get millions of dollars to the bank on a timely basis, a total shutdown and move was not an option. Consequently, management wisely decided to move the operations in segments.

To accomplish the move, new computers were to be installed in

Bartlesville and loaded with Credit Card software. The plan was then to begin electronically transferring via computer tapes groups of approximately 100,000 customer accounts per day from the Kansas City computers to the Bartlesville computers. It was anticipated that each city's computers would run parallel for nearly a month. The Bartlesville computers would gradually increase their load each day and those in Kansas City would gradually be phasing out. When the new computers in Bartlesville had been installed and tested, the coordinated data transfer process went "live."

Each day a different group of accounts was invoiced on the Kansas City computers and mailed to the customer, but the payment envelope included with the statement/bill had a Bartlesville return address. Those invoice files were then transferred to a computer tape, and the tape was delivered each day to Bartlesville and loaded into the Bartlesville computer. This went on for about four weeks, at the end of which time all of the electronic data regarding the customer accounts were safely on the Bartlesville computers, and all credit card charge slips, and customer payments were being received there.

As noted above, there were two challenges to be faced – first, keeping the financial systems running and second, actually making the physical move. My first assignment as a Methods Analyst was to help design and execute the logistics of the second challenge – making the physical move.

An engineer came up from Bartlesville. Between the two of us, we scheduled the movement and placement of every piece of furniture, file cabinet, and fixture in the office except the synchronized movement of the computing equipment, which required very special attention. Our task also involved assisting in scheduling the movement of jobs – people – to Bartlesville on a timely basis. In the end, we were able to populate three floors of the Adams Building in Bartlesville in a manner that was almost seamless. This project – beginning to end – fully consumed most of my efforts for the first six months of my new job.

During the early days of my job at Phillips, I also had to be concerned with my own physical move. Ultimately, I was just another employee being transferred and would receive no special treatment just because I was part of the planning and moving process. As with most major corporations, employees who were being transferred at the company's request received financial and logistic help with their move. At Phillips, it was no different. Basically, Phillips paid realtor's fees on the sale of an employee's house, and of course, paid all moving expenses. In addition, employees received reimbursement for gasoline, lodging, and meals en route to the new location. A final benefit received was a payment in lieu of a realtor's fee – payable if an employee sold his own house and didn't actually incur a realtor's fee. The amount was significant enough to encourage employees to sell their houses without involving a realtor.

Money at our house was still a little tight with the new baby and all, and I decided to take a shot at selling our house on McHenry Avenue without using a realtor. Someone at the office had recommended a Kansas City lawyer who specialized in litigating cases but enjoyed less stressful legal work when it came her way. I contacted the lawyer, and by the grace of God, she accepted the work. Her fee was only $50 to do all the legal and paperwork on the sale of our house. True, it was 1970, but that was still dirt cheap even then. It also made the payment in lieu of a realtor's fee a nice bonus—another miracle.

Our house was attractive and sold in a matter of a few days, and the buyers wanted possession by April 1. I was not scheduled to actually report to work in Bartlesville until early June, so this situation presented a dilemma. It turned out to be no problem.

If you will recall, I stayed with my Uncle Howard for a month in the summer of 1964 when I worked a short time in Kansas City and again for a few weeks early in 1966 when I reported to work with Phillips the first time around. You will also recall that in addition to my uncle and aunt, there were seven kids in the house, and when I had stayed with them, previously I made person number 10 in the house. Well, they invited Shirley and me and Brent to stay with them for a few weeks after we sold our house, but before we made the physical move to Bartlesville. That now made twelve persons living in a three-bedroom, 1 ½ bath house – but it worked. When Shirley decided to go back to work in the Credit Card Center, my Aunt Mae, Uncle Howard's wife, volunteered to babysit Brent during the day. It was the perfect scenario. God appeared to be working overtime on my behalf.

Sometime in May, Shirley and I ventured to Bartlesville to see about buying a house, and having lived there before, I had some ideas about where I wanted to buy. We caught a break in that the number of Cities Service people leaving town exceeded the number of Phillips employees being transferred in. Translated, that means that good deals were available to be made due to a temporary surplus of houses for sale in the city.

I learned that Sidney Roper, the preacher who had delivered the Baccalaureate sermon at my Bartlesville high school graduation in 1962, had retired from preaching and had become a real estate agent – small world once again. It seemed to me that my old friends and acquaintances were being recycled, and I was still meeting them again in new or different circumstances, as had happened in every move I had experienced since leaving Ada ten years earlier. Anyway, I naturally sought him out to help in the house search. He found a brand-new house at 1248 May Lane, one–half block from Ranch

Heights Elementary school – a perfect location for a family with a young child. The house was brick with a fireplace, three bedrooms, 1 3/4 baths, air conditioning, and it already had a patio. We bought it and thought we had really moved uptown with our new "mansion" – or it seemed like a mansion to us. We then made our physical move to Bartlesville in June 1970.

At the time of our move to Bartlesville, Shirley and I had lived in Independence for almost four years. It had been a great experience, particularly since I had a number of close relatives living in the metro. In addition, we were able to enjoy some activities unique to Kansas City – attending Kansas City Chiefs football games (the year they won the Super Bowl), Broadway-cast musicals at Kansas City's outdoor Starlight Theater, Christmas shopping at the famous Country Club Plaza (one of the first shopping plazas in the country) and dining at Arthur Bryant's Barbecue Restaurant.

During our time in Independence, I spent five months on active duty with the Army, our son, Brent, had been born, we lived in three different residences, and I had worked at three different jobs. It appeared that we were part gypsy, but as will be seen over time, our migratory tendencies were only getting warmed up.

Bill Dye, our friend from Harding, who also worked at Phillips in Kansas City, was also being transferred to Bartlesville at the same time as we. He and his wife, Sherry, had a young son, Allen, who was about four months younger than Brent, and Sherry was a stay–at–home mom. Since Shirley was still working at Phillips following the transfer, Sherry became our babysitter for Brent. It seems like every time we needed someone in a special situation – preacher, realtor, babysitter, etc. – God provided.

Once we got to Bartlesville, we settled in, and we reestablished our membership at the Limestone Church of Christ. Wayne Smethers was still the preacher, and most of our friends and acquaintances from my high school days in Bartlesville were still there. The only difference this time around was that I was bringing a beautiful wife and a cute baby. The congregation swallowed up Shirley in no time at all.

On top of all this, about two years after our move to Bartlesville, I traded cars and was now driving a 1972 Oldsmobile Cutlass S, V–8 engine, A/C, power everything, emerald green with a white vinyl top, white interior, leather bucket seats, console – totally cool.

At this point, everything was going my way. If I would just learn to leave things alone. If it ain't broke, don't fix it. A lesson I was yet to learn.

My work changed dramatically following the move. I was now free to pursue other systems issues at the Credit Card Center and did so with enthusiasm. I had no further projects as large as the move, but I felt an integral part of the team.

Once the dust had settled from the move, there was an impetus to up-grade credit card processes across the board, focusing primarily on intro-ducing additional computerization to existing processes in order to increase speed and accuracy. Although I was not a computer programmer, I was fa-miliar with computing concepts as a Methods Analyst. Consequently, I was assigned to assist in designing and implementing several computer applica-tions in my new job.

An initial project I worked on involved working closely with Lee Tribble and Ralph Okle, two Credit Card Center computer gurus, to further auto-mate the access of credit card financial information. The gist of the project was to install computer terminals to directly retrieve data from computers and wean ourselves from the age-old use of printed reports. The basic benefits of doing so would be increased speed, accuracy, and quality of information, not to mention having to no longer deal with stacks of paper. We were able to introduce a prototype system whereby an analyst could access information via a computer terminal and keyboard in a matter of seconds rather than having to wait overnight or over a weekend to view a printed report. As expected, the new system was eventually expanded to encompass almost every data retrieval function in the Credit Card Center.

By this time, the potential uses for computers in the processing of busi-ness and financial information were starting to explode nationwide. For in-stance, heretofore, virtually all input to computers was via keypunched cards. The physical "holes" in the keypunched cards were recognized by the com-puter and were translated into a usable format, which then fed computer tapes or computer disks. The punched cards were cumbersome to handle, and if one was damaged in some way, it became unusable by the computer and had to be manually replaced. Computer experts everywhere were seeking ways to eliminate the use of the punched cards.

One new technology that was being introduced about that time involved "spraying" input documents with magnetic ink that could be "read" by the computers, thereby eliminating the use of punch cards altogether in some applications. This technology enabled computers to exponentially increase their speed and accuracy in processing input documents over that of punch cards, and in addition, the new style documents were lighter in weight and much less expensive to purchase than the punch cards. The technology was evaluated by Credit Card Center management, and the decision was made to install it.

I was invited to join the project, and my responsibility was to design all the forms used in the process. I caught some good-natured flak regarding my design of the new monthly customer statement. I had incorporated some colors on the statement as trim and highlighted several items such as amount due and date due. However, the design was approved, and the statement was used for several years.

Another project I worked on involved Phillips 66 brand automobile tires. A bit of nostalgia here. In 1970 when I came back to work for Phillips Petroleum, the gasoline industry had not yet evolved into convenience stores. Most gasolines of all brands were still sold at "service stations," and most service stations also had service bays, which offered a wide range of automotive services, from tune-ups to engine overhauls to the sale of automobile tires. Starting maybe as early as the 1930s and continuing into the late 1960s or early 1970's most Phillips Petroleum branded stations sold and installed Phillips 66 brand tires, batteries, and accessories – belts, hoses, oil, antifreeze, etc. These items were commonly referred to as "TBA," for "tires, batteries, and accessories." TBA is another issue that will be revisited later in my career and, consequently, again a little later in this book.

However, around the year 1971, the government issued some mandatory safety standards and requirements regarding the manufacture of tires. The new law required that individual tires be assigned Department of Transportation Identification Numbers (DOT IDs) upon manufacture so that they could be traceable to the manufacturer if there were any recalls. With the addition of the DOT ID requirement, it became necessary for the retail sellers of tires to record the DOT ID'S of all tires sold and when they were sold and to whom they were sold. Since Phillips at the time sold tires at Phillips 66 stations in all 50 states, it became incumbent upon the company to establish a tire sale tracking system that could be fed by the stations selling the tires, with the master file being maintained in the Phillips corporate offices. Of course, it not only required merely the recording of the sales but also the ability to generate reports, notifications, and statistics as needed. It would be a complex system.

As a Methods Analyst, I was called upon to aid in developing and implementing the new system. I did not write any computer code but rather worked with the corporate computer programmers developing the design. The leadership of this project was assigned to corporate computing assets rather than Credit Card Center personnel.

I said all that to say this. The lead programmer for the corporate team was Lonnie Porter. I had never met him before, but I worked with him on the project, and it was successfully implemented. I didn't think much about it at the time – just another day at the office. However, three years later and three employers later – when I was rehired by Phillips for the third time (more on that later) – I was assigned to a unit whose manager was Lonnie Porter (more on that later). However, it doesn't end there. Four years after that, I was transferred into another Phillips job, and my new boss was Lonnie Porter (more on that later, also). In retrospect, it seems that there are only so many possibilities in life, and I apparently keep exhausting those possibilities so that they start repeating themselves.

My entire life has been blessed with these events. I just seem to have the unusual habit of making friends with someone and then moving away to another city only to reunite with the friend years later in circumstances which, if not miraculous, were at least unusual. It had happened with Larry Quinalty, Eddie Roark, plus several preachers over the years, plus numerous other friends who had reentered my life at critical junctures.

Lonnie Porter was a new friend who would eventually contribute to that continuum, but there was another new friend that we met in Bartlesville during this second stint with Phillips (1969–1973) who would have a profound effect on our family in an event that occurred in 1980 – a lady by the name of Karen Davis.

There were two congregations of the Church of Christ in Bartlesville – Limestone, where we attended, and Sixth and Dewey, where Kay Spearman, Martha Koger, and Sidney Roper had attended. There was also another congregation in Dewey, Oklahoma, only three miles from Bartlesville. As would be expected, there was considerable visitation and mingling among the members of the three congregations. Karen Davis attended the Dewey congregation, and we had come to know her through that association. As will be revealed a little later, Karen is personally responsible for an entire miraculous event that occurred in 1980. Stick around for the details.

Overall, my time in Bartlesville on this tour of duty with Phillips was exceptionally rich from personal, career, and family standpoints. As described earlier, I had been able to transfer my military service to Bartlesville and managed to avoid injuring my commanding officer in a Phillips league basketball game. Credit Card fielded a slow–pitch softball team on which I played, and friends and I attended stock car races at the Dewey racetrack. The smaller city combined with the many people I already knew provided a considerable number and variety of activities which Shirley and I participated in. Eventually, I was even selected as a deacon at the church – in charge of building and grounds. I should also mention that I loved my current job. I performed responsible work, was well thought of, and, frankly, I had a pretty bright future within the Phillips Petroleum Credit Card Center. Everything was going very well – great job, a great church, great friends, great things to do. I even started playing golf pretty regularly. The Adams Municipal course in Bartlesville is one of the best and most difficult municipal courses I have ever played. As it turned out, enjoying golf was my downfall.

Then Robley Barber called me.

Rob Barber was a classmate of mine at Harding and had been a member with me on Harding's National Champion Intercollegiate Marketing team. He and I were pretty good friends, and Rob was a go-getter. He passed all four parts of his CPA exam on the first try, and in 1973, only seven years following his graduation from Harding, he had become a vice–president of the Gulf South Corporation. Gulf South was headquartered in Oklahoma City and was in the business of developing high-end vacation/retirement communities with all the trimmings – a golf course, spa, restaurants, vacation, and retirement home construction – the whole nine yards.

At the time, Gulf South had purchased an existing but faltering company by the name of Horseshoe Development Corporation – HDC. HDC was in the process of developing a retirement community by the name of Horseshoe Bend Estates in the beautiful Ozark Mountains in the north-central part of Arkansas. A horseshoe-shaped bend in the Strawberry River ran through the town, from whence the town got its name. The development itself consisted of, I think, 40,000 acres and already had a population of around 1,000 plus a 9–hole golf course. Two brothers, William and Richard Pratt, had started the project but discovered they didn't have sufficient capital to complete the community's development as it should be, so they sold their interest in the development to the Gulf South Corporation. Gulf South then spun it off as a subsidiary and named Rob Barber as its president. Rob was now not only VP of Gulf South but also President of HDC. Accordingly, his office was located on-site in Horseshoe Bend.

North-central Arkansas was an area of the country with which Shirley and I were very familiar. Shirley had been raised in Yellville, Arkansas, a small town very near Horseshoe Bend. In addition, we were familiar with the concept of a vacation/retirement community. We had previously frequented Bella Vista Village, an excellent and successful vacation/retirement community in northwest Arkansas. Therefore, we were somewhat aware of the lifestyle that a retirement community offered as well as the beauty of the mountains, forests, and lakes in the area.

Rob Barber had just moved into his position as president of HDC and was looking to fill out a management team. The current Advertising/Public Relations Vice President, Malcolm Miller, was nearing retirement, and it was becoming necessary to groom a replacement for him. Rob thought of me and gave me a call. Rob was dangling the job of Director of Advertising for HDC before my eyes. I think he recalled that during our Intercollegiate Marketing competition at Michigan State, my duty on the team was to manage the advertising. He told me he thought I was a good fit.

He then told me about the golf course. It was currently 9–hole but expansion to 18 holes was in the planning stage. Of course, I could play all the golf I wanted to there by merely walking onto the course. He then told me he would build me a house at the cost of $11.00 per square foot. This was 1973, and our new house in Bartlesville had cost a little more than $13 per square foot when we bought it in 1970, so this sounded like a good deal. He told me that I could be making $25,000 within five years. At the time, I was bringing in $12,600, so he was telling me that I could double my salary in only five years – an average 16% raise compounded every year for five years. Unheard of. He said there were churches and schools available, and the scenery was unbelievable – they call the fall colors in that area the "Flaming Fall Revue," and that pretty well nails it. Being very familiar with Bella Vista Village in northwest Arkansas, I thought that Horseshoe Bend was on the verge of significant growth – if adequate capital were committed to its further development – and might eventually be on a par with Bella Vista. Everything appeared to bode very well. As a cherry on top of the cake, Rob also informed me that early each year, the management team was treated to an expense–paid trip to Las Vegas for a week – transportation, lodging, food, shows, everything except gambling cash.

It all sounded too good to be true. Big raise, all the golf I could play, a big house at cost, a prestigious job, working for a good friend, beautiful mountains, free trips. All of the "good things in life" were mine for the taking. We would be living in Eden. What was not to like?

As time would tell, I approached this issue with blinders on, but that sad story will be fully revealed later in this chronicle. However, I mulled it over for a few days and then told Rob I would like to see the place before I made a final decision.

Prior to making that decision, one Saturday morning Shirley and I drove over to check out the development – it was about 260 miles to Horseshoe Bend from Bartlesville through some magnificent scenery. In retrospect, I really believe that during the trip to Horseshoe Bend and for hours after we arrived there that God was speaking to me about the wisdom of even considering the job. It rained on us for the entire journey – we didn't even get to enjoy the scenery en route – and during the weekend, Horseshoe Bend recorded nine inches of rainfall.

Everything that could be underwater was underwater. The development included a large, picturesque lake – Crown Lake – that was fed by the Strawberry River and was formed by an earthen dam with a spillway. The rainfall was so severe that engineers had to go out in the middle of the night and bulldoze an alternate spillway because the existing spillway could not handle the volume of the water, and the water was in danger of going over the top of the dam. If that occurred, the earthen dam would quickly fail, and everything downstream for several miles would be flooded. It could conceivably have washed away the small town of Franklin located just south of the town of Horseshoe Bend, ironically near the "horseshoe bend" in the Strawberry River.

However, I disregarded the flooding, which I later came to believe was a legitimate omen, and, rather, dwelt on the beauty and serenity of the area, which, admittedly, was difficult to enjoy due to the downpour. The worldly opportunities – prestige, money, golf – which seemed to be mine merely for their taking overrode my better judgment and, as I reflect back, I must have been in complete denial.

As we toured the development, ignoring the rain, we dined at a fine restaurant there, met some of the corporation management, and observed that the properties were well maintained. We visited the hotel/spa and the golf course. Rob mentioned that the second 9 holes on the golf course were due to be developed beginning in the fall. Rob drove us past a vacant lot that had a sign proclaiming, "Future Home of the Church of Christ." He said that the corporation had donated several lots free of charge to any church which would build there. It seemed that he had all the bases covered.

We discussed salary, and he reiterated my potential to be making $25,000 in five years but offered me $1100 per month – $13,200 per year – to start plus a $100 per month auto allowance. Overall, a nice raise, not to mention the amenities that I could enjoy free of charge. It gave me some concrete information to think about.

Despite all the amenities and potential benefits that had been presented to Shirley and me that day, there were still some negatives that needed to be considered. I did notice that the houses were generally small, but it didn't dawn on me at the time that the reason for that was because they were populated almost entirely by retirees, void of any playmates for our young children. Did I mention that Shirley was seven months pregnant with our second son, Greg, at the time? Hardly an opportune time to uproot the family entirely, given all the difficulties associated with such a move. In addition, I currently had a great job and was well thought of by management. Also, there was the issue of abandoning lifelong friends in Bartlesville without a likelihood of ever replacing them. Finally, there was no chance I could ever approach my Bartlesville church experience in a rural place that had only a "Future Home of the Church of Christ" sign planted in a vacant lot with no plans to build. What could the move possibly offer that my present situation did not?

How I could have disregarded all these issues is beyond me. I have only one answer – I was out of my mind. More than likely, however, I was blinded by the promise of "a big raise, all the golf I could play, a big house at cost, a prestigious job, working for a good friend, beautiful mountains, all the good things in life." Consequently, I obviously went brain dead, and before we returned home to Bartlesville on Sunday, I informed Rob that I would accept the job.

The adversity that would ensue was not Rob's fault. He was operating in good faith and was trying to do a friend a favor, but it would turn out to be the single worst decision I made in my entire life.

Back in Bartlesville, I turned in my resignation at Phillips, much to the dismay of the managers up to and including Mr. Montgomery. They attempted to reason with me, but as mentioned, I was both blind and in denial. My last workday would be in just a few weeks.

I called Rob and notified him that I had turned in my resignation and would plan to start work with HDC effective April 1 – April Fool's Day, ironically. That should have been an omen, but I didn't recognize it at the time. Thankfully, however, I had once again managed to avoid burning any bridges at Phillips, but I didn't realize its importance at the time.

We put the house up for sale, and since HDC did not provide financial assistance with realtor's fees, I decided to try to sell it by myself. Once again, I was able to do so. I sold it to John Lanning, a friend whom I had known in high school – he had graduated the year ahead of me – and who was a lawyer whom I trusted. That being the case, we worked the deal and paperwork and were able to transact the sale with only nominal legal costs. John later was elected to a judgeship in Washington County and served honorably for many years.

We were able to stay in the house until June in order to allow Shirley to deliver our second son Greg who was due in early May.

However, the immediate plan was for me to head to Arkansas on April 1 to begin work there. Rob had agreed to let me live free of charge in the hotel/ spa located on the property and to dine in the fine restaurant HDC owned and operated. I would continue to use these amenities until I got the rest of my family moved. I was also allowed to go back to Bartlesville each weekend, primarily due to Shirley's pregnancy, so I put a lot of miles on my car each weekend.

Since we only had one car at the time, I needed to acquire a second vehicle for Shirley's use during the time I was gone. Consequently, I bought a used Chevrolet from my friend Jim Phillips that sufficed, and when it came time to move the family to Arkansas, I sold the car to Ted Lockin. Ted had been the one to hire me when I returned to Phillips from Hallmark, and he had tried to talk me out of moving to Arkansas – I should have listened. Then he helped me even further by taking an old car off my hands to give me one less headache to deal with during my move. I have always admired Ted and have been blessed to know him.

I had really enjoyed and appreciated my time in Bartlesville and with Phillips this second time around. What I did not realize at the time was that I was getting ready to enroll in the school of hard knocks, and the lessons taught there have teeth. The wounds I sustained at that school are chronicled in chapters to come, but I was blissfully unaware of what was coming at the time of my job change. Not only that, I am sure that I raised some sort of Ebenezer at the time because I mistook my new job, which on the surface appeared to be a really attractive job in a really attractive locale with a really great future, as my "good fortune." Little did I know.

THE PROVIDENCE OF GOD

Although my time in Bartlesville this time around did not specifically prepare me for the job in Arkansas, I did derive from some very great blessings during the three years we lived there:

1. We made friends with Karen Davis, which would positively and dramatically affect our future forever, beginning in only seven years – 1980.

2. I performed at a professional level at my job in Bartlesville, which stood me in good stead when I came around to Phillips Petroleum again for a third time – on bended knee.

3. Shirley safely delivered a healthy son, Greg, while we were there.

Hither by His help, I had come, but I was now stepping out on my own. In so doing, I would learn that it is never a good idea to leave God out of your life and plans.

Twenty-Five

HORSESHOE BEND – SIGNS AND WONDERS (1973–1974)

After saying goodbye to all my friends at church in Bartlesville, I drove over to Horseshoe Bend on April 1, a Sunday. I had loaded my spiffy Olds Cutlass with my clothes and my precious golf clubs and was ready for my new beginning.

Upon arriving, I immediately began taking advantage of Rob's freebies during my transition – I checked into the spa/hotel. I then went to the restaurant for Sunday evening dinner.

To this point, except for the Noah–esque rainfall that occurred during my initial visit, everything had gone "swimmingly." But that was soon to change.

My previous job changes had largely focused on increasing my value as an employee by providing me with broader business experiences. However, this last job change had been an exercise in self–aggrandizement—no matter how you sliced it—for all the wrong reasons, totally ignoring common sense. In this move, I had forced the issue. I had excluded God from the equation and instead had chosen to make the move for very selfish reasons. I have to believe that God was disappointed in me and perhaps chose to rap my knuckles to get my attention in the events that followed in Horseshoe Bend.

In support of this thesis, I will relate both some very flagrant signs and some very conspicuous wonders that I experienced following my move to Horseshoe Bend. I have to believe the events that occurred between April 1973 and May 1974 were intentional interdictions by God in my life to encourage me to refocus on the things that mattered – God and family.

The signs, which began almost immediately upon my arrival in Horseshoe Bend and continued for more than a year until May 1974, were more like omens. They were an agonizing series of consecutive, individual, adverse, annoying, and sometimes painful events. Individually, the events were not unusual but taken as a group over a condensed time period they could not have been accidental. Either I was the unluckiest guy on the planet, or God was speaking to me. I choose to believe the latter. After all, my entire life to that point had been filled with unusual, statistically impossible events.

The wonders and the great blessings started a little more than a year later, in May 1974, and lasted until August. They were totally unexpected, against all odds, powerful and timely. However, only after I had fully realized the consequences of my ill-fated decision to move to Horseshoe Bend did the wonders actually begin to materialize.

Overall there were thirteen separate easily identifiable adverse signs/events that occurred during my employment at Horseshoe Development Corporation, all of which were physically, financially, and/or emotionally challenging to my family and me. Is it not ironic that there were thirteen events, thirteen being universally recognized as an unlucky number? Also, as will be revealed, my employment at Horseshoe Bend encompassed - you guessed it! - thirteen months. I happen to believe that this was not an accident but rather a series of celestial admonitions to encourage me to get my head on straight.

As you will notice, I use the words "irony" and "ironic" frequently during this book simply because my life has been replete with ironic events. Such events keep a person guessing and keep things interesting.

Two of the signs – omens – inflicted grave wounds on me and my career at HDC and produced broad adverse nationwide pain. The other eleven signs/events were very personal, and all were byproducts of my unfortunate decision. For that reason, I do not believe the events could possibly have been coincidental. I believe God was talking to me. I believe He was allowing me to experience the folly of my bad judgment in order to redirect me back between the ditches on the road of life, so to speak. And they were effective because it appeared that by May 1974, my head had indeed been screwed back on straight, and my priorities regarding God and family had been recalibrated. At that time, the signs ceased and the wonders began to kick in. As with the signs, due to their nature and timing, I cannot believe the wonders were accidental or coincidental. I can only believe it was God working in my life, His wonders to perform.

Here is what happened.

As mentioned, I was hired as Director of Advertising to assist the VP of Public Relations. Horseshoe Bend's advertising consisted mainly of ads on the Memphis, Tennessee, TV stations, newspaper ads placed in metro newspapers throughout the north-central states, and some direct mail color brochures. The newspaper ads included coupons and were placed weekly in Chicago, St. Louis, Minneapolis, Detroit, and other metros. They advertised an offer to spend a free weekend at Horseshoe Bend to look the place over. "Free weekend, three days and two nights at Horseshoe Bend Estates," the ads screamed. We also used color brochures in limited direct mailings, which were produced and mailed by advertising agencies. These brochures contained photos and descriptions of the community and the coupon that could be used in the same way as those in the newspapers to schedule a vacation. The management of scheduling the ads, placing the ads, paying for them, and then tracking their results were becoming more of a burden than the current VP could effectively handle, given the fact that his job responsibilities were far broader than mere advertising.

It was especially essential to track the results generated from all the advertising sources – TV, newspaper, color brochures – in order to judge their effectiveness and to allow the company to better know where to spend its advertising dollars. So, I was hired to handle those duties, reporting to the VP.

I might add that in early 1973, in our country, the economy was booming, and gasoline was about 50 cents per gallon. There were discretionary dollars to be spent for vacation and retirement homes, and it cost very little to drive to Horseshoe Bend and check it out – particularly since lodging during the tour was free. No one was paying any attention to some possible dark economic clouds just over the horizon.

At that time the processing of the completed reservation coupons which were received was a monumental task, given their volume. All the recording and tracking of the coupons were done manually on huge spreadsheets. One of my first recommendations to management was that we automate the process – enter the data into the computer and let the computer sort and spit out the results. It would save probably at least 120 hours of manual labor each week and provide more accurate and timely reports. I had brought a little computer data entry moxie with me from the Phillips Credit Card Center. Rob thought it sounded like a good idea and turned me loose to develop the system.

Our computer resources were located at the Gulf South office in Oklahoma City, but we had terminals in the Horseshoe Bend office that could be used for data entry. I worked long distance with a programmer in the Oklahoma City office, and we got the system up and running pretty quickly.

While all this was going on, I still had to schedule ads with newspapers and order brochures to be mailed by the advertising agencies. At some point, everything melded, and we were running a pretty efficient advertising department.

This pretty well summed up my early weeks on the job. It was still spring, and sales of lots and construction of houses were actually booming, and my job had smoothed out to the point I felt competent and was enjoying the work. What could go wrong?

As mentioned, people say that "13" is an unlucky number, an omen, such as on Friday the 13th. Ironically, I encountered a Friday the 13th in my first month on the job, April 13, 1973. In the case of my sojourn in Horseshoe Bend, the superstition regarding the number 13 manifested itself in spades. As mentioned, I was employed at Horseshoe Bend for thirteen months, and during that period my family and I had to endure thirteen specific, separate adverse "trials," omens if you will. Some of the omens were painful, some were merely uncomfortable, but taken together in such a compact time frame, they sent a message. In retrospect, I can only believe these were not only God's way of chastising me for making such a selfish decision in taking the job and but also His means of "encouraging" me to get back on the straight and narrow. This is not to indict Horseshoe Bend in any way, for the corporation and its operation were honorable in every way. Rather, I believe the signs and omens were specifically directed at me personally and were the result of the poor choices I made in taking the job in the first place.

May I elaborate?

The First Sign – The Recession (Painful)

The first sign was not a single event but rather a 21–month nightmare. It actually began before I had even contemplated changing jobs and did not conclude until well after my last chapter at Horseshoe Bend had been written. It began in very early 1973 when the United States fell into a recession, which, I would later discover, created an extreme disincentive for discretionary spending on things such as vacation homes and retirement communities. The initial stages of this omen were not dramatic and were completely overlooked by me and much of the financial world early in the year. When it was over, official statistics disclosed that the Standard & Poor's stock index declined by 48.2% during those 21 months – more than 2% per month. The recession had actually quietly begun even before I even made the decision to change jobs, and had I been paying attention in early 1973, it is likely I would never have made the change. However, all I could see were stars before my eyes when I was offered the job at Horseshoe Bend.

Early on, the recession did not affect my new job. As things turned out, the recession crept in on little cat's feet – with apologies to Carl Sandberg – and spring and early summer sales of lots and construction in Horseshoe Bend were near normal. However, by mid-summer, the recession was roaring, and the typical mid-summer and autumn tours and sales had tanked. Although there was some attrition among the sales force, there were no layoffs of management or staff as everyone expected that we could ride out the recession and hit high gear again the next spring. Meanwhile, in response to the economy, we cut back on advertising, and I seemed to be having a lot of spare time in my new job. It is an understatement to say that, looking back, if I had only read the tea leaves regarding the economy before I made my fateful decision, I would never have made the fateful decision. God gave me a heads–up that I ignored.

The Second Sign – The Flood (Uncomfortable)

As previously mentioned it rained nine inches in Horseshoe Bend the day Shirley and I visited the community for our first look-see. The roads were flooded, the road to the next town was under water, and the dam on Crown Lake in the center of the town nearly failed due to the monsoon. However, as it was still early in the game, I ignored this omen. Despite the torrential downpour, the visit had been otherwise positive with regard to community, amenities, offices, and homes, and, despite the rain, I had accepted the job during the visit.

The Third Sign – Initial Family lodging (Uncomfortable)

When I arrived at Horseshoe Bend on April 1, as mentioned, I was provided with a complimentary room at Hill High, the spa and motel, until I could get my family moved over there. I went back to Bartlesville every weekend to be with my wife and family. This obviously was not an ideal plan. My wife, Shirley, was now eight months pregnant with our son Greg, and I could not have picked a worse time to be absent from home. Shirley's mother and dad came to stay with her and our 3–year old son, Brent, while she was still in Bartlesville, but it was still really inconvenient for Shirley. Throughout it all, to her credit, Shirley bit her tongue and went along with my adventure.

Our son Greg was born on May 6, a little over a month after I had begun my new job. I was there for the birth and took a few days off to help get things settled. Sometime in June, we felt it was safe to move the family to Horseshoe Bend. We were able to sell our house in Bartlesville without any trouble. Our new house in Horseshoe Bend was under construction but would not be available until October. I had arranged to rent a well–used 2–bedroom duplex in Horseshoe Bend, so I abandoned the spa/hotel, and we stored most of our furniture and moved into the tiny apartment until our new house was finished. The four of us, including the baby, had to live in a cramped, 600 square foot duplex with noisy neighbors for more than four months. This was not the housing I had anticipated living in when I took the job. This adventure was certainly not starting out as I had imagined.

At this point, I do need to interject one small kernel of good news among the omens I had already encountered and would yet encounter. Another "small world" event occurred shortly after my family arrived in Arkansas. At the Limestone Church of Christ in Bartlesville and at two churches in Independence, we had been greeted on our first visit to the congregation by the preacher who was a friend or college classmate. Consequently, Shirley and I had never been total strangers at any church we had attended to this point. This unbelievably continued on our move to Arkansas. As mentioned, there was no Church of Christ yet established in Horseshoe Bend, but there was one in Melbourne, Arkansas, about 20 miles away. When we attended there on our first Sunday in Arkansas as a family, we were greeted in the foyer by a Harding grad who had been preaching there for about two years. Due to the senility associated with my current advanced age, I cannot recall his name or that of his wife, but, nevertheless, we were welcomed as a family on the first day. This was getting to be weird, and it was not over by any means. But, more on that later.

The Fourth Sign – I Am All Alone (Uncomfortable)

The fourth sign occurred following the movement of my family into the duplex at Horseshoe Bend. At that point I had crossed the Rubicon, so to speak, and there was no turning back. When Rob had recruited me for this job, he told me that he was also contacting several of our Harding classmates and offering jobs to them in the hope that we might be able to turn Horseshoe Bend into a "little Harding." That really appealed to me at the time, and, truthfully, it was a huge factor in my decision to make the move. However, shortly after I had crossed the Rubicon, Rob informed me that every one of the friends from Harding had declined his offers of employment. So it was just going to be Rob and me, and, as it turned out, Rob was required to travel a lot, and we didn't get to spend much time together. It was a real disappointment that cast a real pall on the job because half of the reason I accepted the job was to be working with old friends. The free golf and the house built at cost suddenly did not seem so attractive.

The Fifth Sign – Automobile Problems (Painful)

The fifth sign kept up the theme of Murphy's Law as it applied to my tenure in Horseshoe Bend. My one car, my pride, my beautiful 1972 Oldsmobile Cutlass S laid down on me, metaphorically speaking. It had an automatic shift lever in the floor console. The cable between the shift lever and the gear mechanism snapped, and I could not shift gears. I was advised of a really good mechanic in the town of Franklin, just a couple miles from Horseshoe Bend. I contacted him, and he brought out his tow truck and took my car away. He told me it would take about three days for the repair since he had to order a part. One intelligent thing I had done following our move was to purchase a Honda 175 motorcycle so that my wife could use the Cutlass as she needed and I could still get around. After about a week with no response from the mechanic, I rode my motorcycle to the garage in Franklin. My car sat outside untouched, and the business was closed up tighter than a drum. I was a little concerned, so I asked around in Franklin as to what had happened to the mechanic. I was told that there had been a death in his family in Texas and that he had been gone a few days, and they did not know when he was coming back. What next? Consequently, I then rode my motorcycle over to Melbourne, about 20 miles away, and located an automobile repair shop, explaining the situation to them. They sent a tow truck over to Franklin to retrieve my car, towed the car to Melbourne, and repaired it, and I then got it back in two or three days. However, the several days I was without family transportation were very inconvenient. I felt that the untimely absence of the mechanic in Franklin was just another kick in my shin, so to speak.

After five whacks, the bruises were beginning to show, but I had no choice but to keep on keeping on.

The Sixth Sign – The $14,400 Lesson (Painful)

The sixth sign was really painful. Since Horseshoe Bend was primarily a vacation/retirement community, the homes built there were primarily intended as vacation homes or as retirement homes. In either case, mansions were not the order of the day. The typical house being built in the community was two or three-bedroom with one or 1½ baths, usually about 1200 square feet. All, and I emphasize all, such homes were single story. Vacationers didn't need two-story houses, and retirees, in their advanced age, did not want two-story houses. The house I chose to build was nearly 2600 square feet, had four bedrooms, three bathrooms, and was tri-level. Not just two-story – actually three-story. Totally atypical of the homes being generally built there. However, at the time I contracted for it, I had the intention of living in it for years and then retiring in the community.

The 2600 square foot house at the promised price of $11.00 per square foot, by my calculations, came to just short of $29,000. In my naivety, I assumed that the price of the house included the ground it was going to sit on. However, that is not the way things were done at Horseshoe Bend – the house was priced separately from the lot. It made sense because lots were

239

priced from $2500 to more than $12,000, depending on location. A house was designed, and its construction was priced, regardless if it was to sit on a low– or high–priced lot. I just didn't ask the question when I first spoke with Rob months ago if the $11.00 per square foot was the turnkey price. My bad.

As a concession to the situation, HDC had offered me a $4000 lot at a deeply discounted price of $2400, which I snapped up. It was in a choice location.

However, this sixth sign/omen just would not quit. It turns out that $11.00 per square foot bought me a frame house with no frills – no carpet, no fireplace, no stone or brick, one set of bathroom fixtures, basic kitchen appliances, single-story, and a one-car garage. This was the typical house being built there due to the clientele – retirees and vacationers. As mentioned, we had designed a much larger and more complex house trimmed in native stone. For our house, the stone for the exterior would cost another $800. I wanted a fireplace, and it needed to be built of stone, which required not only more stone but extra work by a mason. The carpet was a few hundred dollars more. Non–standard light fixtures were expensive, as were kitchen appliances and the fixtures for the two additional bathrooms. That was the bad news. The good news was that all these "extras" were actually being sold to me at cost. I can't imagine what the final price would have been if there had been any markup on them.

When the smoke cleared, the house, instead of $29,000, cost me $41,000 ($15.76 per square foot just for the house) plus the lot – $43,400 in total. So here I was with a house that was totally out of character with the community, costing $14,400 more than I anticipated. The builder was not trying to scam me. Rather he assumed that I was aware of how houses were built there. Many years later, I built another house in Amarillo, Texas, and I am here to tell you that I had every single cost documented and nailed down before I signed off. The price of that education, however, was $14,400 in 1973 dollars.

By the time we moved into our house that October, I was already making plans to sell it due to the omens which had manifested themselves by then, not realizing that I was less than halfway through the string of adversities that were to occur. Although I could not put a "For Sale" sign in my front yard, I nevertheless listed the house with the HDC realty office.

A word of explanation. In Horseshoe Bend, as was the practice in many vacation/retirement communities, it was not permitted to post a "For Sale" sign in your front yard because, truthfully, in most such communities, half the houses would have had a For Sale sign out front. The rule was not due to anything illegal or underhanded but rather because it might have been a powerful "turn–off" for any potential buyer touring the community and seeing so many houses or lots for sale. The purchases of lots and construction of houses in vacation/retirement communities are frequently high dollar, discretionary, impulse purchases, which buyers sometimes wish they had given a little more thought to before signing on the dotted line. As a result, a higher percentage of houses are usually on the market in a vacation/retirement community than would be found in a typical city. This would lead to a disproportionate number of For Sale signs being posted if such signs were allowed. In such a situation, the presence of so many For Sale signs would definitely give pause to any potential buyers, perhaps asking themselves, "Why?" Ergo, For Sale signs were not allowed. Ironically (there's that word again), houses or lots that had been sold were encouraged to post "Sold" signs out front. This was legitimately viewed as an incentive to prospective buyers, implying that if they bought, they could also sell without much trouble.

The sixth sign – I had apparently saddled myself with debt on a house that exceeded my entire personal financial net worth at the time with no potential buyer on the horizon.

The seventh through thirteenth signs all occurred between October 1973 and May 1974 and constituted, I thought, cruel and unusual punishment.

The Seventh Sign – Utility Cost (Painful)

There is no natural gas in that part of Arkansas, so most houses were totally electric, meaning an electric furnace. Fate chose to send the harshest weather in decades to northern Arkansas that winter. At one stretch, there were eleven consecutive days when the temperature did not reach as high as 32 degrees. Not only that, there was so much snow that I had to walk to the supermarket, about a mile away, to buy a gallon of milk and then carry it home. Do you realize how heavy a gallon of milk gets while walking through the hills in the snow for a mile?

My electric bill for that winter averaged nearly $300 per month. During that winter my electric bill plus my $300 per month mortgage payment ate up more than half my monthly take-home pay. Not only that, during the Ice Age that was northern Arkansas that winter, my plumbing froze up, and I had to hire a plumber to thaw it out. That alone should have warranted being counted as a separate omen. As with the sixth sign, the seventh sign was cruel and unrelenting, and the eighth sign was lurking, waiting to pounce.

The Eighth Sign – The Oil Embargo/Sky High Gasoline Prices

Fate was still laughing at us. As mentioned, despite the onset of the recession, the spring and early summer of 1973 had been boom times for Horseshoe

Bend. Most of the reservations had already been made before the serious effects of the recession kicked in, and visitors kept coming. There were thousands of visitors, a high percentage of sales, everyone smiling, money flowing, and record profits January through June of that year. However, things were getting ready to change dramatically. The adverse effects of the recession, which actually began in January 1973, were compounded when in October of that year, OPEC declared an oil embargo against the United States and its allies as a result of our support for Israel in the Yom Kippur War. The embargo immediately caused a dramatic increase in gasoline prices and also eventually resulted in nationwide gasoline shortages.

Whatever impetus remained for exploring life in a vacation/retirement community waned substantially when gasoline prices went out of sight. It suddenly became very expensive to drive for a "free" weekend at a resort all the way from Ohio or Michigan. The high gas prices drove down the number of potential buyers and, as a result, the number of sales and the positive financial activity at Horseshoe Bend turned due south. As mentioned, a few of the sales force had already left town due to the recession, but management was still maintaining a stiff upper lip, hoping that gas prices would return to normal levels along with normalized sales revenues the following spring. However, the full effect of the embargo had not yet been felt as 1973 turned into 1974. The embargo still had some wicked blows to deliver, and they were swift and merciless in coming.

After all the adversity that had occurred just in a matter of months, I was beginning to get more than a little apprehensive that this grand plan of mine was not going to turn out as I had hoped. I had already surrendered to the fact that for the immediate future anyway, I was not going to be able to afford to live in the "mansion" I had built and had initiated plans to sell it. I was not yet worried about my job, but on the other hand, I was not getting any positive vibes regarding it either.

The Ninth Sign – Gasoline Shortages (Painful)

For the ninth sign, the embargo introduced another cruel setback – gasoline shortages and gasoline rationing. Due to the embargo, the amount of gasoline available nationwide was significantly reduced. Gasoline became in such short supply, particularly in large metro areas, that many localities placed a limit on the amount of gasoline that could be purchased a single visit to the station. Unbelievably, a common limit in some large cities was four gallons per visit. Even the gasoline stations in and around Horseshoe Bend established a four-gallon limit. This made long trips by automobile virtually impossible in most parts of the country, including the upper Midwest –

Horseshoe Bend's golden goose. Probably 80 percent of all HDC sales came from Iowa, Missouri, Illinois, Ohio, and points north. Consequently, about 80 percent of potential customers were immediately dissuaded from making the drive to Arkansas, and that is even if they were able to afford the high gas prices. The embargo had become a two-headed monster. For our potential customers, this situation reduced visits to a trickle.

The financial crisis brought on by the recession and the embargo official-ly lasted from January 1973 until October 1974, finally abating five months after I had left Horseshoe Bend. If that is not a slap–in–the–face omen, I will eat my hat. But we were not finished yet.

The Tenth Sign – Soaring Interest Rates (Painful)

The tenth sign was very "interesting," pardon the pun. Let's see – by this time, the country was deep in a recession, gasoline was in very short supply and, what you could buy was very expensive. As if there had not been enough personal adversity, another sign soon manifested itself. As with the oil em-bargo, the recession also had deadly tentacles, and it did not hesitate to put them to use. One such tentacle was its devastating effect on interest rates. Interest rates on everything, including real estate loans, soared to more than 10%. At this point the effects of high gasoline prices, gasoline shortages and now usury–level interest rates destroyed every legitimate incentive to invest in a retirement community.

And the pain caused by high-interest rates was not limited to the Horse-shoe Development Corporation. I also shared the pain. When I moved into my new house in October, I was forced to take out a mortgage loan having a 10% interest rate – and by that time, the $300 monthly electric bills not even started arriving yet. My personal financial situation had quickly deteriorated to an untenable condition.

Did I not mention in an earlier chapter that years later, I taught a Per-sonal Finance course at the college level? Given my own financial situation in the fall and winter of 1973, how in God's name did that ever happen? I can only think that the Louis L'Amour quote I used in chapter 9 made that occasion even possible. "Good judgment comes from experience, and a lot of that comes from bad judgment." Apparently, over time I had exercised enough bad judgment that some good judgment finally emerged. However, in the fall of 1973, I had apparently regressed to a Kindergarten level in fi-nancial acumen.

I was now saddled with a 10% mortgage loan on my large, unaffordable house that was virtually unsellable under the then existing socio-economic conditions, and, in addition, I soon began receiving exorbitant electric bills.

I thought I heard my personal financial death knell sounding. My future was very uncertain. As mentioned, by the time my house was completed in October, I was already making plans to sell it – or even abandon it if it came to that. Things never looked bleaker.

The Eleventh Sign – Another Automobile Failure (Uncomfortable)

They just kept coming. The eleventh sign was also just an annoyance, but nevertheless a pain. It was like fate ran out of plagues and had to start recycling them. This sign was very similar to my ordeal on I–35 near Guthrie, Oklahoma, several years ago (car quitting on a Sunday night, bad generator and towing) and to the one involving my Olds Cutlass just a few weeks earlier (gear problem and towing by a Melbourne mechanic). This one involved an alternator instead of a generator, a distinction without much of a difference, and also involved towing by the Melbourne mechanic again.

Shortly after Christmas, in the midst of the awful winter, my mother decided to drive over to visit us. She and my dad and sister, Drew, still lived in Okemah, Oklahoma, about 400 miles of hard driving from Horseshoe Bend. Most of those miles were on 2–lane mountain highways, a lot of it after dark. Thankfully the treacherous winter had not started yet, and no snow was on the ground at that time. My mother had never been to Horseshoe Bend before and had no idea how to find us once she arrived in town. When we spoke on the telephone, I advised her to follow the signs to Horseshoe Bend and then park in the driveway of my office, which was near the entrance to the community. I would be waiting for her. She arrived at about midnight, and her headlights looked like candles. They were barely burning. She stopped the car at my office and turned off the engine. We greeted one another, and then I told her to follow me to my house. She got in her car, and the starter would not even make a sound, much less turn over the engine. It was dead as a doornail.

We put all their suitcases in my car (luckily I had my car operable again) and we piled in and went to my house. The next morning I was unsuccessful in being able to start her car, so I called the automobile garage in Melbourne and asked him to send a tow truck, which he did. When the tow truck driver arrived, he mentioned something about this getting to be a regular thing with me and my cars. I told him I was trying to help him fund his retirement. Anyway, he dragged the car to Melbourne and called us later the same day, informing us that it had been repaired. It was the alternator. It would have been the generator if they still installed generators in cars. This must be a family thing. It's just a good thing it was only about 400 miles from Okemah to Horseshoe Bend. If it had been any further, my mother and Drew might still be stranded beside the road in the dark someplace. I guess that was at least one blessing in that trauma.

The Twelfth Sign – Fear in the Air (Uncomfortable)

For a change of pace, the twelfth sign involved neither finances nor an inoperable automobile. It involved an airplane with much more dire possible consequences. Not long after my mother and sister returned to Oklahoma, winter hit Arkansas with a vengeance. This was the period when there were below freezing daytime highs for eleven consecutive days plus lots of snow. At this time, of all times, it was necessary for me to make a trip to St. Louis to visit a potential new advertising agency.

The Gulf South Corporation had a corporate airplane, a Cessna 340 having twin-turbocharged engines, a pressurized cabin, and seating for four plus the cockpit. Sometime along the way, a commercial quality airstrip had been constructed at Horseshoe Bend that could accommodate most aircraft smaller than a commercial jetliner. HDC personnel were permitted to requisition the plane as needed. I had commandeered to use the plane several months earlier on a trip to Gulf South headquarters in Oklahoma City.

I now scheduled the plane to fly me to St. Louis just ahead of the blizzard that was preparing to devour the Midwest. Harry Meade was the pilot, and a nicer gentleman I have never met. We flew up one morning and landed at Lambert International Airport in St. Louis. Since the meeting with the advertising agency was scheduled for late that afternoon, we planned to spend the night in St. Louis and return to Arkansas the following morning.

The arrival of the blizzard had been anticipated not only by the airport management but also by every owner of any plane that called Lambert home. As a result, Harry was unable to secure storage overnight in a hanger and had to leave the plane outside exposed to the elements. When we arrived at the airport the next morning to head for Arkansas, the plane was coated with a half-inch of ice in some places. Harry managed to pull the plane into a hanger that had been vacated, and after a while, some of the ice melted off. However, if it were to have been necessary to wait for the entire plane to deice itself through melting, we would have been there all day. As I have mentioned, I had worked for Phillips Petroleum Company in their Credit Card Center, and I faithfully carried a Phillips 66 gasoline credit card, as did Harry. In those days, there were neither magnetic stripes on the cards nor any chips. Rather, they were heavy-duty plastic cards that had to be run through manual credit card imprinters. The cards were tough and semi-thick. As God is my witness, Harry and I took our Phillips 66 credit cards out of our billfolds and finished deicing the wings of the plane as far as necessary by scraping the ice with our credit cards. To the cards' credit, neither of our credit cards split while we were deicing the plane.

I had been keeping track of the signs/omens for the past few months, and I believed that this was the twelfth sign/omen and that we had managed to defeat it without further problems. But I was mistaken. The twelfth sign was still alive.

Outside it was still hovering around zero degrees, but we taxied outside to the runway and cued up for takeoff. It was almost hilarious in that our little twin-engine, 4-passenger airplane was in the midst of a whole line of 747's, 727's and other large commercial aircraft. We could only see the bottoms of the others in the takeoff line. I truly would like to have had a photo of that.

However, we soon discovered there was still life in the twelfth omen. After we took off and headed south, Harry attempted to retract the landing gear but was unable to do so. The wheels were apparently frozen in the "down" position. We had neglected to deice the wheels and struts, and the wheels would not retract. At that point, Harry uttered the one and only profanity I ever heard him use. It probably would not have been fatal for us to fly with our landing gear down, but he didn't want to risk it. The plane was pressurized, so its cruising altitude was up to 20,000 feet. Harry had been paying attention to the weather reports, and he remembered that there was an atmospheric inversion – the air at ground level was colder than that at 10,000 feet and above. So he increased our altitude to 15,000 feet or so, and then a few minutes later once again attempted to retract the landing gear – hoping that perhaps the ice had thawed on the struts. After he pressed the button, or whatever he did to retract the gear, he heard the familiar "pop" of the landing gear retracting. The outside temperature at that altitude turned out to be 50 degrees. The remainder of the return trip to Horseshoe Bend was blissfully uneventful, and we had survived the protracted twelfth sign.

A Brief Respite

Prior to the onset of the thirteenth omen, Shirley and I received a brief respite from the uncertainty we had been encountering. As mentioned, one of the perks offered upon my accepting the job with HDC was the news that every winter, HDC management was awarded an expense-paid week-long trip to Las Vegas. Despite the dreary financial outlook for the upcoming spring and summer, the trip to Las Vegas went on as scheduled. There were about a dozen of us that were invited. Shirley and I drove to Okemah and dropped off our kids for a brief vacation with Grandma and Grandpa, and then we drove to Dallas to catch a flight to Las Vegas.

Our lodging in Las Vegas was the famous and iconic Landmark Hotel, at the time the tallest hotel in town. Accommodations were wonderful, the food was great, and overall we had a fantastic week. The highlight of the week was our attendance at an Elvis concert at the Hilton Hotel. We had been to a previous Elvis concert in Tulsa three years earlier, but we were anxious to see him again. At this time, however, he and his wife, Priscilla, were going through a divorce. He fumbled a few lyrics, and it was evident that he was under some stress, but, nevertheless, he gave us everything we expected and more.

We also attended Roger Miller and Wayne Newton concerts that week, and though they were great, they were not Elvis.

At week's end, sadly, we boarded the plane for our flight back to bleak reality, but the week in Vegas had really been a blessing for us during this time.

The Thirteenth Sign – So Long Rob (Painful)

The thirteenth sign hit in late February of 1974. By that time, the economy and gasoline shortage had taken a huge toll on Horseshoe Bend. Reservations for vacations during the coming spring and summer had basically dried up. As mentioned, many of the sales staff had abandoned ship. At that point, under the circumstances, it appeared that the grand plan at Horseshoe Bend had crashed and burned, with no reasonable expectations of resuscitation in the foreseeable future. My hope to be the eventual VP of Advertising had vanished, and my employment future was very tenuous. I was the newcomer among the management employees of the corporation and expected to be laid off at any minute. I had one real asset which I hoped would keep me employed – my personal relationship with Rob Barber, the President of the corporation. However, the thirteenth sign kicked in, and that asset vanished by the end of February when Rob told me he was resigning and leaving – getting out of Dodge while the getting was good. He had no immediate plans, and he had no advice for me. At this point, whatever safety net I had at Horseshoe Bend had just gone away. Although the new President, Len Garner, called me into his office and assured me that my job was safe, I was pretty sure that all of us, including Mr. Garner, were short-timers due to circumstances. I suspect that, as with most corporations, HDC would apply the "LIFO" accounting principle when it came to layoffs – "Last in (me), first-out (likely me)."

This was the straw that nearly broke the camel's back for me. By this time, I was completely worn out physically and emotionally and expected to soon be extremely financially distressed. However, mercifully, no further sign/omens were immediately sent my way. Instead, there began a lull which providentially provided me a time of soul–searching and contemplation and

247

lots of prayers. HDC's prime time for reservations and potential sales traditionally started in mid-spring and continued through early autumn, so consequently, there were no major movements made by the company as of the first of May. Rather, during this time, management was treading water until springtime reservations started coming in.

Come the first of May, my family and I had been exposed to thirteen adverse signs during our thirteen months in Horseshoe Bend, each of which had ranged from uncomfortable to painful. It should be noted that I do not in any way blame HDC for any of these trials. The corporation acted in good faith with me from the beginning and throughout, and none of the trials can be laid at HDC's feet. However, thankfully, as time would tell, these thirteen signs would be totally defeated before we left Horseshoe Bend. In the meantime, however, I was asking myself if this nightmare would ever end. I was very weary with the succession of signs/omens that had come my way and was praying fervently for relief. How about a few blessings?

Then things changed almost overnight. Life did a one-eighty.

The First Wonder – I Sold My House (Relief, Joy, and Thanks)

I have to confess that as the tribulations continued to pile up, I did a lot of soul searching. I considered everything I had done and why and basically came to two conclusions. First, it was stupid and selfish of me to have grabbed at what appeared to be the brass ring without fully considering the possible consequences. Second, I must have quoted – pleaded – 1 Corinthians 10:13 a thousand times over the past several months.

> *No temptation has overtaken you, except what is common to mankind. And God is faithful; he will not let you be tempted beyond what you can bear. But when you are tempted, he will also provide a way out so that you can endure it.*

If you truly believe in God and believe that all Scripture is His will revealed, then you have to believe that this passage is true and faithful. I eventually came to believe, in reflection, that I had succumbed to temptation by accepting the job at Horseshoe Bend. Not that the job in itself was sinful but rather that my motives were impure for accepting the job that subsequently resulted in my uprooting my entire church and family life. I rued the decision and prayed continually that this scripture was applicable to my situation. If it wasn't, then I was at great risk of my entire world collapsing, but if the scripture did apply, then there was hope. If it did apply, then what Shirley and I had endured over the past several months was, I assumed, not punishment but rather consequences of bad judgment, which, as Louis L'Amour

248

explained, would eventually lead to good judgment.

As quickly as the thirteen plagues had struck, they vanished, replaced by true wonders.

In early May of 1974, the first wonder manifested itself. Prior to that time, Ebenezer had disappeared from my mind, and I was just praying for wisdom and deliverance. The more I considered the situation, the more I came to the conclusion that the only way to extract myself and my family from this morass was to be able to leave without the burden of a house to worry about. I had to dispose of the house one way or another. There were only two possible solutions to that problem – either sell the house or allow foreclosure. Foreclosure was the most extreme solution because it would likely require that I declare bankruptcy. I still had some Phillips Petroleum Thrift Plan savings that I had not touched, and if I faced foreclosure, those funds would be drained, and we would be essentially flat broke. Kind of a sad situation for a "star" business student who had been part of a National Intercollegiate Marketing championship team in college.

During the dark days, as the omens continued to pile up, I recalled the Biblical story of Joseph and his youthful arrogance among his brothers and what happened to him. In the story, of course, God allowed Joseph to be severely tested in many ways before His Providence was revealed. In the end, Joseph became a ruler in Egypt, second only to the Pharaoh, and through Joseph's righteousness and wisdom, God helped him create a plan to save the Israelites from extinction from famine. Although I was no Joseph, I had to believe that God was allowing me to learn and mature through my trials and that eventually I would be rescued from my present dilemma. I prayed a lot – continually quoting 1 Corinthians 10:13 – and repented a lot, and made a lot of promises to God.

Consequently, I decided to expend all my energies on selling my unsellable house. I would accept foreclosure only as a very last resort. The last thing I wanted to do was declare bankruptcy and have to start over.

I then focused all my attention on selling the house, temporarily foregoing any efforts to find a new job. My rationale was that I would likely be able to find a job elsewhere before I would be able to sell the house, and that would present another dilemma – incurring costs associated with maintaining two houses. Instead, my decision was that if/when I found a buyer, my family and I would immediately move out and store our furniture at my parents' house in Okemah, Oklahoma. Only at that time would I start the job hunt. In the meantime, I polished up my resume to include "Director of Advertising" among my work experiences to go along with "Credit Analyst," "Shipping Supervisor," and "Computer Systems Analyst." Since word processing software was still basically unknown at that time, I laboriously typed it up on my Remington manual typewriter.

As mentioned, I had first listed the house for sale the previous October with Horseshoe Realty, a subsidiary of HDC. The paint was hardly dry on the house when I listed it. Bear in mind that my house was twice as large and three times as tall as the typical house in the community, and finding a buyer among the population of potential buyers in this community would require a miracle. By early May of 1974 – six full months later – there had been exactly zero showings. The realtor had not identified a single potential buyer in all that time. Of course, the fact that I could not post a "For Sale" sign in my front yard did not help.

I had originally listed the house at $43,400, only attempting to recover its cost, including the lot. I then dropped the price to $38,000 and spread the word among the employees of Horseshoe Bend. A price of $38,000 would barely allow me to pay off the loan against the property. Then, out of the blue, a retired Horseshoe Bend salesman approached me and told me he had heard my house was for sale at a reduced price. I could hardly breathe, but I was able to respond to him without stammering that this was indeed correct. He looked over the property and made me an offer for $38,000, and I signed the papers that same day without any realtor involvement in any way. The retiree that bought the house was more than 70 years old with bad knees and had no business buying a tri-level house, but he did, and he intended to live in it. At that time, I raised a huge Ebenezer, for this very unlikely event had to be the work of God. There is no other explanation under the circumstances. It seemed that perhaps my "luck" had changed.

The Second Wonder – The Vanishing Realtor Fee (Relief, Joy, and Thanksgiving)

The second wonder started out on a very positive note, but then things changed. The potential sign/omen raised its ugly head when word got around that I had sold the house. As mentioned, I had listed the house for sale the previous October with Horseshoe Realty, and the agent was, therefore, also an employee of HDC. The typical sales commission of 6% of the sales price was written into the contract with the real estate office. However, as mentioned, from October to May, the agency had not brought a single person to look at the house. After I sold the house by myself, the agent approached me and reminded me of the sales commission in the contract, which came to $2280 on the $38,000 sales price. He was legally correct but morally out of bounds since he had done exactly nothing to try to sell the house. After we discussed the situation, he decided to concede a portion of the commission and told me he would settle for a payment of $600. Being hard-headed and a little sore and worn out from the way the whole Horseshoe Bend experiment had unfolded, I was in no mood to compromise in this matter. Rather, I approached his boss, who was a VP in HDC, and asked for mercy. He was familiar with all that was happening at Horseshoe Bend, including my situation. He took the sales contract and tore it up in my presence, and threw it away. This was the manifestation of the second wonder. I had to believe that maybe the spring of my discontent was coming to an end.

As the date of our vacating the house neared, I made arrangements to rent the largest U–Haul truck available plus their largest trailer. We contacted Shirley's brother, Darold Swayne, and asked him to help us with the move. He would drive the truck and pull the trailer when we left, and I would drive our car. I made arrangements with my parents to make space in their garage for our furniture and that we would be moving in with them for the foreseeable future. Bringing two young grandsons for an extended visit made us very welcome. They told me to take my time in the job hunt. When the day came, we loaded up the truck and trailer and headed west.

I will say that the timing of my exit from Horseshoe Bend was providential in one other way. Horseshoe Bend Estates, the official name of the Horseshoe Bend community, was not the only real estate holding of Gulf South Corporation in Arkansas. The company also owned a piece of property a few miles west of Horseshoe Bend, which they referred to as Whitewater. During the last weeks of my employment at HDC, there was some effort made to sell that property, and at some point, after I left the company, it was sold and eventually became the focus of the Whitewater scandal that rocked the nation two decades later. I don't know how many owners it passed through before it wound up making the headlines, but I am just glad that I was long gone by then.

One other tidbit – one of the attractions to the job at HDC was the unlimited golf I could play while there. Ironically, during my thirteen months at Horseshoe Bend, I probably did not play more than 20 rounds of golf, and, basically, when I left there, my golf game was worse than when I came.

Thus ended my saga at Horseshoe Bend, Arkansas. It had been a trip to remember, with a few highs and many lows and many learning experiences. I would ever be grateful to Rob Barber for having the confidence in me to offer me the job, but I would have a tough time forgiving myself for accepting the job for the reasons I did. Most of all, I would eternally be grateful to God for delivering me from my Egypt to the Promised Land and to the many blessings for both myself and for others that would later manifest themselves.

As this narrative continues, I will relate many other events in my life which I believe to be the Providence of God. For the time being, anyway, the signs and omens took a rest and allowed peace to reign.

THE PROVIDENCE OF GOD

After reviewing my thirteen months in Horseshoe Bend, it was challenging to find many things to raise an Ebenezer in response to. Most of my time, there consisted of my climbing out of holes that I had dug for myself due to my decision to change jobs. Many years later, my daughter advised me that when I found myself in a hole, I should quit digging and put the shovel away. I wish I had received that advice much sooner. However, in spite of the difficulties I faced during my time in Arkansas, there were nuggets of blessings that I unearthed:

1. First and foremost, I learned the importance of thinking things through, looking at all the angles, before I made any significant decision – such as changing jobs.
2. Second, I learned that there are consequences for all decisions, and bad decisions usually lead to bad consequences.
3. After the thirteen signs/omens had been effectively applied, I received a reprieve by selling an unsellable house to an unlikely customer – a miracle most certainly.
4. In addition, I received another blessing when the realtor tore up a contract and forgave a $2280 realtor fee that a written contract had provided for.
5. The Las Vegas trip and the Elvis concert were additional blessings that provided some cheer at a time when it was really needed.
6. In the end, the blessings I received as a result of my time in Arkansas outweighed the signs/omens, and I managed to escape with both my dignity and my financial situation only slightly bruised.

As a result, I raised my largest Ebenezer ever.

Twenty-Six

A SUMMER EXTRAORDINAIRE (1974)

Although I had struggled with many adversities during my tenure at Horseshoe Bend, toward the end of my time there, my luck changed dramatically. Eventually, I came to believe that it was not luck but rather Romans 8:28 and 1 Corinthians 10:13 kicking in on my behalf. Upon arrival at my parents' house in Okemah, it seemed that the troublesome signs began being replaced with more of God's wonders.

My parents owned a three-bedroom house with 1½ baths, which could easily accommodate my family, including four-year-old and one-year-old grandsons. In addition, they had a two-car garage, which was rarely used and could easily accommodate the furniture I was storing. Mom and Dad were sorry that things had turned out the way they had in Arkansas, but they were very glad to welcome us into their home for however long it was necessary. While we lived in Arkansas, they did not get to see the grandchildren (and Shirley and me) very often.

However, I was still unemployed. Immediately upon arriving and getting settled in Okemah, I began my job search. I journeyed the 70 miles to Oklahoma City and made contact with an employment agency. I gave them my original, hand-typed resume, and the agent made copies, returning the original to me. Despite the recession and gasoline shortage, the situation in mid-America was not as dire as in other, more heavily populated areas. Jobs could still be had in this part of the country, and gasoline was available.

At the time, I also called my former boss at Phillips Petroleum, Lewis Woods. Woody and I had had an excellent relationship when I was working for him at Phillips. He had really hated to see me leave the company. When

I called him, he was sympathetic to my plight, but he said they had no openings at present. He asked me to send him a resume, however, and he would circulate it at Phillips to see if any other opportunities were available. The only copy of my resume that I still possessed was the original, hand-typed copy. Xerox machines were not so readily available in 1974, so it would be difficult for me to make a copy to send him. Once sent, I would have to put together a new resume from scratch if others were needed. I swallowed hard, crossed my fingers, uttered a prayer, and sent the original and only copy of my resume to him.

Given the fact that I had bailed on Phillips Petroleum twice, I did not have a lot of hope that they would be interested in taking another chance with me. I really expected that any job possibilities would emerge from the employment agency in Oklahoma City rather than this latest Hail Mary attempt on my part with Phillips. Little did I know.

A few days later, the employment agency lined up an interview with Johnson & Johnson at their plant in Sherman, Texas. I drove down from Okemah and participated in a plant tour and the interview. The plant was a manufacturing facility, and the job was a shift supervisor. Although my supervisory experience at Hallmark was not unpleasant nevertheless, I was not particularly interested in once again taking a similar position in a production facility. I was still clinging to the Computer Systems Analyst reference in my resume and really had no interest in the supervisor job. To his credit, the interviewer picked up on my nonchalance in the interview and asked me if I really wanted the job. His language indicated that I could probably have the job if I wanted it, but if I was hesitant, he was very clear that it probably wouldn't be a good fit. We more or less agreed that I should not actively seek the job, and he would not attempt to sell me on it. It was a great tour and a great interview that turned out exactly as it should have. This effort didn't work out, but there was always tomorrow. It was still early in the game. Time to wait for God to perform another wonder.

"I will wait for the Lord, my whole being waits, and in his word, I put my hope." Psalms 130:5-6.

Then two significant events occurred, one of which impacted my immediate future and one which had a profound effect on my long-term future.

In the first significant event, the employment agency set me up with an interview at the Hertz Corporation office in Oklahoma City. I was eager to interview with Hertz. After all, it was a well-established company with a solid past and a bright future. The oil embargo was easing somewhat by then, the economy was rebounding, and I viewed this as an opportunity for long-term, secure employment. I showed up at the Hertz office, and the interview commenced.

A SUMMER EXTRAORDINAIRE (1974)

The interviewer explained the job I was interviewing for. That particular Hertz facility handled all the billing and receipts for Hertz rentals in the United States. Bank credit cards (VISA, MasterCard, etc.) were still in their infancy in 1974 and were still not in widespread use. Consequently, almost all Hertz rentals at that time were on the basis of individual rental contracts drawn up between Hertz and the customer at the time of the rental. Balance owing statements and invoices were then mailed to customers by Hertz with the expectation that payment would be received. And as was to be expected, some payments to Hertz became delinquent, and collection efforts were necessary. My experience in the Phillips Petroleum Credit Card office made me a natural candidate for employment in the Hertz credit office.

However, the job Hertz had in mind for me was slightly different from that which I had held in my original job with Phillips. Rather than dealing with the day-to-day customer credit issues, I would be dealing with customers whose accounts were severely delinquent and who were on the verge of being referred to a collection agency. When letters and phone calls do not result in payment, accounts are frequently referred to professional collection agencies for handling. A usual fee for the collection agency's effort is 50% of the monies collected. That's a huge chunk of the amount owed, but it is also 100% more than would be received if no further collection efforts were made. Not only that, by nature collection agencies are usually more aggressive in their collection efforts than are their clients, and it is not unusual for such agencies to resort to legal action to effect collection. To possibly forestall such action, Hertz employed what I would call a "last chance intermediary." The intermediary's job was to make a single last-ditch phone call to the customer, informing them of the action that was likely to be taken. No threats, no coercion – just a sympathetic, polite phone call encouraging them to pay their debt before they were turned over to a collection agency. The customer was also reminded that their credit rating would be severely damaged if they were referred to a collection agency.

With Hertz, this gentle last-ditch effort at collection had been very effective. Thousands of dollars were collected every month through these efforts, half of which would otherwise have gone to collection agency fees. In addition, this type of collection allowed Hertz to retain its goodwill with customers and did not discourage future business with the customer.

This was a job I felt I could do with my eyes closed, and I more or less said so.

Then the interviewer, looking at my resume, said, "You have had four jobs in the past six years. What makes me think you will stick with this one?"

It was a fair question, and I gave him an honest answer, something to the effect that my last job was compromised by circumstances. The two-horned beast of the gasoline shortage and the downturn of the economy had sabotaged my position and, in fact, basically bankrupted the company I worked for. Obviously, my job performance at HDC had nothing to do with either of the issues that hurt HDC, and I reminded him that I left that job voluntarily rather than being terminated. The interviewer seemed satisfied by my response and then told me he would be getting with me in a day or two. I didn't know if that quick of a response was good news or bad. It turned out that he had to go through my employment agency to offer the job.

Two or three days later, I received a letter from my employment agency advising me that Hertz offered me the job. I was to be a salaried employee with a monthly pay of $750 (remember, this is 1974), and that I would be working in the debt collection area of Accounts Receivable. This was a reduction in my HDC pay of $350 per month plus the $100 per month car allowance. The car allowance loss was irrelevant because, unlike my work at HDC, I would not be using my car for company business. The loss of the $350 per month hurt, but I felt fortunate to receive the offer and reminded myself that beggars can't be choosers. I also remembered that I likely had a decent future with the company, given my background and the company's financial stability.

I considered my options and accepted the offer.

I was to begin employment at Hertz two weeks later, on July 1, in its Accounts Receivable Department.

Shirley and I then began the task of relocating to metro Oklahoma City. We felt that since things had been so hectic and unsettled over the past few months that we should make this move by taking baby steps rather than a giant leap. Consequently, we decided to rent a home initially rather than jump right in and buy one. As time would tell, my decision-making was improving because this proved to be one of the best decisions we ever made.

The Hertz office was located on the northwest side of Oklahoma City, and we decided to look for a rental in Yukon, Oklahoma, a suburb just west of Oklahoma City. We found a nice brick home at 509 Ranchwood Drive in Yukon and rented it. Three bedrooms, 1½ baths 2-car garage, but no fireplace, for $200 per month with no contract. Not a bad deal. With my dad helping, we rented another U-Haul truck and toted our belongings tour new home. The house was smaller than our house in Horseshoe Bend, and we had to store quite a few pieces of furniture in the garage. However, we still only had one car, so it was not a problem.

It should be noted that Garth Brooks also lived in Yukon at that time, but he was only four years old. It would be many years later before we could enjoy the music of our local celebrity.

On Monday, July 1, 1974, at 7:55 a.m. I walked into the Hertz office to begin my new job.

I settled into the job with only minimal training and was actually productive on the first day. My supervisor's name was Frank Cunningham, and he was excellent. Although he was not the man who interviewed me for the job, he had read my resume and knew my background pretty well. He was very encouraging as I began to work, and, as will be revealed shortly, he was very tolerant of some other events that occurred.

Shirley and I located the Yukon Church of Christ and showed up for services on July 7, and what had happened so many times happened again. Small world. The regular preacher did not greet us in the foyer, but rather a young man named Charles Cosgrove stuck out his hand and said, "You look familiar." Charles was a junior at Oklahoma Christian during my freshman year there, and we had gotten acquainted with one another at the time. Charles had been a Bible major, and even though he was not the regular preacher at this congregation, he was going to preach this day. This keeps happening, and it will not be the last time it happens – but more on that later.

In addition to Charles, we ran into Perry and Faye Frazier. They had been members at the Southwest Church of Christ in Ada when we worshipped there 14 years ago. However, they still remembered us, and we revisited old times. Their son, James, had been a stud on the Ada High School football team, which was a perennial state champion in the 1950s and 1960s, and I had really admired James. God kept dropping familiar faces in our path wherever we seemed to go. Once again, it can't be happenstance.

The quickly-found Hertz job was the first of the two previously mentioned significant events following my departure from Horseshoe Bend that helped shape my future. The second would manifest itself very, very shortly.

Only ten days after I began my new job, on July 11, the second significant event occurred. I received a call from Phillips Petroleum saying that they had reviewed my resume and asked if I were available to come for an interview in Bartlesville.

No promises were made during the telephone call, but I could read between the lines. I had had an excellent rapport with all my previous bosses and co-workers at Phillips, and I had received excellent reviews for my work there. My current salary at Hertz was forty percent lower than I could likely expect to receive at Phillips. We still had many good friends in Bartlesville, both in the community and at church, and I was familiar with life in general there. To accept the offer of an interview was a no-brainer and was worth about any risk that could arise. The question was – how could it be arranged?

As a less-than-two-week employee of Hertz, I had not yet accumulated any vacation time or any other paid personal time off. Bartlesville was a three-hour drive from Yukon. To take the interview in the middle of a week would likely necessitate taking an entire day off from Hertz. I had my doubts that Hertz would willingly grant me a day off for a job interview with another company, given the question that arose during my initial interview with Hertz regarding my job-hopping, I desperately wanted to go for the interview, but I did not want to jeopardize my current job in the event that the interview with Phillips did not produce a job offer.

In my phone conversation with Phillips regarding an interview, I asked if it was possible to hold the interview first thing on a Monday morning, July 15. The Phillips HR person, fully aware of my current employment situation with Hertz, also read between the lines and said he thought that could be managed. We agreed on an interview at the Phillips offices in Bartlesville on the following Monday morning at 8:00 a.m.

Shirley and I then made the decision that we would go to Bartlesville the upcoming weekend for a visit with friends and would then stay over on Sunday night for the interview on Monday morning. That still did not deal with the fact that I also needed to be in Oklahoma City at the Hertz office at 8:00 a.m. that Monday morning. Since it was impossible to be in both places at once, I had to make a choice – either Bartlesville or Oklahoma City at 8:00 on Monday morning. I rolled the dice and chose Bartlesville, realizing I would have to deal with Hertz regarding missing some work.

I did not want to be dishonest with Hertz, yet the full truth could not be revealed either, at least at that time. Therefore, I decided to call Hertz from Bartlesville on Monday morning and explain vaguely that we were not able to get back home on Sunday evening but that I would be able to make it to the office by noon. Mercifully my boss at Hertz, did not ask any questions and told me to be careful driving home.

I obviously had no trouble locating the interview site at Phillips in Bartlesville. It was in the Adams Building on the 9th floor. I had worked in the Adams Building on the 7th floor only 16 months earlier. The interview went very well. In fact, I interviewed with three managers - and I was told they would be in touch very shortly. I left the interview walking on clouds, so to speak, feeling very confident that I would be receiving an offer.

Only one thing left that could turn the clouds to rain was my return to work later that day at Hertz. However, my fears were assuaged because when I walked back into the Hertz office at 1:00 p.m., no one, including my boss, took notice.

Apparently, what sold Phillips on taking yet another chance with me were the facts that I had performed well during my two previous Philips employments, I had excellent recommendations from my previous bosses, and I now had "Computer Systems Analyst" included in my resume.

As I anticipated, I received a letter from Phillips on Thursday of that same week that made me a firm job offer job in Information Technology (IT), corporate computing, as a Computer Programmer/Analyst. This job is a cousin of my prior job there as a Methods Analyst but with significantly more interaction with the computer. They offered me a monthly salary of $1100, which reinstated my Horseshoe Bend salary, and agreed to pay for my move to Bartlesville. I gratefully raised an Ebenezer, for, truly, hither by His help I had once again been blessed.

When I read the letter from Phillips and told Shirley that I had been offered a job in Bartlesville, she was not too excited. By this point during 1974, we had already moved four times in in just a little over a year – from Bartlesville to the apartment in Horseshoe Bend, from the apartment to our new house in Horseshoe Bend, from Horseshoe Bend to my folks' garage in Okemah, and finally from Okemah to Yukon. Given the fact that she had a four-year-old son and a 3-month-old son to take care of, Shirley was understandably exhausted and in no mood to pack up and move again. She told me that she would be willing to move again this soon only if Phillips would do the packing and move us. When I told her that they had agreed to do so, she was ecstatic.

I decided to wait until the following Monday, July 22, to inform my boss at Hertz of the development. When I met with him and explained the nature of the offer, the work I would be doing, and the salary they were providing, he was very kind in accepting the news. He was the first to acknowledge that it would be foolish to decline the offer, given the terms of the offer, particularly the salary. We agreed that I would work at Hertz through July 31. This worked well because I ultimately made an arrangement with Phillips to commence work there on Monday, August 5.

I had worked at Hertz exactly two weeks when I interviewed with Phillips, I had worked there only three weeks when I announced my resignation, and I ultimately worked for Hertz exactly one month – the month of July 1974. My tenure at Hertz was very short, but it was very good. I had an excellent boss, and I made solid contributions to the company's bottom line while I was there. I will always be grateful for their contribution to sustaining my family while we were in turmoil and transition. Obviously, Hertz was one of the wonders which God dispenses to His children. Could it be that Hertz was an unseen angel? Throughout this book, it is evident that I have been exposed to and been greatly helped by what can only be described as unseen angels.

Also, as described, we continued our trend of meeting friends we knew every time we changed churches, and God had to hustle in Yukon. We attended church there only on three Sundays – July 7, our first visit, and July 21 and 28, our last two before we moved again to Bartlesville.

We bade our goodbye to Yukon and began our latest odyssey.

THE PROVIDENCE OF GOD

Once we made it out of Arkansas and from the plagues of my bad decision to move there, it just seemed that God started heaping blessings on us. There had been a 16-month moratorium on blessings, and it was as if He was just trying to get caught up. Among the current and future blessings were:

1. Through either faith or desperation I sent the last copy of my resume to Phillips Petroleum in hopes of finding work there once again. I'd like to think that it was an act of faith.

2. I was quickly provided with a good intermediate job at Hertz.

3. We were able to rent a nice house that accommodated our needs that did not require a lease.

4. As we were becoming accustomed to, we were once again able to reunite with old friends at church.

5. I was able to interview with Phillips Petroleum without consequences at Hertz.

6. My manager at Hertz was very understanding in allowing my exit from there to be without conflict

7. Phillips' paid for our move to Bartlesville, which was not a benefit usually accorded new hires in those days

8. I was placed in a job with Phillips under extraordinary managers that enabled my career to blossom.

Given my experiences over the past nearly two years, I was finally able to take a deep breath and deeply thank God for His help in the adventure. Certainly, many Ebenezers were raised.

It had truly been a summer extraordinaire. And it was only six years until the miracle of 1980.

Twenty-Seven

PHILLIPS PETROLEUM
– PART 3 (1974–1979)

Three tasks had to be accomplished as we moved again to Bartlesville – rent or buy a house, move our household goods into the new residence, and for me to actually begin work (again) at Phillips Petroleum. The third task trumped the first two, and I started work, as scheduled, on August 5, 1974. Shirley and the boys came with me to Bartlesville so together we could look for a place to live.

Unlike when we moved to Bartlesville in 1970 at a time when houses were plentiful, in 1974, the surplus of houses had been soaked up, and housing was very tight – translation, not a lot of houses for sale, and prices were non–negotiable. However, as had been the case when we first moved to town, we wanted to locate near the Ranch Heights Elementary School. It had the reputation of being an excellent school. The house we had purchased in 1970 was only a half-block from the school, and, also, we loved the neighborhood. However, since we were so picky about the area, we wanted to live in, that narrowed down the number of houses available for sale even further.

To complicate matters, the recession was still in effect, and interest rates were still high. I had just sold a house in Arkansas on which I was paying an interest rate of 10%, and with its exorbitant electric bills, I was just barely able to make the monthly payments. I would be making exactly the same salary at Phillips Petroleum that I was bringing down at HDC.

But we were not dismayed, and we once again selected Sidney Roper as our realtor. Almost miraculously, he located a house at 1231 Saddle Lane, which was just across the alley and three houses north of our previous house in Bartlesville. Same neighborhood, same school, same friends. Although it was on a single level rather than tri-level, it offered almost exactly the same amenities as that of the house we had built in Arkansas – brick, A/C, fireplace, four bedrooms, 1¾ baths, 2–car garage. Except for moving three houses north and across the alley, it was almost like we had never left town.

We had sold our house in Arkansas for $38,000, and – another miracle – our new house in Bartlesville was also priced at $38,000. Since our new house was served by natural gas, I did not have to look forward to $300 per month electric heating bills, and those factors, working together, made the new house affordable. As promised, Phillips paid for the move of our furnishings to Bartlesville.

One of our first tasks following the move was to reunite with our church family at the Limestone Church of Christ, which we did on our first Sunday there. Wayne Smethers was still the preacher there, and almost all of our friends that we had left a little over a year ago were still here, and we were warmly welcomed.

Beginning with my prior tour of duty with Phillips, I had ventured into the world of computers. Since computers were beginning to take over the world, there was a shortage of computer programmers in the labor force. Given my background with at least some knowledge of the concept of computers and my previous work performance at Phillips, the company had apparently rolled the dice and given me a third job offer. As mentioned, my job was now going to be an Information Technology Computer Programmer/ Analyst this time around rather than a Methods Analyst. Although Computer Programmer/Analysts perform many of the activities of a Methods Analyst – system analysis, research, and design – they specialize in creating the code that operates the computer. At Phillips, at the time, there were separate and very different corporate computing departments – Commercial Systems Development (CSD) and Technical Systems Development (TSD). Commercial Systems Development supported all the company's business and financial functions and utilized programs written in the COBOL computer language. Technical Systems Development supported all the technical, R&D, and scientific activities and primarily utilized the FORTRAN computer language.

Much to my delight, I was assigned a slot in CSD since business and finance was pretty much in my knowledge base. However, before I could create any COBOL code, it was necessary for me to learn the language and how to use it.

My training in COBOL was in–house, intensive, and excellent. After not very many weeks, it was determined that I knew enough about the computer language to accept my first assignment. Also, as expected, I would be surrounded by dozens of experienced Programmer/Analysts who would be glad to help me over a rough spot.

Ultimately, I was assigned to a slot that was responsible for the development and maintenance of TBA (tires batteries and accessories – expensive items) invoicing programs. Remember my introduction to the TBA system in my last job at Phillips – regarding capturing automobile tire information? It almost seems that my life has been a series of circles that keep recurring.

Not only that, guess who my supervisor was to be in my new assignment. If you guessed "Lonnie Porter," you would be correct. Another circle. This, however, is not the last time Lonnie would enter my life. More on that later.

This position involved primarily maintaining the daily TBA invoicing system and producing the daily invoices of sales of TBA to Phillips' wholesale marketers across the 50 states. It involved millions of dollars every day, and it goes without saying that it was imperative that sales had to be recorded and invoices printed out within one business day. The actual programs creating the invoices and the associated accounting information ran on the computers at about midnight every night. If problems were encountered with those programs, it was the urgent duty of the computer operator to notify the programmer who was responsible for the program – no matter what time it might be – to fix the problem. Such problems usually involved what was known as an "abend" – the "abnormal ending" of a program – and I periodically received a midnight call from the computer operator when this happened. When I received such a call, I had to get dressed and go into the office and initiate the actions necessary to resolve the problem. We were not required to wear normal office attire at that time of the night, and sweatshirts, shorts, and unshaven faces were familiar sights on those who were called in. In fact, it was sort of a badge of honor to be dressed that way when everybody else showed up for work at 8:00 a.m. They knew we had answered the call. It was intensive work, but I enjoyed it and managed to keep the invoices cranking out.

One problem that cropped up every January was due to the fact that the dates of the TBA transactions carried only a 4-digit date field – 2-digit day and 2-digit month. For example, a date field of 0103 was translated by the computer as January 3, and a date field of 1220 was translated as December 20. There was no "year" code in the transaction because everyone "knew" January followed December. However, the computer never operated on assumptions. It could only process the data as it was presented to it. Consequently, in the absence of "year" information in the transaction, the computer would simply combine the new year's January transactions with the previous year's transactions. Left unaddressed, this processing would totally invalidate record keeping and proper invoicing since all transactions had to be accumulated and processed in the proper year. Therefore, every January it was necessary to run a special program to temporarily jerry-rig the January transactions to "plug" in a "year" in order to segregate the new January transactions from any late-arriving December transactions from the previous year. It was aggravating, but we managed to get through it every year. Eventually, the system was amended to add a 4–digit year field in the transaction, but I was long gone by then.

The only reason I go into detail regarding this issue is that, as things in my life are wont to do, the exact same critical issue would arise a little later on in a different scenario, and my understanding and handling of the issue at the present time would prove helpful in resolving the future situation.

I would remain in my current job for approximately three years. After about two years, Lonnie Porter received a promotion and moved on to the Comptroller's Office in the Chemicals Division of Phillips. Sometime before Lonnie left my area, I had received a promotion which was both welcomed and very much needed. My budget was still as tight as a banjo string following my return to Bartlesville.

During my time in IT, I was introduced to snow skiing by several fellow workers who hit the slopes every winter. The primary target with the best snow was west of Denver in Colorado – Vail, Beaver Creek, the four mountains of the Summit ski area, and, of course, Aspen. Some friends of ours from Harding, Paul and Gayle Kite, had settled in Glenwood Springs, Colorado, 160 miles west of Denver, following Paul['s discharge from the Navy. Glenwood Springs is the third point of a triangle that also includes Vail and Aspen, and about an hour's drive from each ski area. In fact, Glenwood Springs also boasted its own ski area nearby – Sunlight Mountain. With my mouth watering from listening to my friends at work describe their ski adventures, I was determined to give it a try.

Over Christmas break in 1975, Shirley and I planned a trip to Glenwood Springs to visit the Kites and to try our hand at skiing. Paul and Gayle bade us come. While there, Shirley and I took some ski lessons at Sunlight, but Shirley decided they weren't her cup of tea. However, I survived the lessons, and the following two days, Paul and I skied at Buttermilk Mountain at Aspen. There are four ski mountains in and near Aspen, and Buttermilk is the easiest by far. It was a great place for me to test my ski legs. After two days on the slopes, I was totally exhausted but had fallen in love with snow skiing. After resting up for a day, we began our journey back to Bartlesville. I had become hooked on the sport and made pilgrimages, usually to Glenwood

Springs, almost every winter after that for several years. As will be related in a later chapter, my love for skiing almost got me killed.

Back in Bartlesville, following Lonnie's move into Chemicals Comptroller's, Jim Carey became my new boss and remained my supervisor for a year or so. Jim was a super guy, easy to get along with, and had a great sense of humor. He was a pleasure to work for, and I had just gotten used to his management style when another opportunity within Phillips came my way.

The company was getting heavily into online data management. Keypunched cards had basically gone the way of the dodo bird by this time, and this newer technology was being expanded as rapidly as possible company wide. The year was 1978. I was moved from Jim Carey's unit into a unit headed up by Jim Upton. He was director of a development project which intended to utilize the new technology in the management of raw materials across the entirety of Phillips Petroleum. Subsequently, I was designated lead programmer on the project. As I began my work on the project, one thing I remembered vividly during the development and implementation of the new system was the trouble I had encountered with the "year" code in transaction dates from my TBA days. To combat this problem, in recent years, corporate computing management had decreed the use of a 6–digit date field in transaction data – 2–digit day, 2–digit month, and 2–digit year. I am not a prophet, but I was now very experienced in the problems surrounding the proper sequence of transaction dates, and I saw exponential trouble ahead. In 23 years, in the year 2000, it would be necessary to begin using a 4–digit "year" code. For example, to this point, a year code of "77" in a transaction (referring to the year 1977) would always follow a year code of "76" (referring to the year 1976) in the data stream. However, come the year 2000, the system needed to be modified to recognize that a year code of "00" should FOLLOW a year code of "99" in the data stream, not precede it. Retaining a 2–digit year code would only cause trouble.

Consequently, I established an 8–digit date code in my part of the system design – including a 4–digit "year" code – and persuaded the other programmers to do likewise. It is likely that at some point before the year 2000 that someone would have noticed the potential problem, but we managed to sidestep the issue ahead of time with upfront system design.

Due to almost daily advances in computer technology, it was unlikely that my programs would still be operating for 23 years hence, but at worst, they would serve as a model for systems later. It should be noted that 15 years later, in 1992 – only eight years short of the anticipated Armageddon for computers – the dreaded Y2K – a friend of mine who still worked in IT told me that my programs developed in 1977 and 1978 were finally being

265

superseded with newer technology. They didn't last the entire 23 years, but they came close.

At this time, it bears mentioning that an accounting/computing job in the Houston office had been posted. I was not in any way disappointed in either my current work or management, but the job offered a promotion, and I still had some gypsy blood. I applied for the job and was invited to Houston for an interview. My boss at the time reminded me that he really didn't want to lose me. However, I went for the interview anyway, expecting nothing. Lo and behold, when I returned to Bartlesville, I had a job offer waiting for me. I spoke to Shirley about it, and the last thing she wanted to do was move again. She explained eloquently that we had re-established church, friends, schools, and she wasn't ready to start over again, especially in the traffic jam named Houston. Due to Shirley's influence and my eventual good judgment, I politely declined the offer, and everyone stayed happy.

However, there were still things brewing that would affect my future at Phillips and in life. I have to believe God was watching to see what I would do regarding this "opportunity" – whether I would grab the money and run or make an informed decision. I believed that God was still not finished messing with me, that His Providence still had some surprises.

At that time, Phillips Petroleum was highly diversified, and outside of the company's core business – oil production and refining – the Chemicals Division was Phillips' largest business segment. The Chemicals Comptroller maintained overall financial responsibility for the company's chemical-related subsidiaries, which included not only chemical manufacturing but also plastics, fibers, and coal operations, plus a paper manufacturer and some other smaller enterprises. Following his promotion a couple of years earlier, Lonnie Porter was now the Chemicals Comptroller's financial liaison with corporate computing.

In 1978 the Chemicals Comptroller's office sought a Senior Systems Analyst, and guess who came calling. Yep, Lonnie Porter. What goes around, comes around. He was offering me a job in Chemicals Comptroller's, and with it came another promotion. Given my history with Lonnie and the offer of a higher-level job, accepting the promotion was another no–brainer. I got the job promotion that Houston had offered but without having to disrupt my family's life again. I think Shirley may have mentioned a few, "I told you so's."

It should also be noted that my new salary in my new job was $25,000 per year. Although Horseshoe Development Corporation had not been able to deliver the promised $25,000 annual salary within five years, God saw to it that I achieved that level in, of course, five years – 1973 to 1978. These "coincidences" remain inexplicable in the absence of celestial intervention.

I wound up working in the Chemicals Comptroller's office for five years, 1978 through 1983. During that time, I was primarily involved in helping develop or update computing systems in Chemicals facilities in Dallas (American Thermoplastics), Chicago (H.P. Smith Paper Company), Spokane (Phillips Fertilizer), Denver (Phillips Coal Company), Greenville SC (Phillips Fibers), Houston (Phillips Chemicals) and Borger TX (Phillips Copolymer). In visiting remote facilities of those businesses, I traveled to a total of 38 states in the five years. In those days, the airlines did not offer points—a pity.

Early on in this assignment I was heavily involved in developing and installing a cost accounting system at the Phillips Copolymer plant in Borger, TX. My participation in the job required that I be in Borger every week, Monday through Friday, for an anticipated period of at least nine months but possibly up to three years if the project was expanded to include other Phillips operations in Borger. Since the initial project was scheduled to be completed in less than a year, and since there was considerable uncertainty about the project being extended, it was not deemed to be cost-effective to go through the hassle and expense of the company's relocating my family and me to the Borger area at that time. It was less expensive in the long run for me to fly to Amarillo, Texas—about 50 miles from Borger—every Monday morning and return to Bartlesville every Friday afternoon. Even with motels and meals, it was still cheaper to do it this way. If the project were extended, then new plans could be put in place at a later date regarding a potential move.

I started that weekly odyssey in June 1978, and by August, it was taking its toll on my family. Shirley was managing the home front, and with two young boys, things were pretty uncomfortable. I approached Lonnie and suggested that perhaps the company would be willing to pay for an apartment in Amarillo for the project's duration, and I could take my family with me. It would save airfare, expense account meals, car rentals, etc. It was a fair deal, and he went for it. We allowed our church Youth Minister, David Pratt, to use our house for as long as we would be away, and we moved into a 2–bedroom apartment in Amarillo near the Belmar Elementary School. I joined a daily carpool to Borger, and things smoothed out considerably.

At that time, we began attending the Southwest Church of Christ in Amarillo, and we got there just in time to bid the current preacher, Calvin Warpula, goodbye. I think he may have moved to Stillwater, Oklahoma, at the time. He was well thought of, and we had been there just long enough to realize he was a really good and effective preacher. Very soon small world struck again. Once again – a new church, old preacher. Actually, the replacement preacher, Leslie McGalliard, was a friend from my childhood at the Southwest Church of Christ in Ada. From the Southwest Church of Christ in Ada to the Southwest Church of Christ in Amarillo. How about that? Another weird coincidence in my life. During my time in Ada, he had not yet actually begun preaching, but we relived the days back in the late 1950s when we were both lots younger. What can I say?

The cost accounting project progressed smoothly at the Copolymer plant, and in the early spring of 1979, nine months after its inception, it was brought online. The project had been deemed so successful that plans were being made to replicate it on the Phillips Petroleum computers at its offices in Tessenderlo, Belgium, and Stavanger, Norway. At that time further expansion of the system at the other Phillips operations in Borger was tabled. Initial plans included sending our entire 5–man team to Europe to develop and implement the system. I was elated. When Phillips transfers its employees overseas, every effort is made to make them comfortable – housing, periodic travel back to the states, American schools for the children, the whole ball of wax. Also, Brent's best friend in Bartlesville, Brian Hoard, was now in Belgium due to his dad's transfer. It would be a wondrous reunion and a great experience.

Then the bad news came. The system was indeed going to be replicated in Europe, but only the project leader would be making the transfer. The other four of us would remain stateside. We would move back to Bartlesville, and I would assume other projects.

We were crushed.

This was now April 1979, and I moved my family back home, reclaiming our house from our Youth Minister, and the boys re-enrolled at the Ranch Heights Elementary school for the remainder of the semester. We were disappointed, but life goes on, and then it kicked me in the shin one more time shortly after we returned to Bartlesville.

There were labor union issues at the Copolymer plant in Borger. The Oil, Chemical and Atomic Workers (OCAW) labor contract with Phillips Copolymer had expired the previous January. The plant had been on strike for more than four months by the time I was transferred back to Bartlesville. The plant had continued to operate with non–union employees "drafted" from the pool of able-bodied Phillips employees wherever they could be found. Almost immediately upon our return to Bartlesville, I was asked to return to Borger, cross the picket line, and work in the plant.

Those who "volunteered" to work the strike were paid time–and–a–half for all overtime hours. The work shifts were 12 hours per day, seven days per week, which meant we started drawing overtime pay by Wednesday each week. My shift was from midnight to noon, and my roommate at the Sands

Motel in Borger worked the noon to midnight shift. During the entire time I worked the strike, I never met my roommate as, with our schedules, we were never in the room at the same time.

The pay was good, but the work was hard. My job was stacking bales of rubber. The plant manufactured copolymer (synthetic) rubber, a basic ingredient in the manufacture of tires. Copolymer was a generic product, so Phillips supplied it to all the major tire manufacturers – Michelin, Goodyear, General Tire, Goodrich, etc. The bales were large chunks of rubber, slightly smaller than a bale of hay, and weighed 70 pounds, and they arrived at my duty station at the rate of two or three per minute. My job was to encase the bales in clear plastic and then lift them and drop them into large containers for shipment to the customer. We rotated on and off that job about every hour, so in a 12–hour shift, I stacked rubber for only about six hours. By my calculation, I lifted approximately 5000 pounds (2½ tons) of rubber during my shift.

I worked the strike for the month of May, and then I requested that I be sent back home. Management agreed, and I went back home in much better physical shape than when I arrived for strike duty. Shirley and I used the overtime pay I had received during the month to completely furnish our master bedroom. I know of one friend who worked the strike for several months and, in the end, paid cash for a new pickup. I was not that ambitious.

Following my additional month in Borger, we got back into the swing of things in Bartlesville, renewing our church relationships, and began dealing with other issues. One of the friends we re-established friendship with was Karen Davis, whom we had originally met upon our first move to Bartlesville in 1970. And, although we did not realize it at the time, this reunion with Karen was critical and had a massive, unbelievable effect on our family just one year later, in April in the magic year of 1980.

God had had a plan when He denied my transfer overseas, but there was a reason for His decision, which will be explored in the next chapter. The old cliché would prove true, "Behind every dark cloud is a silver lining."

Following my return to Bartlesville from working the strike at the Co-polymer plant, I noticed a posting for a Systems Analyst job in our Denver office. Being a big fan of Colorado and skiing at the time, and apparently not having yet learned the lesson of Horseshoe Bend, I applied for the job. A few anxious days later, Lonnie called me into the office, and he told me that I had come in second in the contest for the job. A friend of mine had landed what I believed to be a plum of a job. I was disappointed but at least not devastated. Fast forward six months. About six months later, I ran into the friend in Bartlesville and asked him how the job was going. He told me that they had pulled the rug out from under him. The job had been cut, and he was now back in Bartlesville attempting to land a position anywhere in the company. I was stunned. I don't know if he got back on with Phillips or not, but God had apparently helped me dodge another bullet. For what was coming down the pike in a very few weeks – in early 1980 – it was critical that I had NOT been selected for the Denver job, for I would most certainly have been out of work, and the events of 1980 would never have occurred.

Since I did not get the Denver job, I was assigned to a project to help convert the computers of Chicago–based H. P. Smith Paper Company, a Chemicals Division subsidiary, from Univac to IBM. This involved not only replacing the computers themselves but also totally reformatting all the information that had previously been processed on the Univacs. I spent most of the winter with two more programmers in Chicago working on the conversion, completing the effort in the early spring of 1980. I learned to really like Chicago as a place to visit, but I would have been overmatched to have lived there.

In what can only be called extreme irony, the Cost Accounting system we had installed on the Copolymer computers proved to be very effective. Not long after the new software had been brought online, it provided conclusive information that the Copolymer plant had been operating at a monetary loss for several years with no relief in sight. The final shoe fell when the Copolymer plant was closed down and razed. I really felt sorry for the employees, but the software system our team had developed had done what had been expected of it. Such is life.

Since our move to Belgium had been deep-sixed, Shirley and I started a conversation about having a daughter. As mentioned previously, boys were the norm on both sides of our family, so we decided to consider adoption. Perhaps part of the impetus in our decision to adopt was due to our observation of other adoptive parents we knew. Several of our friends at church were adoptive parents, and it was always interesting to hear their stories of the why and how they came to adopt. The most common denominator among the reasons they adopted was when the couple could not have children naturally. Several other families adopted due to their resolve to help a child they were aware of who was in dire need. Like my wife and I, others sought adoption simply because we wanted another child to care for, and in our case, we desperately wanted a daughter. We already had two natural born sons, and given the history in my wife's family and mine, the odds of having a girl naturally were very low.

About a half dozen families in our church in Bartlesville had adopted, and they all seemed to be well–adjusted families. We consulted with each of them, and they all highly recommended taking the adoption route. We inquired about what steps we should take, should we decide to adopt, and the Smithlawn Home in Lubbock, Texas, was highly recommended. Smithlawn was associated with the Church of Christ, so it seemed a perfect match.

This was late 1979, and although I had received some raises at work, we were still a one-income family with two growing boys. Home loan interest rates were still sky high, and our budget was still pretty tight. Shirley and I anticipated that once approved for adoption it could be two or three years before we actually received a child. We believed that was good because it would enable me to enjoy some additional salary increases during that time and therefore be in a better financial position to handle the costs of adoption and the additional mouth to feed. But we both wanted a little girl, so at that point, we were not dissuaded.

With this attitude in mind, we contacted Smithlawn and inquired regarding the hows and whats of adoption. They were very courteous and forthright. They explained three things that gave us pause. They explained that it could take up to five years to complete an adoption, their fee to cover all the medical, housing, and legal fees was a flat $4000 (remember, this was 1979), and they could not totally guarantee that we would receive a little girl.

First, we thought that two or three years was pushing the limit, and in five years, we would be 39 and 40 years old, a little long in the tooth to be dealing with an infant. Second, $4000 cash would be a steep hill for us to climb even with a few raises. Third, we were determined to adopt a little girl, and we were not inclined to sit still for the amount of time required, only to be disappointed. Needless to say, we felt defeated.

As the year ended, one final event occurred that was both humbling and educational. At the time, I was reminded that it pays to know your opponent. Late in the year, I found myself in Searcy, Arkansas, and Dr. Clifton Ganus, President of Harding and a good friend of mine, was hosting me in his home. His son, Charles Ganus, was still a student at Harding at the time, and somehow Charles and I got to talking about the game of racquetball. Our conversation was probably inspired by the fact that the new Ganus Athletic Center had been recently completed on Harding's campus. The GAC was a multipurpose building that housed the basketball court, lockers for the varsity athletes, plus several classrooms. It also contained several racquetball courts. During my periods in Amarillo and Borger, I had begun to play racquetball and had become what I thought to be a pretty salty player.

I inquired of Charles if he had ever played racquetball, and he said he had. I should have asked more questions at that point. However, we agreed to play and headed off to the GAC for a game of racquetball. After about a half-hour, I was a quivering pile of gelatin on the floor in the corner of the racquetball court, and Charles had hardly broken a sweat. He had beaten me by a score of 21–1. I have to believe he had, out of mercy, allowed me the one point so I would not be totally skunked.

Afterward, when I had recovered enough to walk and talk, I told Dr. Clifton Ganus of the adventure. Dr. Ganus sympathized with me over the beating but then said, "I'm surprised Charles didn't mention to you that he is the number 3 rated racquetball player in the state of Arkansas." Now you tell me!

When he graduated from college Charles went to work for Murphy Oil and eventually rose to Vice President of Marketing. We became good friends over time due to both our relationship with Harding and our career choices. Under Charles's direction, Murphy Oil came to and still does supply all the gasoline sold at Walmarts and Sam's Clubs. However, Charles and I have never discussed the issue of racquetball since.

And this is the way the year 1979 came to a close. However, the magical year of 1980 was looming, and our Phoenix would arise from its ashes.

THE PROVIDENCE OF GOD

The years 1974 through 1979 were the recalibration of our lives between the omens of the time at Horseshoe Bend and the miracles waiting in the wings. We grew and matured a lot as a family, we had been able to plug back into church and community, and I had been able to be productive in my work and had been rewarded for it. However, as 1979 ended, we didn't feel that joyful – we had been shut down on a wonderful family and employment adventure in Europe, and we were very discouraged in our efforts to add a little girl to the family. We had not given up the faith, but we were not exactly soaring on the wings of eagles at the moment. But, as with the blessings that we were able to identify following our time in Arkansas, some blessings had been showered on us over the past five years:

1. Having learned from the past, we employed better decisions in our family, faith, and financial lives. We were rewarded with much better results than those that we had become accustomed to receiving.

2. We had renewed our friendship with Karen Davis, which, unknown to us at the time, was to later produce a miracle.

3. We were certainly not affluent, but we were now financially stable and were gaining ground.

4. I had learned additional job skills and made additional contacts within Phillips management that would work to my future advantage.

5. Although we did not realize it at the time, our not being transferred to Belgium would turn out to be an extension of the miracle that Karen Davis would be responsible for.

6. It was fortuitous that I chose to decline the offer to move to Houston because had I accepted it, it would have totally upset the apple cart for the rest of my life. It was a God thing.

7. It was fortuitous that I did not get the job in the Denver office for the same reasons I declined the job offer in Houston.

8. I had learned to ski.

No real family or career crises of any type had arisen during these years, and, as I learned later, the disappointments in not receiving either the transfer to Belgium or to Colorado were blessings in disguise. I would later raise several Ebenezers in recognition of God's providence in those issues.

Twenty-Eight

THE RUSTLED CATTLE

I believe that God blesses us in unusual ways, and frequently our recognition of a blessing comes after the fact. Such a blessing occurred during the year 1975.

In April of that year, my Horseshoe Bend adventures and my temporary employment with the Hertz Corporation were in my rear-view mirror. By that time, I had been re-employed with Phillips Petroleum Company for about 8 months in my third and what would prove to be my final stint with the company. As mentioned earlier, I had been rehired by Phillips Petroleum at what I deemed to be a generous salary, but my budget was still a challenge. At that time, I had two growing sons to feed and clothe, the interest rate on my home loan was 9%—typical for the time—and it was going to be necessary very soon to replace my beautiful Oldsmobile Cutlass S with a vehicle which would better accommodate my family. I was looking for opportunities to save a dollar anywhere; it could be found in order to remain financially stable.

The blessing began in the spring of the year and came to fruition in the fall, and I suffered some considerable angst in the intervening months.

As also mentioned earlier, my dad was a pumper for the Exxon Corporation. He oversaw the operation of oil wells scattered over several hundred square miles of central Oklahoma. His job required that he periodically visit each well site, which required him to drive over hundreds of miles of rural county roads each week. The prevalent scenery he "enjoyed" in his work was thousands of acres of fenced pasture land populated primarily by cattle and oil wells. His job also enabled him to become acquainted with farmers and ranchers on whose property the oil wells were situated.

My dad was always looking for a bargain, and my tight budget encouraged me to do the same. He had arrived at a brainstorm that could allow each of us to obtain a side of fresh beef essentially free of charge. His plan was for us to acquire three yearling cows in the spring, feed them out during the summer and into the fall, and then sell two of them in October. He would then have the remaining cow butchered, which would then provide each of us with a side of fresh beef for our freezers. The proceeds from the sale of the two nearly full-grown cows in October would hopefully cover the cost of the purchase of the three young cows and cover the cost of the butchering and processing of the third cow. Dad knew enough ranchers in the area so that purchase of the cattle would be easy, and he knew of one oil well lease-holder who had several hundred fenced acres where we could pasture them free of charge. It seemed like a no-brainer, so I agreed to the plan and paid Dad for my half of the purchase of the three head of cattle.

Dad dutifully contacted another rancher he knew and bought three yearling heifers – a Charolais, a Hereford, and a white-face Aberdeen Angus. A Charolais is a white/cream-colored animal, a Hereford is red-brown with a white face, and an Angus is typically black. However, the Angus we bought was a white-face Angus, which is a crossbreed between a Hereford and an Angus. The offspring had the white face of the Hereford and the black body of the Angus.

Dad purchased the three cattle in April from the local rancher, and they were placed in the unused pasture provided by Dad's friend. The fact that they were heifers would become an important component of the impending blessing.

About a month later, Dad called me and told me that our cattle had been rustled – they were gone.

So much for our money-saving strategy. We had gone from free beef to a several hundred-dollar loss. Dad reported the theft, but there were dozens of ranches in the area, and the cattle might have already been shipped to a feedlot somewhere en route to a packing house. Our hope of recovering the cattle was minimal at best.

In time we licked our wounds and forgot about our loss.

One day, months later, in September, Dad called me and told me that he had found our cattle.

As mentioned, my dad's job took him into virtually all the highways and byways over several counties. One day he was driving on a county road about five miles from where we had pastured our cattle and from which they had disappeared. As he was driving, he noticed that in the pasture adjacent to the road was a huge herd of black Aberdeen Angus cattle – numbering in the hundreds. He also noticed that a white Charolais, a Hereford, and an Angus with a white face stood out like sore thumbs among all the black cattle.

He knew the rancher who owned the pasture and the cattle, so he approached him cautiously and casually and asked him if he was aware of the three head of cattle that were obviously not part of his herd. Dad invited him to go with him to the pasture and look them over. Once there, the situation was obvious – the three strange head of cattle did not belong.

The rancher feigned ignorance and suggested that the three cows had gotten out of their own pasture and wandered into his pasture. The only problem was that there was no damaged fencing in the original pasture, which would have allowed the cattle to escape. Also, the pasture in which they now resided was about five miles from their original pasture, across several roads and bridges. For them to have "wandered off" and gotten into the rancher's pasture was preposterous, and the rancher knew it.

Subsequently, the rancher offered to haul the three cows back to their home pasture, and there was no further interaction between my dad and the rancher. Cattle thieves in Oklahoma are not well thought of, and the rancher was aware of that.

In October, we sold two of the cows as planned and had the third butchered. And, as hoped, the proceeds from the sale covered all the costs my dad and I had incurred during the odyssey.

In the aftermath of our personal ranching adventure, I contemplated all that had happened. I came to realize that the potential disaster had actually resulted in an unambiguous two-pronged blessing. As mentioned, the cattle were heifers, and one of them had been returned to us pregnant which could not possibly have happened had the three heifers remained pastured in isolation. As a result, that heifer brought a premium price when she was sold, an unexpected blessing. Second, the pasturing of the cows in their "temporary" home from April to September relieved my dad of the cost and hassle that would have been associated with feeding and monitoring them for five months, an additional blessing.

Were these blessings simply circumstantial, or were they providential? Given the many inexplicable blessings I had received in my life, I choose to believe this episode was the providence of God, turning what was a small disaster into a welcomed blessing. Our initial angst was replaced by gratitude.

THE PROVIDENCE OF GOD

Several things convince me that God eventually orchestrated this episode to make lemonade out of a lemon:

1. For whatever reason, Dad purchased three separate breeds of cattle in our little entrepreneurial effort, which ultimately made them easy to identify among the herd of black Angus.

2. Dad's job providentially took him down a road and at a time, which enabled him to spot our cattle.

3. The rancher who "accidentally" acquired our cattle was cooperative in returning them.

4. The three head of cattle were "housed" and fed free of charge to my dad and me for a period of several months.

5. During their incarceration among the rancher's herd of Angus, our Angus was impregnated and ultimately brought a higher sale price than she would have had she remained under my dad's care for the period of time. We actually received a "bonus" as a result of their being rustled.

This incident could have very well turned out to be a complete failure, but for God's providence and grace. Just another "coincidence" that made me raise another Ebenezer.

Twenty-Nine

THE PLANE CRASH

The year 1978 started with a literal bang. One of my IT friends at work, Paul Taylor, was also an avid skier. Not only that, he was a pilot and a member of the Bartlesville Flying Club. As such, he could rent a BFC airplane for personal use. Paul and I frequently spoke about skiing and were looking for opportunities to get to the mountains. Our favorite ski mountains were out west of Denver, an 18–hour drive by automobile. In early February of 1978, Paul came up with the bright idea of flying to Denver, renting a car, and driving the last 160 miles or so on I–70 to multiple ski areas. The overall driving distance from Bartlesville to the ski areas in Colorado was more than 800 miles. Flying instead would save us at least 15 hours of driving both going and returning. We agreed that was a good idea.

The Bartlesville Flying Club owned a Piper Cherokee, a single-engine, 4–passenger plane (including the cockpit) that was available in February. Since it had two extra seats, we decided to invite two other skiing companions to join us on the trip. Paul scheduled the plane's use, and I recruited two other skiers – David McCluggage, a long–time friend of mine who lived in Bartlesville, and Bill Dye, my long–time friend from Harding who currently lived in Kansas City. Both eagerly agreed to the trip, the dates were set, and Bill came down from Kansas City to join the party.

The plan was to fly to Centennial/Arapahoe Airport on the southeast side of Denver, park the plane, rent a car, and head west. As mentioned earlier, I had contacted my friend Paul Kite, who as mentioned earlier, lived in Glenwood Springs, Colorado, to help us with lodging. We were too many for

279

Paul to provide lodging in his house, but he made unbelievable arrangements for us. He had a friend who owned a large, deluxe, nearly new cabin situated south of Glenwood Springs toward Aspen, who agreed to allow the four of us to stay free of charge for four nights. It was located on a small stream in a spectacular valley with tremendous views of the mountains. Possibly another miracle? Maybe so, but another, larger, miracle was looming.

The day of our departure arrived, and the four of us boarded the plane, and we headed northwest. I occupied the co-pilot seat, and David and Bill sat in the two rear seats. The weather was clear, and it seemed like a perfect day to fly. It was to be about a four-hour flight to Denver. The best-laid plans of mice and men.

It did not take long for things to get exciting. Visual Flight Rules (VFR) apply on flights such as ours and are commonly utilized on flights of small private planes. VFR simply means that radar is not involved, and all flight decisions made by the pilot are based on what he can visibly observe. One of the VFR's specifies that planes flying with a heading from 0 to 179 degrees (NNE through SSE) must fly at "odd" altitudes plus 500 feet. For example, 3000 feet is an "odd" altitude, so an appropriate altitude for someone flying in that direction would be 3,500 feet – the odd altitude plus 500 feet. Planes flying with a heading of from 180 to 359 degrees (NNW through SSW) must fly at "even" altitudes plus 500 feet - for instance, 4,500 feet. By following these rules, all planes flying in opposite directions would maintain a 1,000-foot vertical separation and avoid any possible midair collisions.

En route, we flew at about 280 to 285 degrees (northwest) at an altitude of about 2,500 feet – an "even" altitude plus 500 feet. We encountered another plane flying at about 110 degrees (southeast) at about 2,600 or 2,700 feet, certainly NOT in its prescribed altitude range. It was coming in our direction at 100+ miles per hour, and it was in our air space! The other plane cleared our path a couple of seconds before we would have intersected it, and it was 100 or 200 feet above us. No midair collision was imminent, but it was very disturbing, nevertheless. The four of us looked at one another, and each of us probably privately thanked our own personal Ebenezer.

Very shortly after the incident, one of the passengers in the rear seats proclaimed a very urgent need to visit a restroom. Since there were no facilities present on a Piper Cherokee, it would be necessary to land someplace to take care of the situation. Paul knew that Colby, Kansas, had an airport, and Colby was more or less on our route to Denver – not on a direct line, but not too far off. The decision was made to land at Colby for the rest stop before continuing our flight. As an afterthought, the close encounter with the other airplane may have been the catalyst that made the rest stop in Colby necessary

The landing at Colby also turned out to be very exciting. It had snowed heavily in western Kansas, but the Colby runway was clear. The snow had been plowed from the runway and "banked" on each side and at each end of the runway. The banks were three- or four-foot high mounds of packed snow. As we were approaching the landing strip, everything seemed ideal for the landing. Paul took note of the direction of the wind, which was not a factor at that moment. He lined up with the runway, reduced engine speed, and began our descent. Everything was perfect until mere seconds before we touched down.

The ground on which the airport was situated was uneven, and a hump in the length of the runway created an optical illusion that made it appear to be much shorter than it actually was. At low (landing) altitude, part of the runway beyond the hump disappeared from sight, momentarily creating the misleading illusion. Since this was Paul's first landing ever at this airport, he was unaware of the phenomenon. As a result, he cautiously decided to take full advantage of what he perceived to be a short runway and touch down at the very end of the runway. However, the snowbank at the end of the runway intervened, and then things went crazy.

Paul and I have remained friends over the years, and we periodically reminisce about Colby landing. As I was writing this book, I ran into Paul one day at the golf course, and I asked him to give me his remembrance of the incident. These are his words from an email he replied with:

"It (the runway) looked very short, so I tried to land at the very end. But what I didn't account for was the snow they had piled up at the end of the runway when they cleared it. I could tell I would be a little short, so I goosed the engine and raised the nose. I would have made it just right, but the snowdrift caught the back wheels and caused the nose to drop. These small planes are made to land on the back wheels, and the front one is not as sturdy, so when the front wheel hit first, it buckled up under the plane. As the wheel collapsed, the propeller (now at full throttle) hit the pavement and stopped dead as we scooted down the runway on the collapsed wheel and the two normal wheels. It was a very smooth landing and quickly stopped while we all just sat there for a few seconds. My only recollection was that a ski mask sitting on top of the luggage was the only thing that moved."

When the rear wheels hit the snowbank, it caused the front wheel to almost simultaneously hit the pavement and collapse, allowing the fuselage's nose to crash into the pavement at about 80 miles per hour. When this happened, we heard the loud BANG that I mentioned earlier. Since the nose wheel was now, useless Paul was helpless to control the plane's direction on the ground. As a result, it skidded down the runway and then veered off to the left, through another snowbank, into a muddy, grassy area next to the runway, and finally stopped. Paul's nanosecond response to the situation - increasing the speed and raising the plane's nose - likely saved our lives and avoided a spoiled ski trip.

An analysis of the situation is frightening, and, once again, I believe God's hand was in the outcome. The plane was landing at about 80 miles per hour – 115 feet per second. Paul's quick reaction to increase the speed and raise the nose kept the plane in the air approximately one additional second, thereby allowing it to stay in the air about 115 feet farther than it would have had no action been taken. This additional distance permitted the plane to stay aloft long enough to at least reach the hard surface of the runway. Had the plane come down just short of the runway, it would have hit mud and grass, and the plane would likely have flipped over on its top, and it is anybody's guess as to what that outcome would have been. All of us on board the plane learned the value of time. We learned that sometimes an interval of one second could mean the difference between life and death.

However, despite the near-disastrous landing, a miracle had just occurred. When all the smoke cleared, the only casualty was the plane. The propeller and engine were ruined, and the fuselage was badly damaged. The fuel tank did not erupt, so there was no fire. We and our luggage, miraculously, escaped unscathed.

The FAA was dutifully informed of the incident, and we had no option other than to leave the plane where it was in the condition it was and to attempt to continue our ski trip. Matters regarding removing and/or repairing the plane would be dealt with in the days to come.

But what now? We were still 250 miles from the Centennial Airport and without wheels. One–way car rentals were not available at the Colby airport. However, another minor miracle occurred. On a whim, Paul called the Colby High School and explained our plight to the principal. Paul asked if he knew of any boys there who had a car and who would be willing to haul four adults and their luggage to Denver that day. Not a question the principal dealt with every day. Miraculously, he identified two such young men who met the criteria and ultimately sent them to the airport to pick us up. The boys arrived in a large car, and we agreed on the price for them to ferry us to Denver – which they did, luggage and all.

We made it to the Centennial Airport, rented the car, and headed toward Glenwood Springs and our rendezvous with Paul Kite, arriving just a little later in the day than we had anticipated and with a big story to tell.

We had three delightful days of skiing, staying in deluxe accommodations. We managed to ski Snowmass at Aspen and Vail.

When we returned the rental car to Denver, we also made reservations on a Continental Airlines flight back to Tulsa. That flight was a little smoother than our flight on the way to Colby. When we returned home, we were the talk of the office and the church. Given the other possible outcome, it was a pleasure to relate our adventures.

Retrospective thoughts regarding our landing in Colby...

I have often wondered if the plane crash was actually the will of God. Here's why. The potential mid-air collision we encountered en route to Colby may have been a message. It might have been in our best interest to discontinue our flight at Colby and go the rest of the way on the ground. To have continued the trip in the plane meant we would have been in the mix of the heavy air traffic over downtown Denver, and who knows what might have happened. Perhaps God "allowed" the plane crash but protected us from injury. The only way the four of us could have survived the crash was for the plane to remain upright and not explode. Due to physics – inertia, gravity, momentum, wind, and perhaps the will of God – the plane did not flip on its top upon crashing. The fuel tank did not rupture, and no one sustained even a bruise. Not only that, we were then, miraculously, provided with excellent transportation from Colby to Denver, and we arrived in Glenwood Springs not too much behind schedule. Just an off the wall thought, but it wouldn't be the first time God allowed what was thought to be a tragedy to really be a blessing in disguise.

Whether the crash was entirely an accident or was due to God's involvement, our survival, I believe, was a miracle, and I fully believe it was necessary so that a second miracle could take place two years later, in 1980. I don't think God hands out anecdotal miracles. Rather, I think His Providence takes the whole picture into account and that His works have a plan. Does that sound crazy? I don't believe so. Consider what happened to me in all the prior events of my life – education, career, marriage, stupid moves, rescues from stupid moves, etc. It all has to be connected, and there is only one possible source that could have connected all those dots – God. The sequence of events over the sixteen years between my high school graduation and the plane crash could not have been accidental or "anecdotal."

THE PROVIDENCE OF GOD

All told, the entire ski trip had the touches of God on it. We could have been killed at worst, or we could have been stranded in Colby, Kansas, without any way to finish our trip or to even return home. When my heart finally slowed down, and my breathing returned to normal following our "landing" in Colby, I did indeed raise my Ebenezer.

1. We had avoided a possible mid-air collision en route to Colby.

2. We had survived a plane crash without a scratch.

3. We received unexpected assistance to continue our trip and enjoyed spectacular accommodations and skiing, and a comfortable return home.

4. I was still alive and healthy and able to participate in the very wonderful miracle that was to begin two years later.

These things – miracles? – just keep on happening to me.

Thirty

1980, THE YEAR OF MIRACLES
– RACHEL

Some things initially viewed as setbacks are actually realized later as victories. I viewed my failure in Arkansas, the failure of the transfer to Belgium, my failure to make the baseball team at OCC, my breakup with Martha, my failure to be accepted for admission to Tulane, the failure to secure the transfer to Denver – all these as disappointments at the time. Looking at each of them in my rearview mirror, I have realized that they were not setbacks but rather were providential life course corrections. The plane crash in 1978, however, was more than a mere course correction. The way it happened was an outright miracle, and my survival was necessary for everything that had happened to me in my life to that point to have made sense and for and everything that would happen to me in the remainder of my life to occur. If any of the events had turned out differently, I would have wound up in the ditch, metaphorically speaking, or maybe even in the grave.

And now, in 1980, it appeared that God had in mind to fill in one more blank. Evidently, God had heard Shirley's requests over the years regarding how much she wanted a daughter and decided that maybe we should be so blessed after all.

Our daughter Rachel's story is an incredible series of events, miracles, if you will, that cannot be explained in any way other than the Providence of God. Each event in the adoption process seemed choreographed to deliver the ultimate miracle – Rachel – to Shirley and me at just the right time and under the most favorable of circumstances. Any event in the adoption decision process, had it been modified or eliminated, could have voided the entire adoption.

As mentioned, the year 1978 got off to a dicey start with the misadventure in the airplane. Throughout my life, I have always believed that if you were fortunate enough to dodge a bullet that there was a reason for it. Consequently, I had to believe there was a reason I had survived the incident with the plane, and fate did not linger long before providing an answer.

Early in the year 1980, things started getting interesting. Shirley and I had been sort of in the doldrums following our conversation with the Smithlawn Home the previous year. We had not given up on adopting, but we didn't see any practical way in which we would be able to do so. Sometime in late January or early February, we ran into Karen Davis at the Northeast Oklahoma Gospel Songfest, hosted annually at that time by the Limestone Church of Christ. Karen attended the Dewey congregation, and people from many congregations in northeast Oklahoma attended the festivities. Karen knew we were still studying the adoption issue, and she asked us if we had ever applied for adoption with the Church of Christ Homes for Children in Federal Way, Washington – a suburb of Seattle. We admitted we had not since we had never heard of it. She told us that her father was an elder of the Federal Way Church of Christ and was also a member of the oversight committee for the Home. In addition, she had worked at the Home while she was in college. She said that she would be willing to provide the Home with a personal reference if we chose to apply there. She really did not know much about the adoption procedure there or the costs involved, but, she said, "There's nothing to lose by applying."

So, we contacted the Church of Christ Homes for Children and applied for the adoption of an infant girl. At that time, the Home was unable to give us any concrete information regarding wait times, costs, and the like. First, we had to get our name on the list.

It should be noted that the Home did not handle prospective adoptive parents like the local automobile tag agency – "Take a number, and we will call you when it's your turn." Instead, the Home was small enough to offer much more personal service in adoptions. What the Home did – and successfully, I might add – was to accumulate information on prospective adoptive parents and then match the available babies to, in the Home's judgment, the best possible home environment for each baby. When possible, the baby's mother was permitted to view the applicants and assist in the selection process. As will be seen, Shirley and I will be eternally grateful for the Home's adoption protocol.

Very shortly after we contacted the Home and put our name in the hopper, things started to get crazy. Just a month or so later, in mid–March, we received a phone call from Barbara Grimm, a caseworker at the Home, and the call was unbelievable. First, to have received any sort of personal reply in that short amount of time is unprecedented. But it gets better. Mrs. Grimm said that it was Spring Break at the high school in Federal Way, and she was driving a small group of high schoolers from there for a visit to, of all places, the Harding College campus. She explained that she and the children would be actually coming through Bartlesville and spending one night at Karen Davis' house, and she was wondering if it would be convenient for her to conduct an in-home visit the evening she was in town.

Is that not incredible? I'm not making this up. It could not have been merely a "coincidence" that we lived exactly on the route she would be driving from Federal Way to Searcy.

After I regained my composure, I told her that the timing was convenient for us and we would welcome her visit. So a date in early April was set, and when that evening came, she rang our doorbell.

The interview went very well, routine, in fact. We were quizzed regarding our individual upbringings, our marriage, our education, our church commitment, our health, and our financial stability – all the things that would seem pertinent to proper Christian parenting. Did we drink? She observed the behavior of our boys – who were perfect gentlemen that evening – and walked through our house to see what sort of living conditions we would provide. We already had a separate bedroom set aside and furnished to accept a little girl. She apparently decided that if the Home gave us a little girl that we could and would care for her properly and assimilate her into our family as just another child.

An important issue did arise during the interview, which left us a little unsettled. We asked the caseworker what we should expect the adoption to cost and told her that Smithlawn had a flat $4000 fee. She explained that each adoption was different, and the Home simply passed on to the adoptive parents the medical costs, foster parent costs, and legal fees incurred with the birth and adoption process. Given typical hospital and doctor charges plus lawyers' fees, we just swallowed hard but decided we would just plow on ahead. At least the Home came highly recommended by Karen Davis, and the Home gave us a little more optimistic outlook than having to wait five years to adopt. It was truly in the hands of God.

We felt at the conclusion of the interview that we had given the caseworker an accurate picture of the life a little girl could expect in the Vaughan home, and we hoped that she was satisfied. We got a little hint of her assessment just as she was preparing to leave. She mentioned that a young lady in the Home was preparing to give birth within three or four weeks, and if it were a girl, they would seriously consider placing her with us. Sonograms were not in general use by that time, so there were no promises that the baby would be a girl, but it set our spirits soaring. And then she was gone, continuing her journey to Searcy.

It was now mid–July. More than three months had come and gone without further word, and we were getting a little antsy. We spoke to some of the other adoptive parents at church, and to a person, they stated that the birth and the immediate aftermath were fraught with medical and legal issues, and there was just no way to hurry it up. They said the waiting was awful, but there was no way to avoid it. So, we bit our tongues and bided our time and hoped that the new baby was indeed a girl.

On July 20, I came home from work at about 5:15, and Shirley was on the telephone. She was dancing around and fidgeting like she had ants crawling all over her. I asked her what was happening, and she just waved me off and stayed glued to the phone. Eventually, she hung up, and she uttered five words that I will remember forever – "We got our little girl!"

After I caught my breath, we hugged and danced around and laughed and giggled like a couple of children. We were overwhelmed with happiness because this was a scenario we could never have imagined just a few months earlier. We had once again totally beaten the odds. We both happily and thankfully raised an Ebenezer because, truly, hither by His help, we had come.

I asked Shirley for the details. She said a healthy little girl had been born in Federal Way on May 5 (within the three or four–week period the caseworker had mentioned) and had subsequently been designated for us. She said the mother was a 19–year–old unmarried single girl who was currently in training to become an airline flight attendant. She said the mother had no bad habits – drinking, drugs, etc. – but felt that as a single mother, she could not effectively pursue both a career filled with travel and at the same time raise a child. She courageously decided to give up her little girl. In addition, the mother had been given the opportunity to influence the decision regarding which of the contending families the child would be placed with. She selected us from among all the others who had been vetted. Shirley was told that it would take another few days to wrap up all the legal and medical issues associated with the adoption and that they would advise us when we could pick up our little bundle of joy.

We called all our family and friends and broadcast the news. We were floating on air. Then, reality began to sink in. At this point, no figures had been presented as to what it would cost us to complete the adoption. Per the caseworker, each adoption is different, and the fee charged by the Home varied case by case, depending on what the costs were. With the hospital, doctors, and lawyers' fees, it could actually exceed the $4000 that Smithlawn charged. We faced a potential financial dilemma. In addition, the baby was in western Washington, almost 2,000 miles from Bartlesville. How would we get her "home?"

Regarding the question of how to bring the baby to Bartlesville, there seemed to be only two possible solutions – either drive to the state of Washington to pick her up and drive her back, or fly to Seattle and bring her back on an airplane. Driving was out of the question since it was at least four long days of driving each way, not an ideal situation for a newborn. The other possible solution – flying to Washington and carrying her back on the plane – would also be very difficult financially. We considered flying out together and bringing her back. That would have required two round–trip airline tickets, which would have cost near $1000 – never mind the pending costs of the adoption. That seemed out of reach. So, we considered having only one of us fly to Seattle, which would have reduced the cost to about $500. Manageable under the circumstances, but still problematic. Not counting the cost of the tickets, the question then arose as to which of us would make the trip. Shirley was the obvious candidate, but her total experience flying commercial airlines to that point consisted of flying round–trip to Las Vegas in 1974, accompanied by about a dozen other friends and me. A trip to Seattle solo would have been stressful enough without having to deal with a 3–month old infant. It seemed there were no reasonable, workable solutions to this problem.

In the meantime, there was nothing we could say or do at that point except pray and hope and do what we were told.

A little later in July, we attended a Brock family reunion at Roaring River State Park, near Cassville, Missouri. We swam and picnicked and ventured to Table Rock Lake for water skiing, all the while treading water emotionally and awaiting "the" phone call.

On July 31, the call came. We were advised by the Home that we could pick up our new daughter on August 8. Now, all we had to do was figure out a way to do so. How to pay for one or two round–trip airline tickets, plus the logistics of the operation, were still completely unsettled.

At that point, the continuing miracle of our adoption just kept on giving – another miracle manifested itself. We received a telephone call the next day, August 1, and surprisingly, the person on the other end of the line was Karen Davis. Karen told us the baby was doing fine and was about ready to come to Bartlesville. Then Karen disclosed the miracle. She said, "Right now, I am in Federal Way at my parents' house. I know you are anxious to have your baby, but if you can wait until August 13, I will be flying back to Tulsa and can bring the baby with me. That might make things a little easier."

289

After Shirley and I picked ourselves up off the floor and became able to speak again, Shirley said, "That would be wonderful. We really didn't know how we were going to get her to Oklahoma. We have waited this long. We can probably endure for five more days."

Shirley and Karen then briefly discussed the trip and the transition a little further, and we hung up the phone and rejoiced and danced some more. Another huge Ebenezer was raised.

A few days later, we had communication from the Home regarding the cost of the adoption. When we received the letter, I broke into a cold sweat and was really dreading opening it. At this point, the miracle once again kept on giving. The statement said the total amount we owed was $724, which covered the legal costs involved. The father of the baby's mother had insurance, and all the doctor and hospital bills had been paid by insurance. The foster home for the baby during the interim, of course, charged nothing.

Frankly, at this point, we felt like we were living in a different dimension or in an alternate universe. It was unreal. Everything had worked to our favor in the adoption process. To begin with, we had an influential advocate with the Home, Karen Davis, whom God had providentially placed in our lives ten years earlier. The caseworker made a timely visit to Searcy, passing through Bartlesville on the way, which ultimately resulted in an invaluable in-home visit. The baby's birth was routine without any problems. We didn't have to wait several years to get our little girl. Insurance was in effect to cover the hospital and doctor fees. The legal costs were minimal. The baby arrived at our front door—special delivery.

You may try, but you will never be able to convince me that miracles no longer occur. This entire episode had God's fingerprints all over it. If you get nothing else out of this book, please realize that our adoption of our little girl was truly a miracle – the Providence of God.

Karen brought our daughter – Rachel Annette Vaughan – home on August 13. Shirley and the boys and I met them at Tulsa International Airport, and we were introduced to our baby girl for the very first time. Unexpectedly, she smiled.

Karen recalls Shirley's immediate reaction when Rachel smiled. "Shirley was so awestruck. She just stood admiring the baby. So I asked her if she would like to hold her."

"Oh, yes," said Shirley as she returned to reality.

Karen handed her to Shirley, and, even more unexpectedly, our son Greg smiled right back. Greg had not been thrilled with our adding another child, especially a girl, but his whole attitude did a 180 when his new little sister smiled at him.

We drove to Bartlesville and treated Karen and her children to breakfast at the Pannekoeken Huis, a German pancake restaurant in Bartlesville at the time. Rachel grinned and cooed at all the attention she was receiving, and this really was a herald of her personality for years to come.

Then we all went home and began the next chapter of our lives as a family of five, now with a little girl at hand.

The adoption of Rachel was without question the highlight of the year, but there was one more miracle to be experienced before the year's end. At least, I believe it was a miracle.

In my job, I was still traveling at least half the time to Chicago, Houston, Denver, Borger, and all over. Late in the year, I was assigned to lead a project to develop computer data transmission capabilities between our American Fertilizer office in Spokane, Washington, and the fertilizer manufacturing facility at Kennewick, Washington, a couple of hundred miles southwest of Spokane. During Phillips' expansion a few years earlier, the Chemicals Division had acquired American Fertilizer, and it was incumbent that the subsidiary's communications capabilities be brought in line with Phillips corporate standards.

Beginning in December, I spent most of a month in the state of Washington, traveling between Spokane and Kennewick, along with some other Phillips IT personnel, working on the project. Mt. St. Helens in southwestern Washington had erupted in May of 1980, shortly after Rachel's birth, and ash from the volcano was still covering a lot of geography in eastern Washington. In many places on the drive between Spokane and Kennewick, the ground was just a light gray. Fortunately, although the volcano was located only about 80 miles south of Federal Way, the force of the eruption had been toward the east and, in addition, the prevailing winds had blown the ash to the east and away from Federal Way instead of toward the city. Although the volcano caused chaos for several weeks, Rachel's temporary home in Federal Way had been spared, and she had not been adversely affected. Another miracle? You tell me.

During Christmas break, Shirley took Brent, Greg, and Rachel, to visit with her sister Dorothy who lived in Searcy, Arkansas. Shirley's parents also lived with Dorothy, as Shirley's mother was in very bad health.

Each evening I would call Shirley from Spokane, and we would chat about how things were going and how her mother was doing. At some point, while in Searcy, Rachel came down with some sort of virus and got pretty sick. One evening when I called Shirley, she said that she had taken Rachel to the doctor that day and he had prescribed some medicine, but the doctor also had said that if Rachel was not considerably improved by morning, he would have to hospitalize her. Here was the situation. My 7½ month-old daughter, who had been delivered to us by a series of incredible miracles, was now very sick, and we were ostensibly in danger of losing her, and I am stuck in Spokane, Washington, more than 2000 miles away, totally unable to provide any kind of help. Except for prayer.

It goes without saying that I was in deep and fervent prayer that evening regarding our daughter's health. I reminded God that we had faced numerous trials, travails, and uncertainties – moves, job changes, a plane crash, and the miracles associated with the adoption itself – just to even arrive at our present situation and that I could not believe we had survived these tests only to lose our little girl. I told God that I believed everything I had done and experienced in my entire life had led to that moment the previous August when Rachel had been placed in Shirley's arms. I told God that I had faith that He would heal Rachel, and this crisis would pass.

I cannot say that I then experienced any supernatural intercession or viewed any celestial beings, but almost immediately after I laid out my case to God, my mind was suddenly at peace. My faith kicked in, and it became almost blatantly obvious to me that Rachel was going to be OK. I went to bed and slept soundly.

Early the next morning, I called Shirley, and she told me Rachel's fever had broken, and she was on the mend. No hospital for her.

Was this a miracle – maybe an extension of the miracles that had already occurred in our adoption of Rachel? I strongly believe it was, and I raised another Ebenezer. This was becoming a habit, but a good habit.

This concluded the miraculous year of 1980. It started off with the miracles of the adoption, and then Rachel's fast recovery from her sickness occurred. I have to believe that our faith in God – Shirley's and mine – contributed to the things that happened not only during the year but in the events in prior years that led up to this fantastic climax.

The word "faith" is associated with some irony in the whole adventure of adopting Rachel. When the Home delivered her to us, they had gone to great lengths to eliminate any possible confidential information regarding Rachel's birth and care immediately following her birth – with the exception of the general information about her birth mother and the circumstances of her giving her up for adoption. All the details were sealed. Following her birth, as all adoption agencies practice, they gave Rachel a "temporary" name by which they could manage her until we received her. During the days following Rachel's birth, she had required normal new-born natal care, and some prescriptions were issued on her behalf. The Home was diligent in removing all references to her, including her temporary name, on the prescription containers they gave us. However, they overlooked one small prescription label that my detective wife discovered that contained her temporary name – "Faith." It could not have been more appropriate.

The foster parents had named Rachel "Faith" while she was still in their care.

Is that not ironic? Faith is the basis of this entire book. Faith has been the cornerstone of essentially my entire life. Faith is what convinced me to believe that God does actually take an active role in the lives of believers – providential miracles if you will. By faith, Abraham was justified, and by faith, I believe, young "Faith" was placed in our home. Over the years, having seen and experienced what is essentially impossibly far–fetched and complicated events, I believe it has become more logical to believe in miracles than to pass those events off as happenstance. Do you believe in miracles?

THE PROVIDENCE OF GOD

The year started off slowly with discouraging information regarding the possibility of adopting a daughter and ended with some grave concern about the health of our new daughter. The middle of the year highlighted all the "coincidences" – miracles, really – that eventually gave us Rachel. As I think back, I must have raised a whole quarry's worth of Ebenezers. As I review what I have written, it seems almost unbelievable that all these things could have happened as they did – but they did and are documented. My head still swims when I think of the blessings God showered my family with during the year.

1. We were initially discouraged in our attempt to adopt, with the projected costs and time involved being prohibitive in our circumstances.

2. We received encouraging words from friends who were adoptive parents and from Karen Davis, who was able to give us not only advice on how to proceed but also to provide us with invaluable personal references with the adoption agency.

3. A caseworker from the agency "just happened" to be visiting Harding University in Searcy, Arkansas, and came through Bartlesville en route to give us an in-home study.

4. A baby girl was born without blemish to a courageous mother who sought a better life for her daughter and agreed to give her up for adoption.

5. The eruption of Mt. St. Helens had not damaged nor adversely affected the Federal Way area.

6. From the initial interview with the agency until notification of our receiving the baby girl was only six weeks – unheard of.

7. Karen Davis saved us hundreds of dollars and tons of stress by delivering our baby to Bartlesville herself.

8. The birth mother's family had medical insurance, so we incurred no medical costs for the adoption. Rather, only having to pay legal fees, which were only $724, which was in itself miraculous.

9. Our new daughter survived a medical crisis near year-end without consequences.

10. Years later, after Rachel was married, she had a daughter, and she named her Morgan Faith Allyn. Faith. This whole odyssey was, I believe, an outcome as a result of faith.

Against all odds.

Thirty-One

NOT OUT OF THE WOODS YET

The year 1980 had been remarkable in every way – probably the best year of our lives, all things considered. The year ended with angst as Rachel got very sick, but the angst disappeared when she recovered very quickly without complications. We did not expect the future to be filled with such an abundance of "good luck," if you want to call it that, and those less-than-optimistic expectations were fully met early on.

Following the implementation of the computer communication capabilities at the Spokane/Kennewick American Fertilizer facilities, it was then necessary to survey the other Phillips Fertilizer facilities scattered across the country to ascertain if they had proper computing equipment in place to handle the new communications process. This involved my visiting the Fertilizer facilities in California, Colorado, Nebraska, Texas, and Kentucky. I made the trips, evaluated their equipment, and turned in my report. The proposal to develop Division-wide digital communication capabilities was approved but was not put on the development schedule as another higher priority project was already underway. The higher priority project was a payroll/personnel software upgrade at the Phillips Driscopipe headquarters in Dallas. It required an all–hands–on deck effort by the computing personnel resources to bring it online. Phillips Driscopipe was a major player in the world plastic pipe industry.

I was assigned along with three or four others in the Chemicals Comptroller's office to head to Dallas every week to assist in the effort. To Dallas on Monday morning, returning to Bartlesville Friday afternoon. This went on for several weeks, and finally, we were able to see the light at the end of the tunnel. Sometime in late summer, I returned to Bartlesville, awaiting my next assignment.

Following my return to Bartlesville, world events intervened ominously. They ultimately affected not only me but all of Phillips Petroleum and, in fact, all of the major oil producers in the Western world over the next four or five years.

The exceptional year of 1980 was now in the rearview mirror, and things got pretty hairy in mid–1981. I believe the problem actually started with the Iranian takeover of the American embassy in Teheran in 1978 and came to a climax in January 1981. During this period, the U.S. was importing most of its oil, and most of that from the Middle East, including Iran. In November 1980, Ronald Reagan had been elected President, and he assumed office on January 20, 1981. Until that time, President Jimmy Carter had remained in a stalemate with Iran on the issue of getting the hostages released, but we were still importing Iranian oil. When President Reagan – whom the Iranians viewed as a "cowboy" who didn't take prisoners – was sworn in as President, the hostages were immediately released, actually, within minutes of President Reagan's swearing-in, after 444 days in captivity. The Iranians didn't want anything to do with a President who was not afraid of them.

For some time, oil had been running at $30 or more per barrel for sweet crude and had gone as high as $37. Since Iran was unwilling to take on the U.S. militarily, they decided to try a different tactic by punishing the U.S. financially. They responded to the Reagan Presidency by flooding the world with cheap Iranian oil. They opened their taps wide and let the oil flow, and the inevitable result of their actions was to greatly depress the price of oil worldwide. The price quickly fell to $20 per barrel. Oil companies such as Phillips, which had become accustomed to selling oil at $30 or more per barrel, had to reduce the price of their crude to compete with the Iranians. This directly and dramatically affected the company's financial bottom line and pretty much created chaos among all of the major Western oil producers.

The reason that low oil prices did not adversely affect Iran and the Saudis was that the cost "lift" a barrel of oil at the wellhead for the Middle Eastern countries was something like $1.75 per barrel at that time. In contrast, the U.S. and other Western countries' oil could cost more than $10.00 per barrel just to get it out of the ground. Labor was cheap in the Middle East, and the oil was easy to find. Whereas most Middle Eastern oil wells were in the desert and relatively close to refineries, major oil companies in the United States faced very high drilling costs in places like the North Slope of Alaska, the Gulf of Mexico, and the North Sea. The oil produced in those wells had to be transported long distances via pipeline or oil tanker to refineries in the lower 48 United States. Hence, at $20 per barrel, the Middle Eastern countries were thriving while the Western world struggled.

Although $20 per barrel of oil did not completely trash the world oil market, it did portend present and future financial pain. Pretty much everyone had anticipated some sort of Iranian shenanigans with oil price, but no one anticipated the depths to which they would eventually reduce the price. To its credit, Phillips had anticipated such a scenario and the likely resulting drop in company revenues. Phillips management had set in place emergency austerity measures to enable the company to continue to function even if the price dropped as low as $20 per barrel.

Many of the Phillips' subsidiaries, particularly in the Chemicals Division, used petroleum as a raw material in their manufacturing. The lower oil price helped those subsidiaries financially by allowing them to buy their feedstock at substantially lower prices. Due to the lower cost of their feedstocks, many of those subsidiaries had boom years, but overall, they could not carry the financial load for the entire company. Philips' largest investments were in oil drilling and production, and its cash cow just got sick.

Phillips kicked off its austerity plan early in 1982 by initiating the tried and true remedy universally employed when financial crunch times hit – corporate layoffs. However, while helpful, management's best plans did not provide a long–term solution to the crisis as $20 per barrel of oil was merely a pipe dream for what would eventually happen.

Meanwhile, layoffs were widespread and were scheduled to be universal in that no particular group within the corporation would be immune, including Chemicals Comptrollers of which I was a member. Everyone from the Managers on down was sweating what was to happen, myself included—particularly myself. Even though I had enjoyed several consecutive years of feast and good fortune, I remained ever the pragmatist – attempting to read the tea leaves objectively rather than being in a state of Pollyanna–Esque denial. With arbitrary computer system development funding getting ready to dry up, I felt that my job, which focused on developing new systems, would be high on the priority list of job cuts. When the layoffs started every morning, every member of Chemicals Comptrollers would steal into the office and look for any unusual memos on their desks. Then they would look around to see if anyone was missing. Eventually, Comptrollers got hit with about 10% or 15% layoff, but my flag was still flying when the smoke cleared, and I still had a job.

I once again raised an Ebenezer. Later, when I considered the situation from all the angles, I concluded that the fact that I was still working was providentially connected to everything that had happened in the last 18 months

– specifically the events associated with Rachel's adoption. My track record while in Chemicals Comptrollers was average at best, and I didn't possess a CPA certificate, as did most of the others in the group, including some who were laid off. So, why did they retain me? I can only believe that God intervened on my behalf.

But there is another chapter to this particular story.

Finally, all the layoffs were completed. Phillips was limping along but still solvent. After the dust had settled following the layoffs, a good friend of mine, Lonnie Valentine, who was a Chemicals Division Human Resources employee, told me something that took my breath away. Lonnie had not been involved in the decisions as to who would go and who would stay. Rather, he had been the grim reaper whose unenviable task at that time was to inform those Chemicals personnel who were being laid off and to actually escort them out of the building. One day, months later and out of the blue, Lonnie told me that my job had actually been on the chopping block in the lead–up to the layoffs, but for some reason, at the last minute, it had been pulled off the list. He did not know who made the decision but that it had to have been approved at the highest level within the Chemicals Division. He was very glad for the outcome, but it left both of us scratching our heads and asking, "why?"

Another miracle? This was becoming a pattern. It is one thing not to have been laid off. It is quite another thing for one's job to have actually been on the elimination list and then be mysteriously (miraculously) removed. I had dodged not a bullet this time but rather a howitzer shell. I have to believe that I was able to keep my job in 1982 due to the events that occurred in 1980. For me to have been out of work so soon after the adoption would have been tragic, and I don't think God deals in the tragedy with those who love Him and believe Him and trust Him.

This latest event brought to mind a quote from Shakespeare where Macbeth says, "I bear a charmed life" – pronounced "charm–ed" by Macbeth. The thing is, if this is true about me, I deserve none of it, but I am eternally grateful for all of it. (My English teacher at OCC, James Skaggs, would be so proud of me for remembering this quote.)

Chemicals Comptrollers continued to function under the freaky oil price circus, and everyone was waiting for the next shoe to drop. Our work settled into a "maintenance" mode rather than a "development" mode since the future was so uncertain. Maintenance is considerably less dynamic than development and can get old quickly, especially when you are constantly looking over your shoulder. Personnel in Chemicals Comptrollers – and in fact all across the company – kept their eyes open for new, more stable opportunities.

Then in mid–1983, I caught what I considered to be a huge career break. A new job in IT had been posted, and the job dealt with managing relatively new computer software technology. Corporate IT was introducing another "fourth generation" computer language – FOCUS – into corporate computers. They were looking for an IT-type who would pick up that ball and run with it. According to the job requirements, I qualified for the job, and I applied for it.

Another miracle. I was selected to fill the opening.

Fourth-generation languages were "short–cut" languages that allowed the generation of computer update or reporting programs with significantly less coding than required by conventional COBOL coding. They did not provide the level of detail or complexity that COBOL offered. Still, they offered quick solutions to data management that would ordinarily have taken weeks or even months to develop using COBOL. My job would be to manage the FOCUS software on the Phillips computers. Following some training and attendance at a FOCUS convention in Orlando, Florida, I was named the software manager. My responsibilities would include advising all corporate FOCUS users, scheduling training classes, conducting Beta testing, and eventually installing all new software releases. I also received a promotion shortly after making the move. I was ecstatic.

In my new job, I would interact with virtually every division and segment of the company. I would no longer be tied to the fortunes of a single entity that might be gutted if oil prices went very much further south. This eased my angst considerably. Moreover, I would be pretty much the master of my own destiny in the new position.

The manager of the fourth generation language staff was Charles. S. Gibbs. Charlie was an African–American, and he was perhaps the most effective manager I ever worked under. He was able to balance upper management's desires with the capabilities, needs, and mindset of his subordinates better than anyone I ever worked under. In other words, he was able to toe the company line but in a way that kept both management and subordinates happy and productive.

Meanwhile, the oil price worldwide continued to drop, and there was some panic in the oil industry, particularly at Phillips Petroleum. Phillips was the smallest of the "major" oil companies, which included Exxon, Amoco, BP, Texaco, Chevron, Shell, and the like. There were all sorts of takeover rumors flying around, and with Phillips being the most vulnerable due to its relatively small size, the company was featured in an article in the *Wall Street Journal* in some manner almost every day.

By1984 the worldwide price of oil had dropped from what was already considered a catastrophic price of $20 per barrel to $10 per barrel. It would eventually bottom out at $8 per barrel, but that would not occur for another year. Phillips was bleeding dollars, and Phillips stock had sunk in value dramatically. Late in 1984, a Texas oilman named T. Boone Pickens rode into town and tried to buy Phillips. Phillips attempted to fend off Mr. Pickens' overtures by taking many bold, innovative steps. First, Phillips introduced a company-wide financial "poison pill" that would automatically activate in the event of any hostile takeover attempt. The poison pill would pay an outlandish sum of money to any employee who was separated from the company due to any hostile takeover bid.

Phillips's other steps in defense of the company included another round of layoffs, restructuring its corporate debt, and buying back some of its own stock to stabilize its price. The poison pill's announcement had encouraged many employees to request layoff, reaping the generous benefits associated with it, thus reducing the overall negative impact of corporate layoffs. Phillips's actions rendered any takeover bid much more expensive than anticipated. In early 1985 the company reached a deal with Mr. Pickens that left Phillips wounded but still intact and left Mr. Pickens much richer but legally estopped from further takeover bids of Phillips. To his credit, as I understand it, Mr. Pickens had actually intended to continue operating Phillips Petroleum as an independent and significant oil company while remaining headquartered in Bartlesville.

But the drama did not end there. The dust had barely settled on the T. Boone Pickens ordeal when, a little later in 1985, Mr. Carl Icahn, a New York financial man, came to town and announced his intention to make a run at the company. As mentioned, Phillips was a very diversified company with oil production, pipelines, refineries, and a myriad of successful subsidiaries. According to reports, Mr. Icahn's strategy was to acquire the company and then sell off the individual pieces, of which there were many. He estimated that the total value of the individual parts exceeded the company's value as a whole, and he was probably correct. At any rate, to make a long story short, Phillips took on more debt and wound up paying Mr. Icahn $25 million to cover his costs and also purchased his shares of Phillips stock at a profit of between $50 and $60 million for Mr. Icahn.

During all the drama with T. Boone Pickens and Carl Icahn, I was safely ensconced in my world of FOCUS. The use of the software continued to grow quickly, basically company-wide, and my job was worry-free with regard to potential layoff. Very little travel was required, and the only trips I specifically remember taking during the three years I was in the group were to FOCUS on conventions in Orlando, New Orleans, and San Diego. During the time I was heading up FOCUS at Phillips, we installed three new, up-graded releases of the software, and all went online without a hitch. Considering all the talented help I had around me to make these happen successfully, perhaps the upgrades were not miracles – but maybe they were.

The seed of another miracle was planted unobtrusively following the Carl Icahn struggle's conclusion, a miracle that would not bear fruit for fourteen more years. However, I need to set the stage at this point because I cannot believe it was anything but a miracle – and a miracle that, frankly, tested my faith.

At the time of the agreement with Carl Icahn, Phillips stock was sitting at $50 per share. Part of the settlement with Mr. Icahn required Phillips to trade each share of $50 Phillips stock for three shares of new Phillips stock with an original issue price of $12. In addition to the three shares of new lower-priced Phillips stock, each shareholder was to receive security valued at $14 to make up the difference between the $50 stock and the three shares of the $12 stock. At the time, I had in my Phillips Thrift Plan about 100 shares of Phillips stock valued at approximately $5000. I traded them in for 300 shares of the new Phillips stock plus $1400 in interest-bearing securities.

Upon receiving my 300 new shares of Phillips stock, I immediately turned around and sold them at $12 per share and received around $3600 in cash. Within a couple of days, Phillips stock had plummeted to $9 per share, so I felt pretty good about my decision to sell. I now had the $3600 from the Phillips stock sale plus the $1400 in securities – around $5000 – to play with. I decided to sit on the cash for a while to see what was going to happen.

During my term as FOCUS coordinator, I had had numerous conversations with a fellow employee, Johnnie Tucker, who also happened to be a member of the Adams Boulevard Church of Christ. Johnnie messed around in the stock market some and had enjoyed pretty good success in doing so. I was aware of his reputation and asked him if he had any good stock tips since I had some cash from my Phillips stock sale burning a hole in my pocket. He said he had made a habit recently of buying and selling Walmart stock. The stock had wavered between $46 per share to around $53 per share for some time. He would buy the stock in the mid–$40's and sell it when it reached the mid–$50's and wait until it fell to the mid–$40's again and then repeat the cycle. He had apparently done this for several years and had had pretty good success.

Following his example, I watched Walmart stock, and when it hit the mid–$40's, I bought 100 shares – roughly a $4500 investment. Sure enough, a few months later, it hit $53, and I sold. Soon it fell in price again. It seemed like it might go lower than $45 per share, so I decided to wait until it bottomed out. The price of the stock did not stop until it had fallen to $32 per share. I asked for his advice, and he told me it might be a good time to buy. So I bought another 100 shares.

Not long after that, in the summer of 1986, I had an opportunity to move into Phillips Marketing as a Wholesale Rep in Alabama. I had grown weary dealing with FOCUS daily and longed to get some field experience. I accepted a Phillips transfer to Wetumpka, Alabama, a suburb of Montgomery, in the fall of the year. At the time, I still owned 100 shares of Walmart stock. In the year or so that I had owned, it had appreciated to $40 per share, but I had visions of it reaching mid–$50's again and decided not to sell just yet. However, by mid–October 1987, Walmart stock had fallen to $32 per share. Sensing an opportunity to buy some more of the stock cheap – totally anticipating its rising back to the $40+ level shortly – I bought another 100 shares at $32. I made the purchase on October 16, 1987. Now I owned 200 shares at the cost of $6400.

Three days later, on Black Monday, October 19, 1987, the Dow Jones Industrial Average fell 508 points, a 22.6% loss, and Walmart stock closed the day at $20 per share. I was now $2400 in the hole, and I had no other option but to sit on the stock until or if it would rally.

Fast forward to 1999. Although I will relate other anecdotes of my life after 1987 in later chapters, still, I feel it is necessary at this point to describe another miracle that was unknowingly initiated in 1985 and manifested itself in spades in 1999.

As mentioned, in 1985, I had purchased 100 shares of Walmart stock at $32 per share. In 1987 I had purchased another 100 shares of Walmart stock at $32. In 1999 our daughter Rachel was in college at Harding, and I had hoped to be able to put her through college without debt as I had been able to do with both of our sons. I had held on to the Walmart stock that I had purchased so many years ago, and eventually, it started to grab my attention. In the intervening years, the seed had begun sprouting. By around 1990, the stock price had increased to a point where it made sense to Walmart to initiate a stock split, which they did. Suddenly I had 400 shares of Walmart stock. Over the next couple of years, the company grew and became more profitable, and the stock price once again rose to a point where another stock split made sense, so they did it again. Suddenly I had 800 shares of Walmart stock. The economy continued to boom, and Walmart continued to prosper. Eventually, somewhere around 1996 or 1997, the stock price had once again risen to the point where another stock split was in order, so they did it once again. Now I found myself with 1600 shares of Walmart stock, and by 1999 the price per share had risen to around $75. My original $6400 investment was now worth around $120,000, not counting its dividends over the years. I cashed in the stock and was happy to pay the capital gains tax on the profit and be able to pay cash for Rachel's college. Tell me that was not a miracle, and I will have to politely disagree.

But I digress—back to 1986.

Following my transfer, we spent three wonderful years in Alabama. My District Manager was Perry Hammond, and he was another in a line of superior bosses I have had. Perry was stationed in the District Office in Birmingham. I inherited a great set of customers who proudly flew the Phillips flag at their stations, and over time I was able to add new customers and new stations. We made many friends while there and worshipped with the Carriage Hills Church of Christ in Montgomery. John W. Smith was the preacher there, and I believe he has been the biggest single influence in my Christian life. His lessons were always crystal clear, scripture-based, and very interesting. Our daughter, Rachel at the time, was in elementary school, and when we got home from church each Sunday afternoon, she would tell us what Brother Smith had spoken about – his sermons even held the attention of grade school kids.

Our son, Brent, graduated with honors from Wetumpka High School and had lettered two years there in football. Our son Greg was valedictorian of his junior high class. While in Alabama, I was awarded a company–paid Caribbean cruise on the Royal Caribbean Cruise Line as a result of my efforts in the state. All in all, our years in Alabama were a great experience.

Meanwhile, Brent had graduated high school and was enrolled at Harding, which had now attained university status. Phillips 66 awarded sixty-six four-year college scholarships each year to employees' children in those days. Yes, sixty–six. I wonder where they came up with that number. Anyway, Brent, based on his academic standing and extracurricular activities at Wetumpka High School, was awarded one of the Phillips scholarships. The scholarship was for $2000 per semester and was renewable each semester for four years as long as the student maintained a 3.0 or better GPA in college. The scholarship did not fully cover the cost of college, but it made a large dent in the cost. (Brent eventually graduated Magna Cum Laude from Harding with a major in Communications, so he had no trouble maintaining his scholarship.) However, the drive between Searcy, Arkansas, and Wetumpka, Alabama, was 427 miles, and a significant portion of the trip was over two-lane, mountainous roads. It was a long and dangerous drive home for holidays and other occasions, so we considered attempting to move a little closer to Searcy. After three years in the same job, I was open for a transfer.

In the early summer of 1989, I spoke to Perry Hammond about possibly transferring and the reasons for it, and he promised to see what he could find. A few weeks later, he said a new job had opened in Bartlesville, which was still in Marketing and was heavily involved in computing. He asked if I was interested. Since the job sounded like it was right in my wheelhouse, I agreed to pursue it. I would be working for a man named Jim Glass, and the job entailed managing the desktop and laptop computer assets of Marketing Division employees. Not only that, it would also cut at least 2½ hours off the drive time for Brent when he came home, and, in addition, most of the highways between Bartlesville and Searcy were 4–lane. It sounded like another miracle to me. After a brief interview with Jim Glass over the phone, I accepted the new position, and we made plans to move in the summer of that year.

Our move back to Bartlesville brought the incredible decade of the 1980s to a close. The year 1980 started out with an amazing and miraculous series of events that led to the adoption of our daughter Rachel. However, upon our return to Bartlesville from Alabama, I was unaware that the turmoil of the mid–1980's was still an albatross hanging around the neck of Phillips Petroleum and that adverse residual effects of the takeover efforts still lingered. Although things seemed hunky-dory upon our return, in due time, I would learn that we were not out of the woods yet.

THE PROVIDENCE OF GOD

After the bad decisions and resulting travails to which I had exposed my family during the 1970s when the 1980s began, we felt like we had won the lottery. EVERYTHING finally seemed to go our way – finances, career, family, church, friends, and dumb luck in an airplane. I have thought deeply and frequently about the decades of the '70s and '80's and their relationship with one another. I can come to no other conclusion than the fact that God was very active in keeping me between the ditches, so to speak, in life and Christianity. His earlier "influence" regarding my decision to take the job in Arkansas simply for the glory, recreation, and potential money had helped me get my head on straight(er) by the beginning of the 1980s and helped me endure the new trials that came my way later in the decade. From 1981 through 1989:

1. Two years following the adoption of Rachel, I was scheduled to be laid off from my job but received a reprieve as the order was never executed

2. I received a promotion in 1983 to a strategic job, which also minimized my chances of being laid off.

304

3. Two years later, due to the company's hostile takeover attempts, Phillips put in place a "poison pill" policy that would discourage hostile takeovers and, as will be revealed, the policy was of great benefit to me just a few years later when I retired.
4. I welcomed a brief respite from company woes and enjoyed a successful segment of my career after being transferred to Alabama.
5. I fortuitously purchased some Walmart stock, which, over the years, God granted an incredible increase.

It is impossible to ascertain how many Ebenezers I raised during that decade and how many times I had verbally stated, "Hither by Thy help I have come."

However, the question posed by my friend at Jude's Coffee Shop had not yet been fully answered. Just how did I finally manage once and for all to put down roots in Bartlesville, given my nomadic propensity? Quoting *Amazing Grace*,

Thru many dangers, toils, and snares I have already come.
Tis grace hath bro't me safe thus far,
And grace will lead me home.

By the grace of God, I had come this far, and only His grace could eventually lead me home – if only I would stay out of the way and let God work His wonders.

There would be more to the story before my friend's question could be fully answered. I was again living in Bartlesville in 1989, and I would make three more moves within the next eleven years before I finally settled in Bartlesville for good and started going to Jude's for coffee. Providence and Ebenezer would visit my family and me many more times over the several years, even beyond my final move to Bartlesville in 2000.

However, in 1989 we were still not out of the woods yet.

Thirty-Two

HOME AT LAST (AFTER ONLY
THREE MORE MOVES)

Upon this latest return to Bartlesville, we bought another house within a couple of blocks of the Ranch Heights Elementary School since Rachel was only in the third grade. We renewed all our friendships from the church but were surprised to learn that the Limestone Church of Christ had merged with the Woodland Church of Christ, and the new congregation was called the Adams Boulevard Church of Christ. At Adams Boulevard, the preacher was Art Henley, our preacher at the Limestone congregation when we left Bartlesville three years earlier. Once again, we got a preacher we already knew. We settled into the new chapter in our life, which was not difficult. It was almost as if we had never left.

My new job's main responsibility was to keep the desktop and laptop computers and communications operational and current for all Marketing personnel, both in Bartlesville and in the field. I was responsible for purchasing and replacing, when necessary, all desktop and laptop computers, printers, and associated equipment for the Marketing personnel. I also was to supervise the work of two programmers who maintained Marketing software on the Bartlesville–based mainframe computers. My new Boss, Jim Glass, continued my tradition of having excellent bosses.

As implied in the previous chapter, even by 1990, neither Phillips Petroleum nor I were out of the woods yet, so to speak, due to the residual adverse financial effects of the attempted takeover debacles of 1984 and 1985. By 1991, although the company was no longer in jeopardy of being bought, its financial condition going forward dictated that additional cost-cutting was going to be required. Consequently, the company embarked on a new staffing strategy. Instead of indiscriminate, across–the–board layoffs, the company decided to take a more scientific approach to the process. The company decided to study each job in the company, weed out the repetitive and the non–essential work being done, and combine jobs where possible. The study's title was Activity Value Analysis (AVA), and it kicked off in early 1992. It was a foregone conclusion that when AVA had wrapped up, some jobs would be identified as unnecessary and eliminated. Other jobs would be reclassified – either up or down – to better reflect their value. Also, some jobs would be absorbed into existing jobs, and still, other jobs, where possible, would be combined to enhance efficiency and effectiveness. The net result would be another round of layoffs supplemented by job consolidations and job redefinitions. For several weeks during the AVA process, everyone, including myself, was on pins and needles regarding their potential future with the company.

AVA ultimately decided that the job I had been performing for Mr. Glass could be absorbed into three other existing positions, thus eliminating one more position – mine. Although my job was going away, I was invited to stay. Instead of being laid off, I was offered a position in IT, which was compatible with my work experience. In the new job, I would be reporting to Bobby Culpepper, a friend of mine and a colleague during our days together, reporting to Charlie Gibbs.

However, Mr. Glass was aware that I had really liked all my work within the Marketing Division in times past, and he began snooping around to see if there was anything available out there within Marketing that I might be interested in as an alternative to the IT job I had been offered. He found another Wholesale Rep job opening, very similar to what I had been doing in Alabama, but this one was located in Illinois. I don't know what strings he pulled to unearth the job opening, but he told me I had about 24 hours to decide, and he sent me home in the middle of the day to discuss the issue with Shirley. Shirley was not thrilled with another move, but she understood Phillips's situation in Bartlesville and the good sense it made to get out of Dodge, so to speak, for a while. At least I would still be working in the same company and in a job with which I was familiar, so she agreed to the move. I went back to the office and told Mr. Glass to initiate the paperwork for the transfer. I also called Bobby Culpepper and expressed my thanks and regrets, and once I explained the situation, he said he understood, and there were no hard feelings.

My new job was the result of the realignment of several Wholesale Rep territories and the retirement of some existing Reps. My territory was to be central and southern Illinois, and I would be based in the city of Mt. Vernon. My new boss was to be Jeff Bailey, and the District Office was located in Chicago. Small world once again. Jeff and I had been friends years earlier when we both worked in Bartlesville, and Jeff's son Steven and my son Brent had been friends at the time.

As the title of this chapter implies, we still had three more moves in our future before we finally made it "home" – retirement, as it were. In the summer of 1992, we made the first of the three moves, from Bartlesville to Mt. Vernon. On our first Sunday there, we were greeted in the church foyer by Charles Clark, our Harding friend who had also been our preacher for a time in Independence, Missouri. This small world thing just seemed to keep on keeping on.

When we moved to Mt. Vernon by some stroke of luck – a miracle? – we bought a mid-century house in the best location in town. It was in a great, secluded, very well–maintained neighborhood. The house had great "bones" but had been empty and neglected for about three years. The price had dropped and had kept on dropping. I could tell it only needed cosmetic attention, so I made an offer on the house that was below the already reduced asking price. The ink of my signature on the offer sheet was not even dry by the time we received the approval of the offer. It proved to be the best investment in a house that I ever made to that point. Unlike our house in Horseshoe Bend, when we moved away from Mt. Vernon, this would definitely not be an "unsellable" house.

By this time, Brent had graduated from college and was seeking employment. He was hired a little later that year as a video editor at the NBC television station in Little Rock in keeping with his college major in Communications. By this time, Greg had also received a Phillips Petroleum scholarship at Oklahoma University majoring in Archaeology and Anthropology. Rachel was now in junior high. We quickly made friends at the church with Gale and Patti Evans, who had a daughter, Tiffany, who was in the same grade as Rachel. Rachel and Tiffany became fast friends, and the Evans' and we have remained close over the years.

We spent three great years in Mt. Vernon. Phillips 66 stations were like dandelions in Illinois – everywhere – so I had no trouble selling gasoline. The only trouble I encountered was the fact that there were so many Phillips stations that there were few opportunities to develop new sites that would not infringe on existing stations. Not a bad problem to have.

However, as we discovered after moving there, Illinois is nothing but one huge garden. Due to some primordial glacier movement across the area thousands of years earlier, the topsoil was ten feet deep, and corn and soybean fields were everywhere. Not only that, in the fall of 1992 and continuing into the spring of the next year, the Mississippi Valley – from Minnesota to the Gulf of Mexico – encountered a 100–year flood. To make matters worse, two great rivers, the Missouri and Ohio, drained into the Mississippi, thereby exacerbating its size. The Mississippi River at St. Louis was more than a mile wide, and every plant known to God that produced pollen was thriving. There was a 10–acre field behind our house that could have exported pollen all over the world.

Due to all the airborne pollen plus the extreme humidity exuding from the inland sea formerly known as the Mississippi River, by the time Rachel was a sophomore in high school, her allergies had flared up, and she was regularly missing about a week of school each month as a result. We felt that the only solution was to relocate to a drier climate. Consequently, in mid–1995, I pled my case to Jeff Bailey and requested a transfer to a job where there was less water and flora. Amarillo, Texas, became available, and Jeff Bailey engineered the transfer. I would be a Retail Territory Supervisor, responsible for all the company-owned stations in the Texas Panhandle in my new job.

As I had anticipated, selling our house in Mt. Vernon was a piece of cake. With its great location and the cosmetic improvements I had made, it was probably the most attractive house on the market in Mt. Vernon at the time. On a Friday, I listed the house with a realtor, and his intent was to put a "For Sale" sign in the front yard on Monday morning.

On Saturday, I left Shirley and Rachel in Mt. Vernon and headed to Bartlesville for initial meetings with management regarding my new assignment. Since my parents now lived in Cassville, Missouri, which was midway between Mt. Vernon and Bartlesville, I stopped at their house on Saturday afternoon to spend the night before heading on to Bartlesville on Sunday. Saturday evening, I received a call from Shirley saying that we had already received an offer on the house. After some minor negotiations over the phone with the realtor, we concluded the sale that evening, and the For Sale sign wasn't even in the front yard yet. Needless to say, this turn of events certainly made our move to Amarillo less stressful.

Earlier in the summer, our son, Greg, graduated from Oklahoma University just a whisker short of Magna Cum Laude. Although his degree was in Anthropology and Archaeology, Farmers Insurance had made him an offer he couldn't refuse. He was hired as a claims specialist and eventually rose to the position of senior claims specialist for the state of Oklahoma. His job primarily involved resolving sticky, complicated claims that frequently wound up in a court of law. Shirley and I figured that he had found his perfect job, but what do we know? Several years later, he went back to school and graduated from the University of Oklahoma Medical School as a doctor – but that's another story.

We were now preparing for the second of our three moves that would occur prior to my retirement. Since I had previously spent a lot of work-related time in Amarillo, including moving my family there for nine months in 1978–1979, I was intimately familiar with the city and the area. We looked for a house on the northwest side of the city, a new neighborhood that was destined to boom. We contracted to buy a house that was under construction, so we had a lot of input as to its amenities. We had to live in an apartment for a month or so until the house was completed.

When we had lived in Amarillo during 1978–1979, we had worshipped with the Southwest Church of Christ, but we now lived on the northwest side of town. Since it was now 1995, we assumed that few, if any, of the Southwest members would still remember us after sixteen years, so we opted to first explore the Central Church of Christ, which was considerably closer to our new home than was the Southwest Church. We showed up Sunday morning and experienced a first – we did not know the preacher. His name was Dick Marcear, and he was the preaching minister of a congregation of about 1100 souls.

We dutifully helped Rachel find the high school class and then wandered around until we found an adult class. It turns out that there were about a half dozen adult classes to accommodate the large membership, but by the grace of God, we stumbled into the right one for us. We were welcomed and sat next to a couple who introduced themselves and Mike and Chris Williams. Another couple came in and sat down beside us – Gary and Becky Douglas – and they also introduced themselves.

It bears mentioning that the Williams' and Douglas' had three children among them, which figured into our time in Amarillo and beyond. The Douglas' had two children, Michelle and Paul. Michelle, by "coincidence," was in the same grade as Rachel. The Williams' had one son, Taylor, who was Paul Douglas's age. The Williams' and Douglas' drew us into their considerable circle of friends at Central, and we enjoyed our first experience with church "small groups."

As for my work, I was now a Retail Territory Supervisor. Over the past ten years or so, starting just prior to my transfer to Alabama in 1986, Phillips had transitioned its company-owned facilities from automobile service stations into convenience stores. Phillips had taken the cue from the 7-Eleven and other successful convenience store chains and had expanded its product line beyond gasoline and discontinued selling tires, batteries, and automobile repair service.

I was responsible for the eleven Phillips–owned convenience stores in Amarillo and nearby Borger in my new job. Also, at the time, and primarily for the convenience of the hundreds of Phillips employees in Borger, we maintained a Fast Lube in that city. I inherited twelve excellent facility managers who ultimately made my Retail Territory Supervisor experience pleasant and, for the most part, tension-free.

The only real tension I experienced during my tenure in the job involved two robbery attempts. All of my stores, except the Fast Lube, were 24–hour operations. The first robbery attempt was a spectacular failure and made the local TV news. Ten of the eleven convenience stores had bulletproof glass cages which were to be locked at sundown each day and which protected the cashier and all of the high–dollar inventory behind the cage wall. Each customer transaction in the evening was handled via a bank teller–type pass–through. In this first robbery attempt, a perp came into the store late at night after the cages were locked, and he demanded money. The robber was carrying a shotgun. The cashier began taking money from the cash register to give to the robber. However, she was apparently not emptying the register fast enough to please him, so he leveled the shotgun at the glass door to the cage and pulled the trigger. The door was stronger than the shotgun shell, and all the pellets ricocheted back at the robber. He sustained numerous wounds to his legs and torso and fled the scene without any money at all. The next day an Amarillo TV station gave a live on–the–scene report. We had no further robbery attempts at the stores with cages.

The only other robbery attempt during my time on the job was successful, but the thief only made off with less than $100. This was due to my well–trained cashier's adherence to the company policy of making cash drops into the safe when cash levels in the cash register reached specified limits. This robbery was at the one store which did not feature a glass cage.

As for Rachel, she enrolled at Tascosa High School when we moved there, and it was a rich experience for her. She has a wonderful soprano voice, and Tascosa had probably the best high school choir in Texas. The choir director was a strong Christian and constantly pushed the envelope by incorporating church songs into the choir repertoire. Rachel was able to perform in several school, and civic musicals, including the opera "Carmen," and, in addition, the school choir toured the Baltimore, Maryland, and Washington, D.C. area during Rachel's senior year. They got to sing on the steps of the Capitol Building, and they performed the national anthem at Camden Yards at a Baltimore Orioles baseball game. Rachel got to meet Cal Ripken, and she said he had the prettiest blue eyes she had ever seen.

After graduating high school in 1998, Rachel enrolled at Harding.

HOME AT LAST (AFTER ONLY THREE MORE MOVES)

Among the other blessings she enjoyed at Harding was reuniting with her friend Tiffany Evans, and as a sophomore, she spent a semester abroad at Harding's campus in Florence, Italy. In November 1999, in what was our first trip overseas, Shirley and I visited Rachel while she was in Florence. It was pretty much a dream trip for us. We toured Rome, Florence, Pisa, Venice, Milan, Paris, and the beaches at Normandy and saw all the sights at each place. The most poignant part of the trip was visiting the American cemeteries in Normandy and viewing the thousands upon thousands of white crosses and Stars of David that mark the burial sites of those who died during the D–Day invasion.

Rachel's semester in Florence was a remarkable and enjoyable learning experience. It was what I believe influenced both Taylor Williams and Paul Douglas to enroll at Harding. As it turns out, both boys met and married Harding girls, and Taylor also was able to spend a semester at the Florence campus. In fact, although we no longer lived in Amarillo at the time, we accompanied Mike and Chris Williams when they visited Taylor in Florence. One other interesting note – upon graduation from Harding, Taylor obtained his Master's degree from Tufts University in Boston in Biomedical Engineering and then returned to Harding and joined the faculty. As of this writing, he is on sabbatical from Harding and is enrolled at Purdue University, completing his Doctoral dissertation with plans to return to Harding to teach.

Overall, our time in Amarillo was a wonderful experience family-wise, church–wise and career-wise. Ironically, at church, we were reunited with Mary Lou Barber, Rob Barber's ex-wife. They had divorced sometime after the Horseshoe Bend debacle.

Sometime in late 1999, during the decade's fading days, Shirley and I began giving thought as to where we would like to retire. I was 55 at the time, and the generous separation packages approved for Phillips employees during the hostile takeover attempts back in the 1980s were still in effect. It was still at least three or four years before I would be looking at retirement, but it doesn't hurt to do a little advance planning. We thought about it, and, as well as we liked Amarillo, we concluded that either Searcy or Bartlesville were our best bets for retirement. We had more and deeper relationships with people who lived in those places. The two cities were considerably smaller than Amarillo, which was a serious criterion in Shirley's point of view. She didn't then and still doesn't like to drive in metro areas. Also the issues of the out–of–pocket costs of selling our present house, buying a new one in the new location and the cost of the move itself were in the back of our minds.

We continued to periodically discuss what we would like to do four or five years hence, but the issue was sort of relegated to a back burner. Then

God intervened in a huge way. In early 2000 an old friend from church in Bartlesville, Gary Russell, gave me a call. At that time, Gary was General Auditor for Phillips Petroleum – a VP level position. Phillips Petroleum had recently acquired a company by the name of TOSCO, an oil refiner and operator of approximately 5000 7–Eleven convenience stores across the country. TOSCO owned and operated several strategically located oil refineries plus some strategically located oil pipelines around the country. Phillips was not interested in the 7–Eleven stores and would ultimately sell them off a little later, but the refineries and pipelines filled in some blanks in Phillips' refining and distribution systems. Thus, the decision to acquire TOSCO.

Gary knew that I had had broad experience in Marketing. He was also aware that I had decent accounting experience – I had previously taught some Accounting classes at Bartlesville Wesleyan College a few years earlier. Gary was looking for some people with that background to perform an in-depth audit of TOSCO's operations, and he thought of me. The gist of the conversation was that he wanted me to transfer into corporate Internal Auditing and to relocate to Bartlesville to do so.

This was, of course, just another coincidence, another cosmic accident. It was beginning to appear that our entire lives had been just one beneficial "cosmic accident" after another. This latest accident closely followed our preferred retirement locations' discussions, also keeping in mind that Phillips would pay all our moving expenses. What was there not to like? I had long since stopped believing the blessings we had received were accidents but rather were clear evidence of God's Providence and grace.

It took me less than five seconds to accept Gary's offer.

The first thing we did was list our house for sale. In the five years we had lived there, the neighborhood had doubled or tripled in size, and both an elementary school and mid-high school had been built about three blocks from our house. I had to believe that selling our house would not be difficult. As it turns out, it sold within a week after being listed and at a price higher than the realtor recommended.

We were going to move again to Bartlesville, and as a transferee, all our moving costs and the costs involved in selling our house in Amarillo would be paid by Phillips. In Bartlesville, I would be working for a friend in an arena where I had lots of experience and great interest. I would likely still be in Bartlesville in four years when I was eligible for early retirement. We would be reunited with old friends and would be much closer to family. I thought it was another miracle, but I think to God, it was just another day at the office, so to speak.

However, miracles still had not ceased. When Shirley and I traveled to

HOME AT LAST (AFTER ONLY THREE MORE MOVES)

Bartlesville to house hunt an old friend of mine from College High School, Jerry Pierce, was the realtor. Since I already knew Bartlesville very well, we were able to focus our house search on just the areas where we wanted to buy. It was no longer necessary to locate near a school as all our children were now grown and out of the house. Shirley and I finally narrowed the search to two houses, one in the Park Hill addition on the northeast side of Bartlesville and one in Colonial Estates located on the southeast part of town. Shirley liked the one in Park Hill, and I liked the one in Colonial Estates, and they were priced exactly the same.

While we were considering the two houses, Jerry took us to lunch to discuss the options further. During lunch, Jerry received a phone call informing him that the house in Colonial Estates had just been lowered in price by $5000. Shirley and I took that as a sign, and we agreed to purchase that property. Was that another coincidence, or was it another intervention by God? Given what had happened to me continually during my life, I had no trouble deciding which it was. Against All odds.

Ultimately, in the year 2000, as the chapter title mentions, we made our third move, and it was back to Bartlesville, and we were home at last. However, God was apparently not finished with his blessings.

THE PROVIDENCE OF GOD

The decade of the '90s was dynamic, to say the least. It started out on a very promising note, but our faith was tested again within three years as I was forced to change jobs. Before the decade would conclude, I would change jobs within the company two more times. However, as with previous dynamic and sometimes adverse events, the series of job changes were all blessings in disguise. Among other things, the job changes gave us new lifelong friends, successfully addressed family health issues, and eventually brought us home. In all these events, God proved once again that in all things, He works for the good of those who love Him. Blessings received during the decade of the '90s:

1. I was offered what I have always felt was my favorite job in my career with Phillips, working with computer issues under Jim Glass.

2. At the time of the AVA layoffs, not only was I not laid off, but I was offered two jobs, and the one I accepted required a move to Illinois.

3. In Illinois, I was reunited with a friend and former preacher at church.

4. In Illinois, we made lifelong friends with the Evans family, and their daughter and Rachel became best friends.

5. We were allowed to transfer at Phillips' expense to Amarillo to help resolve Rachel's allergy problems.

6. In Amarillo, we made lifelong friends with the Williams family. We ultimately influenced their son to enroll at Harding, which eventually provided him with a wife and a career teaching at Harding.

7. Shortly after the end of the decade, I received a timely job offer from a friend and was transferred at company expense back to Bartlesville and home.

8. Once in Bartlesville, even the purchase of our house there appeared to be providential.

However, even though we were back "home," the story still had a page or two to be written. Yes, we had returned to my roots in anticipation of retirement, but retirement was not immediately in the offing. As will be seen, God still had a few tricks up His sleeve.

Truly, we had come hither by His help, but there were a few more miles in the journey and another Ebenezer or two to raise.

Thirty-Three

RETIREMENT, FINALLY

In our latest return to Bartlesville, we set about re-establishing our relationship with the Adams Boulevard Church of Christ and with our friends all over town. At this point, we had been absent from Bartlesville for eight years – from 1992 until 2000. Fortunately, most of our friends, particularly at church, were still here and were glad to receive us for what we all hoped would be the last time. As with most of our prior moves, we found a familiar face in the pulpit, in this case, Art Henley, who was the preacher when we had left Bartlesville eight years earlier. We were assimilated back into the congregation with ease. At this point, both Brent and Greg were married and out of the house, and Rachel was going into her junior year at Harding.

I approached my new job as an Internal Auditor with some apprehension but was soon comfortable with it. In a nutshell, auditing is nothing more than a review of accounting principles that have been applied by the individual or business unit. Basically, auditors review financial transactions, test their accuracy and legality, and offer written opinions as to the findings. If problems or irregularities are discovered, they are noted, and appropriate actions are initiated. If everything is in order, we compliment the auditee and move on to the next audit. I was very familiar with basic accounting principles, so my new job was not a huge leap on the learning curve. As a Phillips Petroleum Internal Auditor, every segment of the business, including subsidiaries, was fair game for an audit.

As mentioned, I was brought into the group primarily to assist in TOS-CO's auditing, the large refining, and marketing company Phillips had acquired. However, before diving into TOSCO's audit, it required that I get my feet wet by performing audits in other segments of the company. Also, it should be noted that I had retained my string of working under superior managers – in this case, Gary Russell.

During my time in Internal Auditing, I frequently traveled, sometimes to interesting places, like Alaska, and sometimes to routine places like Borger and Midland, Texas.

My first assignment was an interesting trip involving an audit at a refinery Phillips had acquired in TOSCO's purchase. The refinery was located at Trainer, Pennsylvania, which was just a few miles south of Philadelphia on the Delaware River. It was about a one–week assignment, and I was the only one of the audit team members that had ever been to the Philadelphia area.

Although the audit was pretty routine, we did have two memorable dining experiences while there. First, we got to enjoy genuine Philly Cheesesteak sandwiches at Geno's Steaks – the best ever. The second memorable experience was dinner one evening at the Tangerine Restaurant in Philadelphia, which specialized in Mediterranean cuisine. The restaurant was lighted entirely by hundreds of votive candles, which rendered visibility next to nothing. The limited menu listed nothing that I recognized, and I ended up ordering a very artistically presented dish but not as satisfying as the Philly Cheesesteak I had enjoyed at Geno's. Although the service was superior, I was not convinced that the food's cost correlated with the overall dining experience. But that's just me, I guess. I understand that the restaurant is now closed, which does not really surprise me. However, the meal was enlightening, to say the least.

My most memorable auditing trip was to Houston in September 2001. On the morning of September 11, my team was auditing a supplier for Phillips in its office on the 43rd floor of a skyscraper in Houston. At shortly after 9:00 that morning, my audit team and I were standing in front of a TV watching the Twin Towers fall. As was probably the case with almost everyone, there were no words to describe our emotions. In short order, the office was closed, and the building emptied. There were rampant rumors that other terrorist planes were flying, and if that were so we were working in a likely target. We decided to cancel the audit at that time and return to Houston the following week if possible. Since the airlines were basically grounded, my audit team of four guys made the trip back to Bartlesville in a rental car.

In addition, we had tickets to an Astros–Giants game the evening of September 11 and had planned to watch Barry Bonds in his quest to break Mark McGuire's season home run record. The game was canceled, so we eventually got the tickets replaced for the following week when the Cardinals and McGuire were in town. When we came back the next week, we got to

318

witness McGuire hit two home runs, one of which hit the train that sits atop the left-center field stands. The train is a gimmick that activates and whistles every time an Astro hits a homer. It didn't whistle when McGuire's homer whacked it.

A few months following the Houston audit trip, I was sent along with Jerry Cantu to Anchorage, Alaska, to audit a company that serviced Phillips drilling activities on the North Slope. In jest, I accused someone in the management of punishing Jerry and me since we were being sent to Alaska in January. While we were there, we never saw the sun except when we went out of the office for lunch at noon. When we left for the office at 7:30 a.m., it was pitch dark. When we headed back to the hotel at 5:00 p.m., it was pitch dark. At that time of the year, the sun was basically visible between 10:00 a.m. and 3:30 p.m.

However, that was adequate for snow skiing. As a skier, I thought it worthwhile to do some skiing while I was in Alaska. My friend, Mike Wofford, a Phillips attorney who was based in Anchorage at the time, and I visited Alyeska, a ski mountain southeast of Anchorage, for some fine skiing.

Also, while we were in Alaska, we experienced a pretty good earthquake. Nothing like the quake of 1964, but pretty volatile.

My most vivid memory of that trip involved our return trip to Bartlesville. Jerry and I were scheduled to catch a midnight flight from Anchorage to Tulsa. However, watching the weather report, we learned that a huge blizzard was expected to hit Anchorage by early evening. Jerry did some checking and discovered there was a flight out of Anchorage (not on the airline we flew up on) around noon, which, if we could get seats, would get us safely out of town before the blizzard hit. He and I went to the Anchorage airport to buy tickets.

Remember, this was about four months following 9/11, and people everywhere were still jumpy regarding terrorists and airplanes. Jerry is Hispanic and has dark hair, and could be imagined by some to be Arabic. This, alone, sent alarm bells ringing at the airport. Then, when he and I sauntered up to the counter and asked to buy one–way tickets back to the lower 48, the security people at the airport basically went berserk. They figured they were dealing with a couple of suicidal terrorists. They gave us the third degree and checked everything about us, including our bodies. They took our luggage and opened it, and looked at everything in it, including the dirty laundry. They made phone calls. They may have called Gary Russell – I'm not sure. At any rate, they finally cleared us to board, and we got out of town ahead of the blizzard and made it home safely.

All in all, the Anchorage trip was memorable on several levels.

Management made up for sending me to Alaska in January on the next trip. I was sent as part of a team to Long Beach, California, to audit Polar Tankers, the Phillips tanker ships that hauled crude oil from Alaska to the terminal in Long Beach. Long Beach on an expense account in the spring is hard to beat. Great audit, excellent food, five–star hotel, and we flew in and out of the Long Beach Airport, a throwback to the 1940s. The airport was an art deco style, with low traffic and no need to catch trams or shuttles.

My final audit trip took place in August of 2002 and was in stark contrast to the leisurely and pleasant trip to Long Beach. My final involvement in the TOSCO audit was scheduled at TOSCO's headquarters in Phoenix, Arizona – in August. Whereas I froze in Anchorage, I fried in Phoenix. Overall, however, it was not uncomfortable. Everything in Phoenix is air-conditioned, and I dined at Ruth's Chris Steak House and the Cheesecake Factory. The Cheesecake factory was memorable in that I met Ryne Sandberg, baseball Hall of Famer there.

Following Phoenix, I began gearing down to retire. At some point during my tenure in Internal Auditing, Gary Russell had been transferred to Phillips' New York office as manager of Investor Relations. Gary's working in New York was providential in that, in 2008, my good friend Allen Richmond and I took a baseball tour of New England and New York, and Gary was able to provide us free tickets to a Mets game in the original Shea Stadium and to a Yankees game in the original Yankee Stadium. Both teams later moved to new stadiums.

Gary was replaced as General Auditor by Beth Heaton. I knew Beth already when we had crossed paths previously in our work. Beth was a jewel, and in my mind, Gary could not have been replaced by anyone better. It once again continued my streak of working under excellent bosses. Beth had a significant positive impact on my retirement. It turns out that God was apparently not finished with providential involvement in my life. What happened is a remarkable story.

In November of the previous year, Phillips Petroleum Company and Conoco had merged to form the ConocoPhillips Corporation, making it one of the world's largest oil-producing companies. Several months later, in September 2002, the new company was finalizing all the details of merging, including headquarters, offices, consolidation of jobs, and, yes, layoffs.

After completing the TOSCO audit in late August of 2002, I had had conversations with Beth regarding potential layoff. At this time, Phillips still had in place the generous retirement benefits that had been established during the takeover bids in the mid–1980's, and I was very seriously considering volunteering for layoff. If I were eligible for the layoff package, it was ludicrous to continue working until age 65. The problem was that at the time I was talking with Beth about volunteering for layoff, I was only 58½ years old, a full year short of being eligible for full layoff benefits, however lucrative they might be. For me to be laid off at this time would not be disastrous, but if I could survive until I was 59½ years old, I would be eligible for the whole benefit.

There were many, many favorable conditions written into the retirement plan, but four were immediately significant. First, under the terms of the layoff plan then in place, a retired/laid-off employee was entitled to 60 weeks of full pay following retirement or layoff. Second, Phillips had a bonus plan that each March paid all employees a bonus for their performance the previous year. However, it was necessary for a person to still be under the Phillips benefits umbrella at the end of the previous year to qualify for the bonus payment. Third, when an employee retired or was laid off, if he had a remaining unused vacation that would carry him to the next calendar year, he was entitled to the benefits that would accrue as if he had actually retired in the next calendar year. Fourth, a person who was still associated with the company on January 1 of any year was entitled to vacation pay for that year.

Bottom line, if I was laid off – voluntarily or not – and totally separated from the company prior to year-end 2002, I would qualify for nothing but the 60 weeks of pay. I would forfeit participation in the bonus plan, I would forfeit the six weeks of vacation pay for 2003, and there would be penalties associated with retiring before age 59½, September 25, 2003.

With these things in mind, Beth and I discussed retirement plans and decided to proceed. She was fully up on company policy, and she delivered on my benefit in spades.

My last official day in the office was September 24, 2002. However, it was company policy to release those laid off two months prior to actual separation date. I was puzzled as to why Beth chose September 24, and then the light came on. That made my official separation date November 24, 2002, strangely a Sunday. However, at that time, I still had 25½ vacation days left in 2002. With weekends and holidays (Thanksgiving and Christmas, two days each) removed, there were exactly 25 workdays left in the year, and my vacation carried me through December 31, 2002, with a half-day of vacation to spare. Beth had factored in my remaining vacation and calculated a separation date that would carry me to the end of the year and thus entitle me to all the benefits of being under the benefit umbrella on January 1, 2003.

Not only did that qualify me for the benefits package, it also allowed me to officially be "on the payroll" on September 25, 2003, at which time I turned 59½ years old, thereby avoiding any early retirement financial penalties. Beth afforded me tens of thousands of dollars in additional income by her creative layoff plan. I will always be grateful for her kindness.

At retirement, Phillips retirees could either choose a monthly annuity as their retirement benefit, or they could choose a lump-sum distribution. Generally speaking, the monthly annuity does not provide as much money as does a carefully managed lump-sum distribution. I chose the lump-sum distribution.

Two more blessings were providentially in place when I finally retired and received my retirement check. First was the GATT rate, an acronym for General Agreement on Tariffs and Trades. Many companies, including Phillips, use these monthly interest rates to calculate lump-sum distributions from their pension plans. Basically, the higher the GATT rate, the lower the lump-sum distribution. The lower the GATT rate, the higher the lump-sum distribution. By fate or providence, when I took my distribution, the GATT rate was at a historic low. I received the absolute largest distribution I could have possibly received.

The second-factor blessing I enjoyed at retirement was the DOW Jones Industrial average. At that time, the DOW was sitting at around 7000, which means the money from my distribution, when invested by someone who knew what he was doing, could not go anywhere but up over time. And it did.

I was reluctant to spend so many words describing something as mundane as my retirement. Still, I felt it was another series of providential blessings I have received during my lifetime. It seems that my boss, Phillips company retirement policy, the GATT, and the Dow Jones Industrial average all teamed up to my benefit. Throughout my life, I have often had instances where a whole series of events or circumstances seemed choreographed to my benefit. I continue to be convinced these are not cosmic accidents.

Especially regarding my retirement.

Life did not end for me at retirement. I was contacted shortly after my retirement by a headhunter in Tulsa asking if I was interested in taking a contract job as an Internal Auditor for the Baker–Hughes Company. Baker–Hughes was a leading manufacturer of equipment used in drilling for oil. The company's headquarters were in Claremore, Oklahoma, about 40 miles from Bartlesville. Initially, the headhunter asked me if I was interested in leading an audit of the Baker–Hughes operations in the country of Oman and the United Arab Emirates – Abu Dhabi and Dubai. I was flattered, but, in the first place, I had not really caught my breath from retirement, and secondly, I did not feel qualified to lead such an audit. I politely thanked them and declined their offer.

RETIREMENT, FINALLY

About a year later, they called me again and offered me another opportunity for contract work with Baker–Hughes, but not as a team leader. Under those conditions, I accepted the offer and went to work for the company in August 2004.

The first two assignments were stateside, in Houston and then Midland, Texas. Next came an assignment in Maracaibo, Venezuela. Our team spent two weeks in Maracaibo and learned that we never wanted to spend much more time there. Among other things, there were armed guards in the parking lots of restaurants and shopping malls. It was truly a third–world country in 2004, and it has seriously deteriorated since then.

Then came a dream assignment. Although I was not going as a team leader, I was selected as part of the team to go to the Middle East. We would perform audits in Muscat, Oman, and in the United Arab Emirates of Abu Dhabi and Dubai. It was a part of the world I had never been to and would likely have never gone on my own nickel. The only disappointing part of the assignment was that the team members were required to fly coach to and from the Middle East. At Phillips, when anyone went overseas on business on a flight of five or more hours, they were given either a business class or first-class ticket. Taking this trip in coach was going to be hard on a 60–year–old body.

In Muscat, we stayed at the InterContinental Hotel on the beach on the Arabian Sea. What Baker–Hughes lacked in providing comfort in the air they made up for on the ground. In addition, we had a chauffeur in a Mercedes–Benz to shuttle us to and from the office each day. In the evening, we dined at Trader Vic's on the beach adjacent to the InterContinental. Muscat was grand.

Next, we traveled to Abu Dhabi. Once again, we were housed in an InterContinental Hotel. In Abu Dhabi, the hotel was downtown, and I did some shopping for my very young grandchildren. I bought them stuffed animals and also purchased a small suitcase to carry them in. When we finished there, we were driven to Dubai, just across several miles of desert. In Dubai, we were housed in a Novotel, not quite as luxurious as the InterContinental, but it was OK. Dubai turned out to be our most complex audit of the three, and we spent the better part of a week there.

A couple of interesting things happened during that week. First, our team plus some other Baker–Hughes employees went to the gold souk in downtown Dubai. The gold souk is about a quarter-mile square of nothing but small jewelry stores. Legend had it that the prices were reasonable and could be negotiated. Remember the ¼ carat diamond I bought for Shirley's engagement ring? In one of the stores in the gold souk, I picked out a ring that had five diamonds in it, the smallest being larger than the one in Shirley's engagement ring. I bargained with the proprietor and finally settled on what I thought was a fair price. However, before we finalized the deal, one of Baker–Hughes employees that had accompanied us stepped in and said, "No."

She then commenced further negotiations with the proprietor and got the price down another $300. This obviously wasn't this lady's first rodeo. I thanked her profusely and purchased the ring at the new price. (When I returned home and had the ring appraised, and its appraised value in Bartlesville exceeded the price I had paid in Dubai.) Shirley liked the ring.

The other interesting thing that happened in Dubai was our final meal the night we departed for home. We were taken to a restaurant named, of all things, "Alamo," and I enjoyed the best Tex–Mex meal I have ever had. The guacamole was created tableside, and the food was delicious. It was rumored that an Emir from Dubai had visited a Tex–Mex restaurant while on an oil-related trip to Houston at some time in the past and had been so impressed with the food that he had hired the chef and the entire staff to open and operate a similar restaurant in Dubai. There may be some truth to the story, for the service staff did appear to be Hispanic rather than Arabic.

Following dinner, I was taken to the airport for the trip home.

Even at the airport, strange things continued to happen to me. As mentioned, I had bought some stuffed animals for my grandchildren while I was in Abu Dhabi and had also purchased a small suitcase to carry them in. I didn't check the small suitcase as luggage at the Dubai airport but rather planned to carry it on as a second item of "carry–on," along with my briefcase. Also, as mentioned, I was flying coach.

The plane was huge and held almost 300 passengers. Not unsurprisingly, the first-class passengers were invited to board first. In fact, the first-class had its own separate door into the plane. An announcement was made, "All first-class passengers may have two carry-ons."

At the time, I didn't pay much attention to it. When the first-class passengers had finally completed boarding, the thralls and fellahin – the coach passengers – were invited to board. At that time, they made another announcement, "All coach passengers are limited to one carry–on."

When I heard that, I became considerably uneasy, wondering how I would be able to smuggle my second carry–on onto the plane. As I was stewing over my dilemma, time dragged on with 200+ coach passengers boarding, most apparently clogging the aisles to get themselves situated. It may have been due to the fact that the plane was not likely to make its take–off as scheduled, or it may have been intervention by God, but for whatever reason, the airline personnel decided to speed up the boarding process. Another announcement was made. "To expedite boarding coach passengers may enter the plane through the first-class door."

By the grace of God, I was well back in the line of coach passengers boarding, but I was directly in front of the first-class entry door. I simply made a left turn, boarded the plane through the first-class door carrying my two items, threaded my way through the first-class seats, and arrived in the coach section behind the back of the flight attendant enforcing the "one carry-on" rule for coach passengers. I found my seat, stored my briefcase and suitcase in an overhead bin, and settled in for the first leg of the flight home, the flight attendants never the wiser.

Now I ask you. Was that blind luck, happenstance, or Providence? If I had been nearer the front of the line of boarding, I would never have had the opportunity to enter through the first-class door. They say timing is everything, and I think even God believes that.

One thing more – even though I was flying coach Emirates Air made the flight feel like first class.

Upon our return to the Baker–Hughes office in Claremore, we learned the destination of our next audit. It was to be in Australia in just a few days. A typical flight to Australia can take 12 hours or more, but the requirement that we fly coach instead of business or first class remained in effect. At that point, realizing that my knees were too old to endure that type of torture for that many hours and that, due to my generous retirement package, I didn't need the money, I thanked Baker–Hughes for the fantastic experiences they had provided and resigned. I had worked for them for about three months and had visited three continents. Thus ended my professional work experience, and I formally retired for good.

THE PROVIDENCE OF GOD

Miracles, it seems, continued to follow me even after we finally got "home." My last job at Phillips was an excellent experience, and my bosses were exceptional. Even my contract work with Baker–Hughes was rewarding and provided worldwide experiences in locations I never dreamed that I would ever see.

The blessings associated with my return to Bartlesville, in my mind, have to have been the Providence of God. And I continued to raise my Ebenezer in response:

1. Out of the blue, I had been offered an opportunity to take a new job that, "coincidentally," turned out to be located in the city where we had hoped to retire.

2. During the term of my new job, I was blessed with two superior bosses.

3. My second boss worked the timing and logistics regarding my retirement from Phillips Petroleum to provide me with maximum financial retirement benefits.

4. Following my retirement from Phillips, I was given the opportunity to perform contract work in some exotic and exciting locations overseas.

5. I was able to resign from my contract work on my terms and on my timetable.

6. I was able to separate myself from the everyday working world in good health and in a position to be able to serve and enjoy God, family, friends, and community, for which I was unbelievably grateful.

At this point, the question posed by my friend at Jude's Coffee Shop regarding how I wound up in Bartlesville had been fully answered. Truly by the grace of God, I had come this far – through trials and tribulations from which I hope I learned and grew, through victories and celebrations for which I will be eternally grateful. I had been the recipient of what I can only describe as almost continuous miracles over a period of more than 50 years, for which I stand in awe.

It is impossible to ascertain how many Ebenezers I raised during those years and how many times I had verbally stated,

"Hither by Thy help I have come."

The Providence of God and the Provenance of Ebenezer.

Thirty-Four

IT'S A SMALL WORLD AFTER ALL
(And a Few Close
Encounters of the Third Kind)

Several times over the years, I had the opportunity to visit Disney World in Orlando, Florida. In many of those visits, I was accompanied by our young grandchildren, and invariably, they wanted to ride the "It's a Small World" attraction. I have nothing in particular against that attraction because, after all, it presents a very worthwhile philosophy – the world is indeed very small in that it is populated by people of every culture, language, and color. And, after all, we should all try to understand each other and try to get along.

However, the cute song that is played continually during the ride, "It's a Small World After All," has just enough clever, easy–to–remember words and a catchy tune that has haunted me for at least 50 years. It is almost like an audio narcotic. As much as I am exasperated from not being able to rid my subconscious of that song, nevertheless, it does make a meaningful title for this chapter of my book. So, at least I have gained one benefit from having endured this discomfort for so many years.

As I have emphasized throughout this book, I am unworthy in the sight of God and am just another regular "Joe" among my friends and acquaintances. I am deserving of nothing special. However, for whatever reason, I have been blessed almost since birth with a wide array of amazing "small world" events that have greatly enriched my life. Some of the events have been described in the previous chapters of this book, and a few others are mentioned in the pages that follow. It just doesn't seem possible that I could have "accidentally" been the recipient of so many of these occurrences. Even though the other obvious blessings – miracles – that are documented in this book are considerably more powerful than small world events, nevertheless I feel that these events were also worthy of mentioning in that they occurred against all odds and, if nothing else, qualify as small miracles that have enriched my life.

Most of the small world events I will describe occurred in unusual places and frequently in unusual circumstances and involved either meeting friends or meeting friends of friends. However, in a couple of instances, my path crossed those of total strangers who personally provided a very interesting and memorable experience.

Anchorage, Alaska

Phil Dixon was the best man at my wedding, and we have been fast friends with him and his wife Ann since our Harding days. In 2005 Shirley and I were on a tour of Alaska, and our last stop on the tour was Anchorage. I had been in Anchorage on two previous occasions on business trips, but this was Shirley's first exposure to the city. We decided to take a trolley tour of the city, so we bought our tickets and sat in the office of the tour company awaiting the arrival of our trolley. The office had large windows that faced the sidewalk and street outside. As we sat there, a woman who looked just like Ann Dixon happened to stroll past. What was Ann Dixon doing in Anchorage? At any rate, I got up and went outside to investigate, and it was indeed Ann. While we were talking, Phil moseyed up and joined the conversation.

This was not a street in Little Rock or Oklahoma City. This small world event took place in Anchorage, 3000 miles from home. However, Anchorage was still not finished with its surprises. A couple of minutes later, a small world struck again.

Anchorage, Alaska, continued

As mentioned earlier, I worked with Lonnie Porter on a computer project in 1971 and then worked for him on two different occasions in two different departments, first in 1974 and again in 1978. He had since retired and moved from Bartlesville, and I had not seen him in more than 20 years. While Shirley and I were visiting with Phil and Ann, our trolley arrived. We bid the Dixon's goodbye and boarded the trolley. As I was sitting down, I heard a voice from across the aisle ask, "Is your last name, Vaughan?" The word "startled" greatly understated my immediate reaction. However, I looked toward the voice, and there sat Lonnie Porter. Not in Bartlesville or Tulsa but in Anchorage, Alaska. Two very small world events in the space of two minutes. All I could do was shake my head and wonder.

Fort Dix, New Jersey

I have already alluded to my chance meeting with an old friend and future Major General of the United States Army, Perry Dalby, while I was stationed at Fort Dix, New Jersey. Admittedly, this small world event was not earth-shaking but was nevertheless welcomed and provided a temporary boost to my morale at the time. God moves in mysterious ways.

Portland, Oregon

As mentioned earlier, during my first four semesters at Harding – before I met Shirley – I had an appropriately active social life. I dated several young women during that time; all were exceptional, but none more so than Marlene Hall. Marlene and I dated during the first semester of my senior year. She was a freshman from Alma, Arkansas, a small town near Fort Smith. She was active in campus activities, including the Chorale, where we first met. We never established any traction in our dating, and she eventually met Gary Kelley, and I met Shirley Swayne, and the rest is history.

Fast forward to 2016. Shirley and I celebrated our 50th wedding anniversary by taking a river cruise down the Columbia River from Clarkston, Washington, to, eventually, Portland, Oregon. We concluded our cruise on a Saturday, spent that night in Portland, and made plans to attend church Sunday morning in a suburb of Portland. We had friends, Tom and Judi Hinds, who lived there, and we were planning on meeting them at church and then having lunch together.

We found the church with no problem and went into the foyer to meet with the Hinds. There were between 75 and 100 people in the large foyer chatting and moving about. I was looking around for Tom and Judi when I noticed that Shirley had zeroed in on one single woman among the 75 or 100 people in the foyer and was apparently deep in discussion with her. I walked over and discovered that of all the people in the room, Shirley had found the only one in the entire state of Oregon that I had once dated – Marlene Hall, now Marlene Kelley. What are the odds? Marlene had married Gary Kelley, and they had been married approaching 50 years at the time. Half a continent away, and my wife strikes up a conversation with a young woman I used to date. Stuff like this keeps happening to me.

Hilton Head, South Carolina

In 2005, a few months after we toured Alaska, where we had encountered some small world events, we took a trip to Hilton Head, South Carolina, with Mike and Chris Williams. As mentioned earlier, we had taken a trip with them to Florence, Italy, to visit their son who, like our daughter Rachel, was spending a semester abroad at the Harding campus in Florence. In our trip to Hilton Head, the objective was to play as much golf as possible because there were many fine golf courses in the Hilton Head area. We and the Williams' and Bill and Jan Knebush had made plans to spend about a week at Hilton Head. Before our arrival, Mike had made golf tee time reservations at several different courses for the week of our visit.

We arrived in Hilton Head on a Saturday, planned to attend church on Sunday, and then begin our golfing adventure on Monday. Sunday morning, we got up, found the church, and settled in for the worship service. During the announcements, the preacher made a reference to a "Glenn Barber." Shirley whispered to me that I knew Glenn Barber. I replied that Glenn Barber is a fairly common name, and there are probably thousands of men with that name nationwide. I thought nothing more of it until the service was over and we were in the foyer preparing to leave. At that point, a man pointed his finger at me and said, "I know you."

You could have knocked me over with a feather. It was THE Glenn Barber.

If the name Barber sounds familiar to you, it should. Glenn is the younger brother of Robley Barber, who hired me as Advertising Manager for Horseshoe Bend Estates in 1973. Glenn had also been a student at Harding, and I had gotten acquainted with him at that time. Like his older brother, Glenn was very smart, a go-getter, and was also a CPA.

Glenn and I shook hands, and he inquired what we were doing in Hilton Head. I replied that Mike and I and Bill Knebush were going to play golf every day for the next four days. Glenn then asked where we were going to play, and Mike named the courses we had signed up for. I remember Glenn's words like they were yesterday. He said, "We can do better than that."

It turns out that Glenn, like Robley, and gotten involved with developing luxury golf/retirement communities. He was CFO of a company that had just completed development at Cabo San Lucas and was currently completing the development of a new one near Hilton Head. And his statement that "we can do better than that" came to fruition when he set up a complimentary tee time for all of us at the Port Royal Golf and Racquet Club just outside Hilton Head. It was a world-class golf course. Harding's beneficial tentacles had reached me again. What are the odds of running into Glenn Barber at that time in that place under the circumstances?

Also, it seemed that, as mentioned earlier in this document, we had encountered so many strange adventures that we exhausted all the possibilities, and now they had begun repeating themselves. This made our third encounter with the Barber family in unusual circumstances – first with Robley and the Horseshoe Bend adventure and then with Mary Lou Barber, Rob's ex-wife, at church in Amarillo in 1995, and now with Glenn in Hilton Head. It had been a wild ride.

I have had numerous other small world encounters with friends and acquaintances over the years, but these are among the most memorable. I have also met people who know people that I know. Here are a few of the most unusual of such meetings.

Flagstaff, Arizona

In 2008 we and our good friends Quinton and Helen Martin decided to take a driving trip to the West Coast. The trip's ultimate objective was to attend the Pepperdine University Lectureships, which are held each May at its campus in Malibu, California. The beautiful campus is located on a picturesque hillside above the Pacific coast, and just to enjoy the scenery makes the trip worthwhile. Combining that with the great speakers and the activities of the week makes for an unbelievable experience.

In making the drive to Malibu, it was convenient for us to spend a night in Flagstaff, Arizona, en route. We arrived in Flagstaff on a Saturday afternoon, checked into a hotel for the night, arose on Sunday, checked out of the hotel, and headed to the Flagstaff Church of Christ. We planned to leave immediately following the Sunday morning service and continue our trek to California.

I need to interject at this time that a young man named Doug Oaks had been the youth minister at the Adams Boulevard church until about 2003 or 2004.

Upon entering the Flagstaff church, we were greeted in the foyer by one of the elders. While I did not personally know him, during our conversation, we learned that he was once a missionary supported by the Sixth and Dewey congregation in Bartlesville. In addition, he had spent a lot of time in Bartlesville in the early 1950s and knew Sidney Roper very well. Everywhere I go, it seems I find some connection to back home.

While our short visit in the foyer was amazing – but not entirely unexpected, given my history – "small world" in Flagstaff was not finished yet. As we left the foyer and made our way to the auditorium, we were greeted at the door to the auditorium by the Youth Minister. He introduced himself and asked where we had come from. When we told him Bartlesville, Oklahoma, his next words were, "How is Doug Oaks doing? He and I are pretty good friends." So we brought him up to date on the fact that Doug and his family had moved to California a few years earlier. It was a small world double play.

This habit of meeting some kind of friend or friend of a friend every time I entered a new church building was starting to work on my mind. And now we were headed for Pepperdine University, where several thousand of my Christian brothers and sisters would be gathered. What are the odds that I would encounter another small world event there? Pretty good, I would say, and I would be proven right just a few days later.

Pepperdine University, Malibu, California

As I expected, Pepperdine proved to be a treasure trove of reunions with friends from Harding and Oklahoma Christian plus members and preachers from many of the congregations I had attended over the years. I was reunited with a Harding TNT club brother who was a missionary in New Zealand. In addition, I had a good visit with my old friend John W. Smith who was a featured speaker at the Lectureship. I don't count any of these reunions as small world events because I more or less expected to see many of my friends at the Lectureship. However, there was one significant and unexpected event that still amazes me.

I had lost track of my good friend Steve Thornton following his wedding. I went to Kansas City, and he had eventually headed to Lancaster, California. Steve was a mechanical engineer and had been hired by one of the large defense contractors located there. When I spent time in 2002 in Long Beach, California, I had ventured one weekend to Lancaster to find him. He had no listed telephone number, and this was before you could find anyone or anything on the internet. Someone in Lancaster told me that he thought Steve had moved to Rosamond, a few miles north of Lancaster, and he gave me an address. I drove on to Rosamond, hopeful. It was a Sunday, and I drove to the address. It appeared that the address was legitimate, but no one was home. I returned to Long Beach, knowing I would be unable to return to Rosamond the following weekend as our project was due to complete in the middle of the coming week.

Six years later, I was now sitting in the Pepperdine Lectureship's closing ceremony in the gym among about 4000 people. Shirley and I had selected random seats in the balcony. A lady sat down beside us, and we began a casual conversation. When we asked her where she lived, she said, "Lancaster, California." I couldn't believe it. I asked her if she knew Steve and Sue Thornton, and she said she did. She then related the sad story that they were divorced and that Steve had remarried. She said Sue had moved back to Texas, and apparently, Steve still lived in Rosamond with his new wife.

It was sad news regarding the Thornton's, but it still amazes me that out of the 4000 people in the meeting that night, there was probably only one other person in the building besides Shirley and me who knew Steve and Sue Thornton, and that one person sat down beside us. Small world once again.

Paris, France

As mentioned earlier, after our visit with Rachel at Harding's Florence, Italy, campus, we extended our tour to include, among other places, Paris. While there we visited all the usual touristy places – Versailles, the Louvre, the Eiffel Tower and Notre Dame Cathedral. While at Notre Dame, we stopped for lunch in a restaurant by the name of L'Ombre, which was across the street from the cathedral. As I think most Americans do, while we were overseas, we constantly listened for English being spoken, particularly English with an American accent. As we were dining that day, a couple with two children occupied the table next to us, and they were speaking very American English. I spoke to them and mentioned their command of English, and asked if they happened to be from the U.S. They replied that they were living in Brussels but added that they were ex-pats temporarily on assignment in Belgium. I asked where they lived in the U.S., and they said they lived in Houston, Texas. The man also mentioned that he was an engineer working for Shell Oil. Not expecting anything, I nevertheless asked him if he happened to know Carlton Ash, who I believe was also an engineer at Shell in Houston. Carlton and his wife Jayne had worshipped with us at the Adams Boulevard church in Bartlesville until he took the job with Shell in Houston.

The man answered, "Yes, we know Carlton and Jayne very well." We then chatted for a few minutes about our common friends. Another amazing event – running into someone across the pond with whom you have common friends. In the movie "Six Degrees of Separation," the thesis is the idea that all people are six or fewer social connections away from each other. As a reesult, theoretically, a chain of "a friend of a friend" statements can be made to connect any two people in the world in a maximum of six steps.

I believe that thesis is too conservative. I have had too many situations in my life where I have encountered significant people with only one or two degrees of such separation. The meetings described in Flagstaff, Malibu, and Paris are cases in point. And there are others that I will discuss. As I think about it, it is kind of eerie. But, bear with me.

Maracaibo, Venezuela

As mentioned earlier, in 2004, I took a contract auditing job with the Baker-Hughes Corporation, and one of my assignments was a two-week stint in Maracaibo, Venezuela. Also, as mentioned, the experience there was almost frightening, and I was glad when it came time to leave. When I was preparing to depart, I happened to get in line at the airport ticket counter behind a lady who appeared to be herding a group of 15 or 20 teenagers. The lady addressed the teens in unaccented English, and the entire group appeared to be American tourists. When I had an opportunity, I spoke to the lady and commented that she did not sound like a Venezuelan and asked her if she happened to be American. She replied that she was indeed from America, was a high school teacher, and that she and the group of teens were from Searcy, Arkansas. She explained that she and the teens had been in Maracaibo on a mission trip for one of the Baptist churches in Searcy.

She about fainted when I told her I was a Harding grad and had spent a lot of time in Searcy even following graduation. We had a nice chat reminiscing about Searcy and Harding. She was very familiar with Harding, particularly the Harding Academy, plus several Harding people she had known there, including Dr. Clifton Ganus. We also agreed that Colton's Steak House in Searcy served some of the best steaks we had ever tasted, and their baked sweet potatoes were exceptional.

Of all the places to meet a person from Searcy—in Maracaibo, Venezuela. However, events like this appeared to be becoming commonplace.

Kruja, Albania

The Adams Boulevard church maintains a thriving mission in the city of Durres, Albania. The church supports two congregations in that city, and Shirley and I have been heavily involved in that mission point for years. Consequently, we have made several trips over the years to visit with the missionaries and the Christians there. On one occasion, one of the missionaries drove us into the mountains of Albania to the city of Kruja. In that city is located the Skanderbeg Museum. Skanderbeg is the Albanian national hero for delivering the country from the tyrannical control of the Ottoman Empire in the 15th century.

We were touring the museum, enjoying the history and the museum's quiet dignity, when we heard a voice cry out, "Y'all come back real soon now. Heyeah?"

Shirley said, "That cannot be an Albanian."

I said, "Sounds like a Texan."

We tracked down the voice and discovered that it was a man who did indeed live in Texas. He said he was originally from Michigan. Somehow the conversation got around to his participation in a gospel singing group in Michigan with one John W. Smith, our friend, and preacher when we lived in Montgomery, Alabama. We had gone halfway around the world to a remote town in the mountains of Albania and had encountered a person who knew a person we knew well. It had to be a God thing. These things just happened too frequently for them to happen without the help of some sort.

Stonehenge, England

In late 2001 we had planned to take a tour of England, Wales and Scotland with our good friends Jim and Joyce Phillips. However, 9/11 took place, and our trip was canceled. We were able to reschedule it for the spring of 2002. At that time, Rachel was finishing her senior year of college at Harding.

Since the tour of England was going to take place in the spring, we expected to incur cool, wet weather. Accordingly, I packed a slicker that bore a Harding logo. Part of our tour included a day excursion to Stonehenge, the ancient stone monument out west of London. It was raining on the day of our trip to Stonehenge, so I wore my Harding slicker.

As we were waiting to board the bus back to London following our visit to Stonehenge, a young lady ran up to me and excitedly asked, "Are you really from Harding?" She had noticed the jacket I was wearing.

It turns out that she was a student at Harding and knew Rachel. She was doing a semester abroad at Harding's London campus. Another of those really interesting small world events to which I was becoming accustomed.

Athens, Greece

In 2009 we and the Andersons – Jerry and Debbie – took a Mediterranean Cruise that started in Athens and included visits to ancient Ephesus, ancient Corinth, Istanbul, Sochi, Russia, Jerusalem, and Cairo. When we arrived in Athens, we checked into the Marble House Hotel – so named because everything but the ceilings was constructed of marble. When we checked in, I wanted to determine if the desk clerk spoke any English to see what I was up against in communicating with her during our stay there.

Before I even had an opportunity to say a word to her, she looked up from our reservation form, which contained our U.S. address, and in pretty much unaccented English said, "From Oklahoma, huh?" I was speechless.

She then told us that she had spent four years in the Norman and Chickasha, Oklahoma, area. I knew she was authentic because she pronounced Chickasha as ChickaSHAY rather than ChickaSHAW, which is the way non–Oklahomans tend to pronounce it. She said she had spent some time at Oklahoma University.

Needless to say, our short stay at the Marble House Hotel was enjoyable and relaxing thanks to another small world event.

Normandy, France

Following our visit in Paris with the friends of the Ash's we took a tour of the beaches of Normandy, the site of the D–Day invasion of France by the Allies on June 6, 1944. It was during our tour of Normandy that we experienced another most remarkable small world event.

We had hired a tour guide who gave us a very thorough and interesting tour of the Normandy area. Our tour had concluded that day at about 5:30 p.m.. Still, our train back to Paris did not depart the Normandy area until about 8:00 p.m., so our tour guide took us to his "chateau"—a bed and breakfast—for a light meal and to await the train. While we were there, another couple arrived. They were from London and were on their annual "wine run." So, they would come to France and load up with dozens of bottles of Beaujolais, a favorite wine that becomes available in France on the third Thursday of November each year. They made the trek every year, so they were regular guests at the chateau and well-known by our tour guide. They were a couple in their 30's and were very genial. During our visit, they inquired extensively about life in the "Colonies," and we engaged in comfortable and amiable conversation during the hour or so we spent with them. We did not really have an opportunity to inquire into their life in London, and they did not offer to send the conversation in that direction.

At a little after 7:00 p.m., it became time for our tour guide to deliver us to the train terminal. We bade the English couple goodbye and left with the tour guide. On the drive to the terminal, the tour guide informed us that the couple was kind of special. The husband was an executive in the financial department of the city of London. His wife was currently the personal secretary to Prince Charles of England and had been secretary to Princess Di until her death two years earlier. Who would have ever guessed? God just kept on dropping little kernels of enjoyment and amazement into our life. I guess, theoretically, we were only two degrees of separation from the Queen of England at that time.

IT'S A SMALL WORLD AFTER ALL

Florence, Italy

The mother of all small world events occurred in Florence, Italy, during our trip there with Mike and Chris Williams in 2004. As we had done during our trip to Florence to visit Rachel five years earlier, we worshipped on Sunday with a congregation in downtown Florence. The building was about four hundred years old and was constructed of stone with a dome over the auditorium. The acoustics were so good that someone could have dropped a coin on the dais, and its sound could have been heard in the back row. Needless to say, the singing was heavenly, and the 50 or so Harding students in the audience contributed significantly to the quality of the music.

Since this was an Italian congregation and most of those in attendance were Italian, the sermon was likewise delivered in Italian. We understood nary a word, but we greatly enjoyed the service and the atmosphere and especially the singing. Besides the Harding students, there were also several other non–Italians in attendance. Consequently, following the service, as we were wont to do, we listened for people speaking in "American" English.

We were approached by a couple who met that criterion. They introduced themselves as Gary and Jennifer Williams. Gary headed up a missionary organization there by the name of "Avanti Italia," and its purpose was to provide lodging for, primarily, college-age students who would come to the area to evangelize. The organization had some attachment to Harding if I recall, but I do not remember exactly how it all worked.

After Gary and Jennifer had introduced themselves, we followed suit. When Mike Williams introduced himself, Gary broke in and said, "I think I am your cousin."

The silence was deafening.

It turned out that Gary and Mike were indeed cousins who had not seen one another for several years and now met almost halfway around the world. What a remarkable small world event.

But God was not finished yet. Gary asked where Shirley and I lived. We told him we lived in Bartlesville, Oklahoma, and asked if he knew where that was.

Gary then responded, "My wife, Jennifer, was Jennifer Bybee before we married, and her father, Howard Bybee, preached at the Sixth and Dewey congregation in Bartlesville for years. Jennifer is very familiar with Bartlesville." This small world thing was getting out of hand.

But God was still not finished.

Gary then said, "Jennifer's best friend was Tammy Windle Ross. Do you know her?"

After I metaphorically picked myself up from the floor, I responded, "Yes, we see Tammy and her husband and her parents in church every Sunday. In fact, for a short time, my wife worked for Tammy at her father's jewelry store in Bartlesville."

At that point, Florence's small world adventure concluded, but it was, in effect, a small world triple play. What are the odds of something like that happening without divine intervention by God?

That pretty well concludes the narrative of our most significant small world encounters. From Anchorage to Albania, with stops in Athens, Paris, Normandy, Stonehenge, Florence, Maracaibo, and several American cities scattered almost from coast to coast. Incredible is the only word I can think of which comes close to describing them.

Earlier in the narrative, I briefly mentioned many prominent people I have met and visited with, including Ronald Reagan, Kenneth Starr, George Romney, and others. However, other well–known people I have personally met and who have added considerable drama to my life include:

1. Stan Musial, Hall of Fame Major Leaguer, at a golf course in St. Louis

2. Guy Hunt, Governor of Alabama, at a Phillips station in Enterprise, Alabama

3. Shari Lewis, TV personality and puppeteer, at Opryland Hotel in Nashville

4. Mickey Carroll, actor (a munchkin in the movie "The Wizard of Oz") at a golf course in St. Louis – he claimed Judy Garland was a very interesting person

5. Al Hrabosky, ex–Major Leaguer and TV broadcaster, at a golf course in St. Louis

6. Eddie Sutton, Hall of Fame Basketball coach, at the airport in Atlanta

Stan Musial, Guy Hunt, Mickey Carroll, Al Hrabosky, and Eddie Sutton were kind enough to pose for a photo.

I have also been privileged to be invited by Harding University to attend speaking engagements by the following:

1. George H. W. Bush

2. Gerald Ford

3. Margaret Thatcher

4. Prime Minister Brian Mulroney of Canada

5. Condoleeza Rice

6. Gen. Colin Powell

7. Mikhail Gorbachev

Gerald Ford (unintentionally) posed for a photo.

Although invited, I was unable to attend the speech by Mikhail Gorbachev due to a work conflict, but Shirley was able to attend.

I attended the U.S. Air Force Officer's Training School graduation ceremony when my son Brent received his commission as a Second Lieutenant in the Air Force. The ceremony was conducted at Maxwell Air Force Base in Montgomery, Alabama, and former President Jimmy Carter was the featured speaker.

Also, as the chapter title implies, I have experienced several "Close Encounters of the Third Kind." The phrase is derived from a classification of potential close encounters with aliens as set forth by American UFO researcher J. Allen Hynek. Close Encounters of the First Kind refer to the sighting of a UFO. Physical evidence of a UFO is classed as a Close Encounter of the Second Kind. Actual contact with an alien is a Close Encounter of the Third Kind. (Not to imply that any of those on my list are aliens, but the principle of a Close Encounter still applies, even if it only refers to actual contact with an earthling.)

My Close Encounters of the Third Kind:

1. Ryne Sandberg, Major League Hall of Famer, at Cheesecake Factory in Phoenix

2. Jill St. John, actress, in downtown Aspen

3. George Jones, singer, on a flight between Houston and Dallas

4. Bob Hope, actor, at DFW Airport

5. Ozzie Smith, Major League Hall of Famer, on a flight between St. Louis and Philadelphia

6. Olga Kurylenko, actress, at Jude's coffee shop in Bartlesville

7. Kurt Russell, actor, at Buttermilk Mountain near Aspen

8. Phil Donahue, TV personality, at Buttermilk Mountain – Aspen

9. Jaclyn Smith, actress, on Rodeo Drive in Beverly Hills

10. Ben Afflack, actor, at Phillips 66 station in Bartlesville

11. Jesse Jackson, political activist, at a hotel in Birmingham

12. Jimmy Johnson, ex-college and pro football coach at Tulsa International Airport

13. Billy Sims, Heisman Trophy winner, at Washington Park Mall in Bartlesville

Billy Sims and Kurt Russell graciously agreed to pose for photographs.

Any way you slice it, my life has been richly seasoned with unexpected encounters all over the world with people I know, and with friends of friends, and with celebrities of every sort.

It truly is a small world.

Thirty-Five

AND IN CONCLUSION

In the previous chapters, I have faithfully related events and situations that have taken place in my life. There is no logical explanation other than to believe they had celestial help. I am not tall, nor handsome, nor strong, nor swift, nor musically talented, nor rich, nor powerful, nor famous, nor particularly intelligent. So it simply begs the question, "How have I managed to arrive in old age healthy, happily married, surrounded by an exceptional family, with plenty to eat and a roof over my head, without scars or regrets, and unafraid of what lies ahead?"

I believe the reason I find myself in my present situation is that I eventually embraced a two-fold truth: Keep the faith, and then stay out of the way and let God work His wonders.

As this chronology has continually revealed, although I have always tried to keep the faith, I have on innumerable occasions attempted to tell God what to do and how to do it. Only when I stood back and let Him work his wonders did the road of life begin to smooth out.

I also should point out that "keeping the faith" also includes truly believing in what scripture says. The following are some of my favorite scriptures which have guided me through my journey:

1 Samuel 7:10–13

10 While Samuel was sacrificing the burnt offering; the Philistines drew near to engage Israel in battle. But that day the Lord thundered with loud thunder against the Philistines and threw them into such a panic that they

were routed before the Israelites. 11 The men of Israel rushed out of Mizpah and pursued the Philistines, slaughtering them along the way to a point below Betha Kar. 12 Then Samuel took a stone and set it up between Mizpah and Shen. **He named it Ebenezer, saying, "Thus far the Lord has helped us."** 13 So the Philistines were subdued, and they stopped invading Israel's territory.

Job 13:15 (KJV)

15 Though he slay me, yet will I trust in him.

Job 37:5

5 God's voice thunders in marvelous ways; he does great things beyond our understanding.

Psalms 25:9

9 He guides the humble in what is right and teaches them his way.

Psalms 38:15

15 Lord, I wait for you; you will answer, Lord my God.

Mark 11:23

23 Truly I tell you, if anyone says to this mountain, 'Go, throw yourself into the sea,' and does not doubt in their heart but believes that what they say will happen, it will be done for them.

Romans 5:2–5

2 . . . And we boast in the hope of the glory of God. 3 Not only so, but we also glory in our sufferings, because we know that suffering produces perseverance; 4 perseverance, character; and character, hope. 5 And hope does not put us to shame, because God's love has been poured out into our hearts through the Holy Spirit, who has been given to us.

Romans 8:28

28 And we know that in all things God works for the good of those who love him, who have been called according to his purpose.

1 Corinthians 1:25

25 For the foolishness of God is wiser than human wisdom, and the weakness of God is stronger than human strength.

1 Corinthians 10:13

13 No temptation has overtaken you except what is common to mankind. And God is faithful; he will not let you be tempted beyond what you can bear. But when you are tempted, he will also provide a way out so that you can endure it.

Philippians 4:4–7

4 Rejoice in the Lord always. Again I say, rejoice. 5 Let everyone see your gentleness. The Lord is near! 6 Do not be anxious about anything. Instead, in every situation, through prayer and petition with thanksgiving, tell your requests to God. 7 And the peace of God that passes all understanding will guard your hearts and minds in Christ Jesus.

1 Thessalonians 5:16–18

16 Rejoice always, 17 pray continually, 18 give thanks in all circumstances; for this is God's will for you in Christ Jesus.

Hebrews 13:2

2 Do not forget to show hospitality to strangers, for by so doing some people have shown hospitality to angels without knowing it.

1 Peter 5:6

6 Humble yourselves, therefore, under God's mighty hand, that he may lift you up in due time.

These scriptures are buoyed by hundreds of others which teach of faith, patience, thanksgiving, acceptance of discipline, God's love for us individually, the fruit of the spirit, and the list goes on. Also, I fully believe God is both willing and able to perform miracles in the current age – perhaps more discretely than in the days of the Apostles – but miracles nonetheless. I just can't explain away what has happened to me over the years as happenstance or coincidence.

My personal philosophy of life is summarized in the statements below, and I believe they bear out spectacularly what has happened to me throughout my life.

- Have faith in God and trust in Him.
- Realize that sometimes bad things will happen, for whatever the reason, but when those do things happen, God will work for your good.
- God will not allow us to be tempted beyond what we can bear, and will always provide a way out.
- Learn from your mistakes.
- Faith produces perseverance.
- Realize that God is smarter than you are.
- Wait on the Lord. Realize that God may not choose to solve your problem overnight, but given time He will.
- Realize that sometimes a defeat is actually a victory in disguise.
- Give thanks, even when it doesn't seem like you have anything to be thankful for.

And finally,
- Believe that God still performs miracles and that angels still appear from time to time.

It is impossible for me to believe that all the wondrous things that have happened to me during my life were not choreographed by God. They are statistically impossible and had to have happened in the exact sequence in which they occurred for anything to have made sense. Truly, as the old hymn says, "God moves in mysterious ways His wonders to perform."

The thoughts also bring into stark focus the last line in another hymn, "Amazing Grace," where it says, "I was blind, but now I see." Hindsight is 20/20, but sometimes it takes a while for things to come into focus.

Finally, there are the very familiar and inspirational Biblical stories of Joseph, Job, Peter, Abraham, Moses, Jacob, Daniel, and friends, the Virgin

Mary, and Joseph the husband of Mary. Each of these people faced potentially negative life–altering events, but each, by the Providence of God, emerged stronger and more full of faith than if they had succumbed to the adversity. I will never rise to the level of any of those people, but as the years have passed, I have attempted to emulate them to the best of my ability, trusting in God to fill in the blanks. This brings to mind another of my favorite scriptures because it applies to powerfully to me:

2 Samuel 7:18

1. 18 Then King David went in and sat before the Lord, and he said: "Who am I, Sovereign Lord, and what is my family, that you have brought me this far?

And I have gratefully raised my Ebenezer innumerable times over the years in recognition of the fact that . . .

Hither by Thy help, I've come.

COINCIDENCE OR GOD'S PROVIDENCE?

Okay, you have now read the book. Is it coincidence or God's Providence? Did I need to raise an Ebenezer or just thank my lucky stars? Early on I listed my lifetime objectives which were developed and fleshed out as I grew and matured:

1. A happy marriage to a wonderful woman and, later, children
2. A college education
3. A good job which would support my family
4. An opportunity to serve my country honorably
5. A life situation which would enhance my walk with God

Eventually, after my marriage and the birth of two sons, another objective surfaced:

6. To have a daughter

Every one of these objectives has been realized in spades.

So how did that happen? The simple answer is to first recognize that the achievement of all of these life objectives is the direct result of only four significant events in my life.

First, while I was in high school my dad was transferred from Ada to Bartlesville by his employer, the Exxon Corporation.

It was necessary for my family to be living in Bartlesville, Oklahoma, during my high school years in order for me to be able to meet people there who would influence me to enroll at Harding College. Further, it was necessary that my dad be an Exxon employee there in order for him to eventually be transferred to Okemah, Oklahoma, by Exxon.

Second, I enrolled at Harding College

For my spiritual and social well–being it was imperative that I study in an environment such as was found at Harding in order to prepare me for real life – education, marriage, career and enhancement of my walk with God. My enrollment at Harding was a direct result of my years in Bartlesville.

Third, my dad was transferred to Okemah, Oklahoma, during my college days

It was necessary that my mom and dad be living in Okemah in order for me to meet and become acquainted with members of the Oklahoma National Guard. This connection with officials of the National Guard enabled me to enlist and allowed me to serve my country honorably without delaying or cancelling either my wedding or my career with Phillips Petroleum.

Fourth, Shirley and I lived in Bartlesville 1970–1973 and again 1974–1986

It was necessary that Shirley and I establish an extended personal history in Bartlesville in order to place us in a position to eventually adopt our daughter, Rachel. Living in Bartlesville enabled us to meet people who would be influential and provide personal references in the adoption process.

Of course, each of these four events was supported, complemented, seasoned and frequently enhanced by an amazing array of life situations and events described in the narrative. All of the side shows ultimately contributed to both the journey and its outcome.

To me it is totally unreasonable to explain away these four events and their effect on future events as random or coincidence or happenstance because they are too well choreographed. They are too improbable and statistically impossible to have been the result of merely blind luck. I have to believe that they are the Providence of God, helping a struggling Christian and his family in its Christian journey.

So, it begs the question – What or who is responsible for this amazing journey? It can be due to only one of two possibilities – either coincidence or the Providence of God. I certainly didn't earn these blessings.

To once again quote John W. Smith, this time in his editorial of May 14, 2020, entitled "The Redhead and the Brunette" he states, "Think about all of those totally unplanned meetings, incidents, and conversations that changed the entire course of your life, and ask yourself – "chance" or "providence?" For Disciples of Jesus, there is only one possible response."

In fact, I even believe my reading of his comments was providential in that I was in the final stages of proofreading my manuscript when his note popped up in email. Was it chance or providence that the email with that particular subject came to my attention at the exact time it did? It was much too timely and relevant to have been chance.

Also, when the events mentioned above are examined in concert with the "Small World" and "Close Encounters" meetings highlighted in Chapter 34 it seems to me totally improbable that they could all have been "coincidences."

So, the jury is out. You are jury. You make the decision. Coincidence or God's Providence? I cast my vote for God's Providence and continue to raise my Ebenezer, for . . .

Against all odds, "Hither by Thy help I have come."

Made in the USA
Coppell, TX
12 June 2022